The URBANIZATION of MAN: A SOCIAL SCIENCE PERSPECTIVE

Compiled and edited by

Thelma S. Baker

The Pennsylvania State University

McCutchan Publishing Corporation
2526 Grove Street
Berkeley, California 94704

LC: 72-5704
ISBN: 0-8211-0122-6

Manufactured in the United States of America

PREFACE

This reader, designed to introduce students to the social sciences and then to see how the social sciences focus on a problem, was developed to meet a specific need. The need for such a book is a natural outgrowth of the developing General Education Program at The Pennsylvania State University. The Social Science courses in General Education at Penn State were first conceived as capstone courses, similar to those discussed by Daniel Bell and others. Such courses were taught or directed by senior faculty members; the students were upperclassmen; the courses attempted to synthesize the discipline-oriented courses such as sociology, psychology, political science, anthropology, economics, and sometimes history into a significant fabric called Social Sciences, and thus give a dimension of unity to a set of otherwise fragmented experiences.

Several factors, however, have altered this concept over the past several years. An increasing emphasis on professional standards has pressured senior faculty into giving more attention to their departmental courses. Ideally, alternative rewards could provide the necessary faculty stimulus toward greater participation in General Education programs; but other, perhaps more significant factors have emerged. Somewhat unconsciously, the students have played a significant role in reshaping the emphasis of the former capstone philosophy. They simply do not view the capstone idea as valid and have avoided scheduling these courses late in the baccalaureate program. Instead, they have scheduled these courses earlier and earlier until the specific course for which this reader is designed has become an introductory course, taken by freshmen or sophomores, and taught primarily by advanced graduate students or faculty from the junior ranks. Such a transition seems to have been prompted by necessity. For example, when *does* a student learn *about* the social sciences? Not by taking a typical introductory course in a discipline.

In its new form, Social Science 1 at Penn State is both an introduction to the social sciences and a focusing of the social sciences on a given topic. This reader provides a basic tool for teaching such a course.

Part I, "The Social Science Perspective," provides the reader with some insights into the enthusiasm, expectations, and enjoyment that social scientists bring to their work, as well as a vision of their horizons and the intellectual excitement that comes with trying to understand man and society. The methodology of the social sciences is analyzed in Section B of Part I. Various selections provide some specific instructions and generalized rules for gathering information as well as some cautions about the misuse of statistical information or raw data. Two readings provide in lucid detail the theoretical framework that directs the collection, analysis, and interpretation of data. The goal here is for the reader to appreciate the diversity of viewpoints and to evaluate their relative strengths.

Part II, "The Urbanization of Man" has been selected as the problem to which the principles of Part I will be applied. Hopefully, the reader will become an informed participant in this analysis. Beginning with pre-urban man and moving to the industrial city, Part II presents the development of the city, not as history, not in a kaleidescope fashion, but as a series of still photographs or views taken at significant points in its development. So even though three-fourths of all Americans live in cities and all Americans live in a city-dominated culture, the reader should gain some new insights from the awareness that man has also lived, and still lives, in societies in which the city is not even a dream. From the beginning, the reader considers the social, political, and economic dimensions of urbanization, and also compares and contrasts these dimensions at varying stages in the evaluation.

Thus, the reader discusses the Greek "city-state," the polis, and discovers that its influences are more significant than the architectural style of so many First National Banks. He looks next to Rome, a pattern for so much— the United States Senate, excellent highways connecting cities, and even urban violence. After the "fall" of Rome, both roads and cities decayed over a period of centuries. Like the mudfish that burrows into the mud to survive a drought and then resumes his aquatic life with the rains, the Roman cities in Europe, except in one or two places, faded into the countryside when the requisites of urban life dried up. But they too were ready to come alive again and did, when conditions were right, with remarkable vigor. One of the concerns of the reader is to examine the causes of decline and later rebirth of cities. Much can be learned about the nature of social science by reviewing the arguments regarding the relative importance of the many factors involved in those social changes.

The cities that appeared in the late Middle Ages are worthy of our careful scrutiny, for they were our direct urban ancestors. The political and economic changes accompanying and related to late medieval urbanization provided the impetus that thrust Western society on its present course. The rise of commerce, of the middle class, of representative government and national states, the Renaissance and Reformation—all were important aspects to the formation of the culture we take so much for granted.

The later Scientific and Industrial Revolutions also contributed to the making of the modern city. The reader is encouraged to look further for these later factors. The task of the present book is completed.

If this venture proves successful, and it should insofar as it provides a perspective on the social sciences, the following people should be thanked for their contributions. Let me express my sincere thanks for their cooperation and help to all faculty members at University Park campus and the branch campuses who have offered suggestions; to Mrs. Thelma Baker, who served as editor, and her assistant, Miss Sarah Harbison; to Dr. Vincent Norris, who aided in several ways; to Mrs. Maureen P. Lewis who helped coordinate various phases of this effort; and to Mrs. Lonni Swanson, who typed much of the material for the reader.

Theodore E. Kiffer
Director, General Education
*   in Humanities and Social Sciences*
The Pennsylvania State University

CONTENTS

PART I. THE SOCIAL SCIENCE PERSPECTIVE

Section A. Logic and Function of the Social Sciences

The Logic and the Functions of Social Science   1
Robert Redfield
The Promise   11
C. Wright Mills
The Social Sciences in General Education   15
Vincent P. Norris

Section B. Methodology of the Social Sciences

Discovery and Explanation   26
George C. Homans
Methods of Inquiry   38
Bernard Berelson and Gary Steiner
Steps in the Scientific Method   56
Matthew Enos
The Idea of Chance   59
J. Bronowski
How to Lie with Statistics   69
Darrell Huff

Section C. The Social Sciences and Society

Scientific Principles and Their Consequences   78
Daniel C. Reber
Value-Free Social Science   89
Stephen B. Baier
Social Science and Ideology   95
Raymond E. Ries
Social Science and Social Policy   102
Karl R. Popper

PART II. THE URBANIZATION OF MAN

Section D. The Scope of the Problem

The Origin and Growth of Urbanization in the World   110
Kingsley Davis

Section E. Some Operational Definitions of Urbanization and the City

The Nature and Rise of Cities   123
     Ralph Thomlinson

Section F. The Emergence of Early Urban Forms

The Urban Revolution   128
     V. Gordon Childe
Ur as an Urban System Ca. *2800 B.C.*   137
     Henry T. Wright
*Teotihuacán: Completion of Map of Giant Ancient City in
the Valley of Mexico*   144
     René Millon

Section G. The City and Its Environment

Cultural Ecology of Nuclear Mesoamerica   155
     William T. Sanders

Section H. The Classic Pre-Industrial City

Greece
The Polis   165
     H. D. F. Kitto
Health and the Course of Civilization as Seen in Ancient Greece   176
     J. Lawrence Angel
Rome
The Site of Rome   184
     Donald R. Dudley
*Social and Economic Development of the Empire in the
First Two Centuries*   187
     M. Rostovtzeff
Urban Violence in Imperial Rome   198
     Thomas W. Africa

Section I. The Medieval City

The Making of a Town: Ninth-Century Bruges   215
Manorial Records of the Tenth and Eleventh Centuries   216
The Customs of Newcastle-Upon-Tyne   218
Mohammed and Charlemagne   220
     Henri Pirenne
The Pirenne Thesis: Towards Reformulation   222
     Paul Craig Roberts
City-State   227
     André Piganiol
The Towns   231
     Henri Pirenne
The Ghetto   241
     Louis Wirth

The Influences of the Church on Medieval Culture   247
   Caroline D. Eckhardt

Section J. The Transformation to the Industrial City

The Change in Demographic Patterns
The City   265
   Werner Sombart
The Change in Stratification
Middle-Class Wealth   280
   Werner Sombart
The Class Struggle and the Change from Feudalism to Capitalism 284
   Karl Marx and Friedrich Engels
The Change in Political Systems
The Modern State   292
   Robert Bierstedt, Eugene J. Meehan and Paul A. Samuelson
The Change in Values
The Author Defines His Purpose   305
   Max Weber
A Contribution to the Critique of Political Economy   311
   Karl Marx
The History of a Controversy   313
   Ephraim Fischoff
The Change in Economic Systems and Technology
The Causes of the Industrial Revolution: An Essay in Methodology 323
   R. M. Hartwell

Suggested Readings   343

PART I
THE SOCIAL SCIENCE PERSPECTIVE

Section A. Logic and Function
of
the Social Sciences

THE LOGIC AND THE FUNCTIONS OF SOCIAL SCIENCE

Robert Redfield

In these lectures I propose to talk about the nature of social science. I am reporting something of what I have learned about social science in the twenty years or more during which I have had something to do with it. Into the report will go experience in teaching, in research, and in administration, for it has been my good luck to see social science from the viewpoint which each of these activities provides. But especially will my remarks be shaped by the presumptions and habits of mind of the anthropologist. An anthropologist may study social science just as he would study anything else in a society. Social science is one of the many systems of attitudes and practices that make up a culture and a society. In our present-day society it is an institution, just as the market, the family, and the church are institutions. In these lectures I invite you to consider with me what is done by economists and sociologists and psychologists and other social scientists—all that they study and teach—in the same spirit and asking the same questions that were represented when Professor Fei Hsiao-tung studied the agricultural and industrial institutions of communities in Yunnan, China, or that were represented when Professor Everett C. Hughes studied the familial and industrial institutions of a French-Canadian town. Social science and social scientists as a part of modern society and culture: that is my subject.

In investigating this subject we are prepared, as anthropologists of some experience, for the necessity to look at our subject freshly, as if we had not seen it before. We must come to it from the outside, so as to free ourselves from the limiting effects of our own close association with it. We know we

From *Human Nature and the Study of Society* ©1962 by Robert Redfield. Reprinted by permission of the University of Chicago Press.

1

cannot accept, as full understanding of what social science is, what the social scientists themselves are in the habit of saying about it. We cannot do this any more than the student of the kinship system of an unfamiliar people can accept as a complete and adequate understanding of the nature of that system what the people who use that system say about it. What they say about it only partly represents the scientific "truth." Social scientists, until they come to study the actual nature of their social science, as it really is in our society, may merely repeat what they have learned to say about their social science. No, now we must approach social science, as if we were anthropologists come to study this society, and we must look at what particular people, social scientists and others, in fact do think and feel about social science. We must look to see how the social science that is taught and studied actually affects the lives of social scientists and people who are not social scientists. It is a kind of anthropological field work.

It is useful to have some preliminary concepts to guide us in arranging our facts and in reaching our conclusions. I propose to adopt a distinction that is common among anthropologists: the distinction between structure and function. When we look at the structure of a cultural object or institution, we need not consider any of the other objects or institutions of the society in which we find it. We consider it as if it were alone, and, having recognized it as something separable from all else, we attend to the way in which its parts are related to each other. We are concerned with its internal order. I can recognize a table, and describe its structure by describing the way in which the legs support the top. I can describe the structure of a clock by showing how its parts go together so as to produce the movements which make a clock something different from a phonograph. But in doing this I need not take account of what use people make of a clock or what they think and feel about clocks as regulators of their lives or perhaps disturbers of their sleep.

When we consider the function of the clock or the table or the institution, we do have to think of what it means in the lives of the people of that society. Then we ask ourselves what contribution this thing that we are studying makes toward fulfilling the needs and desires of people. Also we look to see what contribution it makes toward enabling all the parts and institutions of the society to work together so as to enable the society to persist. The function of anything, in this sense, is its place in making up the going concern in which the activity of that thing is one element.

In speaking of the "structure" of social science, we are then concerned with its internal order. We attend to the way in which men use their minds, the way in which they apprehend and make order of their experiences of man in society when they do what we recognize as "science." As this way is constituted of rules and habits of observing and thinking, we might speak of the structure of a science as its "logic." We distinguish the scientific ways of getting understanding of man in society from other ways of getting such understanding by looking at the rules and habits of observing and reasoning— and also of communicating—which characterize science.

Science is one of the ways men have to make sense of experience. It is, perhaps emphatically, a method, a kind of procedure for getting understanding. Also we think of "science" as the product of that method: this is "science" in the sense of "scientific knowledge." And also we sometimes use the word "science" as in the phrase "A Science of Society," in the title of a book which records this kind of knowledge; "a science" is one kind of written work.

Let us here think of science as method, as a way of understanding. From what other ways of understanding, of making order of experience, is it to be distinguished? For one thing, it is to be distinguished from common sense, and for another it is to be distinguished from mysticism. Common sense and mysticism are also ways of getting understanding of society as of anything else; the one is open to everybody with normal wits, common sayings perhaps to the contrary; the other is open, apparently, only to those having the inclinations and the powers of the mystic. The mystic's ordering of experience is on the whole a matter private to him—its very incommunicability is the test of its mystic nature—while common sense has a considerable currency: what one man learns by that way he can in many cases make known to others.

It is from common sense that we feel the need to distinguish science. The nature of that distinction is a commonplace in treatises on scientific method. There we read how scientific method is objective. It requires a detachment of the scientist's personal attitudes from his subject matter and from his conclusions. Science is "impersonal." The scientist must deliberately doubt his own thoughts on the matter at hand and subject his procedures and his conclusions to testing. He has the word "hypothesis" to dignify these temporary conclusions in the process of testing. Moreover, we are told that science aims for perfect communicability—so far as possible the propositions must be formulated so that they will mean the same thing to any two scientists. So propositions in the form of numbers have high value in science: 92 percent, we are told, is 92 percent to everybody.

We are talking also of the form or logic of science when we say that it tends to become systematic and comprehensive. Common-sense knowledge is a medley, a collection. But scientific knowledge seems always to be struggling toward an architecture of description. Its effort is to represent the world in the form of propositions that are related to each other by a sort of natural order. Lesser generalizations are marshaled under generalizations of wider scope. A proposition that follows from acceptance of an anterior proposition is declared and shown to be so related. The connections between some particular facts and more inclusive propositions are made plain, and like matters are grouped because they are alike. The likeness is felt to arise within the facts, and without necessary relation to the practical interests of men. The movement is toward compendency, toward linking of propositions with one another; and at the same time toward comprehensiveness: the propositions are widened as observations authorize the widening. For a comprehensive proposition that scientists are at the time not interested in proving or disproving, we have the phrase "natural law."

This characterization of science in its formal or logical nature, made familiar to us in treatises on the subject, applies to social science. It applies, but not so well as it applies to physics or mathematics. In coming to understand man in society we can use more than common sense and more (or shall we say less!) than the occasional private insight of the seer. Social scientists are in no small part engaged in making order of experience, an order that is objective, systematic, and comprehensive. For society, as for matter and organisms, there grows a structured body of knowledge that belongs to no one thinker, that is accessible to all who will study it, and that is the work of many men. The result is perhaps less objective than is the corresponding result in physics or biology, for it is harder to be objective about a famine or the threat of war than it is about a star or a starfish. In some of his work the physicist or the chemist may be as anxious about the results of what he does as is the social scientist. The physicists and chemists who saw their studies of nuclear energy go into the making of atomic bombs were certainly anxious. But the situation of the social scientist is different in that many, probably most, of his scientific problems are also problems of immediate practical concern and in the further fact that his very subject matter is made up of human beings, rather than of matter or animal life. As the subject matter of social science is humanity, it would be inhuman not to care. Indeed, in my opinion, a good social scientist does care. He cares about the race relations or the village economy that he studies; he would not do as good a job if he looked at the village or the racial situation with inhuman indifference to it. At the same time he must be self-critical; he must be ready to give up any conclusion for another nearer the truth. Now this is harder to do when the very thing you are looking at, as scientist, is a thing that as a man you feel for and with. Yet it is done, and as it is done social science results.

Nor is social science as systematic or as comprehensive as physics or biology, and in my opinion it is not likely to catch up with the "natural" sciences in these qualities. Perhaps the generalization in social science has there a somewhat different role to play. Perhaps it is not so much a final or nearly final summing up of accepted understanding as it is a provider of a more tentative and yet illuminating point of view. Perhaps the generalization in social science is a sort of searchlight on each particular case. It throws light on it—from one side—but it does throw light. Another generalization, also tentative and not too substantially reported, will perhaps be offered to illuminate the case from another side. I think that in much of social science the generalizations tend to be constructions some considerable way from thoroughly acceptable "truth." They guide us among real cases that always escape the generalization, and escape by amounts and in ways that are less definable than is the departure of an actual falling stone from the law of falling bodies. But we grasp and deal with the case the better for looking at it with the generalization.

The remarks so far made may be reduced to a sentence: Social science, looked at with regard to its inner or logical nature, as one of the ways men use to understand the world around them, has the chief formal characteristics of other sciences, although in less degree, although as modified because of the peculiar humanity of its subject matter.

So far I have talked about social science as if social scientists did what they do without consequences to other people or to themselves and without significance in the society of which they are a part. But we know at once that what they do does have significance for social scientists and for other people. The money given for social science research is not given to keep the research workers happy; it is given because the givers suppose some good to result to people generally from the performance of the research. And when an economist or a sociologist expresses a result of his studies that seems to threaten some established attitude or interest of some of the people in his community, those people may feel uneasiness or alarm and may indeed complain to the university or foundation that employs the social scientist. In times of social and political insecurity it is the social scientist, among men of science, who is likely first to feel the curb of government or of public opinion. It is the social scientist whose work suffers most when a ruler begins to control what is written or said. A physicist or a chemist may continue to do honest physics or biology, even though a tyrant may put the result to evil uses, but many an economist or sociologist cannot continue as an honest social scientist and still please such a ruler. The very work he does, the very findings as to monetary policy or the nature of racial groups, will offend the tyrant. The social scientist becomes a propagandist for the ruler or he ceases to be.

The trend of these remarks has carried us into consideration of the functions of social science. Before I make the attempt to identify these functions, I should like to say that it is the societal functions, the parts played by social science in the lives of the people of the community, in which I am here interested. There are also what we may call the personal functions. (The readers of the works of A. R. Radcliffe-Brown will be familiar with that anthropologist's emphasis upon the societal functions of the institutions of primitive and other societies, and the readers of B. Malinowski's writings will have found there an attention also to the ways in which cultural activities meet the human needs that are supposed to characterize all people.) Social science "does things" for the social scientist himself, but here I am not concerned with how he may by social science earn a living or with how research meets his need for adventure or distracts his mind from the troubles he may be having with his wife. No, in this excursion into the place of social science in our lives, I am thinking of the lives of all of us. What is social science, in a wide sense, "good for?"

The obvious answer is that it is good for all of us because it helps to get useful things done. This is a true answer. Social science does tell us how we may do things we want to do more effectively than if we acted only according to common sense. The economist may be able to tell the maker of financial policy what is likely to happen if he makes a certain change in the interest rate in the centralized banking system. Professor Louis Thurstone has developed a method of administering tests to individuals and of analyzing the results of these tests in such a way as to enable one to determine what are the capacities of these individuals for one kind of work or another, for one career or another, with much greater success than one can determine these capacities without the benefit of his science. It is a useful consequence of psychology that it helps to pick out—among many other things that it does—the airplane pilot who is not apt to have an accident. Another of my colleagues, Professor Burgess, has with others developed ways of predicting the probability that a paroled criminal will not return to crime and the probability that marriage between two persons he has investigated will endure. In hundreds of other ways social scientists are getting work done.

Looked at this way, social science is the making of useful inventions. Just as physicists and chemists and biologists discover or invent penicillin or atomic energy, so social scientists discover or invent what helps man. The help may not be as critical, and the value of the invention is sometimes less clear, but the help is there. In his recent book, *The Proper Study of Man*, Stuart Chase has collected mention of some of these inventions. They occur in all fields of social science. I had a small part in one social science invention as a member of a group of men who drafted a possible constitution for a federal world government. We wanted to find a way of electing representatives that would induce men to come to think of themselves as responsible to a world community rather than to a nation or local community. It occurred to us that it might be required that some of the elected delegates be chosen from a unit of federation other than that of the electors who chose them. We proposed that, for example, the United States choose some Asians among its representatives. This is, of course, an invention not in effect, and indeed it is probably a not wholly original invention. But it suggests that social inventions occur in matters of government as in matters of economics, psychology, or sociology.

In my experience it is in the discharge of the utilitarian function that social scientists commonly find justification to themselves and to society for what they do. They put forward their practical usefulness. In the United States, where practical usefulness is not undervalued, it is the popular justification. On the whole I think the argument prevails, and, in so far as the American community values social science, it is for its contribution to practical affairs. During the First World War it was the psychologists especially who enlarged their foothold on the good opinion of the public for useful work done in classifying soldiers and in other such tasks; and my own science of anthropology obtained a similar lodgment in the bureaus and offices of government and even of business in the course of the more recent world conflict. Now anthropologists advise the government as to the administration of American Indian communities and as to problems arising in rural communities. It is not rare now for a business organization to hire an anthropologist or a sociologist to study what goes on among its employees with a view to learning something that will help the business. Anthropologists in America now have their society and their journal of "applied anthropology."

In Europe, or in parts of it, the application of scientific thought about society to the solution of practical problems is probably not quite so characteristic. Here social science has less vigorously separated itself from the philosophy and speculative thought in which it in part began. At any rate, it is written works by Europeans that chiefly come to my mind when I think of illustrations of the exercise of a second and to me very important function of social science. We might call it the illuminating function, the humanizing function, the enriching function, the making-wise function. The great works about society do not present inventions that can be directly applied to the solution of practical problems. They clarify one or another aspect of man in society. In this clarification they not only suggest to the social scientist problems for further investigations; they also make a revelation of significance to any man who reads and understands. The revelation is as to his own life, to himself, to his own neighborhood perhaps, or to his situation familial or political. When Henry Maine recognized in the history of Roman law and the changes taking place in East Indian villages a great historic and sociological generalization as to the transformation of society from an organization of families to a collection of individuals, he provided a view of social change that helps many people to understand their own places in the social universe. A similar illumination is provided by the related generalization of Durkheim as to social segment and social organ, and by that of F. Tönnies as to *gemeinschaft* and *gesellschaft*. In understanding these ideas, one is helped to understand oneself. I have seen the effect of these ideas upon a young Chinese college student. By their means he saw, almost as if it were a revelation, what was happening to him, in the breakdown of the older familial institutions of China, and saw it as a part of what is happening in many other parts of the world. The realization came to him, as it has to many, as an enlargement of vision, a release of spirit. He saw himself as a part of a great historical trend, as an illustration of an aspect of the nature of changing society.

Do not many of the great works in social science bring this sense of illumination and understanding to the reader? Apart from the influence they have had on the progress of research, have they not played important parts in the liberal education of men and women? When Tocqueville and again when Lord Bryce published their works on America, it was, in each case, as if the European had taken the American by the hand and led him to a mountain top outside his land and from there pointed out to him aspects of his country which he had not noticed while living in it. Many of the works in social science give this sense of personal understanding. At another hour I shall say something more as to how Sumner's *Folkways,* and the writings of Veblen, Freud, Marx, and others have helped many people to think about themselves and their societies and to reach an understanding of their society and of their own places in it.

From this second point of view the function of social science is one of illumination. Social science is needed by society that men may be wiser than they would be without it. From this point of view social science is seen not as an inventor but as a source of light. The books I have just mentioned cannot be directly put to work. They contain no formulas for the solving of practical problems. Their value lies in large part in their power to enlarge vision, to improve the power of judgment, and to lift the human spirit. So regarded, social science helps to show us where we are and what we are. It provides a point of view or a variety of points of view. For the research worker the viewpoint is a guide to his studies—or a challenge to adopt some other viewpoint in his studies. For the man it is a contribution to general education.

The illuminating function is to be recognized in all science, physical as well as social. When the Copernican view of the universe came to be generally accepted, it surely made a difference in the religion of men and in their conception of their place in the universe. Perhaps the recognition of the convertibility of matter and energy or some of the other more recent conceptions of physical science will come to make important changes in the way in which men see themselves in nature. In the case of social sciences the illuminating function is even more apparent. Its subject is man himself, and man is to man more important than is a star or a fish. Social science helps the individual to understand his difficulties, his powers and his limitations. From this way of looking at it, the place of social science in life is like that of philosophy or of art. The reflective person will see that *The Bleak Age* by the Hammonds or the fifth chapter of E. H. Carr's book on *The Conditions of the Peace* is saying what is also said in T. S. Eliot's poem, "The Waste Land." The illumination given by social science issues from its power to show the universal in the particular. Where the poet speaks in symbols, and speaks from his own intuition and personal experience, the social scientist states a generalization derived from the objective and public study of special and verifiable facts. In keeping to its formal and logical character, social science exercises its influences over men's minds. Its contribution to liberal education is made by the fact that it is science, and not art or philosophy. It is the very impersonality of social science, the fact that its vision rests upon the careful studies of many men, that gives it its peculiar authority. But it works together with art and philosophy in performing the illuminating function.

No, the place of social science in modern life is not fully described when its practical usefulness is declared. If social science were merely a servant, it might serve a bad master. If social scientists accomplished nothing but the turning out of devices for governing men, or for making men believe what someone with force at his command wanted them to believe, social science might be a human disaster. In the effort of social science to become truly objective, to make itself descriptive of the nature of man in society without sermonizing on the subject, it became usual for social scientists to deny that their social science had any concern with what people ought to do. "We tell what is, not what ought to be," became the established doctrine.

I have myself not come to deny the soundness of this declaration. But I think I have come to see its shortcoming. In so far as it implies that social science has no influence over the decisions men make as to what they ought to do, I think it is mistaken. I think that in studying society and man in society the social scientist affects his own views and feelings as to what ought to be done and those of other people. On a later occasion I will try to say how I think that this happens. Now I will merely recognize that there is yet a third societal function of social science. We may call it the value-making function. This function is continually exercised as social science makes clear to people what are the probable consequences of one course of action rather than another. Description of something that you cannot help being concerned with often changes the way you feel about it. Men may cling to their opinions on the tariff when they come to understand the effects of the tariff on international trade, but it may also happen that they change their views as a result of the understanding. And there is evidence that those who become concerned with the study of the relations between racial groups modify the attitudes they have had toward racial groups different from their own, although it is probably also true that the existence of an interest or strong attitude about one or another racial group may tend to draw a person into the scientific study of race relations. At any rate, I do not think it can be maintained that the study of any social problem or matter goes on without influence on men's conceptions of what ought to happen, but I suppose it rather to be true that the two, science and scheme of values, are interrelated. Later I will explore with you some of these interrelations.

At another hour I propose to consider a fourth function of social science which is perhaps a special case of the third. The recognition of a fourth function becomes necessary when you see that the formal operations of science are carried on by men who have to control these operations in accordance with principles of conduct. Objectivity in science may be greatly helped by the use of machines and measures. But the machines and measures are of no avail if the scientist is a cheat and a liar. A social scientist, like any other scientist, is himself not a machine but a moral being. He is moral in the laboratory and in the library, as well as at home, or he is no scientist. The morality of the laboratory and the library is a form of altruism. The scientist must subordinate his personal success to the truth. He must be willing to abandon a theory or hypothesis that is shown to be unsound. In all this he serves a general truth and to it sacrifices his own more immediate interests. The morality that he thus exhibits is a necessary part of his science. It is a morality that is not by any means inconsistent with the ideal morality of the communities I know best, but it demands of him conduct that is in some respects nearer that ideal, more altruistic than is the general level of conduct. This is not because scientists are by nature better than other men. It is because their work requires it of them in certain respects. In so far as they meet these exactions of their discipline, the scientists are upholding and strengthening a part of the moral system of the whole community. This is what I mean by the moral function of science.

The case of social science is not different with regard to this fourth function from that of physics and chemistry, except to the degree that the direct concern of the social scientist with the immediate human problems of social life makes it so much the more difficult for him to realize the morality of science. Archimedes studied mathematics during the siege of Syracuse, until the soldiers interrupted him as he drew figures on the sand. The detachment—and the heroism—might have been all the more impressive if Archimedes had been studying politics or the sociology of war. And in that case the soldiers would probably arrive all the sooner with their swords. In a world of partisanship the physicist may be seen as a potential weapon-maker, a specialist whose physics is to be encouraged in the interests of the partisans. But a social scientist is seen, not as a useful inventor, but rather as a source of danger to the cause of the partisan. To every partisan a social scientist is a potential enemy. It is the nature of the social scientist to doubt, to test, or criticize, to reject an unproven view that is popular or powerful. A partisan is one who has adopted a view and now is concerned only with making it prevail, by force if necessary. To be an honest and truly scientific social scientist is to stand for free inquiry and humility before the facts in the face of partisans and power politics.

The people are right—the ordinary people—when they feel that social science is somehow affecting their interests and beliefs. The businessman who fears that the teaching of social science may modify sentiments and convictions to which he is attached, and make people turn away from them, is not wholly wrong. When the proponents of an American National Science Foundation decided not to include, at least expressly, the social sciences in the provisions of a bill which would have given federal financial support for scientific research, they took account of an uneasiness as to social science among the laity that is real. The uneasiness does not arise from a fear that social scientists, like physicists, may invent something that will destroy cities. It arises from the fear that the conduct of social science, in teaching and research, disturbs existing attitudes and values of the community. So it is disturbing. Social science, in my opinion, both strengthens established ideals and also disturbs existing attitudes and values. The beneficial influence of social science upon society is only in part acknowledged when its practical usefulness is declared. The influence is further good, if we want reason to be used in understanding and acting as to the social and political and personal questions that trouble men. Its influence is good for all who think that the mind should be free to inquire and decide. In a society of free men, dedicated to the realization of the generous and altruistic and creative qualities of humanity, social science is as much moral as technical.

The utilitarian function of social science is so well known that I will not deal with it in these lectures. But in the lectures that follow I shall have something to say as to the illuminating function, the value-making function, and the moral function.

THE PROMISE

C. Wright Mills

Nowadays men often feel that their private lives are a series of traps. They sense that within their everyday worlds, they cannot overcome their troubles, and in this feeling, they are often quite correct: what ordinary men are directly aware of and what they try to do are bounded by the private orbits in which they live; their visions and their powers are limited to the close-up scenes of job, family, neighbourhood; in other milieux, they move vicariously and remain spectators. And the more aware they become, however vaguely, of ambitions and of threats which transcend their immediate locales, the more trapped they seem to feel.

Underlying this sense of being trapped are seemingly impersonal changes in the very structure of continent-wide societies. The facts of contemporary history are also facts about the success and the failure of individual men and women. When a society is industrialized, a peasant becomes a worker; a feudal lord is liquidated or becomes a businessman. When classes rise or fall, a man is employed or unemployed; when the rate of investment goes up or down, a man takes new heart or goes broke. When wars happen, an insurance salesman becomes a rocket launcher; a store clerk, a radar man; a wife lives alone; a child grows up without a father. Neither the life of an individual nor the history of a society can be understood without understanding both.

Yet men do not usually define the troubles they endure in terms of historical change and institutional contradiction. The well-being they enjoy, they do not usually impute to the big ups and downs of the societies in which they live. Seldom aware of the intricate connection between the patterns of

From *The Sociological Imagination* © 1959 by C. Wright Mills. Reprinted by permission of Oxford University Press.

their own lives and the course of world history, ordinary men do not usually know what this connection means for the kinds of men they are becoming and for the kinds of history-making in which they might take part. They do not possess the quality of mind essential to grasp the interplay of man and society, of biography and history, of self and world. They cannot cope with their personal troubles in such ways as to control the structural transformations that usually lie behind them.

Surely it is no wonder. In what period have so many men been so totally exposed at so fast a pace to such earthquakes of change? That Americans have not known such catastrophic changes as have the men and women of other societies is due to historical facts that are now quickly becoming "merely history." The history that now affects every man is world history. Within this scene and this period, in the course of a single generation, one-sixth of mankind is transformed from all that is feudal and backward into all that is modern, advanced, and fearful. Political colonies are freed; new and less visible forms of imperialism installed. Revolutions occur; men feel the intimate grip of new kinds of authority. Totalitarian societies rise, and are smashed to bits—or succeed fabulously. After two centuries of ascendancy, capitalism is shown up as only one way to make society into an industrial apparatus. After two centuries of hope, even formal democracy is restricted to a quite small portion of mankind. Everywhere in the under-developed world, ancient ways of life are broken up and vague expectations become urgent demands. Everywhere in the over-developed world, the means of authority and of violence become total in scope and bureaucratic in form. Humanity itself now lies before us, the super-nation at either pole concentrating its most coordinated and massive efforts upon the preparation of the Third World War.

The very shaping of history now outpaces the ability of men to orient themselves in accordance with cherished values. And which values? Even when they do not panic, men often sense that older ways of feeling and thinking have collapsed and that newer beginnings are ambiguous to the point of moral stasis. Is it any wonder that ordinary men feel they cannot cope with the larger worlds with which they are so suddenly confronted? That they cannot understand the meaning of their epoch for their own lives? That—in defence of selfhood—they become morally insensible, trying to remain altogether private men? Is it any wonder that they come to be possessed by a sense of the trap?

It is not only information that they need—in this Age of Fact, information often dominates their attention and overwhelms their capacities to assimilate it. It is not only the skills of reason that they need—although their struggles to acquire these often exhaust their limited moral energy.

What they need, and what they feel they need, is a quality of mind that will help them to use information and to develop reason in order to achieve lucid summations of what is going on in the world and of what may be happening within themselves. It is this quality, I am going to contend, that journalists and scholars, artists and publics, scientists and editors are coming to expect of what may be called the sociological imagination.

The sociological imagination enables its possessor to understand the larger historical scene in terms of its meaning for the inner life and the external career of a variety of individuals. It enables him to take into account how individuals, in the welter of their daily experience, often become falsely conscious of their social positions. Within that welter the framework of modern society is sought, and within that framework the psychologies of a variety of men and women are formulated. By such means the personal uneasiness of individuals is focused upon explicit troubles and the indifference of publics is transformed into involvement with public issues.

The first fruit of this imagination—and the first lessons of the social science that embodies it—is the idea that the individual can understand his own experience and gauge his own fate only by locating himself within his period, that he can know his own chances in life only by becoming aware of those of all individuals in his circumstances. In many ways it is a terrible lesson; in many ways a magnificent one. We do not know the limits of man's capacities for supreme effort or willing degradation, for agony or glee, for pleasurable brutality or the sweetness of reason. But in our time we have come to know that the limits of "human nature" are frighteningly broad. We have come to know that every individual lives, from one generation to the next, in some society; that he lives out a biography, and that he lives it out within some historical sequence. By the fact of his living he contributes, however minutely, to the shaping of this society and to the course of its history, even as he is made by society and by its historical push and shove.

The sociological imagination enables us to grasp history and biography and the relations between the two within society. That is its task and its promise. To recognize this task and this promise is the mark of the classic social analyst. It is characteristic of Herbert Spencer—turgid, polysyllabic, comprehensive; of E. A. Ross—graceful, muckraking, upright; of Auguste Comte and Emile Durkheim; of the intricate and subtle Karl Mannheim. It is the quality of all that is intellectually excellent in Karl Marx; it is the clue to Thorstein Veblen's brilliant and ironic insight, to Joseph Schumpeter's many-sided constructions of reality; it is the basis of the psychological sweep of W. E. H. Lecky no less than of the profundity and clarity of Max Weber. And it is the signal of what is best in contemporary studies of man and society.

No social study that does not come back to the problems of biography, of history, and of their intersections within a society, has completed its intellectual journey. Whatever the specific problems of the classic social analysts, however limited or however broad the features of social reality they have examined, those who have been imaginatively aware of the promise of their work have consistently asked three sorts of questions:

1. What is the structure of this particular society as a whole? What are its essential components, and how are they related to one another? How does it differ from other varieties of social order? Within it, what is the meaning of any particular feature for its continuance and for its change?

2. Where does this society stand in human history? What are the mechanics by which it is changing? What is its place within and its meaning for

the development of humanity as a whole? How does any particular feature we are examining affect, and how is it affected by, the historical period in which it moves? And this period—what are its essential features? How does it differ from other periods? What are its characteristic ways of history-making?

3. What varieties of men and women now prevail in this society and in this period? And what varieties are coming to prevail? In what ways are they selected and formed, liberated and repressed, made sensitive and blunted? What kinds of "human nature" are revealed in the conduct and character we observe in this society in this period? And what is the meaning for "human nature" of each and every feature of the society we are examining?

Whether the point of interest is a great power state or a minor literary mood, a family, a prison, a creed—these are the kinds of questions the best social analysts have asked. They are the intellectual pivots of classic studies of man in society—and they are the questions inevitably raised by any mind possessing the sociological imagination. For that imagination is the capacity to shift from one perspective to another—from the political to the psychological; from examination of a single family to comparative assessment of the national budgets of the world; from the theological school to the military establishment; from considerations of an oil industry to studies of contemporary poetry. It is the capacity to range from the most impersonal and remote transformations to the most intimate features of the human self—and to see the relations between the two. Back of its use there is always the urge to know the social and historical meaning of the individual in the society and in the period in which he has his quality and his being.

That, in brief, is why it is by means of the sociological imagination that men now hope to grasp what is going on in the world, and to understand what is happening in themselves as minute points of the intersections of biography and history within society. In large part, contemporary man's self-conscious view of himself as at least an outsider, if not a permanent stranger, rests upon an absorbed realization of social relativity and of the transformative power of history. The sociological imagination is the most fruitful of this self-consciousness. By its use men whose mentalities have swept only a series of limited orbits often come to feel as if suddenly awakened in a house with which they had only supposed themselves to be familiar. Correctly or incorrectly, they often come to feel that they can now provide themselves with adequate summations, cohesive assessments, comprehensive orientations. Older decisions that once appeared sound, now seem to them products of a mind unaccountably dense. Their capacity for astonishment is made lively again. They acquire a new way of thinking, they experience a transvaluation of values: in a word, by their reflection and by their sensibility, they realize the cultural meaning of the social sciences.

THE SOCIAL SCIENCES IN GENERAL EDUCATION

Vincent P. Norris

> And whereas it is generally true that people will
> be happiest whose laws are best and are best adminis-
> tered, and that laws will be wisely formed and honest-
> ly administered in proportion as those who form and
> administer them are wise and honest; whence it be-
> comes expedient for promoting the public happiness
> that those persons, whom nature hath endowed with
> genius and virtue, should be rendered by liberal educa-
> tion worthy to receive and able to guard the sacred
> deposit of the rights and liberties of their fellow citi-
> zens . . . .
>
> Thomas Jefferson, *Bill for the More*
> *General Diffusion of Knowledge*

No man was more convinced than Thomas Jefferson of the people's right and ability to govern themselves. Nevertheless he was fully aware that the success of the American experiment in self-government is ultimately dependent upon the knowledge which Americans bring to the solving of public problems. Thus he was a life-long advocate of liberal education which was, A. Whitney Griswold tells us, "perhaps the principal inspiration of his life. It runs as a major theme through all his works—his public papers and his private correspondence—informing and promoting him at every state of his career."

If men are to be ruled by despots it is better that they be kept ignorant, for they are then the more malleable. In the early empires, from the beginnings of civilization onward, the newly found literacy was the exclusive property of the ruling caste; the peasantry was kept illiterate and ignorant.

In classical Greece, where the first experiment in democracy was conducted, liberal education was born. The Greeks recognized that although ignorance is good preparation for servility it is poor training for the making of significant public decisions. Thus, while the children of the slaves received only vocational training for the performance of whatever tasks they were destined to carry out, the children of the citizens studied what have come to be called the "liberal arts." The world "liberal" here is kin to the word "liberty." The liberal arts are those branches of knowledge that men through the centuries have considered prerequisite to the living of a fully human, self-governing life.

This tradition still lives in American universities. We grant the usefulness of vocational, or as it is now called, professional, education. Who would want his brain tumor removed or even his plumbing repaired by someone who knows only philosophy? That is not intended as a slur against plumbers, or philosophers either, for that matter. As John Gardner pointed out, a nation must have excellence both in its philosophy *and* in its plumbing, or else neither its ideas nor its pipes will hold water.

No, it is not that we do not need skilled professionals, technicians, and artisans; of course we do. It is rather that no man is complete if he is *merely* a professional, or technician, or artisan. He is, in Alfred North Whitehead's words, no more than a highly trained barbarian.

THE SOCIAL SCIENCES

It is impossible to trace, in these few pages, the evolution of the liberal arts from their beginnings to our own age. We have space only for some introductory remarks about the social sciences and their role in "the More General Diffusion of Knowledge." Our concentration here on the social sciences is not meant to imply that they enjoy a place of special importance. Liberal education involves the arts and humanities, the life and physical sciences, and the social sciences. All of them are ways man has devised in his struggle to understand himself and his world. No one can call himself educated who is ignorant of any of those fields.

The social sciences are distinguished from the arts and humanities in that they are "scientific" and from the life and physical sciences in that they are concerned with things "social." It is generally agreed that the social sciences include anthropology, economics, political science and sociology, but there agreement ends. There is a strong argument for including social psychology, that hybrid which lives in the interstice between psychology and sociology. About psychology itself, however, there is considerable dispute. Although some psychologists consider their discipline a social science, others insist that it is a biological science, a close kin of physiology; still others insist that it is a physical science, not far removed from physics. Now and then one hears that it is one of the humanities. To a great extent, it depends on *which* psychology they are talking about.

Another discipline about which the argument continues is history. Is it a social science or one of the humanities? In *The Uses of the Past,* Herbert Muller answers "that history is more genuinely scientific in spirit as it takes into account the reasons why it cannot be utterly objective or strictly scientific in method." Without doubt, history informs all the social sciences, for it explains how things came to be as they are. Every social science has its historical aspects and its practitioners whose interests are primarily historical.

Most people, remembering their sixth-grade geography, think of it as the study of mountains, deserts, jungles, oceans, climates and ore deposits. And, in part, it is. But a growing number of geographers are interested in the human populations scattered about the earth—their densities, movements, and relationships to the earth's physical features.

Linguistics is the study of languages—their forms, their underlying structures, their histories, and geographical distributions. Traditionally, it has been considered a branch of anthropology. Recently, however, it has developed into an independent discipline. It has been described as "the most scientific of the humanities and the most humanistic of the sciences." In any case, language itself is a part of culture. In all likelihood it is the most important part, for its influence seems to pervade every other aspect of culture. It has even been hypothesized, but not conclusively demonstrated as yet, that even the way in which a people perceive reality is determined by the form of their language. Naturally, learning the language of a culture, whether it is contemporary or extinct, is an important key to the discovery of other aspects of that culture.

Communications, in which advanced degrees have been awarded for less than a generation, may be the youngest of the social sciences. It is the study of the processes and institutions by means of which the members of a society exchange the symbols which inform, influence, enculturate and entertain them. Its scope includes both interpersonal or face-to-face communication, such as the patterns of gossip and rumor; and mediated or mass communication, such as the structure and functions of the mass media and their relationship to other aspects of the culture.

But "young" is a relative term when applied to the social sciences; none of them is very old *as a science.* Because the questions with which they deal are of such fundamental importance to mankind, philosophers have always been concerned with them. But the social sciences, as such, came into their own by breaking away from philosophy only about a century ago. Economics is a bit older than that, Adam Smith's *Inquiry into the Nature and Causes of the Wealth of Nations* having been published in 1776; but Adam Smith was a moral philosopher, not an economist in the current sense. He has been called the grandfather rather than the father of economics.

It is to their youth that we may attribute, in part, the social sciences' many imperfections. But it is not only that; another factor, if we may use unscientific language, is the sheer cussedness of their subject matter, *homo sapiens.* Even though the physical sciences now recognize that they too must deal in probabilities rather than certainties, the behavior of Mars or of an atom of chlorine is highly predictable compared with that of man. The story is told that someone once attempted to compliment Albert Einstein by contrasting his successful formulation of the theory of relativity with the dismal failure of governments to preclude its possible application to the destruction of mankind. "Ah, but physics is easy," he replied, "and politics is very hard."

Let us return to anthropology, economics, political science and sociology—the generally agreed-upon social sciences, and say a few words about each of them. Anthropology is usually defined as the study of man, although one distinguished anthropologist has suggested that it is really the study of *kinds* of men. Anthropologists have a number of specific research interests but the discipline is now usually said to comprise three basic divisions: physical and cultural anthropology, and archeology. Physical anthropologists are students of the biology of living and extinct populations. They study the evolution of man from his primate forbears to his present racial variations and his adaptation to all varieties of environments.

Cultural anthropologists are students of man's ways—the ways in which different societies are organized to conduct their affairs, and with the products of men's minds and hands. That is, they are interested in *culture*—"That complex whole which includes knowledge, belief, art, morals, law, customs, and any other capabilities and habits acquired by man as a member of society."[1] Cultural anthropologists occasionally study men in modern industrialized societies, but their concern is usually with men in simpler societies: with the members of nonliterate folk societies, and with the peasants who live on the margins of civilization.

Whereas cultural anthropologists are almost exclusively concerned with living men, archeologists devote their energies to reconstructing, from their remains, societies that have disappeared. Surely the best known example is the fellow in khaki shorts and pith helmet, digging into the sands of the Middle Eastern desert or groping along the dark and mysterious corridors of the pyramids. But not far from Penn State University, archeologists have been working hurriedly to unearth the riches of Sheep Rock, where Americans lived seven thousand years ago, before the site is lost forever to the waters rising behind Raystown Dam.

Economics, according to the classic definition of Alfred Marshall, is the study of man in the everyday business of life. But that doesn't tell us much, and it seems a better definition of cultural anthropology than of economics, which has been concerned almost exclusively with capitalistic and other modern, "monetized" economies while ignoring all the others.

Another common definition, found on the first page of many introductory texts, is that economics is the study of how scarce resources are allocated to satisfy man's insatiable wants. But a few economists leave man entirely out of their definitions, thus raising the question whether economics is indeed a social science. Frank Knight, for example, has insisted that economics is purely a *formal* science, like mathematics; and Kenneth Boulding claims that the "economist's interest is not in human behavior but in the behavior of *commodities.*"[2] Marston Bates, a biologist, complained that the world of the economists is a world "of abstractions—money, labor, market, goods, capital. There is no room for people . . . people loving and hating and dreaming. People become the labor force or the market."[3]

It is true that the entire structure of economics has long rested upon a mere handful of *a priori* postulates about the behavior of men, the validity of which has often been challenged. But there is no doubting the imposing edifice of theory built upon these postulates, and no modern government would dream of conducting its affairs without the advice of a staff of economists. The disagreements among economists are many and are often the source of humor ("He predicted nine of the last six recessions," jibed one economist about a rival), and their diagnoses as well as their prescriptions are rarely free of ideological influence. But if these are faults of economics they show that for all their abstractions, economists have not lost sight of the fact that at bottom, they *are* concerned with people—perhaps not loving and hating and dreaming, but people struggling for a better life for themselves and their children. Perhaps Marshall's definition isn't so bad, after all.

Political science, naturally, is the science of politics. Not in the narrow sense in which the word is used in ordinary conversation by Americans, but in the larger sense of men trying to govern themselves and create a good society. Man is *zoön politikon,* said Aristotle—an animal who lives in the polis. He who does not is either a beast or a god, but he is certainly not a man. Although we might not go as far as Aristotle we are aware that, with rare exceptions, men prefer to live in the company of others. But men do not just live together, in physical proximity; they live in a structure of organized relationships. There must be rules. Otherwise, as Thomas Hobbes insisted, life would be "poor, nasty, brutish and short." Security and order must be maintained; justice must be provided for; decisions must be made which will affect the fortunes of the entire group. In modern societies, whether democratic or authoritarian, those are the tasks of government. Simpler societies do not have governments in the modern sense, but every one of them has a political order, a system of institutions for coping with those problems of order, security, justice, sovereignty. They are problems that man has never really solved, problems which never go away; this may be what makes political science so interesting.

Finally, sociology—of all the social sciences, sociology may be the hardest to define. Practically all the interests attributed above to the other social scientists are also those, at one time or another, of sociologists. "Sociology studies the processes and patterns of individual and group interaction, the forms of organization of social groups, the relationships among them, and group influences on individual behavior."[4] This definition excludes very little that is social. There are sociologists who study men at work and men at play, or the members of age groups, ethnic groups, social classes or entire communities, or even entire societies. There are specialists in stratification, social mobility, juvenile delinquency, gerontology, crowd behavior, public opinion, and religion, to name just a few areas. Another area, which its proponents argue is the very core of sociology, is the sociology of knowledge. It is the study of the relationships between social organization and belief systems, between institutions and ideas. Surely institutions, such as universal suffrage, and beliefs, such as "We hold these truths to be self evident, that all men are created equal," are interrelated. But the debate as to the precise nature of that relationship goes on and no solution is in sight. Several readings in this book deal with this relationship and with the relative importance of ideas and social organization as determinants of social change.

THE SCIENTIFIC METHOD

What sets the social sciences apart from other means of striving to understand man and society is their dependence upon the scientific method. The novelist or artist or theologian is just as eager as the anthropologist or sociologist to discover and present the truth about his subject, but he doesn't go about it "scientifically."

Unfortunately, it is necessary to pause here to point out that the above remark is not intended as a criticism. In our society, science has become a "sacred cow," and most Americans are guilty of some degree of idolatry from time to time. This has been encouraged, and no doubt exploited by Madison Avenue. How often have our television screens presented us with the spectacle of a fellow in a white lab coat, holding up a product and saying, "Science proves..." This overdone reverence for science is unfortunate for it has led to the misapplication of science, or we should say *pseudo-science,* in areas where it is inappropriate. This is known as *scientism,* "the pernicious exaggeration of both the status and function of science."[5] It is a kind of fanaticism and like every other kind, it should be recognized for what it is.

In short, to criticize the artist or humanist for being unscientific is as absurd as to criticize the economist for being untheological or the archeologist for being unmilitary. Science is not better than art or philosophy, it is simply *different.*

One way of characterizing this difference is to say that whereas the painter or musician pours himself into his work, the social scientist tries as much as possible to keep himself *out* of his. That is, he tries to prevent his own biases, values, and tastes from influencing the outcome of his research, although of course they will influence his choice of *what* to research. The artist strives for individuality. The good artist succeeds ("Ah, that's a Picasso!"). The social scientist, on the other hand, strives for replicability; his work is validated as other social scientists come up with the same answers. And that is what the scientific method is all about, when all the convoluted jargon is over and done with.

But it is not easy for a social scientist to keep himself out of his work. Indeed, it may not be possible. The astronomer may not be influenced by his political views as he studies a quasar in distant space, but it is much more difficult for the political scientist or economist to forget his politics as he studies a proposed foreign policy or the rising level of unemployment.

At the risk of complicating matters, we must admit that not every social scientist accepts the desirability of keeping oneself out of his work. Near the end of a lifetime of significant research, Robert Redfield argued the opposite case:

I am an anthropologist, and have taken the oath of objectivity. Somehow the broken pledge—if it is broken—sits lightly on my conscience. In me, man and anthropologist do not separate themselves sharply. I used to think I could bring about that separation in scientific work about humanity. Now I have come to confess that I have not effected it, and indeed to think that it is not possible to do so. All the rules of objectivity I should maintain: the marshaling of evidence that may be confirmed by others, the persistent doubting and testing of all important descriptive formulations that I make, the humility before the facts, and the willingness to confess oneself wrong and begin over. I hope I may always strive to obey these rules. But I think now that what I see men do, and understand as something that human beings do, is often with a valuing of it. I like or dislike as I go. This is how I reach understanding of it.[6]

Nevertheless, the recognition that there are so many opportunities to be misled, and to mislead oneself, causes social scientists to be concerned with methodology. Sometimes, unfortunately, they become too concerned. The charge is often heard that physics has a subject but sociology has only a method. There is some truth in it, as sociologist Peter Berger admits:

... it is quite true that some sociologists, especially in America, have become so preoccupied with methodological questions that they have ceased to be interested in society at all. As a result, they have found out nothing of significance about any aspect of social life, since in science as in love a concentration on technique is quite likely to lead to impotence.[7]

Sociology, however, should not be singled out in this regard. All the social sciences, and other disciplines too, have their rampant methodologists. Abraham Kaplan says that like a small boy who has been given a hammer for Christmas, they find that everything in sight needs pounding. The pounding, in fact, is no longer the means to an end; it is an end in itself.

Percy W. Bridgman, the famous physicist and philosopher of science, once said he had "no other method than doing his damnedest" to be scientific.[8] That means, among other things, that one must have a high regard for the facts. Or, as we otherwise say, science is empirical. The scientist doesn't want to take anyone's word for anything, no matter how reasonable it seems; he wants to see for himself. Students sometimes equate that with experimentation. This is a mistake. Conducting an experiment is one way to see the facts for oneself, but it is not the only way by any means. A good deal of experimentation goes on in some of the social sciences but others are almost entirely devoid of it. There is little opportunity for experimentation in archeology, for example. But there is as little in astronomy. Archeology is none the less scientific for that; neither is astronomy.

Social scientists in the various disciplines have a variety of ways of seeking the facts. To some extent these are dictated by the nature of the field, as astronomy requires the telescope and microbiology the microscope. An anthropologist may live among the members of another society for a year or more, observing, interviewing, and making careful notes. A sociologist may become a "participant observer" of some segment of his own society. An economist, however, would never say that he studies the American economy by living, working, and consuming in the United States all his life. Especially as his discipline becomes more quantitative in method, he believes he needs more "rigorous" data, which usually means a variety of business and government documents and, in some cases, polls of consumers.

Speaking of polls brings us to statistics. Since the 1930s there has been a great development of statistical and sampling techniques for the collection and analysis of data gathered from samples of the population. Everyone has heard of the public opinion polls by George Gallup and of the various Nielsen, Trendex, and other ratings of television audiences. But no one has ever been included in such a poll, or even knows of anyone who has—or so it seems— and as a result great skepticism exists in the public mind concerning their validity. Well, sampling, like anything else, can be done badly; and in the short history of polling there have been some colossal disasters. But when done properly, sampling can provide the researcher with remarkably accurate information.

The widespread use of sampling in the social sciences (and in other sciences and in government and business as well) arises from immense difficulty and expense of conducting a *census* (which means asking everyone). Even the United States government, with all its resources, attempts that only once a decade. Social scientists make considerable use of census data, but when the answers they are looking for are not there, they must gather their own. In that effort they resort to sampling because they practically never have the time or the funds to conduct a census unless the population they are studying is very small.

But sampling must be carried out with great care because of the variation within the population being studied. One cannot just ask his friends, or people he meets on the street. A chef doesn't have to eat the entire pot of soup, or even one percent of it, to see if it needs more salt. If he has stirred it well before tasting, the batch will be so homogeneous that a single spoonful will be representative. But people are different—different from soup, and more important, different from one another. Thus the social scientist does not dare to take a single taste, for fear of falling into the absurdity of the mythical visitor to the American frontier who reported,

"Indians always walk single file."

"Are you sure?"

"Well, the one I saw did."

That kind of conclusion-jumping is as commonplace as it is unfortunate. Most of the notions people carry around in their heads about other identifiable groups of men are stereotypes of that sort, based on equally flimsy evidence.

But if the question is asked, how many Indians must one watch before he is justified in saying that they always walk single file, then the answer is that he must watch every Indian, forever. Such is the logic of induction. Fortunately, for the social scientist, he need not often make such categorical propositions. In fact, it is rarely possible for him to do so, since as we have already said, people are different. Therefore, statements by social scientists usually take a more cautious form: "At least in the United States, the timing of marital dissolution reaches a peak around the third year." Many statements simply point out tendencies, such as "Human conflicts cannot usually be settled by removing the original source of conflict," or "The greater the sexual freedom of women the less prostitution." In just a few instances, however, it is possible to arrive at an almost universal proposition: "Every known human society, certainly every known society of any size, is stratified."[9]

SCIENCE AS THEORIZING

One often hears that the facts speak for themselves. But as the distinguished historian Carl Becker said, the facts never say anything at all. They just lie there. In other words, facts in isolation are useless, like a heap of automobile parts. They get us nowhere. It is only when facts are organized, assembled into a structure, and explained, that they help us to make sense of the world. Certainly, science is empirical. But just as certainly, the goal of science is to get as far away from empiricism as possible. That is, to go from fact to theory. And the more general the theory—the further removed it is from individual fact—the better.

Perhaps no scientific term is more abused in ordinary converstion than "theory." Laymen seem to believe that a theory is some kind of personal hunch, or that it has nothing to do with the real world. "I have a theory . . ." they say, or "That's all right in theory but it won't work out in practice." Well, a theory that doesn't "work" is a bad theory, for the function of a theory is to explain, *successfully,* the facts one observes. Not only the facts one has already observed, but the facts one will observe in the future. John Dewey was the greatest of pragmatists; thus we may believe him when he tells us "There is nothing so practical as a good theory."

THE UNITY OF THE SOCIAL SCIENCES

In the eighteenth century, the German scientist and philosopher Leibniz could take all knowledge as his province. Thomas Jefferson, whose statement of concern that the people be liberally educated introduced this article, may have come as close as any modern man to mastering all the knowledge of his day. President Kennedy once invited all American Nobel Laureates to dine at the White House. Geniuses from a great variety of fields were there. The President toasted them thus: "Never before has so much wisdom been gathered under this roof at one time, except when Thomas Jefferson dined alone."

Genius and wisdom are not confined to any one historical epoch, any more than to one color of men or to one part of the globe. But knowledge has increased explosively since Jefferson's day, and is now said to be doubling every few years. No longer can any man hope to master all knowledge. Hence it has been divided, rather arbitrarily, into all the disciplines currently listed in university catalogs. It is a way of reducing that knowledge to manageable chunks. As knowledge continues to grow this division and subdivision goes on constantly. Most social scientists, and for that matter scholars in other fields too, will admit that they cannot know even the entirety of their own disciplines, much less the others. For better or worse, continually increasing specialization seems to be a fact of life in academe as elsewhere.

Nevertheless, it is a rare social scientist who would deny that the social sciences are really branches of a single science, or that the lines of demarcation among them are vague, fuzzy, and in fact fictitious. Not only are all the social sciences related, but *all knowledge.* The universe is not divided into watertight compartments; everything in it is related to everything else. Some things are more *directly* related than others, that is all.

Those who work in General Education in the social sciences believe that just as there is a need for intradisciplinary specialization there is a complementary need for interdisciplinary integration. One means of working toward that end is to select a topic that has significance for all the social sciences and then to study that topic in such a way as to cast light on those aspects of the several disciplines which united them as well as on those which differentiate them.

One eminently suitable topic for such an investigation is the city, a phenomenon of overwhelming significance in human experience. For millenia, of course, men got along quite nicely (by their lights) without the city, and a sizable number of men still do—in the jungles of South America, on islands in the Pacific, and across the frozen tundra of the Arctic Circle. But when certain requisite conditions were met in a few places on the globe, the city appeared— and spread. The city was in no sense inevitable, but once here it is inexorable. As Redfield said, "After the rise of cities, men became something different from what they had been before."[10]

FOOTNOTES

1. This definition of culture is attributed to Edward B. Tylor, one of the important pioneers in anthropology. See George and Achilles Theodorson, *Modern Dictionary of Sociology* (New York: Thomas Y. Crowell, 1969) p. 95.

2. K. Boulding, *The Skills of the Economist* (Cleveland: Howard Allen, 1965) p. 29.

3. M. Bates, *The Forest and the Sea* (New York: Random House, 1965) p. 251.

4. Theodorson, *op cit,* p. 401.

5. A. Kaplan, *The Conduct of Inquiry* (San Francisco: Chandler Publishing Co., 1964) p. 405.

6. R. Redfield, *The Primitive World and Its Transformations* (Ithaca: Great Seal Books, 1953) p. 165.

7. P. Berger, *Invitation to Sociology* (Garden City: Doubleday-Anchor Books, 1963) p. 13.

8. A. Kaplan, *op cit,* p. 27.

9. These several statements can be found in Berelson and Steiner *Human Behavior* (New York: Harcourt, Brace & World, 1964) pps. 312, 622, 632, and 460, respectively.

10. R. Redfield, *op cit.,* p. ix of the Introduction.

Section B. Methodology
of the Social Sciences

DISCOVERY AND EXPLANATION

George C. Homans

For our purposes—my readers' and mine—the social sciences include psychology, anthropology, sociology, economics, political science, history, and probably linguistics. These sciences are in fact a single science. They share the same subject matter—the behavior of men. And they employ, without always admitting it, the same body of general explanatory principles. This last truth is so obvious that it is still highly controversial.

The question most often asked of these sciences is the one question I shall not ask: whether they are sciences at all. The very effort to answer it by demonstrating in action that they are truly no-nonsense, brass-instrument, experimental scientists has damaged some sociologists: they have gotten diverted from the matter of science to the manner. Yet in all these fields even scholars less preoccupied with their status would have no trouble agreeing that they were scientists—except perhaps the historians. The historians get the best of both worlds: they become humanists when judged by the scientists and scientists when judged by the humanists. Not all the physical scientists, of course, would agree that the social sciences were sciences. They would argue that social science was not exact and could not make many specific predictions. By these standards Darwin's theory of evolution would not qualify as scientific: it makes no very exact statements, nor can very precise predictions be made from it. Yet not a scholar in the world would deny scientific status to the theory of evolution, even without its underpinnings in modern genetics. What makes a science are its aims, not its results. If it aims at establishing more or less general relationships between properties of nature, when the test of the

From *The Nature of Social Science* ©1967 by George C. Homans. Reprinted by permission of Harcourt Brace Jovanovich, Inc.

truth of a relationship lies finally in the data themselves, and the data are not wholly manufactured—when nature, however stretched out on the rack, still has a chance to say "No!"—then the subject is a science. By these standards all the social sciences qualify—even history. The humanities do not. Much fiction, for instance, is very true to life, but the standard by which fiction is judged is certainly not in general this kind of truthfulness.

Much less often asked, though much more interesting, is the question: What sort of science is social science? Yet I shall go wrong at the very beginning if I seem to imply in this question that social science differs radically from other science. The differences are matters not of kind but of degree. The enterprise of science faces everywhere the same characteristic problems. What forms do they take in the social sciences? How successful are the social sciences in coping with them, compared with one another and with the physical and biological sciences? If there are different degrees of success, what are the reasons for the differences? These are the questions I shall address myself to, without any hope of answering them fully.

I believe the questions are worth trying to answer, both to dampen the high hopes and to lighten the deep disillusion that sometimes afflict the students of the social sciences. I shall work on both the manic and the depressive phases of our collective psychosis. Briefly, you shall know the worst—and the worst shall make you free.

Though I sometimes teach history and have published papers in anthropology, I shall speak here primarily from the point of view of a sociologist, not only because that is by title my profession but also because sociology, it seems to me, suffers from the manic-depressive psychosis more severely than do the other social sciences. Its aims are larger, and its confidence smaller. In both directions it protests too much, and accordingly it stands in greater need of therapy.

If mine were questions to be answered by the philosophy of science, I should keep quiet, for the philosophy of science is well advanced. I shall need philosophy, but I shall need something more—the qualities of a student of comparative science—and I do not know that there is such a thing. If there were, how would he differ from a philosopher? Let me illustrate. Supposing explanation to be one of the aims of any science, a philosopher may hope to make clear to us what explanation is. In so doing he may well cite examples of the types of explanation developed in different sciences, and in this sense he will be comparative. Less often will he compare the sciences with respect to the practical difficulties they encounter in attaining to any explanation at all. It is just this latter sort of comparison that I shall need to make here.

Let me say at once that if the social sciences are in some ways less successful than the physical sciences, and some of the social sciences less successful than others, I do not—at least not in my sober moods—believe the reason to be that the scholars in the less successful fields are less intelligent, though success does tend to attract intelligence. And I never believe, though it is a common belief, the reason to be that the less successful fields are younger, and so have not had time to show what they can do. Sociology, for one, is not all that young—if it begins with Aristotle it is practically as old as physics —and in recent years it has been very energetic. No, I think the reason is of a different kind. An occasional thoughtless thinker asserts that science is a free creation of the human spirit. But how free? And where free? There is something intractable out there—call it the world, call it nature—intractable especially in not being all of a piece, all of the same grain, which may make it more difficult to create in some fields than in others. The difference finally lies neither in the mind nor in the subject matter but in the relation between the two—the problems that the materials of the different sciences present for the mind trying to bring order out of their different kinds of chaos.

PROPOSITIONS

Any science has two main jobs to do: discovery and explanation. By the first we judge whether it is a science, by the second, how successful a science it is. Discovery is the job of stating and testing more or less general relationships between properties of nature. I call this discovery only because in many sciences the relationships were unknown before research revealed them: for instance, the discovery that bats navigate on the sonar principle. As we shall see, discovery in this sense, particularly discovery of the more general relationships, is much less characteristic of the social sciences than of the others, making one of the most striking differences between them.

A discovery takes the form of a statement of a relationship between properties of nature. Let us be sure we understand what this means. Take Boyle's familiar law: The volume of a gas in an enclosed space is inversely proportional to the pressure on it. A statement, a sentence like this, consists of two parts: first, a reference to what the relationship applies to—gas in an enclosed space—and second, a specification of the relationship between the properties, which must, of course, be at least two in number. Here the two properties are volume and pressure, and the relationship is inverse proportionality: if pressure goes up, volume will go down. Volume and pressure are continuous variables. In another variety of this kind of sentence, the properties, to speak loosely, can take only two values, as in the sentence: A man who loses his kidneys is dead. Here the variables are really classes: first, having kidneys or not having kidneys, and second, being alive or dead. And the relationship between the two is association: not having kidneys is definitely associated with being dead. Sentences of these two varieties I shall call "propositions." Propositions are the one essential product of any science.

In the words of Percy Bridgman, all propositions are accompanied, implicitly or explicitly, by a "text."[1] In the case of Boyle's Law, the text would include answers to such questions as: What is a gas? What are pressure and temperature? How are they defined and measured? The text might also include a statement of the conditions within which the relationship held good. Boyle's Law holds good under the condition that the temperature of the gas is constant.

I have heard that propositions, statements of relationships between properties of nature, were "more or less general." When I assert that the battle of Hastings was fought on October 14, 1066, I am certainly stating a relationship, but it is a relationship of association between a single event and a single time. If I asserted that all decisive battles were fought in October, the statement would, if true, begin to have some generality. And if I asserted that all battles whatsoever were fought in October, the generalization would be, in the terms used here, more general still. In the same way, Boyle's Law, which applies to all gases in an enclosed space and at constant temperature, is less general than a law applying to all gases at any temperature. But let us not worry much at the moment about the degree of generality of propositions. To have stated and tested a proposition of any degree of generality is no mean achievement. Let us remember Mr. Justice Holmes's dictum: "I always say that the chief end to man is to form general propositions," and let us not altogether forget what he added: "And no generalization is worth a damn."[2]

NONOPERATING DEFINITIONS

I suppose every professor has horrid moments of feeling that he is teaching his students everything but what they really need to know, everything but the fundamentals. One reason why I have made the, after all, rather obvious points of the last few paragraphs is that I seldom teach my students how to recognize the different kinds of sentence that appear in the literature of social science, and I take the opportunity, belatedly and vicariously, of doing so now. Especially they need to be able to recognize a real proposition, or rather how to tell a real proposition from other kinds of sentence, for these nuggets are often few and far between. If, as Bridgman says, every proposition is accompanied by a text, the text in much of social science seems to take more room than it does in physical science. Indeed in some sociological writings no room is left for anything else.

Yet real propositions do appear in the literature of social science, and so do definitions of the terms that occur in them, the equivalents of the definition of pressure that accompanies Boyle's Law. These I call "operating definitions," because we actually work with them. An example might be a definition of the term "frequency" to accompany the proposition: The more valuable a man perceives the result of his action to be, the more frequently he will perform the action. I want my students to be able to distinguish operating definitions and real propositions from two other kinds of sentence, similar in form to definitions and propositions respectively, which appear very often in the literature of social science, particularly in introductory texts and in "general theory." These I call "nonoperating definitions" and "orienting statements."

Examples of nonoperating definitions include the definitions of some so-called central concepts in sociology and anthropology, concepts the workers in these fields take to the glories of their sciences. Thus a "role" is the behavior expected of a man occupying a particular social position. And a "culture" is the inherited pattern of living of the members of a society. These are nonoperating definitions because they do not define variables that appear in the testable propositions of social science. Though "roles" and "cultures" could each perhaps be analyzed into clusters of variables, they certainly are not such themselves. It would be absurd to say: "The more the role, the more the something else." We might indeed say: "The more specific the role, the lower the social position in which the behavior is expected." But here the variable would be specificity and not role itself.

This example suggests that "role" may have the status in sociological propositions that "gas" has in Boyle's Law: we might speak of the specificity *of* the role as we speak of the pressure *on* the gas. But I am not sure that the parallel holds. Certainly the status of the two is not exactly alike. For some propositions, like Boyle's Law, that hold good of gases do not always hold good of non-gasses—liquids and solids—but it is far from clear that there are propositions that hold good of roles but not of non-roles (whatever they may be). That is, the word "gas" makes a difference in meaning, and "role" may not.

I think the same sort of thing is true of "culture." But here I add a comment that gets me a little ahead of my argument. An anthropologist friend once said to me, in pointing out the usefulness of this concept: "If someone asks me, for instance, why the Chinese do not like milk, I can only say, 'Because of the culture.' "[3] All I could say in turn was that, if that was all *he* could say, he was not saying much. All that the use of the word "culture" implied was that disliking milk had been characteristic of the behavior of some Chinese for some generations. But we knew that already; "culture" did not add anything. What we should have liked to know was why milk, specifically, rather than, say, tea was disliked. Talking about culture did not answer this question at all—not at all. More generally, "explanation by concept" is not explanation.

Yet I am loath to argue that the concepts "role" and "culture" are useless. What I want to be sure of is that we recognize the sort of usefulness they possess. They tell us roughly the kinds of thing we are going to talk about. They and their definitions tell us that we are going to talk about expected behavior, and it may indeed be well for a new student to be forewarned. But sooner or later we must stop "being about to" talk about something and actually say something—that is, state propositions. Lingering over nonoperating definitions may actually get in the way of this primary job of science. This happens, I think, when nonoperating definitions are multiplied and elaborated into a nonoperating conceptual scheme (called a "general theory"), as in much—not all—of the work of Talcott Parsons. Some students get so much intellectual security out of such a scheme, because it allows them to give names to, and to pigeonhole, almost any social phenomenon, that they are hesitant to embark on the dangerous waters of actually saying something about the relations between the phenomena—because then they must actually take the risk of being found wrong. The failure to state real propositions leads in turn to a failure to create real theories, for, as we shall see, a real theory consists precisely of propositions. I sometimes think we need not be at such pains introducing our students to social science. Start them out at once with real propositions. They would find out soon enough what we were going to talk about: we should already be talking about it.

ORIENTING STATEMENTS

Just as "role" and "culture" are famous concepts, so what I call "orienting statements" include some of the most famous statements of social science. One is Marx's statement that the organization of the means of production determines the other features of a society. This is more than a definition and resembles a proposition in that it relates two phenomena to one another. But these phenomena—the means of production and the other features of a society—are not single variables. At best they are whole clusters of undefined variables. And the relationship between the phenomena is unspecified, except that the main direction of causation—determination—is from the former to the latter. Whereas Boyle's Law says that, if pressure goes up, volume will assuredly go down, what Marx's Law says is that, if there is some, any, change in the means of production, there will be some unspecified change or changes in the other features of society. Put the matter another way: Boyle will allow one to predict *what* will happen; Marx will only allow one to predict that *something* will happen. Accordingly, I cannot grant his law the status of a real proposition.

In taking Marx's statement thus out of context, I do not in the least mean to imply that this is all he had to say about the relations between the infrastructure and the superstructure of society, or that his writings do not include other statements that are real propositions, or that this particular statement is unimportant. That is far from my view.

Another example of an orienting statement is the assertion by Parsons and Shils that, in social interaction between any two persons, the actions of each are sanctioned by the actions of the other.[4] This is an important statement in that, in my view, the beginning if wisdom in the study of social behavior is to look at it as an exchange between at least two persons, in which the action of each rewards or punishes—that is, sanctions—the action of the other. But the statement in itself does not say what effect a change in the behavior of one will have on the behavior of another. Like Marx's Law, it implies that there will be *some* effect, but does not begin to say what. Only if Parsons and Shils had gone on to say, for instance, that the more rewarding (valuable) to one man is the action of the other, the more often will the first perform the action that gets him the reward—only then would they have stated a real proposition. Much of what they say suggests that they believe this proposition to be true, but they manage to avoid coming right out with it.

For my third example I do not take an isolated statement but a passage from a book, chosen for no better reason than that I read it recently. If it were a bad book, that fact would get in the way of my making the point that passages more or less like this one have been appearing for many years and in immense numbers in all the best literature of social science:

An individual is born into a social system that possesses a culture. The social-ization of that individual is a threefold process. It involves the inculcation of the culture upon the individual by the social system. The transmission of culture through socialization is never complete. The individual learns only a selected number of elements in the culture of his society. He introjects, or commits himself to, even fewer elements of that culture. In so doing he brings to bear the influence of his own personality upon the survival and growth of the culture. Also, the social system itself does not act upon the individual in his socialization. It is individual members of the system who act upon him. Their influence upon him reflects the uniformity of relationships that comprise the social system. Their influence also reflects their own idiosyncratic response to culture, based on the dynamics of their personalities. In this way, the individual is trained in the common bonds of society. But the pattern of his being taught and the lessons he learns are unique to him.[5]

In a way, this is all sound as a bell. I suppose we could find out, for instance, what words like "culture" and "socialization" meant, and would even agree that culture was transmitted through socialization. But let us ask ourselves this question: Where in the passage do we find a single statement from which we could tell what specific change would occur, or even probably occur, along any one dimension of human behavior if there were a specific change along another? Yet it is the business of a science to make such statements. The passage tells us that things like culture, socialization, and the social system are all important and all somehow related to one another, but it tells us nothing *about* them. It is all true—and all powerless. After so many years of orientation, do we and our students really need so many weak truths?

Much writing in social science consists of orienting statements when it does not consist of nonoperating definitions. Orienting statements do not qualify as real propositions: they are of little use in prediction and of none at all, as we shall see, in explanation. Yet I should be slow to argue that they did no good in other ways. I must testify, perhaps complacently, that I personally have been greatly helped both by Marx and by Parsons and Shils. I claim that statements of this sort are really imperatives, telling us what we ought to look into further or how we ought to look at it. This is the reason why I call them orienting statements. Look at the relations between the means of production and the other features of society, for if you look, you will surely find! Look on social behavior as an exchange, for then you will begin to make progress! And, God knows, with the help of Marx at least, scholars have made progress. Looking where he pointed, they have discovered and tested statements that, if of smaller scope than Marx's, still have more of the character of real propositions.

Yet the very success of Marx's Law in being useful in its particular way teaches us that we should not mistake orienting statements for either the empirical or the theoretical results of science. A statement that tells us what to study or how to study it is an important statement. But it tells us little about the thing studied. In Merton's words, it gives us an approach, not an arrival.[6] Let us not exhaust ourselves in the preliminaries, lest we fail at the consummation. We are always getting around to saying something we never actually come out with. But sooner or later a science must actually stick its neck out and say something definite. If there is a change in *x,* what sort of change will occur in *y*? Don't just tell me there will be *some* change. Tell me *what* change. Stand and deliver!

THE FINDINGS OF SOCIAL SCIENCE

And the social sciences do this. Though nonoperating definitions and orienting statements are comparatively prevalent in them, especially in anthropology, sociology, and political science, and are comparatively often mistaken for real definitions and propositions, yet the social sciences now have a very large number of solid findings to their credit. At the turn of the century the mathematician Poincaré could sneer that " . . . sociology is the science that possesses the most in the way of methods and the least in the way of results."[7] He could not fairly say so now. Though we still talk endlessly about methodology, the other side of the balance has been redressed. Anyone, for instance, who reads the useful book by Bernard Berelson and Gary A. Steiner, *Human Behavior: An Inventory of Scientific Findings,*[8] should be impressed with the number of generalizations (propositions) in this field that have now been pretty well tested against data.

Choosing almost at random, let us get an idea of their variety within some subfield, such as social stratification.[9] Every society, certainly every society of any size, is stratified by class or status. The rate of inter-generational mobility between classes is currently about the same in all highly industrialized nations. Family instability (divorce, separation, and abandonment) is greatest in the lower class, next in the upper, and least in the middle. The higher the class, the later the average age at marriage. And so forth. If the first job of a science is to establish generalizations, social science has established a great many.

But look at the characteristics of these propositions. Except for the first—that all societies are stratified—all of them state only central tendencies. It is not true of all members of an upper class that they marry late, but only of the average. And when the propositions state relationships between variables, the nature of the relationship, the function, is not very specific. We know that a rise in class position means a rise in the age of marriage; what we cannot say is, for instance, that one increases as the logarithm of the other. Sometimes a social science can get a little closer to specifying the shape of the function, as in the so-called law of diminishing marginal utility in economics: the curve relating the quantity of a good received by a man and the value to him of a unit of the good is concave downward. But few of our propositions ever state the exact function—which is one of the reasons why our science is not an exact science. Still, they are likely to say at least this much: that, for instance, as the value of one of the variables increases, the value of the other increases too—which is enough, just enough, to make them real propositions and not simply orienting statements.

Even more important, our propositions, though they are generalizations all right, are seldom very general generalizations. They are known to hold good only within rather narrow limits, only within western industrial societies, for instance. Or if the limits are not known, they are still shrewdly suspected of being narrow. And finally, with one class of exceptions, which I shall speak of much later, even our apparently most general generalizations, like the proposition that all societies are stratified, do not possess much explanatory power. Thinking of these, I have sometimes entertained the hypothesis that in social science the greater the generalization, the less its explanatory power. But explanation brings in a new kind of consideration.

THE NATURE OF EXPLANATION

Most people interested in comparing the social sciences with the natural sciences, especially those interested in making sure that social science *is* a natural science, emphasize the greater difficulty the social science faces in establishing, against data, the empirical truth of its propositions. It is certainly less easy in the social sciences than in some physical and biological sciences to manipulate variables experimentally and to control the other variables entering into a concrete phenomenon, so that the relationship between those the scientist is interested in at the moment shall be, beyond question, unmasked and stand out clearly. It is less easy to control the variables because it is less easy to control men than things. Indeed it is often immoral to try to control them: men are not to be submitted to the indignities to which we submit, as a matter of course, things and animals. Hence the relative prominence in some of the social sciences, even increasingly in history, of other methods of controlling variables, methods thought somehow to be less satisfactory, such as the use of statistical techniques.

I shall have no more to say about this difference between the social sciences and the others. Admittedly it is important, but it is also rather well understood, and much intelligence of a high order has been devoted to finding methods of dealing with the problem. Moreover, some of the biological sciences, such as medicine, suffer from difficulties of control almost as much as do the social sciences. Much less well understood are the differences between the social and the other sciences in the matter of explanation.

Though stating and testing relationships between properties of nature is what makes a science, it is certainly not the only thing a science tries to do. Indeed we judge not the existence, but the success, of a science by its capacity to explain. If there is one thing I should like my students to learn but seldom teach them, it is what an explanation is—not that it is hard to do. Again, no "big" word is more often used in social science than the word "theory." Yet how seldom do we ask our students—or, more significantly, ourselves—what a theory is. But a theory of a phenomenon is an explanation of the phenomenon, and nothing that is not an explanation is worthy of the name of theory.

I am, of course, using "explanation" in the special sense of explaining why under given conditions a particular phenomenon occurs and not in one of the vaguer senses in which we use the word, as when we "explain" how to drive a car by telling a youngster what to do with the controls in various circumstances. In the special sense, the explanation of a finding, whether a generalization or a proposition about a single event, is the process of showing that the finding follows as a logical conclusion, as a deduction, from one or more general propositions under specified given conditions.[10] Thus we explain the familiar finding that there are two low and two high tides a day (actually a little longer than twenty-four hours) by showing that it follows logically from the law of gravitation under the given conditions that the earth is largely covered with water, that it rotates on its axis, and that the moon moves in orbit around it.

But let me go into more detail, using a humble example but one that in the past had good reason to interest me. As a boy swimming in the fundamentally rather chilly waters of Massachusetts Bay in summer, I discovered, as others had done before me, that for comfort in swimming, the water near the shore was apt to be warmer when the wind was blowing onshore—towards the shore—than when it was blowing offshore. By thoroughly unsystematic statistical methods I tested the discovery and found it true. But why should it be true? I shall try to give the essentials of what I believe to be the correct, though obvious, explanation, without spelling it out in all its logical, but boring, rigor.

Warm water tends to rise. The sun warms the surface water more than the depths. For both reasons, surface water tends to be warmer than deeper water. The wind acts more on the surface water than it does on the depths, displacing it in the direction of the wind. Accordingly an onshore wind tends to pile up the warmer water along the shore, while an offshore wind tends to move it away from the shore, where, by the principle that "water seeks its own level," it is continuously replaced by other water, which, since it can only come from the depths, must be relatively cold. Therefore water along the shore tends to be warmer when the wind is blowing onshore than when it is blowing offshore. Q.E.D.

Simple though it is, the characteristics of this explanation are those of all explanations. Each step of the argument is itself a proposition stating a relationship between properties of nature: between, for instance, the temperature of water and the direction of its movement, up or down. That is why propositions are so important. Some of the propositions are more general than others. In the example, some of the more general propositions are that warm water tends to rise and that water seeks its own level. They are more general in that they apply to all water and not just water along a coast. Some of the propositions state the effect of the given conditions, such as that the wind sometimes blows onshore and sometimes offshore. By calling them given conditions we mean simply that we do not choose to explain them in turn—we do not choose to explain why the wind sometimes blows onshore—though no doubt we could do so. And the proposition to be explained, the *explicandum* —in this case the difference in temperature of coastal water under onshore and offshore winds—is explained in the sense that it follows as a matter of logic from the general propositions under the specified given conditions. That is, the *explicandum* is deduced from, derived from, the other propositions, the whole set forming a "deductive system." The reason why orienting statements cannot play a part in explanation is that little in logic can be deduced from them.

Note that, if the *explicandum* can be deduced from the general propositions under the given conditions, the general propositions cannot be deduced in turn from the others in the set, any more than in the classic syllogism we can deduce that all men are mortal from the facts that Socrates is a man and that Socrates is mortal. That is, the process of deduction runs in one direction but not the other in the set of propositions. If it did both, the argument would be circular. On the other hand, the general propositions in our example can themselves be explained by, can themselves become the *explicanda* of, other deductive systems containing still more general propositions. That hot water rises is ultimately explained by propositions of thermodynamics relating the temperature of any substance to its volume and thus to its weight per unit volume. That water seeks its own level is ultimately explained by the law of gravitation. But as we move towards more and more general propositions, we reach, at any given time in the history of science, propositions that cannot themselves be explained. If we can judge from experience, this condition, for any particular proposition, is unlikely to last forever. Newton's law of gravitation stood unexplained for some 200 years, but can now be shown to follow from Einstein's theory of relativity. Nevertheless at any given time there are always at least a few unexplainable propositions.

The explanation of the relation of water temperature to wind direction is also the theory of this phenomenon. But of course scientists generally use the word "theory" in a broader sense than this. They use it to refer, not just to an explanation of a single phenomenon, but to a cluster of explanations of related phenomena, when the explanations, the deductive systems, share some of the same general propositions. Thus someone might write a book called *The Theory of Water Temperatures,* which might explain the relations between variations in temperature and a number of other conditions besides the one chosen in our example, and which would apply, in doing so, a number of the same general propositions from thermodynamics and mechanics. Naturally any scholar is free to use the word "theory" in any way he likes, even for something different from what I call theory, provided he makes clear just how he is using it and does not, by slurring over the issue, claim for his kind of theory, by implication, virtues that belong to a different kind. All I submit here is that, normally in science, "theory" refers to the sort of thing I have described.

If we like, we can look on theory as a game. The winner is the man who can deduce the largest variety of empirical findings from the smallest number of general propositions, with the help of a variety of given conditions. Not everyone need get into the game. A man can be an admirable scientist and stick to empirical discovery, but most scientists do find themselves playing it sooner or later. It is fascinating in itself, and it has a useful ulterior result. A science whose practitioners have been good at playing it has achieved a great economy of thought. No longer does it face just one damn finding after another. It has acquired an organization, a structure. When Newtonian mechanics reached this sort of achievement it became the first thoroughly successful science, and other sciences have since become successful in the same way. But if theory is a game, it must like other games be played according to the rules, and the basic rules are that a player must state real propositions and make real deductions. Otherwise, no theory!

FOOTNOTES

1. P. W. Bridgman, *The Nature of Physical Theory* (Princeton, N.J.: Princeton University Press, 1936), pp. 59-61.

2. M. DeW. Howe, ed., *Holmes-Pollock Letters* (Cambridge, Mass.: Harvard University Press, 1961), II, 13.

3. For the notion that the concept of culture explains something, see, especially, Clyde Kluckhohn, *Mirror for Man* (New York: McGraw-Hill, 1949), pp. 17-44.

4. T. Parsons and E. A. Shils, eds., *Toward a General Theory of Action* (Cambridge, Mass.: Harvard University Press, 1951), pp. 14-16.

5. R. C. Hodgson, D. J. Levinson, A. Zaleznik, *The Executive Role Constellation* (Boston: Harvard Graduate School of Business Administration, 1965), p. 37.

6. R. K. Merton, *Social Theory and Social Structure*, rev. ed. (Glencoe, Ill.: The Free Press, 1957), p. 9.

7. H. Poincaré, *Science et Méthode* (Paris: Flammarion, 1909), pp. 12-13.

8. New York: Harcourt Brace & World, 1964.

9. *Ibid.*, pp. 453-91.

10. The view of explanation adopted here is, I think, that of R. B. Braithwaite, *Scientific Explanation* (Cambridge: Cambridge University Press, 1953) and of C. H. Hampel, *Aspects of Scientific Explanation* (New York: The Free Press, 1965), pp. 229-489. Philosophers will note that I have dodged the issue of the implicit definition of "theoretical" terms. See also G. C. Homans, "Contemporary Theory in Sociology" in R. E. L. Faris, ed., *Handbook of Modern Sociology* (Chicago: Rand-McNally, 1964), pp. 951-77.

METHODS OF INQUIRY

Bernard Berelson and Gary Steiner

Behavioral scientists, someone has observed, can talk about methods with a capital M or with a small m. The capital M is used for the large questions: How are the scientist's values involved in the selection of problems or the interpretation of results? What is the proper relationship of observation to conceptualization? Do findings operate against their own further verification by changing the very actions to which they refer? Is man truly capable of being objective about himself? Is a science of human behavior possible at all?

The small m, on the other hand, is used for detailed questions of technique: How can a proper sample be selected? How can unwanted bias be reduced or eliminated from a questionnaire? How can proper experimental controls be set up? How can a valid measuring instrument be developed? How can a study be designed most economically?

In a book of this kind, devoted to findings, why give any attention at all to Method and method? There are two reasons.

The first is that the procedures by which the behavioral sciences work help to define the very nature of the field itself. Just as doctors or lawyers or engineers are defined by a set of techniques that they, and normally only they, are trained and even licensed to use, so are behavioral scientists. In the large, we have actually employed this criterion in deciding what to include as findings: that is, we have omitted many contributions to the understanding of human behavior made by novelists, historians, playwrights, biographers, and poets, not because their contributions are less true or less interesting than those included, but because they stem from techniques other than those used by the behavioral sciences.

The second reason is that an intelligent evaluation of these findings requires some acquaintance with the kinds of assumptions and evidence they are based on, as well as an awareness of the potentials and limitations of various types of data. Armed with such critical understanding, the reader should be better able to judge the validity of the findings, and hence to appraise their contribution without going overboard in either direction.

To begin with, we need to say a few words about the nature of science as applied to human behavior.

This is not the place to argue the Big Questions as to whether there can be a science of human behavior at all, or whether these disciplines are really sciences, or whether the assumptions and procedures of the natural sciences can properly be transferred to the study of human beings. It should be obvious that there are several ways other than the scientific by which men have come to an "understanding" of man (we use quotation marks because the meaning of the term changes with each method): common observation, intuition and self-inquiry, reflection and philosophizing, revelation, creative and artistic expression. By claiming that the scientific approach to understanding human beings is valuable, we do not necessarily mean to devalue any of the others. But we do claim that the scientific approach is distinctive and that scientific procedures in the behavioral sciences produce factual evidence that demands respect from men of reason, however skeptical they may initially be.

In any case, whatever the behavioral disciplines are—sciences or otherwise—they have more or less established the hard knowledge about human behavior that appears in the following pages, and that is a final test. By "established" we mean that they have produced evidence for these findings using the methods usually attributed to science. Only ideal science, of course, always lives up to all of the following; but real science, behavioral science included, strives to do so:

The Procedures Are Public. The results and the methods are both communicable and communicated. The scientific report contains a detailed description of just what was done and how. The description is adequate if, and only if, another competent practitioner of the science can follow each step of the investigation as though he had been there. And scientific reports are, of course, honest: they are minutely true down to the finest detail. In addition:

The Definitions Are Precise. Here again, the procedure must be crystal clear. As an example, the statement "aggressive subjects were found to have greater dependence on their fathers than nonaggressive subjects" is inadequate as a scientific report. How was aggression defined and measured? By what test or procedures and by what specific scores? Where was the cut-off point between aggressive and nonaggressive subjects? How was dependence on the father revealed?

The Data-collecting is Objective. Once the investigation is under way, the investigator is bound to follow the data, whatever way they may fall—for or against his hypothesis (however cherished), for or against his personal preferences as a man. Biased procedures in collecting data have no place in science, nor has biased perception of the results. As a result:

The Findings Must Be Replicable. Because of the openness of the inquiry, another scholar can test the finding by seeking to reproduce it. This is why "artistic sensitivity" or "clinical insight" is itself not sufficient, though it may of course suggest hypotheses for subsequent verification.

The Approach Is Systematic and Cumulative. Scientists strive to unify whole bodies of knowledge through the use of central concepts, and hence to build up an organized system of verified propositions, which is usually called a theory. Here is another important difference between scientific operations on the one hand and artistic ones on the other.

The Purposes Are Explanation, Understanding, and Prediction. The scientist wants to know why and how, and to be able to prove it. If he can, then he can predict the conditions under which the specified behavior will occur. And if he can do that, then the question of control enters in as well. We have achieved a great deal of control over nature in the physical and biological sciences, and some in economic affairs; but the matter inevitably becomes more sensitive at the prospect that the behavioral sciences will enable us to control ourselves, i.e., one another.

Moreover, the outlook of the scientist is important. He assumes, first of all, that there is some order in nature—otherwise, why seek for uniformities? As a scientist, he tries to look at human behavior as part of the order of nature, along with animals, organisms, rocks, and galaxies. In short, he assumes no special causes in the case of man, no divine intervention, no capricious will.

Nor, as scientist, is he directly concerned with good and bad, right and wrong, moral and immoral, but only with what is true and false. Indirectly, he is concerned: moral considerations may lead him to study a certain subject, such as ethnic relations, but once engaged he is supposed to proceed in an impartial and dispassionate manner. This point of view is much harder to achieve in the behavioral sciences than it is in the physical or biological sciences, since it is much more difficult to view objectively such phenomena as murder, incest, personality, or love than it is to take a disinterested view of the finger, orbits of the stars, or an inclined plane. This is perhaps a principal reason for the belated development of the behavioral sciences and for much of the present resistance to some of their findings.

Finally, science is characterized by a certain point of view toward the acceptance of new findings and ideas, involving both extreme open-mindedness on the one hand and extreme skepticism on the other: that is, willingness to accept the possibility of everything but reluctance to accept anything as fact until it is demonstrated. ("I am certainly willing to accept the *possibility* that people have extrasensory perception, but I am not willing to state that they *do* have it until I have definitive evidence.")

These few paragraphs, plus the details on various methods that follow, must serve to suggest what is meant by the scientific study of human behavior. . . . We might say, by way of condensation, that in our view the study of human behavior has made considerable progress toward the status of a science in the past half-century or more, and in several respects has achieved it. This is especially the case when one considers how extraordinarily difficult it is to establish sound, valid, objective information on human affairs. The subject matter is itself highly complicated, often obscure if not hidden, hard to observe fully let alone control experimentally. Consider the technical difficulties in observing the psychological development of a child; or in discovering how many people not in mental hospitals act like those who are in; or in learning precisely what effect campaign speeches have on a presidential election; or in validly finding out what Negroes really think of white people; or in isolating the causes of juvenile delinquency; or in establishing in fact just what relationship exists between childhood experience and adult personality. We are not speaking here of having ideas or even convictions about such matters—that is easy. We are speaking of having data, collected in a scientific manner according to the criteria discussed above.

The reader would do well to keep this notion in mind in appraising the results reported in this book: these findings have been reasonably well established despite the difficulties, often the intractabilities, involved in the scientific study of human behavior.

As for methods with a small *m,* they can perhaps best be considered under three headings: methods utilized in the design of studies, methods of data collection, and methods of analysis. The other two are discussed in this chapter, with necessarily brief descriptions of the ways behavioral scientists proceed in their empirical inquiries.

DESIGN

In the broadest terms, there are three designs used in the behavioral sciences: the experiment, the sample survey, and the case study.

The Experiment

By *experiment* is meant any investigation that includes two elements: manipulation or control of some variable by the investigator and systematic observation or measurement[1] of the result. In short, it means active intervention on the phenomena of interest to see what, if any, effects are produced by the intervention.

The experiment has had a central place in the history of science. The importance of experimentation depends not so much on its precision, its objectivity, or its instruments as on the inherent efficiency of intervention in disentangling cause-and-effect relationships. Whenever its use is feasible, intentional intervention is the method that most readily exposes cause and effect; and if the behavioral sciences were able to experiment more widely on their materials they would be better equipped today with important findings. For example, we would know much more about the effects on personality of different ways of rearing children if experimentation were not precluded on moral and humanitarian grounds. And the field is currently making some progress on such basic problems as mental disease and emotional disturbance by means of physiological intervention in the nervous system accompanied by controlled observation of the behavioral results. The implantation of tiny electrodes in the brain has been used to induce fear, rage, joy, even "pleasure"; and ultimately such mapping of the brain centers that mediate emotions may have far-reaching clinical implications. Similarly, in human beings, chemical intervention has produced behavior that closely resembles certain manifestations of schizophrenia; and, in animals, certain parts of the brain have been systematically removed to see what effect that has on learned problem-solving.

The Classical Experiment

The prototype of scientific experimentation, and in many ways its most foolproof form, is the classical experiment. The general question it answers is whether, and to what extent, one variable (called the experimental or independent variable) affects another variable (the dependent variable).

The logic is simple. Two groups are matched at the outset; one is given the experimental intervention (a piece of propaganda, a new drug that affects behavior, a French lesson taught in a new way, a special procedure that can introduce changes in working procedures in a factory); the result of the intervention is subsequently measured (i.e., its effect on attitudes, or personality, on the amount of French learned, on morale and productivity). The essentials of the classical experiment can be schematized as follows:

Experimental group, but not control group,
exposed to intervention (the experimental
or independent variable)

	Before	After
Experimental group or subject	B_e	A_e
Control group or subject	B_c	A_c

The figures represent measurements of the dependent variable, and the effect of the experimental variable is $(A_e - A_c) - (B_e - B_c)$.

Here is an illustration of a classical experiment concerned with the effects of a new tranquilizer pill on psychotic behavior:

1. Define the population of subjects and draw a sample—e.g., a random sample of all the patients with a given diagnosis at a certain institution.

2. Divide the sample at random into two groups. By definition the two groups will now be similar, within limits of sampling error, on *any* measurement. Thus there is no reason to expect one group to behave any differently in the future than the other. Flip a coin to decide which will be "experimental" and which "control."

3. Define the dependent variable ("psychotic behavior"): How will it be measured or rated? Take a "before" measurement on each group.

4. Define the experimental variable precisely—What doses of the tranquilizer over what period of time?—and administer it to the experimental group only. The control group will probably get a placebo—a pill that looks the same but has no active ingredients—to control for the effects of autosuggestion, and even for the effect of participating in the experiment at all (since that will involve some special attention, at the least). In some cases of this kind, for extra precaution, the experiment is "double blind": not only does the subject not know which pill he gets but, in order to control the expression of his own (conscious or unconscious) wishes in the matter, the experimenter does not know at the time either.

5. Take "after" measurements of the dependent variable on each group.

6. The difference between the two groups after the experiment, beyond any difference that may have existed before, is the effect of the experimental variable. In this case, it is the effect of the tranquilizer upon psychotic behavior.

The glory of the classical experiment is that its logic has no loophole. When all the conditions of the classical experiment have been met, and all four cells have been filled in, the final difference between control and experimental group *must* be due to the effect of the experimental or independent variable: both groups reflect the effects of any other variables not directly manipulated by the experimenter (such as time itself, atmospheric conditions, or the effects of having been selected to participate in the study). Thus the control group protects the experimenter against many of the common fallacies that plague less rigorous studies. Before-and-after observation of an experimental group alone is particularly vulnerable to the fallacy of *post hoc, ergo propter hoc.* Without a control group there is a temptation to attribute any subsequent change in the observed subjects to the experimental variable, whereas the change may have occurred without the experimenter's intervention.

Although there is a logical model for the classical experiment, in actual experiments the design is frequently modified for various reasons: costs, practical difficulties, and so on. In some cases, statistical approximations will do. For example, if the experimental and control groups are truly divided at random, the before-measurement may be omitted in the knowledge that the two groups will vary only within known limits of sampling error. The experiment simply consists of the administration of the experimental condition to one group and the subsequent after-measurements of both. If this after-measurement records a difference between the two groups that cannot be attributed to chance variation, it is taken to be the result of the experimental variable.[2]

Similarly, many experiments add onto the basic four-fold model. Some measure the effect of the experimental variable over time: propaganda may be effective right after its administration, but how long does it last? Others assess the effects of several experimental variables within a single investigation. The simplest form of this involves two or more experimental groups, each of which is measured against a single control group. For example, the patients can be divided into three or more groups: one is the control, one gets tranquilizer A, one gets tranquilizer B, etc.

Moreover, modern statistical designs make it possible to evaluate the relative effects of a number of independent variables acting simultaneously and in combination. An investigation of classroom learning might vary the method of instruction, the sex of the teacher, the room lighting, and student motivation, all at one stage of observations; and then conclude which of these factors is the most important influence on learning, and how they act in combination.

So much for the general logic of experimental design: the principal point, worth repeating, is that the fundamental advantage of experimentation is not its precision or its instrumentation but its inherent logical rigor. Now let us apply the method to the settings and subjects of behavioral science experimentation. In our field we can distinguish experiments in the laboratory and in natural settings.

The Laboratory Experiment—Animal

Behavioral scientists, notably psychologists, conduct intensive studies on animals in the laboratory: historically, the animals have usually been rats, pigeons, or apes. Why study lower animals when the objective is to understand people? The reasons are both practical and theoretical.

On the practical side, many experiments cannot be conducted on human subjects for legal and moral reasons—e.g., the behavioral effect of systematic destruction of various parts of the nervous system. In general, any experimental variable that involves bodily harm or undue pain, discomfort, embarrassment, or psychological or social damage is naturally excluded from experimental intervention with human subjects. In addition, animals are cheap, they cannot resist captivity, they are almost always available, and they do not have to be paid for their services.

On the theoretical side, the environment of animals, unlike that of human beings, can be completely and systematically controlled twenty-four hours a day. The lower animals reproduce more quickly and in greater numbers than human beings, and their mating can be controlled, thus making possible longitudinal studies of hereditary effects. With animals, far greater homogeneity of subjects can be attained by inbreeding, thus reducing sources of behavioral variation that are irrelevant and bothersome for some purposes. Animals are presumably simpler and thus more easily understood than people, hence some scientists argue that the study of human behavior must begin with the simpler forms (in the sense that arithmetic has to be mastered before the calculus). Finally, the acceptance of evolution as a biological fact leads to the assumption that, in principle, the processes underlying human behavior are an outgrowth of those represented in lower forms, and therefore the study of animals cannot be irrelevant. Findings from animal studies are not expected to be directly replicated in human behavior, but they may well provide the foundations on which the elaborations introduced at the human level must be built.

The Laboratory Experiment—Human

Human beings are also studied intensively in laboratory situations, both individually and in groups. Given the practicalities of the matter, the human beings involved are usually college students, and many of the practical advantages of using lower animals apply as well with students as subjects: they do not have to be paid, they are readily accessible, and they often cannot effectively resist the experimentation.[3]

We have reviewed the theoretical justification for studying rats and pigeons. What is the justification for using college sophomores or, more generally, representatives of any selected type of human subject for laboratory investigations?

The answer depends largely upon the expected variation of the phenomenon under study. There is little reason to suspect, for example, that the visual or auditory processes of college students vary considerably from those of other types of people; or that their eye movements, which signal dreams, are unique. Accordingly, the tendency to generalize to people at large on such issues is frequently supported by further studies, and college students turn out to be a reasonably good sample of human beings on such limited topics as those closely tied to physiological processes.

However, when the question deals with political attitudes, feelings toward the family, reactions to stress, life values, or such complicated or culturally determined matters, it is safest to assume, until proved otherwise. that there *are* important differences between college students and other categories of citizens. Hence, a priori generalizations of findings of this character must be avoided.

Another general problem of much experimental work done in the laboratory is that of "translation." Some laboratory experiments deal with phenomena that can be reproduced directly in the laboratory, such as depth perception, small-group problems, or the learning of certain skills. In these cases, the experimenter simply brings the behavior of interest into the laboratory for more careful scrutiny under experimental conditions. Many phenomena, however, cannot be transplanted to a laboratory either in principle or for such practical considerations as time, money, cooperation of subjects, and so on; or the phenomenon that interests the experimenter is a general one (motivation, love, hostility) that must be delineated to one specific instance for a given investigation. Such conditions require acts of "translation": before the experiment, translation of the phenomena of interest to the experimenter into the specific laboratory operations that will "tap" them; after the experiment, translation of the results of the specific operations performed back into the original concepts and phenomena.

An illustration will, we hope, make the point. The psychoanalytic notion of "repression" states that under certain circumstances individuals will force out of their awareness the memories of certain traumatic or psychologically damaging events. In addition, some impulses or desires that are unacceptable (e.g., killing or having sexual relations with one's father) may be repressed, that is, not be consciously acknowledged although they are actively present in the personality. When experimentally inclined psychologists wanted to test some of these notions in the laboratory, one design used was to show subjects a series of pictures—some pleasant, some unpleasant or gruesome—and at a later sitting ask them to describe the pictures seen. So the hypothesis that traumatic events get repressed is translated into the test: "Gruesome pictures will be accurately recalled less frequently than nongruesome pictures."

Evaluation of such experimental results demands critical consideration of the translation involved and its validity. Students of repression might reject the experiment (as many of them did) not because it was poorly designed or failed to produce conclusive results but simply because they considered it irrelevant to their views of the concept of repression.

Note how this example illustrates the scientific requirement that results be reported operationally (what was done) as well as conceptually or theoretically (what they mean). When the experimenter reports that gruesome pictures were not described accurately with the same frequency as nongruesome pictures, behavioral scientists can decide for themselves what relevance, if any, the finding has for issues in which they are interested.

The Natural Experiment

Frequently the major elements of an experiment occur or are produced in the natural habitat of the behavior under study. Such experimentation avoids many of the problems of the laboratory situation discussed above, e.g., oversimplification and artificiality. In the natural experiment the subjects ordinarily do not know they are under investigation and hence do not modify their behavior as a result of being watched. On the other hand, natural experimentation is usually less precise, because the pertinent events are less fully under the experimenter's control.

The Planned Natural Experiment

In this type, as in the laboratory, the investigator intentionally manipulates the independent variable and then makes systematic measurements of the result. The tranquilizer study is an example; so is the illustrative study mentioned above dealing with classroom learning. A planned natural experiment often used in advertising research is the "split-run" technique: metropolitan newspapers frequently offer advertisers the opportunity to run two versions of an advertisement in the same issue, with coupons or other coded devices enabling "returns" from the two versions to be compared.

The Spontaneous Natural Experiment

Sometimes behavioral scientists are fortunate enough to come on a situation that happened by itself yet has most or all of the elements of a successful experiment. In such cases, an approximation of experimental results may be obtained.

For example, when television was being introduced, there was a period during which technical considerations were the principal determinants of which towns and cities would have stations. Thus it was possible to find a number of cities without TV and to know about when the medium would be introduced in them. This provided an opportunity to study "what television does" on a before-and-after basis, as compared with matched towns without TV (the controls). Similarly, studying the culture of a primitive community during and after the advent of technological developments provides an attenuated natural experiment under spontaneous conditions. Since, as noted above, the absence of a proper control is the technical failing of such studies, the investigator must often decide between naturalness and control, or compromise on some of each.

The Sample Survey

The sample survey, as a type of research design, does not refer simply to a public opinion poll, though a properly designed poll is certainly one example of a sample survey, and probably the most familiar one. In our sense, a sample survey is properly named in that it contains the indicated two elements:

A Sample. The investigator first decides what group or "population" he is interested in (American adults, voters, women of childbearing age, college students, etc.) and then selects a sample in the statistical sense. It may be "random," "representative," "quota," "weighted," or any of a number of technical types. The main point is that the sample is so chosen as to enable the experimenter to draw conclusions regarding the entire "population" and not simply those members of the population who happen to turn up in the sample.

A Survey. The investigator then collects some measures on the appropriate characteristics of the population being studied (number of television sets or children in the household; how the members feel about Russia or religion; what they know about India or space; and so on).

Obviously there are certain questions that can be answered only by a sample survey. The question, "To what extent do American psychologists today believe that extrasensory perception exists?" can be answered by specifying a population and then asking a selected sample. No experiment will answer the question once and for all and neither will a case study. In general, whenever the investigator is interested in assessing or estimating the present state of affairs with regard to some variable that changes over time for a large group of subjects, a sample survey is the only practical way to get the answer. If the variable did not change over time, we could probably learn the answer once and for all by experiment; or if there were interest in only one or a few instances, case studies could provide the answer. These are certainly not the only conditions under which the sample survey is useful, but these are the conditions under which it is the imperative form of design.

In addition to simple measures of magnitude (How many people will vote?), sample surveys provide clues to relations between variables (and thus ultimately to cause and effect) by correlation of the various measures obtained. For example, a survey of number of children per family can provide a series of tables showing how fertility varies by families of differing class, race, rural-urban residence, religion, etc. This example, incidentally, illustrates another advantage of the sample survey in the study of relationships: many times the variables of interest are difficult or impossible to manipulate by experiment (years of schooling, race), so the only approach is to compare people who already differ on the characteristic in question and see how their behavior differs.

Such correlations are difficult to disentangle causally, because the direction of the influence is uncertain (and it is often reciprocal, which makes the matter more difficult still). To take a simple example, a correlation between reading an advertisement for a given make of car and buying the car could go either way—reading influenced purchase, purchase influenced reading. Even when the direction is clear, when one characteristic (e.g., race) antedates and is not affected by another (e.g., fertility), the nature of the causal relationship is quite complex, with several other factors usually involved (e.g., income, social position, religion, place of residence, age at marriage).

To handle change over time in certain investigations, a variant of the sample survey has been developed that is called the panel. This requires repeated measures of the appropriate characteristics on the same people, so that the investigation can study how changes were brought about over time. This method is particularly useful in campaigns that bring a variety of stimuli to the subjects' attention, and it is no accident that the method is used mainly in studies of marketing and voting. A major limitation of the panel technique is that, as the same people are queried repeatedly, they may change their behavior simply as a result of panel membership. As a control, panel responses are often checked against samples of "fresh" respondents.

The Case Study

The case study is complementary to the sample survey. The sample survey measures many people on few characteristics, usually at one point in time. The case study intensively examines many characteristics of one "unit" (person, work group, company, community, culture), usually over a long period of time. The goal of such investigations is to learn "all" about the area of interest for the one case involved. Typical case studies in the behavioral sciences might include: the life history of a psychotic; an intensive analysis of a patient's psychological disturbance;[4] an anthropological monograph describing in detail the technology and customs of a primitive culture; a detailed description and analysis of the socioeconomic classes existing in a small Southern town.

As the examples suggest, the detail and the depth of information over time that the case study provides makes this design particularly relevant for questions involving etiology and development: How does a particular neurotic manifestation emerge and change over time? What are the critical incidents that lead up to an industrial strike? How does the industrialization of a traditional society affect the family?

The chief limitation of this method is that the results are based on a sample of one, so that the degree of their generality is not known. Would another individual, another company, another community, another culture respond in the same way? In addition, the case study is often subject to the *post hoc, ergo propter hoc* fallacy, since neither a "control group" nor intervention by the investigator is provided as a safeguard.

Hence, case studies rarely *prove* anything, although they are frequently rich in clues and insights for further investigation. In many areas the case study is the idea-getting investigation par excellence.

COLLECTION OF DATA

These research designs require that information about human behavior be gathered and recorded in some systematic fashion. We now discuss the potentials and problems of some of the major methods for collecting data that are used in the behavioral sciences: observation, report, records.

Direct Observation of Behavior

Frequently it is possible for the scientist to observe the behavior he is interested in as it occurs. He can do this either as a participant in the event or the community studied or as a nonparticipant. In either case, the fact that they are under observation may or may not be known to the subjects. This means that there are four types of direct observation, illustrated thus:

	Participant	*Nonparticipant*
Known to subjects	Social psychologist enrolls and goes through nurse's training program in order to learn how the recruits are taught. Identity is known.	Laboratory experiment in problem-solving in a small group. Psychologist sits in corner and takes notes, tape-records, or watches through a window. Anthropologist lives in primitive culture for a year, collects material on the religious life of the natives.
Not known to subjects	Sociologist gets job as laborer in order to study behavior of workers. Healthy psychologist has himself admitted to psychiatric hospital, with his identity and purpose unknown to the staff or to other patients.	Social psychologist on street corner observes and records behavior of drivers on approaching stop sign: how many stop completely, how many merely slow down, etc.

The relative efficiency of these methods depends, of course, on the character of the problem. A basic consideration is the extent to which the phenomenon under study is likely to be modified if the subjects know they are being studied.

Now in principle there probably is no problem in the behavioral sciences that is not affected at least potentially by the subject's knowledge that he is participating in the study. When people are observed by others, especially in behavior that is personally or socially significant, they frequently behave quite differently than they would otherwise. Tell a woman that she is going to be weighed every morning as part of a study and you run a high risk that she will change the very measurement at interest. Ask parents if you can observe how they treat their children under stress and you are not likely to see the full range of responses. In general, people, at least "in our culture," have a desire to please or impress, to be considered intelligent, acceptable, moral, or good, even (sometimes especially) by an impersonal scientific observer who does not judge their actions as such and who is a stranger unlikely ever to be encountered again.

This tendency on the part of a knowing subject may be irrelevant or insignificant in some studies; it can sometimes be controlled experimentally (as, for example, by a control group that also knows it is under study). But when the investigator wishes to describe behavior of a personally important or private nature, direct observation known to the subjects may be impossible. When the ethical problems of surreptitious observation are considered less weighty than the potential benefits to science, the investigator usually confesses his surreptitious observation subsequently and asks the subjects' permission to use the data so collected.

The actual means of recording direct observations vary from impressionistic field notes to precise and highly quantified ratings or precoded observations. For example, as we shall see later, one such method of quantitative recording and analysis utilizes a system of twelve categories into which all behavior that occurs in a face-to-face group can be classified. The observer, located behind a one-way mirror, can record on a moving belt the complete proceedings of a meeting, indicating who speaks to whom, in what order, and in which category each exchange falls.

Direct observation also includes records made on films, tapes, and other mechanical devices. In many instances, such records may yield quite accurate and comprehensive data since they can be studied at leisure by any number of observers (independently or in unison) and checked and rechecked as often as desired.

Verbal Report

Some phenomena are inherently out of the scope of direct scientific observation: behavior that is private (sexual behavior, arguments between husband and wife) or asocial (criminality and trickery) or protected by custom (certain religious matters) as well as the vast amount of behavior that simply does not exist in directly observable form (ideas, attitudes, feelings, beliefs). In addition, it is frequently not feasible on practical grounds to make direct observations of the number and scope that may be desired for a given study, even though it would be possible to do so.

Thus a great deal of behavioral science is based on (usually solicited) verbal reports of what has happened, what is expected to happen, how one felt, what one thought, and other conditions internal to the subject: "I voted Democratic"; "I was rarely spanked"; "The light is getting brighter"; "The blot reminds me of a turtle"; "I hate my wife"; "I want to get ahead"; "That's the way we do things around here"; "I thought it reasonable to go along with the others." Now there are a variety of techniques for obtaining and recording verbal reports, and they vary considerably in their advantages and disadvantages for particular problems. They can be roughly classified and ordered as follows, according to their characteristic contributions to the collection of behavioral data:

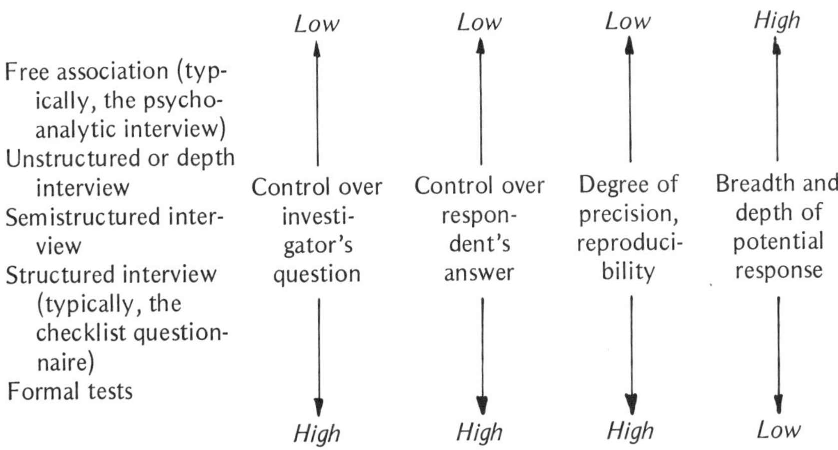

Naturally, a great deal of data on human behavior comes directly from reports of these kinds. In general, as more and more constraint is placed upon both the interviewer and the respondent, the unknown biases introduced by the method of interrogation decrease while precision and reliability increase. Respondents confine themselves more and more closely to a specific topic and their answers typically become more directly comparable one to another.

At the same time, the potential range of responses decreases as constraint increases. The more structured the interview, the less "broad" the information obtained. Ideally, then, as a research project progresses from the initial exploratory or groping stage, through the middle range where the investigator begins to have specific hypotheses about his material, to the final step where he is concerned with pinning down or proving some point, the techniques would move from nonstructured through semistructured to totally structured. If totally structured techniques are applied in the initial stages, the risk is run of ruling out entire areas of response that did not occur to the investigator; applying nonstructured techniques in the final stages makes it less likely that any hypothesis will be rigorously confirmed or refuted. By and large, this general logic is observed in the field as a whole—over the long run in a series of studies of the same problem, as well as within a single inquiry.

Free Association (The Psychoanalytic Interview)

True free association represents the ultimate in freedom of response. Not only does the interviewer refrain from any direct questioning, but the subject himself is supposed to place no constraints whatever on what he says; he simply reports anything that comes into his mind. Ideally, even the ordinarily assumed constraints of speech are removed—logical sequence, rules of grammar, syntax, etc.—and the process approaches the freedom-from-rules characteristic of the content of dreams.

Verbal reports of true free association rarely occur, but they are approximated in some psychoanalytic interviews, where the length and the intimacy of the relationship, as well as the personal and social safeguards in the situation, make such behavior possible. The material in a transcript of such sessions over a period of several years is about as broad and deep a verbal report as can be secured in the form of data. The subject covers an exhaustive series of topics; each is treated at length and on repeated occasions; and the whole includes mention of behavior and feelings probably never before or again reported to anyone.

But the same factors that make such reports possible also restrict their accessibility as well as their controllability. When made, as they only rarely are, psychoanalytic transcripts are ordinarily restricted to the analyst or a small group of his colleagues and are not available for general publication or study.

The Unstructured or Depth Interview

The unstructured or depth interview approximates complete freedom for the respondent in discussing a particular topic, but it does confine him to the area of major concern to the investigator; it frees the answers but limits the questions. The interviewer has no set list of queries but only an outline of topics he wants to cover. The wording, the sequence, and the intensity of questioning are left to the interviewer's discretion; ordinarily, they are tailored to each interview so as to produce the most meaningful material with the particular respondent.

Characteristic depth interviewing involves extensive use of the "nondirective probe," a query designed to produce further elaboration without influencing the content of the response in any way. Typical probes are: "Would you tell me a little more about that?", a nod of the head, a questioning repetition of the last few words spoken by the respondent, and "I don't quite understand," "Really?" or simply "Mmm."

The unstructured interview typically attempts to elicit all the respondent's information and attitudes related to the topic. In some cases, the discussion is recorded verbatim, and the interviewer also makes note of revealing facial expressions or gestures. So it allows analysis of the emotional flavor and the between-the-lines meaning communicated by the respondent's own language and subtle coloration of terms (that are not available when an answer must be given to specific questions in specific terms). It is these characteristics of the material that are appropriately referred to as "depth," and not the degree of consciousness of the attitudes tapped.

The Semistructured Interview

This form gives greater control to the interviewer. It specifies not only the major topic to be stressed but also the questions to be asked and usually their order. Questions are of the "open-ended" type ("What do you think of Russia?"), in which the wording of the question is specified but the wording of the response is left to the respondent.

The semistructured interview is a compromise: as it acquires some of the advantages of reliability, precision, and control associated with the more structured techniques, it sacrifices some of the scope and depth of response obtainable by the less structured interviewing methods.

The Structured Interview

In this case, the interviewer is entirely controlled in the wording and the sequence of questions; in addition, the respondent is confined to a precoded set of answers, made available to him by multiple choice or some other device: "When do you think men will reach the moon—this year, in one to five years, in five to ten years, or never? Or don't you know?" Or the familiar form: "How do you feel about the statement that it's more important to advance our knowledge of people than it is to reach the moon—strongly agree, mildly agree, can't say, mildly disagree, or strongly disagree?" Or the simple dichotomy: "Have you spanked a child of yours in the past two months—yes or no?"

Tests and Inventories

The dividing line between tests and interviews is obscure, if indeed it exists. An ordinary paper-and-pencil, multiple-choice "attitude" test varies in no important respect from the characteristics of the structured interview; the questions merely happen to be printed instead of spoken. Such tests are in effect self-administered interviews and represent the extreme control on both questioner and respondent. The forms that ask the subject to answer fairly direct questions about himself (e.g., "How often do you have nightmares?") are usually called inventories. The term "test" usually refers to the subject's performance on a task as scored or evaluated by the investigator (as in an I.Q. or aptitude test).

Tests and inventories are typically concerned with measuring or evaluating the individual tested, whereas interviews (excluding psychiatric ones) are more generally interested in securing information on some event or topic. And tests are conducted on "subjects," whereas interviews are held with "respondents" (giving information about themselves) or with "informants" (giving information about others: the community, the society, the culture).[5]

Among the tests of personality are included both precoded paper-and-pencil tests and those in which the subject's free response is interpreted clinically. Illustrative of the latter category are the common "projective" tests, such as the Rorschach ink-blot test or the TAT (Thematic Apperception Test), which requires telling a story from a picture.

A useful distinction can be made between theoretical and practical tests. Theoretical tests are devised to answer basic questions about people and are judged by their contribution to basic understanding: What are the fundamental capacities? What is the nature of personality? How does an individual diagnosed as hysteric differ from an individual diagnosed as manic? Practical tests are devised to predict some events in the real world: Who will be a successful pilot? How much achievement can an individual expect in college? What is the probability of nervous breakdown? Which engaged couples will be happily married? Such tests are evaluated very simply, by seeing how much better they do than chance, and a test is as good or as bad as its proved ability to separate the ultimate "successes" from the "failures."

The methods of development and the basic characteristics of these two types differ considerably. For example, one of the principal objectives of theoretical tests is to become as "pure" as possible: to measure one thing and one thing only. If the score on a mathematical aptitude test is also influenced by the subject's reading ability, the test is considered "contaminated." On the other hand, very few of the practical criteria we wish to predict, like success in flying or in marriage, depend on "pure" abilities. Instead, they involve a combination of abilities and skills, with various combinations producing varying degrees of success. Therefore the most successful practical tests often contain a great jumble of items from a theoretical point of view.

Records

Sometimes the material at interest is simply not available for an original investigation—for instance, when it occurred a hundred years ago. At other times behavioral scientists are fortunate enough to have made available to them masses of interesting data that they had no part in collecting. Cases of the first type necessitate the use of secondary data; cases of the second type make analyzing the data inviting and frequently efficient.

Information recorded for other purposes but of great potential interest to students of human behavior comes from many sources: census statistics; life insurance records; medical histories; newspapers, magazines, novels, and autobiographies; admission and release records of psychiatric hospitals; records of prisons, churches, and schools; business transcripts of several kinds. In fact, it is hard to think of any recorded information regarding people and their behavior that could not be of potential value to behavioral science; the application is limited only by the ingenuity and energy of the investigator and the quality of the record. And much of such data is of a scope that no single scientific investigation could afford to collect.

In order to retrieve data from the volume of published material, the method of content analysis has been developed as a way of quantifying the characteristics of interest that appear in communications. This method is used quite extensively, especially for descriptive purposes. It consists, in effect, of classifying the content of books, newspapers, speeches, television shows, documents, or any other communication material into a set of categories so that their relative frequency can be determined. Is there more foreign news in magazines now than there was in the 1930s? How closely do television programs conform to stated standards? What shifts are made in adapting novels into films? How do international wars appear in the history texts of the contending powers? These are some questions to which content analysis has been applied.

The proof of the methods, however, is in the knowledge that they produce. This chapter described how behavioral scientists have secured empirical knowledge of human behavior. The following chapters set forth the results. The reader should keep in mind that the following findings have indeed been documented in one or another, or several, of these ways.

FOOTNOTES

1. By *measurement* the behavioral scientist typically means something broader than what the term means to the layman. The behavioral scientist considers that an attitude has been measured if it can simply be distinguished as "for" or "against," "more" or "less." Finer quantitative distinctions, of course, are also measurements, but so are dichotomies or classificatory categories in general.

2. It is sometimes hard to believe, but it is still true, that when a group has been divided at random into two groups, the groups will differ by no more than chance on *any* characteristic whatsoever. The proportion of blue-eyed people in the two groups, of redheads, of people over and under 5'7", of Catholics, of those who skipped breakfast this morning, of those opposed to capital punishment or in favor of a stronger United Nations—all will be roughly equivalent. There are statistical procedures that determine the probability of a given difference having arisen simply by such random division. Therefore, when a difference is greater than that which could reasonably be expected on the basis of random division, and the groups have in fact been randomly divided, the conclusion is that the difference is not due to their division but to something that happened to them afterward.

3. In this connection, it is worth recalling an observation of the late Edward Tolman, a distinguished psychologist. He once noted how much of American psychology was based on two sets of subjects, rats and college sophomores, and enjoined his colleagues to remember that the former certainly are not people and the latter may not be!

4. In fact, case studies are one of the principal sources of data on many questions in clinical psychology, since the practicing clinician is interested in specific individuals and collects intensive data on his patients. The most important questions in this area revolve around such time-bound issues as how and when the various syndromes arise, develop, and change. Thus, clinical histories have practical significance for the therapist and stimulate many hypotheses in personality theory.

5. The use of persons as informants is particularly common in anthropology, with a few members of a tribe or primitive society providing information on the life of the entire group. In sociology, the interviewer is usually a respondent, and the investigator (being a member of the society under study) is often his own informant.

STEPS IN THE SCIENTIFIC METHOD

Matthew Enos

STEP ONE: FORMULATING THE PROBLEM

A. What *broad topic* will your research investigate?
B. What are your feelings concerning this topic? (What are you angry about? Excited about? Curious about?)
C. Why do you think research is necessary on this topic?
D. Is there a social problem your research might help solve? How?

STEP TWO: SELECTING A QUESTION FOR INVESTIGATION

A. What *specific question* about the broad topic will your research attempt to answer? (Must be in question form.)
B. Can your question be answered objectively? Is it free of *value judgments?*
C. Is your question narrow enough to be answered by your planned research?

STEP THREE: GETTING ORIENTED ON THE TOPIC

A. What *literature* will you survey in order to learn what research and thinking already has been done on your topic?
B. What do you want to find out about your topic from this survey?
C. How may your research plans be changed by what you learn about previous research on your topic?

STEP FOUR: STATING THE HYPOTHESIS

A. What is your *specific hypothesis* (empirically testable proposition)? (Your answer must be a statement—not a question—of your tentative belief about the answer to the question you posed in Step Two.)
B. Is your hypothesis *operational* (capable of being tested objectively)?

STEP FIVE: CHOOSING THE RESEARCH DESIGN

A. What *research design* is most appropriate for testing your hypothesis?
  1. Naturalistic observation (the *case study*).
  2. Correlational study (the *sample survey*).
  3. Experimental study (the *controlled experiment*).
B. What possible weaknesses are there in the research design you have chosen?
C. Specify the *variables* involved in your research.
  1. *Independent* (stimulus) variables (task, environmental, subject).
  2. *Dependent* (response) variables (subject behaviors).

STEP SIX: SELECTING THE SUBJECTS

A. How have you defined the *subjects?*
  1. What is the *population* (people you want to learn about)?
  2. What is the *sample* (people you actually observe)?
B. How will you draw your sample so that it will be *representative* of the population?

STEP SEVEN: COLLECTING THE DATA

A. Explain your *procedure*—your exact plan for gathering the data. List each step.
B. What *apparatus* will be used? How will the data be recorded?
C. What special social science techniques (interview, test, etc.) will be used?
D. What features of your data-gathering procedure insure *objectivity?*
E. How will you guard against subjectivity? What are the dangers of *bias* in your research?
  1. *Experimenter* bias.
  2. *Response* bias.
F. Will your methods of measurement actually test the hypothesis?
  1. Are they *reliable?*
  2. Are they *valid?*

STEP EIGHT: ANALYZING THE DATA

A. Determine the *meaning* of the raw data (the "facts") you have collected.
  1. How will you *manipulate* the data? What statistical operations, tables, charts, etc., will you use?

2. What *decision rule* will you use to determine confirmation or rejection of your hypothesis?
B. What mistakes in procedure can you now see in your research? How would you correct them if you did the research again?
C. Summarize and present the relevant *findings.*

STEP NINE: VERIFYING THE HYPOTHESIS

A. Draw logical *conclusions* from your findings.
    1. Does the data (as analyzed) tend to *support* or *reject* your hypothesis?
    2. What *surprises* turned up in the findings?
    3. What important questions does your research still leave unanswered?
B. What *theory* (or theories) are supported or suggested by your research findings?
C. On the basis of your research, what recommendations do you have for:
    1. Social action?
    2. Further research?

STEP TEN: REPORTING THE FINDINGS

A. Present your research procedures, results, and conclusions in a *written report* for the scientific community (and interested laymen).
B. What audience are you especially eager to inform about your research?
C. What use do you want made of your report? What effect do you hope it may have?
D. In what journals, magazines, books, etc., would you like to have it published?

THE IDEA OF CHANCE

J. Bronowski

I have repeatedly spoken of science as a language. This analogy seems to me so easy and helpful that I found it most natural to begin this book by comparing science with the English language. It seems to me natural to think of optics, for example, as a language to describe seeing and being seen. As a language, it is uncommon only in the single-minded pains which it takes to avoid other topics: to get rid of the confusion which might be caused by color blindness, for instance; and to avoid the more attractive topics of wishing and believing. Optics is the language in which seeing is seeing and nothing else—not even believing.

This analogy would not have occurred at all naturally to scientists in the last century. For a language is no more than a code for describing some chosen features of the world. Of course the purpose of language is to arrange with others how we shall act in the world. But in method it remains a description, which names the facts and mimics their arrangement. The nineteenth century would have thought this too modest a view of science. Its best minds did see science as a guide to action. But they were convinced that it helped them to act usefully because it does not merely describe the world: it explains it. And by an explanation they meant a model which follows nature exactly, link by link, along a chain of causes and effects. An animal is precisely a heat engine, they said; or a gas is a collection of small billiard balls; or the brain is a telegraph office. They believed that in the end there is only one scientific method: to set up a system of causes and effects. If science describes, they held, then it describes the cause by its effects; and if it predicts, it predicts the effect from its causes.

I have said at some length that this belief can no longer be sustained. Very well: we are to give up the universal search for causes. What are we to put in their place? For answer, we must go back to beginnings, and repeat something which cannot be said too often. The aim of science is to describe the world in orderly language, in such a way that we can if possible foresee the results of those alternative courses of action between which we are always choosing. The kind of order which our description has is entirely one of convenience. Our purpose is always to predict. Of course, it is most convenient if we can find an order by cause and effect; it makes our choice simple; but it is not essential.

What we are looking for, in science as much as in the day-to-day of our lives, is a system of prediction: is, as it were, a predictor. The principles which guide us in our predictions are in the end nothing more than steps in the calculation. And life is not an examination; we do not get marks for the steps; what matters is getting the right answer. So it is perfectly possible to base a system of prediction on no principle except trying to get the right answer. This is exactly what all plants and animals do. The bat avoids obstacles by shouting at them that shrill cry just beyond my hearing, and then listens for the echo. Whatever system it has for translating the echo into a prediction it has found by evolution, and evolution has found it by trial and error. The radar set does all this more rationally. Yet the steps in its calculations are no better than the bat's; and they are no worse. For instance, the bat and evolution have long discovered that the best wavelengths for range-finding are the centimeter waves which the radar set also uses. A man catching a ball is a predictor, or a child flying a kite, or a cat at a mouse-hole. They remind us that the business of prediction, and of science, is to get us to do roughly the right thing at roughly the right time.

There is of course nothing sacred about the causal form of natural laws. We are accustomed to this form, until it has become our standard of what every natural law ought to look like. If you halve the space which a gas fills, and keep other things constant, then you will double the pressure, we say. If you do such and such, the result will be so and so; and it will always be so and so. And we feel by long habit that it is this "always" which turns the prediction into a law. But of course there is no reason why laws should have this always, all-or-nothing form. If you self-cross the offspring of a pure white and a pure pink garden pea, said Mendel, then on an average one-quarter of these grandchildren will be white, and three-quarters will be pink. This is as good a law as any other; it says what will happen, in good quantitative terms, and what it says turns out to be true. It is not any less respectable for not making that parade of everytime certainty which the law of gases makes. And indeed, the gas law takes its air of finality only from the accumulation of just such chances as Mendel's law makes explicit.

It is important to seize this point. If I say that after a fine week, it *always* rains on Sunday, then this is recognized and respected as a law. But if I say that after a fine week, it rains on Sunday more often than not, then this somehow is felt to be an unsatisfactory statement and it is taken for granted that I have not really got down to some underlying law which would chime with our habit of wanting science to say decisively either "always" or "never." Even if I say that after a fine week, it rains on seven Sundays out of ten, you may accept this as a statistic, but it does not satisfy you as a law. Somehow it seems to lack the force of law.

Yet this is a mere prejudice. It is nice to have laws which say, This configuration of facts will always be followed by event A, ten times out of ten. But neither taste nor convenience really make this a more essential form of law than one which says, This configuration of facts will be followed by event A seven times out of ten, and by event B three times out of ten. In form the first is a causal law and the second a statistical law. But in content and in application, there is no reason to prefer one to the other. The laws of science have two functions, to be true and to be helpful; probably each of these functions includes the other. If the statistical law does both, that is all that can be asked of it. We may persuade ourselves that it is intellectually less satisfying than a causal law, and fails somehow to give us the same feeling of understanding the process of nature. But this is an illusion of habit. No law ever gave wider satisfaction than the law of gravitation. Yet we have seen that the explanation it gave of the workings of nature was false, and the understanding we got from it mistaken. What it really did, and did superbly, was to predict the movements of the heavenly bodies to an excellent approximation.

There is, however, a limitation within every law which does not contain the word "always." Bluntly, when I say that a configuration of facts will be followed sometimes by event A and at other times by B, I cannot be certain whether at the next trial A or B will turn up. I may know that A is to turn up seven times and B three times out of ten; but that brings me no nearer at all to knowing which is to turn up on the one occasion I have my eye on next time. Mendel's law is all very fine when you grow peas by the acre; but it does not tell you, and cannot, whether the single second generation seed in your windowbox will flower white or pink. Mendel himself ran into this trouble when he tested his law, because he had to do his experimental work in a rather small monastery garden.

So far, this is obvious enough. It is obvious that if we did know what is to happen precisely next time, then we would at once have not a statistical law, but a law of certainty into which we could write the word "always." But this limitation carries with it a less obvious one. If we are not sure whether A or B will turn up next time, then neither can we be sure which will turn up the time after, or the time after that. We know that A is to turn up seven times and B three; but this can never mean that every set of ten trials will give us exactly seven A's and three B's. In fact, it is not possible to write down an irregular string of A's and B's in such a way that every set of ten successive letters which we pick out from it, beginning where we like, is made up precisely of seven of one and three of the other. And of course it is quite impossible to write them down so that any choice of ten letters picked here and there will contain just seven A's.

Then what do I mean by saying that we expect A to turn up seven times to every three times which B turns up? I mean that among all the sets of ten trials which we can choose from an extended series, picking as we like, the greatest number will contain seven A's and three B's. This is the same thing as saying that if we have enough trials, the proportion of A's to B's will tend to the ratio of seven to three. But of course, no run of trials, however extended, is necessarily long enough. In no run of trials can we be sure of reaching precisely the balance of seven to three.

Then how do I know that the law is in fact seven A's and three B's? What do I mean by saying that the ratio tends to this in a long trial, when I never know if the trial is long enough? And more, when I know that at the very moment when we have reached precisely this ratio, the next single trial must upset it—because it must add either a whole A or a whole B, and cannot add seven-tenths of one and three-tenths of the other. I mean this. After ten trials, we may have eight A's and only two B's; it is not at all improbable. It is not very improbable that we have nine A's, and it is not even excessively improbable that we may have ten. But it is very improbable that, after a hundred trials, we shall have as many as eighty A's. It is excessively improbable that after 1,000 trials we shall have as many as 800 A's; indeed it is very improbable that at this stage the proportion of A's departs from seven out of ten by as much as five percent. And if after 100,000 trials we should get a proportion which differs from our law by as much as one percent, then we should have to face the fact that the law itself is almost certainly in error.

Let me quote a practical example. One of the French encyclopedists of the eighteenth century, the great naturalist Buffon, was a man of wide interests. His interest in geology and evolution got him into trouble with the Sorbonne, which made him formally recant his belief that the earth has changed since Genesis. His interest in the laws of chance was less perilous, but it prompted him in 1733 to ask an interesting question. If a needle is thrown at random on a sheet of paper ruled with lines whose distance apart is exactly equal to the length of the needle, how often can it be expected to fall on a line and how often into a blank space? The answer is rather odd: it should fall on a line a little less than two times out of three—precisely, it should fall on a line two times out of π, where π is the familiar ratio of the circumference of a circle to its diameter, which has the value 3.14159265.... How near can we get to this answer in actual trials? This depends of course on the care with which we rule the lines and do the throwing; but, after that, it depends only on our patience. In 1901 a minor Italian mathematician, Mario Lazzerini, having taken due care, demonstrated his patience by making well over 3,000 throws. The value he got for π at one stage was right to the sixth place of decimals, which is an error of only a hundred-thousandth part of one percent.

This is the method to which modern science is moving. It uses no principle but that of forecasting with as much assurance as possible, but with no more than is possible. That is, it idealizes the future from the outset, not as completely determined, but as determined within a defined area of uncertainty. Let me illustrate the kind of uncertainty. We know that the children of two blue-eyed parents will certainly have blue eyes; at least, no exception has ever been found. By contrast, we cannot be certain that all the children of two brown-eyed parents will have brown eyes. And we cannot be certain of it even if they have already had ten children with brown eyes. The reason is that we can never discount a run of luck of the kind which Dr. Johnson once observed when a friend of his was breeding horses. "He has had," said Dr. Johnson, "sixteen fillies without one colt, which is an accident beyond all computation of chances." But what we can do is to compute the *odds* against such a run; this is not as hard as Johnson supposed. And from this we can compute the likelihood that the next child will have brown eyes. That is, we can make a forecast which states our degree of uncertainty in a precise form. Oddly enough, it is just here that Mendel's own account of his work is at fault. He assumed in effect that once a couple has had ten brown-eyed children, the chance that they may yet have blue-eyed children is negligible. But it was not.

This area of uncertainty shrinks very quickly in its proportion if we make our forecasts not about one family but about many. I do not know whether this or that couple will have a child next year; I do not even know whether I shall. But it is easy to estimate the number of children who will be born to the whole population, and to give limits of uncertainty to our estimate. The motives which lead to marriage, the trifles which cause a car to crash, the chanciness of today's sunshine or tomorrow's egg, are local, private and incalculable. Yet, as Kant saw long ago, their totals over the country in a year are remarkably steady; and even their ranges of uncertainty can be predicted.

This is the revolutionary thought in modern science. It replaces the concept of the *inevitable effect* by that of the *probable trend*. Its technique is to separate so far as possible the steady trend from local fluctuations. The less the trend has been overlaid by fluctuation in the past, the greater is the confidence with which we look along the trend into the future. We are not isolating a cause. We are tracing a pattern of nature in its whole setting. We are aware of the uncertainties which that large, flexible setting induces in our pattern. But the world cannot be isolated from itself: the uncertainty *is* the world. The future does not already exist; it can only be predicted. We must be content to map the places into which it may move, and to assign a greater or less likelihood to this or that of its areas of uncertainty.

These are the ideas of chance in science today. They are new ideas: they give chance a kind of order; they re-create it as the life within reality. These ideas have come to science from many sources. Some were invented by Renaissance brokers; some by seventeenth-century gamblers, some by mathematicians who were interested in aiming-errors and in the flow of gases and more recently in radioactivity. The most fruitful have come from biology within little more than the last fifty years. I need not stress again how successful they have been in the last few years, for example in physics: Nagasaki is a monument to that. But we have not yet begun to feel their importance outside science altogether. For example, they make it plain that problems like

Free Will or Determinism are simply misunderstandings of history. History is neither determined nor random. At any moment, it moves forward into an area whose general shape is known but whose boundaries are uncertain in a calculable way. A society moves under material pressure like a stream of gas; and on the average, its individuals obey the pressure; but at any instant, any individual may, like an atom of the gas, be moving across or against the stream. The will on the one hand and the compulsion on the other exist and play within these boundaries. In these ideas, the concept of chance has lost its old dry pointlessness and has taken on a new depth and power; it has come to life. Some of these ideas have begun to influence the arts: they can be met vaguely in the novels of the young French writers. In time they will liberate our literature from the pessimism which comes from our divided loyalties: our reverence for machines and, at odds with it, our nostalgia for personality. I am young enough to believe that this union, the union as it were of chance with fate, will give us all a new optimism.

Let me make this point more explicit. It was assumed in the classical science of the last century that such a phenomenon as radioactivity, or the inheritance of a blood group, or loss of nerve, or the rise in prices in a time of scarcity, is each the result of many influences; and that step by step these could be taken apart and the phenomenon traced to all its causes. In each case, what was happening could be treated as a laboratory experiment. It could be isolated from those events in the world which had no bearing on it, and lay as it were beyond the box of the laboratory. And within this box, the causes could be studied one by one, much as we study how the volume of a gas changes when the pressure is varied while we keep the temperature the same, and then when the temperature is varied while we keep the pressure the same.

But this picture of the phenomenon in isolation from the rest of the world and from the observer turns out to be false. There comes a time when it will not do any longer even as an approximation. Then it turns out that time and space, which Newton thought absolute, cannot be given physical meaning without the observer. The laboratory cannot exist in a void, and the experiment cannot be put in a box. And as we refine our measurements, the limitations of the observer look larger and larger. The liquid on whose surface the microscope is trained leaps and shivers under the lens, until we can see the Brownian movement of its molecules. The stately flow of the gas is shot through and through with the random darting of its particles. Enlarge the pointer on the dial a millionfold, and the instrument can no longer be read, because the turbulent movement of its atoms shifts the point from instant to instant. The experimental errors are woven into the very substance of the world.

And while all this was going on in the laboratory, nature and society outside were of course thronged with a million larger examples. Everything in the plant and the living body, in earthquakes and the weather, in animal society and human workshops and the prices on the ticker tape, is beyond the control of the neatly designed experiment. There had been a moment in history, an imaginary moment but no less important for that, when the weights falling from the Leaning Tower had been a key to open the secret of the stars. Ever since, the mute laboratory worker had gone on in the faith that his little box would sort out the sun-spot cycle and the coming of the Black Death and the Wall Street crash. The world is a machine, and he would repeat the triumph of Newton and make a model which would act out its fate minute by minute. Adam Smith and Jeremy Bentham and Mill, Hartley and Mesmer and Freud, Zola and Proust and Theodore Dreiser, each in his own way worked a lifetime in that hope.

But there were also men who were faced with particular problems which they could not wait three centuries to take to pieces. They were not always respectable scientific problems. The gambling friends of Pascal and Euler were impatient men. The insurance brokers in Florence and Amsterdam and London did not care about theory; they wanted empirical results. And then, most interesting, at the end of the last century Francis Galton and later Karl Pearson began to look at human characters: size and weight and configuration and growth. They formed no tidy theories like Lombroso's theory of criminal types. They seemed even to have a harsh suspicion of Mendel's theory of inheritance. Rather they looked back to work like that of Laplace and Gauss, who had first considered what errors must be regarded as unavoidable even in astronomical observation. Thus they came to formulate the notion of the chance distribution of a set of characters in a population. And from their work in turn has developed the whole theory of statistical differences, which I believe to be the basis of science for the future.

Let me quote an example from my own experience. In 1945 I went to Japan, and since I did not speak Japanese there were sent with my party several full-blooded young Japanese who had been brought up in America. It struck me when we set out that they were on the whole smaller men than the white Americans in the party. When we got to Japan, it struck me as forcibly that the Japanese we had brought with us were themselves taller on the whole than the native Japanese. Here were two differences provided by nature and by society which could not be treated by laboratory experiment. Nor were they invariable differences. Although on the average the group of white Americans was taller than the group of Japanese-Americans, and these in turn taller than the native Japanese, there were men in each group who overlapped into the others. Indeed, the smallest man I set eyes on was a white American, and there was one tall Japanese-American. Nevertheless, I was willing to formulate two personal hypotheses: that the Japanese are by heredity smaller than white Americans, and that Japanese brought up in America are taller than home-grown Japanese, presumably because America provides them with different foods or a different environment.

How do we test such hypotheses? The problem is just like those which Pearson tackled, and the method is due to him and to a brewer with a statistical bent who called himself *Student.* We find the average of each of our three types; and at the same time we calculate from the individuals in each group a measure of the variation round its average which this group itself seems to display. Since in the nature of things we observe only a few members in each group, neither our averages nor our measures of variation are free from error. But in each case, the variation allows us to estimate what is the largest error we are likely to make in measuring these averages. That is, we surround each average as we have measured it by an area of uncertainty. If these three areas of uncertainty do not overlap, then we know with some confidence that my hypotheses were justified. But if two of the areas overlap, then we cannot be sure that the difference between the two averages round which they have been drawn is a real one. We have failed to establish a systematic difference between these two groups, because the random fluctuations within each group, as we have observed them on this occasion, are large enough to swamp the possible difference.

This is the essential content of the statistical method. It has many applications, and they differ one from another in the detail of application. But the underlying thought is the same. Essentially the thought depends not on unlimited accuracy in measuring a character, but on judging the accuracy by a measure of the inherent variation from individual to individual which we cannot escape. We look for a trend or systematic difference. But the line of this trend will itself be blurred by the unsteady hand of chance or random fluctuation. We cannot get rid of this random scrawl. But we can from it determine a measure of random variation, and use that to draw round the trend an area of uncertainty. If the area is small enough by standards which are agreed between us, then the trend is established, and we know the limits within which it is likely to lie. If the area is too large, and the limits too wide, we have not been able to establish a trend. It may exist, but in this set of observations it has been swamped by the random fluctuations.

Let me take another practical instance. We believe that streptomycin is effective in helping to cure tuberculosis. We base this belief on experiment. But in every experiment, patients are themselves in many stages of the disease; they inevitably receive different doses and respond in different degrees; the whole picture is overlaid by unavoidable variation. Can we extract any positive results in so variable a field? Yes, if we choose our statistical technique intelligently. For example, suppose we have measures of the health of each patient from time to time during treatment. Then we can test the hypothesis that on the whole patients get better as treatment goes on. The first step is to find, by taking straightforward averages after each month of treatment, what seems to be the average improvement in each month. This allows us to draw a line of improvement on our graph. The patients are still widely scattered round this line. But we can measure the scatter or random variation round the line of improvement, and we can compare it with the scatter of all results when we neglect the systematic trend or line. And this will be our criterion for judging whether the line of improvement is a real effect or not. We shall see by how much the total scatter is reduced when we compare it with the scatter round our line. If the reduction is substantial by standards on which statisticians are agreed, then we say that we have found a meaningful effect of the treatment; we call it significant. We shall still need further analysis to assure ourselves that what makes the treatment work is the streptomycin. But if the hypothesis that there is a trend with treatment turns out not to reduce the random scatter in the condition of patients, then we have not established an effect at all; the result fails to reach significance.

This approach is very simple in conception. At bottom it divides the phenomenon which we observe in a hundred instances round us into two parts. I have called the parts systematic and random, or trend and fluctuation, or effect and chance. But under all these names, there runs essentially the same conception: that we can isolate the effect only to a certain accuracy. To determine whether the effect is real, we have therefore to compare its area of uncertainty with the accuracy to which we can isolate it. We have to judge the effect by the fluctuation to which our estimate is liable. If the effect stands out plainly above the fluctuation, then we have a significant result. We have established an effect, and although the unavoidable fluctuation still surrounds it with an area of uncertainty, we can apply our finding with this small margin or tolerance. But if the effect turns out not to be large when compared with the inherent fluctuation, then we have not established its significance. Even if it exists, its area of uncertainty is too large to be useful. Our only hope then is to do more experiments, since each experiment reduces the area of uncertainty.

The idea of chance as I have explained it here is not difficult. But it is new and unfamiliar. We are not used to handling it. So it does not seem to have the incisiveness of the simple laws of cause and effect. We seem to be in a land of sometimes and perhaps, and we had hoped to go on living with always and with certainty. We may see, again and again, that smokers contract cancer of the lung more often than nonsmokers; but we go on feeling (as we nervously console ourselves with a cigarette) that the connection has not been "proved."

Yet I believe that the difficulty is only one of habit. We shall become accustomed to the new ideas just as soon as we are willing and as we have to. And we are having to. On all sides science is crowding into fields of knowledge which cannot be isolated in the laboratory, and asking us to come to conclusions in matters where we cannot hope to trace a causal mechanism. It may seem to be overtaxing our notion of science to hope that we shall find some common method of tackling the problems of physics and economics, of evolution and soil chemistry, of medicine and meteorology, of psychology and aerial bombardment. We have grown accustomed to thinking of science itself as divided into smaller and smaller pieces of specialization, an atomic universe and knowledge of its own, which no one and nothing can again hope to master. But this may well be an illusion. The different branches of science may seem so far apart only because we lack the common method on which they grow and which holds them together organically. Look back to the state of knowledge in the year 1600: the branches of science and of speculation seemed as diverse and as specialized, and no one could have foreseen that they would all fall into place as soon as Descartes and Hobbes introduced the unifying concept of cause and effect. The statistical concept of chance may come as dramatically to unify the scattered pieces of science in the future. What Hobbes and Newton did was to change the whole concept of natural law: instead of basing it on the analogy of the human will, they built it on cause and on force. But this analogy with human effort is now breaking down. We are on the threshold of another scientific revolution. The concept of natural law is changing. The laws of chance seem at first glance to be lawless. But I have shown in this chapter that they can be formulated with as much rigor as the laws of cause. Certainly they can be seen already to cover an infinitely wider field of human experience in nature and in society. And it may be that they will give to that field the unity which the last fifty years have lacked. If they do, they will give us all also a new confidence. We have been swept by a great wave of pessimism, which rises from our own feeling of helplessness in the recognition that none of us understands the great workings of the world. As science and knowledge have been broken into pieces, there has come upon us all a loss of nerve. That happened to the old classical culture of the Mediterranean in the seventeenth century. The future lay with the driving and purposeful optimists of the North, who seized the notion of cause and purpose, and with it conquered nature and the world together. We are looking for another such universal concept to unify and to enlighten our world. Chance has a helpless ring in our ears. But the laws of chance are lively, vigorous and human; and they may give us again that forward look which in the last half century has so tragically lowered its eyes.

HOW TO LIE WITH STATISTICS

Darrell Huff

"The average Yaleman, Class of '24," *Time* magazine reported last year after reading something in the New York *Sun,* a newspaper published in those days, "makes $25,111 a year."

Well, good for him!

But, come to think of it, what does this improbably precise and salubrious figure mean? Is it, as it appears to be, evidence that if you send your boy to Yale you won't have to work in your old age and neither will he? Is this average a mean or is it a median? What kind of sample is it based on? You could lump one Texas oilman with 200 hungry free-lance writers and report *their* average income as $25,000-odd a year. The arithmetic is impeccable, the figure is convincingly precise, and the amount of meaning there is in it you could put in your eye.

In just such ways is the secret language of statistics, so appealing in a fact-minded culture, being used to sensationalize, inflate, confuse, and over-simplify. Statistical terms are necessary in reporting the mass data of social and economic trends, business conditions, "opinion" polls, this year's census. But without writers who use the words with honesty and understanding and readers who know what they mean, the result can only be semantic nonsense.

In popular writing on scientific research, the abused statistic is almost crowding out the picture of the white-jacketed hero laboring overtime without time-and-a-half in an ill-lit laboratory. Like the "little dash of powder, little pot of paint," statistics are making many an important fact "look like what she ain't." Here are some of the ways it is done.

Charts by Sigman-ward.

THE SAMPLE WITH THE BUILT-IN BIAS

Our Yale men—or Yalemen, as they say in the Time-Life building—belong to this flourishing group. The exaggerated estimate of their income is not based on all members of the class nor on a random or representative sample of them. At least two interesting categories of 1924-model Yale men have been excluded.

First there are those whose present addresses are unknown to their classmates. Wouldn't you bet that these lost sheep are earning less than the boys from prominent families and the others who can be handily reached from a Wall Street office?

There are those who chucked the questionnaire into the nearest wastebasket. Maybe they didn't answer because they were not making enough money to brag about. Like the fellow who found a note clipped to his first pay check suggesting that he consider the amount of his salary confidential: "Don't worry," he told the boss. "I'm just as ashamed of it as you are."

Omitted from our sample then are just the two groups most likely to depress the average. The $25,111 figure is beginning to account for itself. It may indeed be a true figure for those of the Class of '24 whose addresses are known and who are willing to stand up and tell how much they earn. But even that requires a possibly dangerous assumption that the gentlemen are telling the truth.

To be dependable to any useful degree at all, a sampling study must use a representative sample (which can lead to trouble too) or a truly random one. If *all* the Class of '24 is included, that's all right. If every tenth name on a complete list is used, that is all right too, and so is drawing an adequate number of names out of a hat. The test is this: Does every name in the group have an equal chance to be in the sample?

You'll recall that ignoring this requirement was what produced the *Literary Digest's* famed fiasco. When names for polling were taken only from telephone books and subscription lists, people who did not have telephones or *Literary Digest* subscriptions had no chance to be in the sample. They possibly did not mind this underprivilege a bit, but their absence was in the end very hard on the magazine that relied on the figures.

This leads to a moral: You can prove about anything you want to by letting your sample bias itself. As a consumer of statistical data—a reader, for example, of a news magazine—remember that no statistical conclusion can rise above the quality of the sample it is based upon. In the absence of information about the procedures behind it, you are not warranted in giving any credence at all to the result.

THE TRUNCATED, OR GEE-WHIZ, GRAPH

If you want to show some statistical information quickly and clearly, draw a picture of it. Graphic presentation is the thing today. If you don't mind misleading the hasty looker, or if you quite clearly *want* to deceive him, you can save some space by chopping the bottom off many kinds of graph.

Suppose you are showing the upward trend of national income month by month for a year. The total rise, as in one recent year, is seven percent. It looks like this:

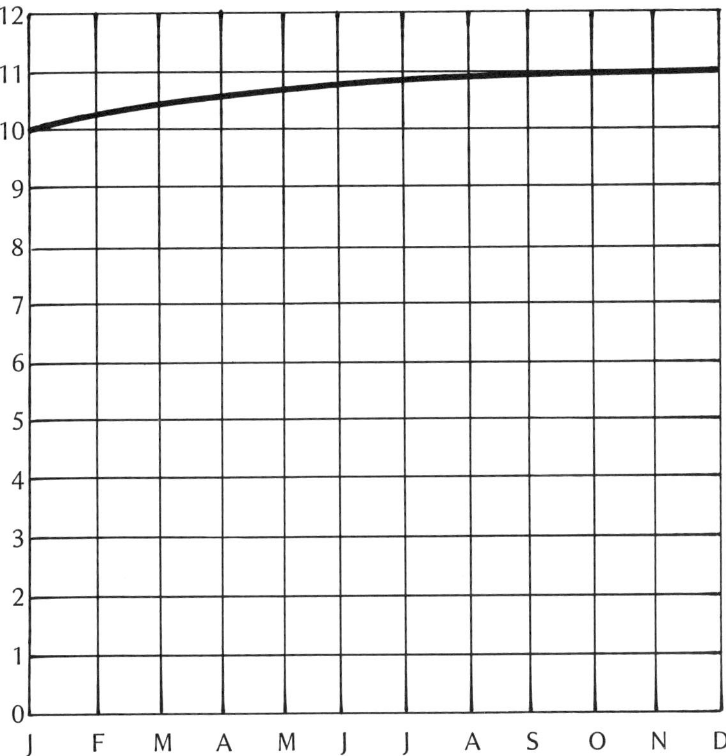

That is clear enough. Anybody can see that the trend is slightly upward. You are showing a seven percent increase and that is exactly what it looks like.

But it lacks schmaltz. So you chop off the bottom, this way:

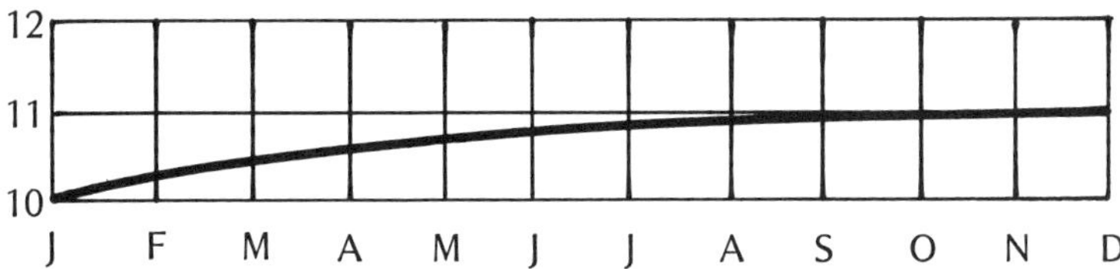

The figures are the same. It is the same graph and nothing has been falsified—except the impression that it gives. Anyone looking at it can just feel prosperity "National income rose seven percent" into "... climbed a whopping seven percent."

It is vastly more effective, however, because of that illusion of objectivity.

THE SOUPED-UP GRAPH

Sometimes truncating is not enough. The trifling rise in something or other still looks almost as insignificant as it is. You can make that seven percent look livelier than one hundred percent ordinarily does. Simply change the proportion between the ordinate and the abscissa. There's no rule against it, and it does give your graph a prettier shape.

But it exaggerates, to say the least, something awful:

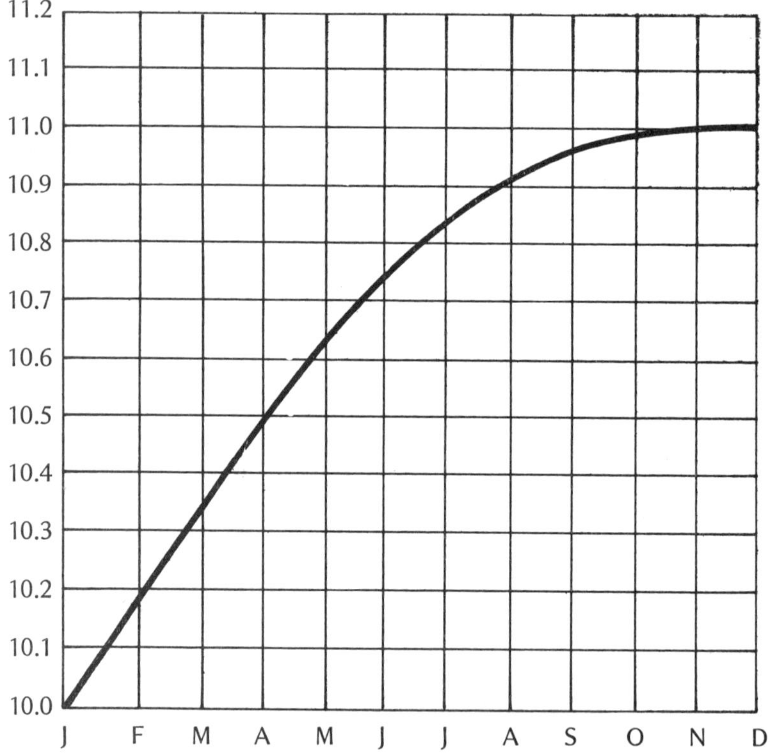

THE WELL-CHOSEN AVERAGE

I live near a country neighborhood for which I can report an average income of $15,000. I could also report it as $3,500.

If I should want to sell real estate here-abouts to people having a high snobbery content, the first figure would be handy. The second figure, however, is the one to use in an argument against raising taxes, or the local bus fare.

Both are legitimate averages, legally arrived at. Yet it is obvious that at least one of them must be as misleading as an out-and-out lie. The $15,000-figure is a mean, the arithmetic average of the incomes of all the families in the community. The smaller figure is a median; it might be called the income of the average family in the group. It indicates that half the families have less than $3,500 a year and half have more.

Here is where some of the confusion about averages comes from. Many human characteristics have the grace to fall into what is called the "normal" distribution. If you draw a picture of it, you get a curve that is shaped like a bell. Mean and median fall at about the same point, so it doesn't make very much difference which you use.

But some things refuse to follow this neat curve. Income is one of them. Incomes for most large areas will range from under $1,000 a year to upward of $50,000. Almost everybody will be under $10,000, way over on the left-hand side of that curve.

One of the things that made the income figure for the "average Yale-man" meaningless is that we are not told whether it is a mean or a median. It is not that one type of average is invariably better than the other; it depends upon what you are talking about. But neither gives you any real information —and either may be highly misleading—unless you know which of those two kinds of average it is.

In the country neighborhood I mentioned, almost everyone has less than the average—the mean, that is—of $10,500. These people are all small farmers, except for a trio of millionaire weekends who bring up the mean enormously.

You can be pretty sure that when an income average is given in the form of a mean nearly everybody has less than that.

THE INSIGNIFICANT DIFFERENCE OR THE ELUSIVE ERROR

Your two children Peter and Linda (we might as well give them modish names while we're about it) take intelligence tests. Peter's IQ, you learn, is 98 and Linda's is 101. Aha! Linda is your brighter child.

Is she? An intelligence test is, or purports to be, a sampling of intellect. An IQ, like other products of sampling, is a figure with a statistical error, which expresses the precision or reliability of the figure. The size of this probable error can be calculated. For their test the makers of the much-used Revised Stanford-Binet have found it to be about three percent. So Peter's indicated IQ of 98 really means only that there is an even chance that it falls between 95 and 101. There is an equal probability that it falls somewhere else—below 95 or above 101. Similarly, Linda's has no better than a fifty-fifty chance of being within the fairly sizeable range of 98 to 104.

You can work out some comparisons from that. One is that there is rather better than one chance in four that Peter, with his lower IQ rating, is really at least three points smarter than Linda. A statistician doesn't like to consider a difference significant unless you can hand him odds a lot longer than that.

Ignoring the error in a sampling study leads to all kinds of silly conclusions. There are magazine editors to whom readership surveys are gospel; with a forty percent readership reported for one article and a thirty-five percent for another, they demand more like the first. I've seen even smaller differences given tremendous weight, because statistics are a mystery and numbers are impressive. The same thing goes for market surveys and so-called public-opinion polls. The rule is that you cannot make a valid comparison between two such figures unless you know the deviations. And unless the difference between the figures is many times greater than the probable error of each, you have only a guess that the one appearing greater really is.

Otherwise you are like the man choosing a camp site from a report of mean temperature alone. One place in California with a mean annual temperature of 61 is San Nicolas Island on the south coast, where it always stays in the comfortable range between 47 and 87. Another with a mean of 61 is in the inland desert, where the thermometer hops around from 15 to 104. The deviation from the mean marks the difference, and you can freeze or roast if you ignore it.

THE ONE-DIMENSIONAL PICTURE

Suppose you have just two or three figures to compare—say the average weekly wage of carpenters in the United States and another country. The sums might be $60 and $30. An ordinary bar chart makes the difference graphic.

That is an honest picture. It looks good for American carpenters, but perhaps it does not have quite the oomph you are after. Can't you make that difference appear overwhelming and at the same time give it what I am afraid is known as eye-appeal? Of course you can. Following tradition, you represent these sums by pictures of money bags. If the $30 bag is one inch high, you draw the $60 bag two inches high. That's in proportion, isn't it?

The catch is, of course, that the American's money bag, being twice as tall as that of the $30 man, covers an area on your page four times as great. And since your two-dimensional picture represents an object that would in fact have three dimensions, the money bags actually would differ much more than that. The volumes of any two similar solids vary as the cubes of their heights. If the unfortunate foreigner's bag holds $30 worth of dimes, the American's would hold not $60 but a neat $240.

You didn't say that, though, did you? And you can't be blamed, you're only doing it the way practically everybody else does.

THE EVER-IMPRESSIVE DECIMAL

For a spurious air of precision that will lend all kinds of weight to the most disreputable statistics, consider the decimal.

Ask a hundred citizens how many hours they slept last night. Come out with a total of, say, 781.3. Your data are far from precise to begin with. Most people will miss their guess by fifteen minutes or more and some will recall five sleepless minutes as half a night of tossing insomnia.

But go ahead, do your arithmetic, announce that people sleep an average of 7.813 hours a night. You will sound as if you knew precisely what you are talking about. If you were foolish enough to say 7.8 (or "almost 8") hours it would sound like what it was—an approximation.

THE SEMI-ATTACHED FIGURE

If you can't prove what you want to prove, demonstrate something else and pretend that they are the same thing. In the daze that follows the collision of statistics with the human mind, hardly anybody will notice the difference. The semi-attached figure is a durable device guaranteed to stand you in good stead. It always has.

If you can't prove that your nostrum cures colds, publish a sworn laboratory report that the stuff killed 31,108 germs in a test tube in eleven seconds. There may be no connection at all between assorted germs in a test tube and the whatever-it-is that produces colds, but people aren't going to reason that sharply, especially while sniffling.

Maybe that one is too obvious and people are beginning to catch on. Here is a trickier version.

Let us say that in a period when race prejudice is growing it is to your advantage to "prove" otherwise. You will not find it a difficult assignment.

Ask that usual cross-section of the population if they think Negroes have as good a chance as white people to get jobs. Ask again a few months later. As Princeton's Office of Public Opinion Research has found out, people who are most unsympathetic to Negroes are the ones most likely to answer yes to this question.

As prejudice increases in a country, the percentage of affirmative answers you will get to this question will become larger. What looks on the face of it like growing opportunity for Negroes actually is mounting prejudice and nothing else. You have achieved something rather remarkable: the worse things get, the better your survey makes them look.

THE UNWARRANTED ASSUMPTION, OR *POST HOC* RIDES AGAIN

The interrelation of cause and effect, so often obscure anyway, can be most neatly hidden in statistical data.

Somebody once went to a good deal of trouble to find out if cigarette smokers make lower college grades than nonsmokers. They did. This naturally pleased many people, and they made much of it.

The unwarranted assumption, of course, was that smoking had produced dull minds. It seemed vaguely reasonable on the face of it, so it was quite widely accepted. But it really proved nothing of the sort, any more than it proved that poor grades drive students to the solace of tobacco. Maybe the relationship worked in one direction, maybe in the other. And maybe all this is only an indication that the sociable sort of fellow who is likely to take his books less than seriously is also likely to sit around and smoke many cigarettes.

Permitting statistical treatment to befog casual relationships is little better than superstition. It is like the conviction among the people of the Hebrides that body lice produce good health. Observation over the centuries had taught them that people in good health had lice and sick people often did not. *Ergo,* lice made a man healthy. Everybody should have them.

Scantier evidence, treated statistically at the expense of common sense, has made many a medical fortune and many a medical article in magazines, including professional ones. More sophisticated observers finally got things straightened out in the Hebrides. As it turned out, almost everybody in those circles had lice most of the time. But when a man took a fever (quite possibly carried to him by those same lice) and his body became hot, the lice left.

Here you have cause and effect not only reversed, but intermingled.

There you have a primer in some ways to use statistics to deceive. A well-wrapped statistic is better than Hitler's "big lie": it misleads, yet it can't be pinned onto you.

Is this little list altogether too much like a manual for swindlers? Perhaps I can justify it in the manner of the retired burglar whose published reminiscences amounted to a graduate course in how to pick a lock and muffle a footfall: The crooks already know these tricks. Honest men must learn them in self-defense.

Section C. The Social Sciences and Society

SCIENTIFIC PRINCIPLES AND THEIR CONSEQUENCES

Daniel C. Reber

THE PRINCIPLES

Science, and the results which it has produced, are what set modern times apart from all previous periods of history, more than any other characteristic or factor. If you and I were suddenly able to take a trip through medieval England, we would be struck with the enormous differences in the conditions of life then and now. Transportation would be primitive; boats, wagons and beasts of burden would be the only means of moving men or wares. Everywhere we would see conspicuous evidence of the ravages of disease and the lack of hygiene: wheezing tuberculars, toothless smiles, faces scarred by smallpox, the small stature of most of the people, and the conspicuous odor of everybody, for whom baths were a rare luxury. Not so conspicuous but equally telling would be the tombstones of those who did not survive: a vast number of infants, young people, and mothers dead in childbirth, victims of diseases and conditions which men knew not how to control. If we looked in on an average serf to check his circumstances, we would discover that he lived in a primitive shack, on a monotonously starchy diet, untraveled, untutored and unclean. If we sought to send a message beyond the range of our voices, the only way would be to send some person with a note. At night, a candle or a lamp fueled with animal fat would be the only source of light.

In modern times many of these repellent, painful and inconvenient problems, which were so much a part of daily life in premodern times, have been

From *Perspectives of Social Science* © 1970 by Frank Zulke, Editor. Reprinted by permission of the editor and the author. Daniel C. Reber is Assistant Professor of Political Science at The Loop College, Chicago, Illinois.

78

overcome by the applications of modern science. While admittedly most people on the globe today enjoy no more than a few of the benefits of scientific technology, the problem now is mainly one of spreading the benefits around. Furthermore, we confidently believe that in the not-too-distant future science and technology will overcome the remaining problems which are still beyond our knowledge; and we take for granted wonders which earlier times hardly dreamed of: antibiotics, skyscrapers, television, Kleenex, H-bombs, nylon and deodorants that won't wear off.

The cause of this monumental change in the comfort, health, and convenience of mankind was a change in the way men approached the problem of finding out about nature, a change in the approach to the problem of how to understand, manipulate and control the environment. The success of modern natural science stems from the fact that it discarded the various older ways of approaching the problem of how to investigate and know, and substituted its own. Observe that the examples above have been taken from natural science, and yet you are beginning a course in *social* science; but social science shares with natural science the same approach to the problem of knowledge, and social scientists, while admitting that in few instances have they been so obviously successful in explaining phenomena and applying their knowledge of it as have the natural scientists, point to a few successes and cherish the hope that the research of the future will give them much greater knowledge than they have enjoyed up to now.

Although we now take modern science and the ways of thought which are based on it for granted, modern science represents something relatively new, and our understanding of it may be aided if, before explaining just what science is, we take a passing look at the way of thinking which preceded it, and which science had to overcome in a long and hard-fought struggle. Before the rise of the scientific way of thinking, which, incidentally, often and properly goes by the name of *Empiricism,* philosophy was dominated more by the thinking of Aristotle than by that of any other thinker. Notwithstanding the influence of Christianity in both philosophy and politics in the Dark and Middle Ages, the power of the philosophy of Aristotle was such in men's minds that the Christians had to eventually come to terms with it. The attempt to resolve the differences between Christian and Aristotelian thinking was most impressively attempted by St. Thomas Aquinas, and it is for that that he has become justly famous. Despite the work of St. Thomas and the temporal, intellectual and spiritual power of the Church, however, the early empiricists, such as Bacon and Hobbes, who were leaders in the successful intellectual battle to overthrow old ways of thinking, considered Aristotle, and not the Christian thinkers, their prime adversary, and his the body of thinking which had to be explained away if empiricism and what we call science was to become preeminent. Some measure of their success can be gained from the fact that today only a few people know anything about what Aristotle thought and hardly anybody cares.

Along with modern science, Aristotle thought that the five senses were useful in the effort to gain knowledge; and, conceding that for some important things the senses were indispensable, he held that any notions which *contradicted* the evidence from the senses was patent foolishness. But Aristotle credited the mind with greater power than empiricism gives it, he thinking that the mind had the power to find certain truths *directly,* by reasoning things out, without the aid of the senses, things which the senses could never perceive. Aristotle thought, for example, that the reason for the world's existence, which cannot be known through the senses, is intelligible and must therefore be intelligent, and that the existence of God could be established. He believed that living creatures were made for certain ends or purposes, from which his philosophy is sometimes called teleological, because it interprets things in terms of ends; and Aristotle thought that man, as the highest animal, must have the highest end, and could find out what it was. He thought that the mind unaided by the senses could acquire knowledge of some things which are eternal, which always were and will be, and which cannot be other than they are. The early empiricists, whose basic approach has yet to be superseded in science, discarded Aristotle by changing the premises on which his knowledge was based, for the explicit reason that Aristotle's approach was not leading to any progress in the areas of physics and biology, and was leading to bad results in the areas of politics, religion and human relations. After 2,000 years of the dominance of the Aristotelian way of thinking, most of the common bodily and environmental complaints of men had gone unalleviated, and men were engaged in the destructive folly of religious wars and the social evil of discrimination on moral and intellectual grounds. The empiricists rejected Aristotle's notion that the mind has an independent power to know things, and confined the objects of knowledge to those things which the senses could detect. In so doing, they rejected any idea that the mind could directly know truths about nature, and rejected the notion that invisible things like right and wrong and the end of life could be known. When you reflect on how much men like to know right from wrong, and want to know the purpose for their lives, you can begin to understand why the triumph of science was such a long and at times such a fierce struggle.

Understanding any philosophical position or any approach to knowledge at its most basic requires a mental effort to wrestle with and grasp the fundamental premises on which its proofs are based. This study of the philosophic fundamentals has a long and hard name which you are hereby assigned to learn: *Epistemology,* a word of ancient Greek origin meaning the study of knowledge, or the study of the first principles of knowledge. Epistemology seeks the answers to the questions, how do we know what we know? What are the basic assumptions on which our understanding is based? By what means do we get the information we have, and what are the limitations on what we can know imposed by the qualities of the mind and the senses?

When you were in high school, you probably took a course in plane geometry. You discovered that geometry is capable of proving many interesting and useful properties and relationships about lines, points and plane figures, but every proof in geometry rests on certain assertions or statements which must be accepted without proof. These assertions are usually called *axioms,* or postulates. They cannot be proved, and yet if they are assumed to be true and turn out not to be, clearly every proof based on such assumptions will be false, too; either false, or true just by lucky accident, as the child who makes several mistakes in adding a column of figures sometimes ends up accidentally with the right answer. Geometry is in the uncomfortable position of being able to prove a vast number of subordinate truths, based on its first assumptions or axioms, but of having to assume without proof that its most fundamental tenets are true.

Geometry is not alone in its affliction with this problem. All knowledge, and all of the various systems of knowledge, are faced with the same difficulty. Every system must assume certain things to be true before it begins its investigations, and these things wholly shape the inquiry which follows. Both Aristotle's way of thinking, and science's, involved basic unproved axioms, and the revolution in the thinking of men which modern science produced, and the resulting revolution in the way of life of men, resulted from a change in the fundamental premises on which knowledge was based. Time and again in your study of social science you will see these premises of science and their consequences implied or explicitly stated, and you will see how the acceptance of these premises of science is the underpinning of momentous conclusions about the nature of men and about their relationships with each other. Three of modern science's premises are most basic, and the other assertions of science about knowledge and how it is gained can be shown to be consequences of these three.

1. "Our access to knowledge is solely through the senses." This postulate has been stated many ways, but the different statements mean the same thing, that the only connection the mind does or can have with the world outside of it is through the senses, and that there is no idea, principle, notion, opinion, conception or other thing in the mind which was not at first derived from an impression on one of the five senses. This axiom is sometimes referred to as "the first principle of empiricism." One of the first of the major blasts fired in the fight to overthrow the old ways of thinking was a book, ostensibly on politics, by Thomas Hobbes, entitled *Leviathan.* Interestingly, and consistently with what we have said above on the basis of knowledge, Hobbes began his book with some metaphysical comments which have come to be regarded as a classic statement of the modern approach.

Concerning the thoughts of man, I will consider them first singly, and afterwards in train, or dependence on one another. Singly, they are every one a representation or appearance, of some quality, or other accident of a body without us, which is commonly called an object. Which object worketh on the eyes, ears, and other parts of a man's body; and by diversity of working, produceth diversity of appearances.

The original [origin] of them all, is that which we call SENSE, for there is no conception in a man's mind, which hath not at first, totally, or by parts, been begotten upon the organs of sense. The rest are derived from that original.

Modern scientists are not always consciously aware that they adhere to this principle, but they would never accept the alternative, which is, that there are things which are real whose existence is not and cannot be confirmed in some way through the senses.

2. The second postulate of science is, "the mind has the power to remember what is perceived by the senses; the power to rearrange and compare what the senses have perceived; and the power to create combinations and abstractions from these sensations that will aid the mind in understanding them." Obviously this second postulate deals with the nature of that which is investigating phenomena, the mind. You will see on reflection that some specification of how the mind works is essential to any theory of knowledge, because it is with the mind that we know whatever it is that we know. No other part of our apparatus can be said to know; that is, to conceive and hold generalizations about anything. The eye, for example, can see red now, and again tomorrow; but it does not have the power of concluding that the color seen today and again tomorrow is the same. When you try to remember something you saw, what you do do? You shut your eyes, and imagine it in your "mind's eye," as we say. Do not forget that according to science the mind depends wholly on the senses for the material it works with.

3. The third great principle of science is most simply stated: "All effects have a cause." This means that nothing occurs spontaneously or unexplainably, nothing happens which cannot be traced to a prior cause, a cause of a type accessible to the senses. "All behavior is naturally determined"; "Nothing occurs without a prior efficient material cause," are other statements of the same notion. Implied in this postulate, and necessary to it for anything to be known, is the assumption that the rules of nature governing causation always operate; that is, what happens now and here under a certain set of circumstances are the same. If water boils now at a certain temperature and atmospheric pressure, then it boiled under the same conditions in 83 B.C. in Rome, and will boil again in 1984 in Accra under the same circumstances. The scientist cannot prove that the rules of nature always apply, but he must assume it or all attempts to obtain knowledge will be fruitless, each event being unique and unable to teach us anything about any other event; no general theories about phenomena could be formed.

These postulates of science fit together logically. If you think about our first postulate, you will see that it forces the acceptance of our second. If our only access to knowledge is through the senses, how does it happen that we have in our minds generalizations about phenomena when a generalization as such cannot be detected through the senses? The only explanation must be that the mind has a power to rearrange and connect sensations into what we call theories, hypotheses, principles and generalizations. Similarly, the implication of our third postulate is essential if our second postulate is to be of any consequence, because the power of the mind to rearrange and compare the sensations received will be of no benefit to it if the sensory data are not consistent in the pattern of their occurrences. The mind will find it both interesting and useful if it can discover that water will turn into a solid at low temperature. The mind's search for knowledge in this respect will be hopeless, however, if sometimes at low temperatures water turns to a solid, at other times under identical circumstances it gets thicker, like molasses, but does not become solid, and at still other occasions it just disappears when the temperature falls. The power to guess at the connection between low temperature and the properties of water will be of no use, i.e. knowledge cannot be obtained, if nature does not exhibit similar results under similar circumstances.

THE CONSEQUENCES OF THE PRINCIPLES

Our next task is to outline the consequences of the premises of science: first, because you will be meeting these consequences constantly, and second, because it sometimes happens that scientists fail to realize that their conclusions and procedure are a result of scientific postulates; indeed, matters sometimes go so far that it is claimed that science involves *no* philosophic premises or any epistemological position, and is simply a method which has been shown to be fruitful in practice and stands above philosophic arguments. We take up first, some methodological consequences of scientific postulates, and later, the social consequences.

What the scientist seeks is general rules about the events of nature which will relate one event to another in such a way as will make it possible for him to predict future events and be able to control them. General rules, however, and the laws and explanations are not themselves things which one of the five senses can perceive: they do not have color, shape, texture, odor, taste, loudness or pitch. Where, then, is the scientist to get the rules to measure against what his senses tell him? The answer is, from within his own mind. What the scientist does when he sets out to investigate a subject is to collect sense experience, think about it, and come up with a *hypothesis,* or a tentative explanation of the relationship between the phenomena, a relationship which should specify the causal relationships between phenomena, since, according to our postulates, that is the only kind of relationship that can exist.

Once the scientist's mind has presented itself with the hypothesis, the next step is to test the hypothesis systematically, to see if the supposed relationship actually exists. Ideally, what the scientist does is set up an experiment, in which all other possible explanations for the observed results will be excluded except for the cause which he has surmised, so that the one cause being tested will be responsible for the result. We hear occasional true stories and frequent exaggerated tales about the excitement and damage which occurred when students added things together in the high school chemistry laboratory just to see what would happen. Real scientists avoid mixing things together just to see what will happen, because such a random mixing will leave the scientist without any conclusion as to what caused what. Suppose we dump a generous quantity of francium, phosphorous, beeswax and water into a tub of sulphuric acid. After the smoke clears, we will still not know what combination of two or more elements caused the blast which wrecked our laboratory. A careful scientist would have conducted his experiment with careful measurements of the materials used, and used methods which would permit him to test the result against his carefully drawn hypothesis, which, of course, would have specified what would happen. In that way he will have a clear notion of exactly what combination was the cause of the result.

In social science we are faced with the grave difficulty which natural science usually avoids, the problem that we cannot isolate the subjects of our tests in the pristine manner that physical scientists are famous for. For this reason the social scientist has to devise tests that strive to at least minimize in one way or another the disturbance to the results and the conclusion caused by factors which are not being tested. A social scientist will try to get a *sample* of the individuals in a class, trying to make up for lack of accuracy of measurement of the results with one individual with a large number of cases, presumably representative, which will show the statistical probability of the truth of his hypothesis. Or he will make a *case study* of a situation which will not be able to prove any hypothesis, but which may help him to improve and refine his theory. Or the social scientist may reduce the precision of his hypothesis by positing only a hypothesis of *correlation* rather than causation. A hypothesis of correlation specifies that when one phenomenon appears or occurs, another will too, in some specified degree. For example the social scientist might hypothesize that, statistically speaking, when the average income of an area is lower than a certain amount, the incidence of assault will be higher. He is not sufficiently confident to say that poverty is the cause, and he would be even less sure how to prove such an hypothesis experimentally, but he *can* say, and undoubtedly prove or disprove by a statistical analysis that poverty and the incidence of assault do or do not go together. Actually, the third premise of science insists that if the connection between two phenomena can be shown, the relationship must be a causal connection: either one of the phenomena causes the other, or they have a common cause somewhere along the chain of causation. The alternative would be that the connection between the two phenomena is by chance, and chance, according to science, cannot exist. But in social science, because the chains of causation are often extremely complicated, we sometimes have to be satisfied with correlative explanations because the causes cannot yet be unraveled.

As a consequence of its premises, scientific knowledge is relativistic: science says, that no matter how much we have learned so far, the future will always bring more experiments and more hypotheses. The number of hypotheses that might be made about cause-and-effect relationships of phenomena is literally infinite; and if the number of hypotheses is infinite, so also is the number of experiments to be conducted. A hypothesis is considered to be true while it provides an explanation for all the phenomena it refers to. But if, in the course of observation, an event is recorded which cannot be explained by that hypothesis, then it must be replaced by a new hypothesis which explains both the observations explained by the previous hypothesis and also the new observation. Even the most highly tested theory is never considered final; the possibility of some new and pertinent but unexplained observation always exists.

Every hypothesis, to be scientific, must be testable through the senses.

When we say that the hypothesis must be testable through the senses, we mean that the hypothesis must predict under conditions which it specifies, a certain sensory result. This predictive quality is essential to any scientific test: the hypothesis says that cause-and-effect have a certain relationship, and that means that when a certain specified cause or causes is or are present, a certain effect or set of effects must be the result. The acceptability or unacceptability of an hypothesis does *not* turn on the actual power of men to investigate, but only on whether the subject is potentially subject to sensory inquiry. For example, an hypothesis that human life can survive on the surface of Venus is not testable at the present level of space technology, but there is nothing in it *intrinsically* untestable by the senses; presumably, when space technology reaches the necessary level, we will be able to settle the question scientifically. Likewise, the hypothesis that eclipses of the moon are caused by changes in the color of the surface of the moon is not an unscientific hypothesis, because the matter can be settled through the senses: the hypothesis is false, but not unscientific. By comparison, take the "hypothesis" that "God loves the meek." This is an unscientific hypothesis because we cannot specify sensory results flowing from either the truth or falsehood of the statement. God Himself is an unscientific cause, because by very definition He is immaterial, invisible, "everywhere and nowhere," having intrinsically no qualities the senses can detect—nor could He, for if He did He would not fit the definition of God. Neither can we specify in sensory terms the results for the meek of God's having loved them.

If any event is detectable through the senses, it must be detectable to the senses of normal people in a position to sense it, and the sensations must recur on another occasion if the conditions which produced the sensations in the first place recur or can be made to recur. Science rules out of the realm of knowledge such unique and private events as Bishop Pike's supposed conversations with his dead son. The dead son talks to Pike, but not to others, and we must doubt the reality of the sensations. Science also rules out the reality of events which require a supernatural or extrasensory cause, such as the Virgin Birth of Jesus. Explanations which require the participation of something intrinsically unique are unacceptable to science, because they rest on a premise that somehow the rules or laws of nature were suspended, the possibility of which is denied by our third postulate; or, that some supernatural and extrasensory cause interfered, which is denied by our first.

Even with its insistence on sensory verification, science can investigate things not *directly* accessible to the senses. Biology, for example examines living creatures too small for the eye to see without a microscope. But even the super-powerful electron microscope, which can even "see" some molecules, fits the scientific requirements because it ultimately produces a picture for the eye to see; and it is that picture which is the verification of what the electron microscope discovered. An atom smasher is another example. No one can see an atom getting smashed; but the event must produce some effect which sensitive equipment translates into something which the eye, or ear, or one of the senses, can detect. Otherwise, we would have no evidence that the atom had been smashed.

The subjects of social science are, for the most part, not detectable through the senses, although perhaps they will become so in the future with advanced technology. Emotions, opinions, motives, purposes, and decisions are not themselves accessible to the senses. But the social scientist says that although these things may not be sensations, they have sensory results or consequences. We cannot see a man's rage, but we can see the results: he shouts perhaps, his fists are clenched, his blood pressure rises, his hands shake. Maybe we cannot tell if a man is lying; but a lie detector measures certain bodily involuntary changes which usually go with telling a lie. Maybe we cannot tell exactly why people assault others, but perhaps we will find those who commit such a crime show a statistically higher incidence of poverty, ignorance and unemployment.

Arguments over "objectivity" inevitably arise in any discussion of scientific material. "Objective" means simply, testable through the senses. "The leaf is green" is considered an objective statement because the statement can be tested through seeing. Subjective statements are those about things inaccessible to the senses. If one says, "our country's wars are always just," that is a subjective statement because justice is not something which the senses can detect. Good and bad, fairness or unfairness, right and wrong, and morality and immorality are regarded by science as simply matters of opinion.

In general, the social scientist, like the natural scientist, tries to exclude "values" or questions of good and bad from his scientific investigations. As a social scientist, he does not make statements such as "we ought to try to eliminate the causes of crime" or "you should study hard," or "killing is immoral." He may have such views, but not in his capacity as a scientist. As a scientist, he will only say that "if crime is to be reduced, X must be done," or "if you want to get a good job, then you should study hard," or "if killing is to be stopped, these measures must be taken." His task as a scientist is only to show how the different social phenomena are related, not to show what ought to be done. Whether right and wrong are real things having an existence independent of the opinions of men is an age-old question which we cannot argue here; but this much is certain, that right and wrong do not have shape, color, texture, loudness or any other of the qualities of material things; and since the postulates of science restrict it to the investigation of sensory and therefore material things, science cannot make morally prescriptive statements. Science can, however, study the material results of certain kinds of moral ideas. Science cannot say, "free love is immoral," but it can investigate the results of people's believing that free love is moral, and compare those results with those in a society in which people believe that free love is immoral.

In spite of his effort to exclude values from his work, the scientist nevertheless cannot avoid depending on his own values for the answer to a question which he must always ask and answer before he does any research, and that is, what should I study? Any choice that he makes leads to the question, Why? and the answer to that must be in terms of a value. There is a literally infinite number of things which could be studied: How many grains of sand are on the beaches around Lake Michigan? How often are fire hydrants in the city of Chicago defiled by dogs in an average year? These are questions that science could answer, but does not waste its time investigating. What directs scientists' attention instead to the number of parts to an atom or to the causes of juvenile delinquency is that those questions are considered important—and considering something important or unimportant is a value.

In spite of science's efforts to be value-free and ethically and morally neutral, the widespread acceptance of the authority of science and its method may lead to the prevalence of certain social values which seem to grow out of the method and principles of science. Some of these, indeed, were actually intended by some of the early empiricists. Others are widespread in our society today, and you may judge for yourself how close the connection is of these to scientific principles.

One such value is the widespread expectation and approval of progress in our society. It is hard for us now to imagine, but in centuries past the idea that time would inevitably or almost certainly bring an estensive improvement in the conditions of men's lives would have been considered preposterous. Men lived the same kind of lives under the same material conditions of their ancestors, and they fully expected the pattern of their children's lives to be basically the same as theirs. Nowadays we take it for granted that the future will hold greater wealth and comfort, and that science will overcome afflictions that yet assail us. No one doubts, for example, that eventually a cure will be found for cancer; such optimism, doubtless well founded, is a product of the progress which science and technology have already produced, and reflects the basic scientific tenet that knowledge is relative and the future will produce more than the present has.

Worldliness or materialism, could also be an outgrowth of scientific philosophy. We say that we live in a secular age, and we are vaguely aware that there was a time past called the Middle Ages in which, we are told, people were profoundly religious and took such ideas as Heaven and Hell seriously, as real alternatives when death would come. Today few people worry seriously about what will happen in the next life, and many scoff at the notion of life after death. People today, it seems, are more concerned with the goods of this world: cars, houses, clothes, sex, having a good time, keeping up with the Joneses. Even those who profess to be unconcerned with material things and occupy themselves with promoting their own principles by one means or another are "doing *their own* Thing," and not God's Thing or the Things prescribed by Scripture. Preoccupation with these things can be connected with science, because science teaches that the only knowable, the only real things, are the "objective" things, the things that can be seen through the senses. Concerning the things not knowable through the senses, every man must be his own guide and judge.

In the field of morals, scientific thinking leads to three results: relativism, tolerance, and a retreat from the idea of individual moral responsibility. Science leads to moral relativism because right and wrong are not among the things which can be detected through the senses, if, indeed, they exist at all. This is easily proved: right and wrong do not have shape, color, loudness, hardness, or any other of the characteristics of material objects. Since there is no knowledge about moral things, that means that each man's views on what is right and wrong are as good as any other's; there are no grounds for saying that one view is better than another, or for promoting one view at the expense of another. Since no view can be proscribed on account of its wrongness, that means that every view must be allowed; that is, tolerated.

The scientific postulate that nothing occurs without a cause forces the retreat of moral responsibility, because, if everything occurs with an efficient prior cause, that means that the thoughts and actions of men must be included in the category of things that are caused. Granting that, since men are not eternal and are born, the chain of causes which causes them to act as they do must extend outside themselves, ultimately if not immediately. If that is so, then a man cannot be held responsible for what he does, because his actions are ultimately not determined by himself.

The affirmation that men are equal is another value that might tend to arise from scientific postulates. We know what we know through the senses; and with regard to our senses, we are much more equal to one another than in other respects. Some may hear a little better than others, and some may see better, but a normal healthy individual, by the time he has his glasses on and his hearing aid adjusted, sees and hears just about as well as any other healthy individual. This is the sensory equality and the scientific position from which the early empiricists asserted that men were in fact equal, and hence entitled to equal consideration and equal rights: and we need only look at and listen to the rhetoric of contemporary society to see how thoroughly our society has become permeated with this view. Today it is hard for us to get even an inkling of the notions of inequality that pervaded the societies of the past, which took for granted the inequalities of men, based on distinctions such as those of birth, strength, wealth, intelligence, beauty and virtue.

As you wend your way through the labyrinth of scientific literature, keep in your mind the connection between method, conclusions and premises; if you do that, you will find that many things otherwise mysterious or difficult will be easily understood.

VALUE-FREE SOCIAL SCIENCE

Stephen B. Baier

In recent years social scientists have emphasized the need to separate the reporting of facts from the expression of values. Social research, as they see it, must avoid statements which express the *values* of the researcher. They feel that science must not be concerned with the scientist's view of how the world *should be.* The task of the social researcher is to tell us what actually exists, what *is,* in the world. Everyone, after all, has a slightly different view of how things should be, and there is no reason why the opinion of the scientist is any better than that of anyone else.

In considering the difference between facts and values, social thinkers usually assume that there are two distinct areas of knowledge. One area of knowledge is characterized by statements about what *is.* The other area, which seems to be fundamentally different, consists of statements about what *should be.* Statements of the first kind, about the world that is, are called empirical statements. Empirical knowledge is gained through the senses and is available to everyone. In order to have empirical knowledge, a person need only see, hear, touch, taste or smell something. We tell ourselves, "this chair is brown" —this is an empirical statement because we can see and feel the chair. Whatever knowledge we have of the chair comes to us through our senses.

Although knowledge of this kind seems very basic, empirical knowledge need not remain simple. It is possible to combine empirical statements in an attempt to explain relationships between events. The social scientist may say, for example, that in a given neighborhood overcrowding is related to arson. Both of the events listed in this statement are elements of empirical knowledge. It is possible to go to the neighborhood and check for overcrowding, defined in a suitable way, and check for arson, also suitably defined. In other words, an observer can have sense knowledge of both overcrowding and arson. But he may be able to go beyond his knowledge of the events. If an observer is careful in the way he investigates, he can show that a rise in crowded conditions is accompanied by a rise in fire-setting. He may then assume that overcrowding is the cause of arson, or perhaps only one of many causes of fire-setting.[1] With the assumption about a causal relationship between the two events, the observer has made considerable progress in finding out something about his surroundings.

The empirical statement, then, enables us to make a range of useful observations about our surroundings. It is possible to say "there are twenty-four chairs in this room," or to use sense knowledge in an attempt to prove that events are related. As long as a particular statement concerns knowledge that is available through the senses, it belongs to the body of empirical knowledge.

The second area of knowledge concerns values. Besides knowing the world as it is, we are able to project our idea to a world that *should* exist. Man's tendency to place values on things and ideas is just as certain as his ability to observe. Some objects in the environment are desired and are of high value; others are not. Similarly, we approve of certain actions because of some real or imagined benefit to ourselves or to mankind. Other actions gain our disapproval for opposite reasons.

When a person expresses a value, it does not mean that the thing he is talking about is inherently valuable to all men. The person who expresses a value is only reflecting his personal history. In the past he has been rewarded and punished for performing some action or having some attitude. For example, someone who has been constantly rewarded for neatness throughout his childhood will be led to believe that neatness is "good." In fact, neatness *is* valuable to him if it led to approval from his mother and some reward, such as a piece of candy. With time, other rewards for valuing neatness take shape— an A on a paper in school or the attention of someone of the opposite sex who appreciates and values neatness, too. It should be remembered that other values are similar. We are rewarded or punished for the length of our hair, for example, and consequently begin to believe that long hair is either "good" or "bad." It would, of course, be impossible to enumerate all the ways that values are formed from previous experiences of the individual. People have widely differing ideas about the value of hard work, the military, the need for competition, and many other things. The diversity of their attitudes merely reflects the way that their experiences of rewards and punishments have differed.

Values are never held in isolation. Since we place differing values on things or ideas, our values have to be arranged in relation to each other. People must choose between two things which are desired, and decide which of the two they value the most. For example, some people will value defending their country more than preserving the lives of certain other people (namely, the enemy's troops). Others, of course, will reverse the order of importance of the two values, and decide that it is more important not to kill, regardless of the reason. The latter group is said to have a differing *value system* from the former group.

Finally, people have enormous difficulty keeping their values to themselves. Friends, relatives, politicians and religious leaders tell us what we *should do*. We must value one brand of toothpaste over another brand, liberty over life, one law over another, the program of one political party over that of its rival. Situations where we must make choices according to our values present themselves to us often in our everyday life.

WEBER AND VALUE-FREE SOCIAL SCIENCE

The German social thinker Max Weber played a decisive role in formulating the idea that social sciences should be value free. Indeed, Weber felt that the value-free concept was essential for progress in the social sciences.[2]

Weber wrote at the beginning of the twentieth century, at a time when the gap between the natural sciences and the social sciences was a wide one. Natural science had been able to use techniques of observation to discover laws in nature. Natural scientists were able to formulate laws stating that whenever certain specific conditions were present, a definite result would follow. The social sciences, however, lagged far behind. The scientific process of observation, inference, then prediction to verify inference was of little use to social scientists. They limited themselves to very broad and somewhat vague statements about social life. Social scientists frequently failed to verify their theories systematically. Furthermore, these general theories were not able to explain instances of specific behavior.[3]

Weber attempted to bring the social sciences closer to the natural sciences, even though he admitted that the two were quite different. Weber believed that man's interest in natural science is directed at understanding for the purpose of control. In the social sciences, on the other hand, man's interest aims at understanding for evaluation. Weber believed that man places value on all elements of culture, on everything which passes from generation to generation. Therefore, almost everything in the social world has a value attached to it. Social science must operate in social surroundings which place "good," "bad" and other value labels on everything.

Yet, Weber felt that the social sciences would be able to make some of the progress that the natural sciences had already made if social science would choose to be free of values. He blamed the lack of progress in the social sciences on the tendency of social researchers to become too involved in their personal values. The correctness of values, he felt, is a matter of faith, not of knowledge. Social science should be an empirical science. In this way, social science could explain causation in society by means of observation. Above all, it was necessary for social scientists to leave behind the influence of their personal, moral or political beliefs. They should not praise or condemn what they saw; rather, as scientists, they should merely describe.

Despite his belief that society cannot refrain from placing values on everything in the human environment, Weber thought that value-free social science was possible. He examined human conduct by applying the categories of "means" and "ends" to it. He felt that men desire something either for its own sake—as an end—or as a means of achieving something else. Weber stated that science is able to analyze means to determine whether or not they will lead to a given desired end. In other words, science can tell us that if a given end is desired, then a certain means should be employed in order to reach it. He felt that science could also tell us what must be given up in order to reach a desired end. But Weber insisted that science is not able to tell us what end should be chosen. That is a question of values, a question of how much a particular end is valued. Weber summarizes this position as follows:

An empirical science cannot tell anyone what he should do—but rather what he can do—and under certain circumstances—what he wishes to do.[4]

Weber felt that the borderline between facts and values should be very important to social scientists. They are not able to choose among ends, but only to say something about the probability of events occurring in sequence. Accordingly, Weber felt that social scientists have a responsibility to make the distinction between facts and values clear to others, and above all to themselves.

IS VALUE-FREE SOCIAL SCIENCE POSSIBLE?

Weber thought that value-free social science was both possible and desirable. But there are others who contend that the possibility of value-free social science is a myth and, further, that it is not even desirable.

One persuasive critic of Weber, Alvin Gouldner, argues that the doctrine of value-free social science was Weber's answer to needs of his time.[5] In Weber's day, professors in German universities competed for students. Career advancement depended on the ability of the professor to attract students, and in some ranks the teacher's salary depended on the size of the enrollment in his class. Professors who expressed a strong stand on some question of value— a political question, for example—were more likely to attract students than those who did not. Observers argued that the lecture hall of the university was a particularly unsuitable place for the expression of value judgments, especially on politics. Since the relationship between the student and the professor was that of unequals, the student would naturally be at a disadvantage and less able to form an independent opinion. Weber's critic argues that he was actually proposing a truce to his fellow professors when he proposed the value-free doctrine. In effect he was saying that they should leave their personal beliefs, and especially their politics, outside the classroom.

In a broader perspective, the idea of value-free social science was useful to the university as a whole. In the early decades of the twentieth century, the universities were trying to gain enough independence from the church and the state to permit an objective study of society. The stance of the social scientist as a totally objective observer would assure him of immunity from the criticism of established social institutions. At that time the universities stood to gain from a position in a world apart. Social scientists attempted to transcend society by insisting that their studies were value free.

From a modern viewpoint, the question of objectivity in the social sciences appears more complex. Is value-free social science possible? Today, there are many who argue that it is not. The social scientist can guard against the overt expression of his personal values. But can he eliminate the subtle influence of values on his selection of problems and on his choice of the theoretical framework he uses to solve the problem? Gouldner argues that the "vain ritual of moral neutrality," the pretense of a value-free social science, only obscures the real issue. If the social scientist is interested in the truth, he must make his audience aware that no scientist can ever completely free himself of values. Values accompany particular ideas and actions which have produced rewards and punishments in the past; the ideas and actions are likely to have similar results in the future. What are the values for which the social scientist is rewarded? He tends to accept the values of his colleagues and superiors, or at least a common denominator of these values. In return, he receives the very tangible reward of employment. He has lived with the values of a certain segment of society, and often he is not acquainted with the value systems of other socioeconomic groups. Finally, the social scientist accepts the values of his culture, and cannot expect to find rewards there for actions which might be highly regarded in, let us say, Japan or India.

One of the most surprising aspects of social science today is that value-free social science is losing ground. Social sciences had established themselves as objective, empirical sciences in our century. But one observer notes "the astonishing reversal of the belief in the scientific, that is, the objective, the detached, the dispassionate character of the social sciences."[6] What group is responsible for this reversal? Surprisingly, the attitude is to be found among social scientists themselves—among an increasing number of younger social scientists and among students of the social sciences. The revolt against objectivity is led by radicals who question the assumption that society should be observed, and assert that it must be radically changed. Yet, many aspects of the revolt against value-free social science have had an effect beyond radical circles.

Today there are many social scientists who reject the possibility of objective social science. Some say that value-free social science is not possible because there is very little human behavior that goes unrewarded or unpunished, and the social scientist cannot claim immunity from this aspect of his surroundings. Consequently, values are at least implicit in his writings. Others argue that members of one ethnic group will never be able to write objectively about members of another ethnic group. Some insist that there is black science and there is white science, and the gap is unbridgeable. They believe that an objective understanding of social behavior is impossible because it will always be limited by the social scientist's political, economic or ethnic position. The conclusion of the researcher necessarily reflects the values inherent in his social position.[7]

Critics of Weber's belief in the possibility of value-free social science can point to the record of the past few decades. Social sciences have not resisted the temptations of money for research from government, the military, political parties, and from the numerous research centers sponsored by big business foundations. Social scientists can repeat their magic formula, insisting that their research is "pure," "objective," or "value free." But there is some reason for disbelief when we ask ourselves who is paying for social science research.

Up to this point, some may agree that separating values from science is indeed a difficult task: difficult, yet not impossible. Another question arises, however: is the goal of value-free social science desirable? Radical social scientists, of course, would answer that it is not. And there are many others who would agree with them. Social science, they feel, ought to show its relevance and its concern for the problems of modern society. The value-free concept should not distract scientists from relevant social questions and lead them to a position of moral indifference. No knowledge can remain purely theoretical after Hiroshima. The seemingly remote work of physicists produced the atomic bomb. Afterwards, moral questions must be posed about all scientific knowledge.

FOOTNOTES

1. It is also possible that two events varying together may be caused by a third factor which affects both of the variables which vary simultaneously. In our example, arson and overcrowding may result from some third variable.

2. Max Weber was born in 1864 to a wealthy family. He was trained in law and economics in the German Universities. Although he was originally a professor of economics, he earned a reputation as a sociologist. He made a number of studies of concrete social problems and also contributed greatly to the theory of sociology.

3. The Social Darwinists, for example, were not able to explain behavior in any specific way. They borrowed wholesale Darwin's explanation for the evolution of animal species which had become popularized as "the survival of the fittest." Applying this idea to society, the Social Darwinists contended that the stronger people did survive at the expense of the weaker. They were unable to go beyond this broad explanation to describe the causes for specific human behavior.

4. Max Weber, "Objectivity in Social Science and Social Policy," *Philosophy of the Social Sciences, a Reader,* ed. Maurice Natanson, (New York, 1963), pp. 360-61.

5. Alvin Gouldner, "Anti-Minotaur: The Myth of Value-Free Sociology," *Sociology on Trial,* (Englewood Cliffs, N.J., 1963), p. 51.

6. Robert Nisbet, "Subjective Si! Objective No!", *The New York Times Book Review,* April 5, 1970, p. 1.

7. *Ibid.,* p. 2.

SOCIAL SCIENCE AND IDEOLOGY

Raymond E. Ries

Modern social science traces its origin to the breakup of traditional society and the rise of the modern industrial state. Traditional society maintained a fairly stable system of social relationships over time and a fixed center of belief. In contrast, industrial society exhibits a pattern of social mobility within a changing class structure and a horizontal movement of people from one residential location to another. In the place of a fixed center of belief, modern society develops a network of central administrative agencies. It is a situation of change in which the adaptations of thought and custom give way to ever newer forms.

But such changes are not experienced by all men in the same way. The structure of society and the varying sensitivity among men filter the impact of change, so that some in varying degrees are sheltered from it and others exposed to it unmercifully. For many of the intellectuals of the past century the problem of the significance of these changes in terms of historical development was of paramount concern.

Auguste Comte, the French philosopher of Positivism, was reflecting on this situation in the early nineteenth century when he wrote: "We find ourselves living in a period of confusion, without any general view of the past, or sound appreciation of the future, to enlighten us for the crises prepared by the whole progress yet achieved. We find ourselves, after half a century of tentative confusion, oscillating between an invincible aversion to the old system and a vague impulsion toward some kind of reorganization." Comte sought an historical orientation, and an end to the uncertainties of the future

From *Social Research: An International Quarterly of Political and Social Science,* Summer, 1964, Vol. 31, No. 2, pp. 234-243. Reprinted by permission of *Social Research* and the author.

and the disorganization of the present. He found his solution in adopting the methods of the natural sciences to these tasks; methods which had proved so fruitful in the exploration and control of nature. It was he who coined the term, "Sociology," as representing a new discipline in the study of man and society. This new discipline would abandon the theological and metaphysical approaches to the study of society, and utilize the "positive" methods of observation and experiment.

Contained in Comte's program were two themes which, however much he felt them united, were nevertheless in tension with each other. On the one hand Comte wished to establish a program for the scientific study of human society, and on the other hand he wished this same program to become the basis of nothing less than the total reorganization of human society. Not only would sociology provide for an empirical study of man, it would also provide the means for the redemption of society from the chaos and disorganization in which he found it. It is one thing to expect some practical consequences from the science of society, but it is quite another thing to expect it to provide the means of salvation.

This combination of themes has had its exponents among Marxists and positivists alike. For Marx the validity of theory required that it have an active effect on the life of man. A few years ago George Lundberg wrote a book entitled *Can Science Save Us?* He was concerned with the political and economic problems of our time, and the answer to his question, although methodologically more sophisticated than Comte's, was in essence the same. At the end of his book he wrote, "To those who are still skeptical and unimpressed with the promise of social science, we may address this question: What alternatives do you propose that hold greater promise? If we do not place our faith in social science, to what shall we look for social salvation?" As with Comte, Lundberg ties salvation to society and human history, and offers the promise of achieving salvation through the science of society. The use of the terms "faith" and "salvation" are indicative of the basically religious nature of his concern.

In its more active form, the insistence that knowledge of society must act as an instrument of social change is known by the term "ideology." The force of ideology is the force of passion and commitment to an idea. An ideology provides its possessor with self-justification and with a claim to action. It is something to believe in and to give orientation to one's life and experience. Ideology has a function analogous to religious commitment. The commitment effects a transformation in the life of the individual and as a consequence in the lives of those about him.

The method of science, however, requires detachment. Not that science has no passion and commitment, for indeed it has. How else could one devote his life to such an enterprise as science? But it is a vocational commitment— not a commitment to the content of information which the scientist may help to add to the accumulative store of scientific knowledge. Indeed, the scientist must reckon with the fact that the bit of information which he adds through the energies of his lifetime may well be cancelled or discarded at some later time.

The ideologist is committed to an idea which transcends the present reality. His aim is to transform existing life, and his knowledge has a "meaning" for him in a personal sense. The scientist is committed to the observation of present reality. His knowledge will consist in the rational, empirical observation of the life of society about him, and personal "meaning" for him is not provided by the content of his tested observations. For this reason the science of society, insofar as it maintains a strictly scientific attitude, can only record the defeat of ideological or religious intention. No matter what the belief, or what the commitment, science can only reveal those everyday realities in the life of men holding such belief and commitment. It may record that such and such ideological or religious attitudes are present, but that these attitudes are contradicted by the realities of current social life. In the place of the "meaning" which the ideologist finds, science will find only the realities of class, status or psychosocial processes. Thus, for example, denominationalism among Protestants appears as a reflection of differences in status and class; the populist movement in the "Age of Reform" appears to be generated by status anxiety and discontent; and authoritarian personality structures appear to be associated with certain political attitudes and movements. By the adoption of its methods, science can neither transcend society nor find its "meaning." Although a science of society may have consequences for the transformation of human history, it cannot require that transformation, nor determine its direction.

As William Graham Sumner pointed out long ago in *Folkways,* the behavior of men in society involves the acceptance of rules of meaning, some of which have the additional sanction of being sacred. That is to say, they are not open to question or trespass. Even such a simple form of social behavior as a college pep rally involves an assortment of sacred meanings, only partly conscious, and most inarticulate, but without which the behavior could not continue. Imagine, if you will, a visiting anthropologist describing this custom among the natives of a college campus. He would record the bodily movements, the words of the chant and songs, the course of the whole affair. He might even indicate the magical potency attributed by the natives to this activity in the winning of football games. And he might try to describe the outward manifestation of the demon or "spirit" invoked on these occasions. Using his comparative knowledge of culture he might find an activity similar in function among the Arunta of Australia, or the Crow Indians of the last century. But in all this he would neither feel nor share the meanings which affect the participants. And his final scientific description of the pep rally will provide not one iota of substance for the value and meaning which the participants find in it.

In this manner the science of society appears to "unmask" human behavior, to discover hidden realities, or the "illusions" by means of which people interpret their own behavior. And this is so because to the scientific observer these values have the status of "facts," and as facts they are merely one element among others which will be taken into account in analysis of behavior. Science is not at war with ideology; it is simply incapable of supporting it.

The final separation of these two themes which positivists and Marxists alike shared was stated unequivocally by Max Weber toward the end of his career. "Science today is a 'vocation' organized in special disciplines in the service of self-clarification and knowledge of interrelated facts. It is not the gift of grace of seers and prophets dispensing sacred values and revelations, nor does it partake of the contemplation of sages and philosophers about the meaning of the universe."[1] Weber made clear that the occupation of science was not a sign of grace, and that science had no authority to assess the meaning of life. To the question: How shall I live my life, and what shall I do? science must perforce remain silent.

This viewpoint, now so much a part of modern social science, had its echo in a remark attributed to the economist, J. M. Keynes, in a conversation with President Franklin Roosevelt. Roosevelt is said to have asked Keynes to tell him as an economist whether the United States should remain on or go off the gold standard. And Keynes is said to have replied that as an economist he might be able to say what might happen if we remained on the gold standard, and what might happen if we went off, but that, as an economist, he could not say whether we should or should not.

Social science, at least in the West, has developed into an empirical, rational form of the self-observation of society. As a source of critical information about the society, social science finds its uses in the administration of the modern state and the other corporate agencies of society. And in this respect it produces what might be called policy-related information. We are accustomed to having available organized forms of information about the society we live in—be it in the form of divorce rates, rates of national growth, or surveys of opinion. Consider for example a simple decision by a local school board regarding classroom needs for the next ten years, and consider the various forms of information it would find available in defining and estimating these needs. But we may not realize that such kinds of information about society were not available even a scant hundred years ago. What we know of population or birth rates of, say, seventeenth century England is largely based on estimates of modern scholars, because no one living at that time had such information. Indeed, we today probably know more in a statistical way about the seventeenth century than anyone living at that time. The task of modern social science has been the development and interpretation of information about society. In this it aids in the achieving of clarity in thinking about our objectives and alternatives, and it may indicate possible consequences of action. And in this manner social science may inform decisions, but it does not in so doing provide the framework of value within which those decisions are finally made.

Whatever the causes, the postwar generation of intellectuals has become disengaged from ideology. The author recalls reading a statement by Dwight Macdonald written shortly after World War II that politics no longer interested him. The decline of ideology among many intellectuals in the West has been marked by apathy in regard to the search for meaning. It is true that the vague ideas associated with economic development exert an ideological claim on some, and certainly the concept of the Peace Corps rests on such ideas associated with the economic improvement of underdeveloped nations. It is hard to predict the future in these matters. Millennial hopes have had a strong grip on the pattern of Western social thought. Perhaps the waiting or the living will become too hard, and the next generation will find a new way to force the "end of days." But for the present at least it would seem that social science has moved beyond ideology. But what is beyond ideology?

First of all it must be recognized that we no longer need to make a virtue of necessity. The self-observation of society in the form of a policy-related social science is a necessity under the present conditions of social organization. This is even more true of the democratically organized industrial state than the totalitarian. Without a dominating ideology, the democratic state requires information about itself as a means of social control.

Nor need one make an evil of the same necessity. The charge that social science will create the means of manipulation for a regimented society is largely misdirected. A recent account of motivational research seemed to suggest just that. But several things are overlooked here: In the first place, whatever the symptoms or motivations that social science may discover, those symptoms and motivations are still chosen by men. Secondly, human beings can and often do alter the rules of their own behavior. And finally, social science has not yet discovered that there are two kinds of people, namely those who are unconsciously motivated and those who are not.

Social science, then, performs a necessary function in our society. It is the practical consequence of this function for the life of society, however, with which we need to concern ourselves. For it is the insistence or the demand that the study of man should have some practical political consequence that we have described as the basis of ideology. Insofar as social science is concerned, beyond ideology means that social science no longer claims to deliver man from the salient predicament of his existence: namely, that he does not fit into his own environment. If the solution to that problem is to come in human history, then the solution will have to come from some other agency than social science.

Social science cannot provide the "solution" for the problems of crime, poverty, or juvenile delinquency. Social science can only clarify our understanding of these problems, indicate means of solution and their cost. All these problems involve the responsibilities of men in their capacity as self-determining agents, and social science cannot absolve man from taking responsibility for what he does.

Yet the demand for a solution, for an orientation, is still with us as it was in the time of Comte. Let me quote from a recent work of the late C. Wright Mills:

> The very shaping of history now outpaces the ability of men to orient themselves in accordance with cherished values. And which values? Even when they do not panic, men often sense that the old ways of thinking and feeling have collapsed and that the newer beginnings are ambiguous to the point of moral stasis. Is it any wonder that ordinary men feel that they cannot cope

with the larger worlds with which they are so suddenly confronted? That they cannot understand the meaning of their epoch for their own lives? . . . What they need, and what they feel they need, is a quality of mind that will help them to use information and to develop reason in order to achieve lucid summations of what is going on in the world and of what may be happening within themselves.[2]

It is instructive that the same sense of disorientation which activated Auguste Comte should appear well over a hundred years later in the writings of C. Wright Mills. At a much earlier time, it was, I believe, this same sense of disorientation that led men to the expectation of the coming of the Messiah. In fact, at various times in Western history this expectation has become so intense that false Messiahs have arisen to fulfill the demands of the time. Perhaps in our age, so organized by corporate activities, this same demand leads men to seek the Messiah in the corporate body: be it a political party, the institution of science, or even a business organization. But if the concept of the Messiah and His coming means anything at all it means at least that He will come in His own time. In the past there were men who have refused to play the role of Messiah even though the demand upon them was great. And I think that social science needs also to refuse to promise the deliverance of man even though the demand made upon it may be equally great.

What then can social science offer in an age when men seek the comfort of an orientation, an image? There is little in the way of consolation which the scientific study of man can give except consciousness. It is a consciousness of the values men have pursued, the roles men have played, and the images they have forged. It is a critical consciousness of the social agencies and forces operative in contemporary life. But someone will say, "All very well and good, but I wish something more than this."

This may be answered by an analogy. The book of Isaiah describes how a person cuts a tree, and with part of its wood builds the fire to warm himself, and with another part builds a fire to cook his roast. Then warmed and fed, with the remaining wood he carves an image to which he bows down, and asks deliverance. The scientific knowledge of society, like the wood of the tree, has its uses. It is written in books, communicated to students, it is used in the lives of individuals and policy makers to clarify and organize the alternatives to action, it is used by individuals to inform and gain understanding of what they have been doing as well as what they may do. But apart from this what would you make out of the knowledge of society? Into what would you carve it? Would you make it into a redeemer? Would you make it into an instrument of propaganda? Would you make it stand in the place of a man?

The injunction against graven images is not simply a matter of bowing down before false gods nor of breaking the First Commandment. The injunction is against giving the authority of a thing to its image or its likeness. An image of man is a likeness but the authority for what a man is, is man, not an image of him. The knowledge of man, even the scientific knowledge of man, cannot take the place of authority for what a man is, for that place belongs to man. We may see this more clearly if we consider the repugnance we may feel, say, toward the image of Soviet man. The problem here is the relation between the image and the Soviet people. And the question is, who is the authority for what that people shall be, the image or the people themselves.

In the end the ideologist and the maker of graven images want the same thing. The ideologist cares only that his idea have some active expression in the life of man and society. The image maker cares only that his image have some bodily expression in the wood which he carves. The image maker, unlike the artist, has no respect for the material in which he carves. It makes no difference to him what the quality of the wood may be, or whether he shapes wood, brass or stone, so long as the image stands apart from him and he can bow down to it. The ideologist in the end cares neither for the men nor the society which is to serve as the bodily expression of his idea. Men may be crushed and society torn asunder so long as this gives evidence of being effected by the force of an idea. Both image maker and ideologist seek deliverance by giving the authority of a thing to its likeness, the one through an image of God, the other through an image of man. The one carves in wood, the other carves his fellow man.

If social science moves beyond ideology, it may make us conscious of the images and the false authorities in the history of man. There is always the hope, of course, that this consciousness of society will make a difference. But what difference it shall make and how it shall make it we cannot ourselves say. The objective, interpretative study of society may entertain the hope of liberating man from some of his idols. But this is a hope and not a promise.

FOOTNOTES

1. H. H. Gerth and C. W. Mills, eds., "Science as a Vocation." *From Max Weber: Essays in Sociology* (New York: Oxford University Press, 1946), p. 152

2. C. Wright Mills, *The Sociological Imagination* (New York: Oxford University Press, 1959) pp. 4-5.

SOCIAL SCIENCE AND SOCIAL POLICY

Karl R. Popper

THE TECHNOLOGICAL APPROACH TO SOCIOLOGY

The term "social technology" (and even more the term "social engineering"[1] which will be introduced in the next section) is likely to arouse suspicion, and to repel those whom it reminds of the "social blueprints" of the collectivist planners, or perhaps even of the "technocrats." I realize this danger, and so I have added the word "piecemeal," both to offset undesirable associations and to express my conviction that "piecemeal tinkering" (as it is sometimes called), combined with critical analysis, is the main way to practical results in the social as well as in the natural sciences. The social sciences have developed very largely through the criticism of proposals for social improvements or, more precisely, through attempts to find out whether or not some particular economic or political action is likely to produce an expected, or desired, result.[2] This approach, which might indeed be called the classical one, is what I have in mind when I refer to the technological approach to social science, or to "piecemeal social technology."

Technological problems in the field of social science may be of a "private" or of a "public" character. For example, investigations into the technique of business administration, or into the effects of improved working conditions upon output, belong to the first group. Investigations into the effects of prison reform or universal health insurance, or of the stabilization of prices by means of tribunals, or of the introduction of new import duties,

---

etc., upon, say, the equalization of incomes, belong to the second group; and so do some of the most urgent practical questions of the day, such as the possibility of controlling trade cycles; or the question whether centralized "planning," in the sense of state management of production, is compatible with an effective democratic control of the administration; or the question of how to export democracy to the Middle East.

This emphasis upon the practical technological approach does not mean that any of the theoretical problems that may arise from the analysis of the practical problems should be excluded. On the contrary, it is one of my main points that the technological approach is likely to prove fruitful in giving rise to significant problems of a purely theoretical kind. But besides helping us in the fundamental task of selecting problems, the technological approach imposes a discipline on our speculative inclinations (which, especially in the field of sociology proper, are liable to lead us into the region of metaphysics); for it forces us to submit our theories to definite standards, such as standards of clarity and practical testability. My point about the technological approach might perhaps be made by saying that sociology (and perhaps even the social sciences in general) should look, not indeed for "its Newton or its Darwin,"[3] but rather for its Galileo, or its Pasteur.

This and my previous references to an analogy between the methods of the social and the natural sciences are likely to provoke as much opposition as our choice of terms like "social technology" and "social engineering" (this in spite of the important qualification expressed by the word "piecemeal"). So I had better say that I fully appreciate the importance of the fight against a dogmatic methodological naturalism or "scientism" (to use Professor Hayek's term). Nevertheless I do not see why we should not make use of this analogy as far as it is fruitful, even though we recognize that it has been badly misused and misrepresented in certain quarters. Besides, we can hardly offer a stronger argument against these dogmatic naturalists than one that shows that some of the methods they attack are fundamentally the same as the methods used in the natural sciences.

A *prima facie* objection against what we call the technological approach is that it implies the adoption of an "activist" attitude towards the social order ... and that it is therefore liable to prejudice us against the anti-interventionist or "passivist" view: the view that if we are dissatisfied with existing social or economic conditions, it is because we do not understand how they work and why active intervention could only make matters worse. Now I must admit that I am certainly out of sympathy with this "passivist" view, and that I even believe that a policy of *universal* anti-interventionism is untenable—even on purely logical grounds, since its supporters are bound to recommend political intervention aimed at preventing intervention. Nevertheless, the technological approach as such is neutral in this matter (as indeed it ought to be), and by no means incompatible with anti-interventionism. On the contrary, I think that anti-interventionism involves a technological approach. For to assert that interventionism makes matters worse is to say that certain political actions would not have certain effects—to wit, not the desired ones; and it is one of the most characteristic tasks of any technology to *point out what cannot be achieved.*

It is worth while to consider this point more closely. As I have shown elsewhere,[4] every natural law can be expressed by asserting that *such and such a thing cannot happen;* that is to say, by a sentence in the form of the proverb: "You can't carry water in a sieve." For example, the law of conservation of energy can be expressed by: "You cannot build a perpetual motion machine"; and that of entropy by: "You cannot build a machine which is a hundred percent efficient." This way of formulating natural laws is one which makes their technological significance obvious and it may therefore be called the *"technological form"* of a natural law. If we now consider anti-interventionism in this light, then we see at once that it may well be expressed by sentences of the form: "You cannot achieve such and such results," or perhaps, "You cannot achieve such and such ends without such and such concomitant effects." But this shows that anti-interventionism can be called a typically *technological doctrine.*

It is not, of course, the only one in the realm of social science. On the contrary, the significance of our analysis lies in the fact that it draws attention to a really fundamental similarity between the natural and the social sciences. I have in mind the existence of sociological laws or hypotheses which are analogous to the laws or hypotheses of the natural sciences. Since the existence of such sociological laws or hypotheses (other than so-called "historical laws") has often been doubted,[5] I will now give a number of examples: "You cannot introduce agricultural tariffs and at the same time reduce the cost of living."—"You cannot, in an industrial society, organize consumers' pressure groups as effectively as you can organize certain producers' pressure groups."—"You cannot have a centrally planned society with a price system that fulfills the main functions of competitive prices."—"You cannot have full employment without inflation." Another group of examples may be taken from the realm of power politics: "You cannot introduce a political reform without causing some repercussions which are undesirable from the point of view of the ends aimed at" (therefore, look out for them.)—"You cannot introduce a political reform without strengthening the opposing forces, to a degree roughly in ratio to the scope of the reform." (This may be said to be the technological corollary of "There are always interests connected with the *status quo.*")—"You cannot make a revolution without causing a reaction." To these examples we may add two more, which may be called "Plato's law of revolutions" (from the eighth book of the *Republic*) and "Lord Acton's law of corruption," respectively: "You cannot make a successful revolution if the ruling class is not weakened by internal dissension or defeat in war."—"You cannot give a man power over other men without tempting him to misuse it—a temptation which roughly increases with the amount of power wielded, and which very few are capable of resisting." Nothing is here assumed about the strength of the available evidence in favor of these hypotheses whose formulations certainly leave much room for improvement. They are merely examples of the kind of statements which a piecemeal technology may attempt to discuss, and to substantiate.

PIECEMEAL VERSUS UTOPIAN ENGINEERING

Notwithstanding the objectionable associations which attach to the term "engineering,"[6] I shall use the term "piecemeal social engineering" to describe the practical application of the results of piecemeal technology. The term is useful since there is need for a term covering social activities, private as well as public, which, in order to realize some aim or end, consciously utilize all available technological knowledge.[7] Piecemeal social engineering resembles physical engineering in regarding the *ends* as beyond the province of technology. (All that technology may say about ends is whether or not they are compatible with each other or realizable.) In this it differs from historicism, which regards the ends of human activities as dependent on historical forces and so within its province.

Just as the main task of the physical engineer is to design machines and to remodel and service them, the task of the piecemeal social engineer is to design social institutions, and to reconstruct and run those already in existence. The term "social institution" is used here in a very wide sense, to include bodies of a private as well as of a public character. Thus I shall use it to describe a business, whether it is a small shop or an insurance company, and likewise a school, or an "educational system," or a police force, or a Church, or a law court. The piecemeal technologist or engineer recognizes that *only a minority of social institutions are consciously designed while the vast majority have just "grown," as the undesigned results of human actions.*[8] But however strongly he may be impressed by this important fact, as a technologist or engineer he will look upon them from a "functional" or "instrumental" point of view.[9] He will see them as means to certain ends, or as convertible to the service of certain ends; as machines rather than as organisms. This does not mean, of course, that he will overlook the fundamental differences between institutions and physical instruments. On the contrary, the technologist should study the differences as well as the similarities, expressing his results in the form of hypotheses. And indeed, it is not difficult to formulate hypotheses about institutions in technological form as is shown by the following example: "You cannot construct foolproof institutions, that is to say, institutions whose functioning does not very largely depend upon persons: institutions, at best, can reduce the uncertainty of the personal element, by assisting those who work for the aims for which the institutions are designed, and on whose personal initiative and knowledge success largely depends. (Institutions are like fortresses. They must be well designed *and* properly manned.)"[10]

The characteristic approach of the piecemeal engineer is this. Even though he may perhaps cherish some ideals which concern society "as a whole"—its general welfare, perhaps—he does not believe in the method of redesigning it as a whole. Whatever his ends, he tries to achieve them by small adjustments and readjustments which can be continually improved upon. His ends may be of diverse kinds, for example, the accumulation of wealth or of power by certain individuals, or by certain groups; or the distribution of wealth and power; or the protection of certain "rights" of individuals or groups, etc. Thus public or political social engineering may have the most diverse tendencies, totalitarian as well as liberal. (Examples of far-reaching liberal programs for piecemeal reform have been given by W. Lippmann, under the title "The Agenda of Liberalism."[11]) The piecemeal engineer knows, like Socrates, how little he knows. He knows that we can learn only from our mistakes. Accordingly, he will make his way, step by step, carefully comparing the results expected with the results achieved, and always on the look-out for the unavoidable unwanted consequences of any reform; and he will avoid undertaking reforms of a complexity and scope which make it impossible for him to disentangle causes and effects, and to know what he is really doing.

Such "piecemeal tinkering" does not agree with the political temperament of many "activists." Their program, which too has been described as a program of "social engineering," may be called "holistic" or "Utopian engineering."

Holistic or Utopian social engineering, as opposed to piecemeal social engineering, is never of a "private" but always of a "public" character. It aims at remodelling the "whole of society" in accordance with a definite plan or blueprint; it aims at "seizing the key positions"[12] and at extending "the power of the State ... until the State becomes nearly identical with society,"[13] and it aims, furthermore, at controlling from these "key positions" the historical forces that mold the future of the developing society: either by arresting this development, or else by foreseeing its course and adjusting society to it.

It may be questioned, perhaps, whether the piecemeal and holistic approaches here described are fundamentally different, considering that we have put no limits to the scope of a piecemeal approach. As this approach is understood here, constitutional reform, for example, falls well within its scope; nor shall I exclude the possibility that a series of piecemeal reforms might be inspired by one general tendency, for example, a tendency towards a greater equalization of incomes. In this way, piecemeal methods may lead to changes in what is usually called the "class structure of society." Is there any difference, it may be asked, between these more ambitious kinds of piecemeal engineering and the holistic or Utopian approach? And this question may become even more pertinent if we consider that, when trying to assess the likely consequences of some proposed reform, the piecemeal technologist must do his best to estimate the effects of any measure upon the "whole" of society.

In answering this question, I shall not attempt to draw a precise line of demarcation between the two methods, but I shall try to bring out the very different point of view from which the holist and the piecemeal technologist look upon the task of reforming society. The holists reject the piecemeal approach as being too modest. Their rejection of it, however, does not quite square with their practice; for in practice they always fall back on a somewhat haphazard and clumsy although ambitious and ruthless application of what is essentially a piecemeal method without its cautious and self-critical character. The reason is that, in practice, the holistic method turns out to be impossible; the greater the holistic changes attempted, the greater are their unintended and largely unexpected repercussions, forcing upon the holistic engineer the expedient of piecemeal *improvisation.* In fact, this expedient is more characteristic of centralized or collectivistic planning than of the more modest and careful piecemeal intervention; and it continually leads the Utopian engineer to do things which he did not intend to do; that is to say, it leads to the notorious phenomenon of *unplanned planning.* Thus the difference between Utopian and piecemeal engineering turns out, in practice, to be a difference not so much in scale and scope as in caution and in preparedness for unavoidable surprises. One could also say that, in practice, the two *methods* differ in other ways than in scale and scope—in opposition to what we are led to expect if we compare the two *doctrines* concerning the proper methods of rational social reform. Of these two doctrines, I hold that the one is true, while the other is false and liable to lead to mistakes which are both avoidable and grave. Of the two methods, I hold that one is possible, while the other simply does not exist: it is impossible.

One of the differences between the Utopian or holistic approach and the piecemeal approach may therefore be stated in this way: while the piecemeal engineer can attack his problem with an open mind as to the scope of the reform, the holist cannot do this; for he has decided beforehand that a complete reconstruction is possible and necessary. This fact has far-reaching consequences. It prejudices the Utopianist against certain sociological hypotheses which state limits to institutional control; for example, the one mentioned above in this section, expressing the uncertainty due to the personal element, the "human factor." By a rejection *a priori* of such hypotheses, the Utopian approach violates the principles of scientific method. On the other hand, problems connected with the uncertainty of the human factor must force the Utopianist, whether he likes it or not, to try to control the human factor by institutional means, and to extend his program so as to embrace not only the transformation of society, according to plan, but also the transformation of man.[14] "The political problem, therefore, is to *organize human impulses* in such a way that they will direct their energy to the right strategic points, and steer the total process of development in the desired direction." It seems to escape the well-meaning Utopianist that this program implies an admission of failure, even before he launches it. For it substitutes for his demand that we build a new society, fit for men and women to live in, the demand that we "mold" these men and women to fit into his new society. This, clearly, removes any possibility of testing the success or failure of the new society. For those who do not like living in it only admit thereby that they are not yet fit to live in it; that their "human impulses" need further "organizing." But without the possibility of tests, any claim that a "scientific" method is being employed evaporates. The holistic approach is incompatible with a truly scientific attitude.

FOOTNOTES

1. For a defense of this term, see note 6 below.

2. Cp. F. A. von Hayek, *Economica,* vol. XIII (1933), p. 123. ". . . economics developed mainly as the outcome of the investigation and refutation of successive Utopian proposals . . ."

3. See M. Ginsberg, in *Human Affairs,* ed. by R. B. Cattell and others [London: Macmillan & Co., 1937], p. 180. It must be admitted, however, that the success of mathematical economics shows that one social science at least has gone through its Newtonian revolution.

4. See my *Logic of Scientific Discovery* (1959), section 15. (Negated existential propositions.) The theory may be contrasted with Mill, *Logic,* Book V, ch. V, section 2.

5. See, for example, M. R. Cohen, *Reason and Nature* (New York: Harcourt, Brace & Co., 1931), pp. 356 ff. The examples in the text appear to refute this particular antinaturalistic view.

6. Against the use of the term "social engineering" (in the "piecemeal" sense) it has been objected by Professor Hayek that the typical engineering job involves the centralization of all relevant knowledge in a single head, whereas it is typical of all truly social problems that knowledge has to be used which cannot be so centralized. (See Hayek, *Collectivist Economic Planning* [London: Routledge & Kegan Paul Ltd.], 1935, p. 210.) I admit that this fact is of fundamental importance. It can be formulated by the technological hypothesis: "You cannot centralize within a planning authority the knowledge relevant for such tasks as the satisfaction of personal needs, or the utilization of specialized skill and ability." (A similar hypothesis may be proposed regarding the impossibility of centralizing initiative in connection with similar tasks.) The use of the term "social engineering" may now be defended by pointing out that the engineer must use the technological knowledge embodied in these hypotheses which inform him of the limitations of his own initiative as well as of his own knowledge.

7. Including, if it can be obtained, knowledge concerning the limitations of knowledge, as explained in the previous note.

8. The two views—that social institutions are either "designed" or that they just "grow"—correspond to those of the Social Contract theorists and of their critics, for example, Hume. But Hume does not give up the "functional" or "instrumentalist" view of social institutions, for he says that men could not do without them. This position might be elaborated into a Darwinian explanation of the instrumental character of undesigned institutions (such as language): if they have no useful function, they have no chance of surviving. According to this view, undesigned social institutions may emerge as *unintended consequences of rational action:* just as a road may be formed without any intention to do so by people who find it convenient to use a track already existing (as Descartes observes). It need hardly be stressed, however, that the technological approach is quite independent of all questions of "origin."

9. For the "functional" approach, see B. Malinowski, for example,

"Anthropology as the Basis of Social Science" in *Human Affairs* (ed. Cattell), especially pp. 206 ff. and 239 ff.

10. This example, asserting that the efficiency of institutional "machines" is limited, and that the functioning of institutions depends on their being supplied with proper personnel, may perhaps be compared with the principles of thermodynamics, such as the law of conservation of energy (in the form in which it excludes the possibility of a perpetual motion machine). As such, it may be contrasted with other "scientistic" attempts to work out an analogy between the physical concept of energy and some sociological concepts such as power; see, for example, Bertrand Russell's *Power* (London: George Allen & Unwin, Ltd., 1938), p. 10 f., where this kind of scientistic attempt is made. I do not think that Russell's main point—that the various "forms of power," such as wealth, propagandist power, naked power, may sometimes be "converted" into one another—can be expressed in technological form.

11. W. Lippman, *The Good Society* (Boston: Little, Brown & Co., 1937), ch. XI, pp. 203 ff. See also W. H. Hutt, *Plan for Reconstruction* (London: Routledge & Kegan Paul Ltd., 1943).

12. The expression is often used by K. Mannheim in his *Man and Society in an Age of Reconstruction* (London: Routledge & Kegan Paul Ltd., 1940); see his Index, and, for example, pp. 269, 295, 320, 381. This book is the most elaborate exposition of a holistic and historicist program known to me and is therefore singled out here for criticism.

13. See Mannheim, *ibid.*, 337.

14. "The Problem of Transforming Man" is the heading of a chapter of Mannheim's *Man and Society*. The following quotation is from that chapter, p. 199 f.

PART II
THE URBANIZATION OF MAN

Section D. The Scope
of the Problem

THE ORIGIN AND GROWTH OF URBANIZATION
IN THE WORLD

Kingsley Davis

ABSTRACT

Although there were a few cities as early as 4000 B.C., the cities of the ancient world were generally small and had to be supported by much larger rural populations. "Urbanized societies," in which a high proportion of the population lives in cities, developed only in the nineteenth and twentieth centuries. The process of urbanization has moved rapidly in the entire world since 1800, and the peak is not yet in sight. A diminution of the rate of urbanization in the older industrial countries is being compensated for by an increase in the rate in the underdeveloped areas.

Urban phenomena attract sociological attention primarily for four reasons. First, such phenomena are relatively recent in human history. Compared to most other aspects of society—e.g., language, religion, stratification, or the family—cities appeared only yesterday, and urbanization, meaning that a sizable proportion of the population lives in cities, has developed only in the last few moments of man's existence. Second, urbanism represents a revolutionary change in the whole pattern of social life. Itself a product of basic economic and technological developments, it tends in turn, once it comes into being, to affect every aspect of existence. It exercises its pervasive influence not only within the urban milieu strictly defined but also in the rural hinterland. The third source of sociological interest in cities is the fact that, once established, they tend to be centers of power and influence throughout the whole society, no matter how agricultural and rural it may be. Finally, the process of urbanization is still occurring; many of the problems associated with it are unsolved; and, consequently, its future direction and potentialities are still a matter of uncertainty. This paper examines the first and last points: the origin, growth, and present rate of progress of urbanization in the world. Since good statistics on urban concentration do not exist even today for substantial parts of the world, and hardly exist for any part during most of the time since cities have been in existence, we are forced to rely on whatever credible evidence can be found and so can reach only broad conclusions concerning early periods and only approximations for recent times. Nevertheless, it can be said that our information, both statistical and nonstatistical, is much better today than when Adna Weber wrote his classic treatise on comparative urbanization at the turn of the present century.[1]

THE RISE OF EARLY URBAN CENTERS

Because the archeological evidence is fragmentary, the role of cities in antiquity has often been exaggerated. Archeologists in particular are inclined to call any settlement a "city" which had a few streets and a public building or two. Yet there is surely some point in not mistaking a town for a city. Moreover, what is important is not only the appearance of a few towns or cities but also their place in the total society of which they were a part. Thus, even though in particular regions around the Mediterranean and in southern and western Asia many towns and a few cities arose prior to the Christian Era, there were severe limitations both on the size that such cities could reach and on the proportion of the total population that could live in them.

Speaking generally, one can agree with the dominant view that the diverse technological innovations constituting Neolithic culture were necessary for the existence of settled communities.[2] Yet one should not infer that these innovations, which began some 8,000-10,000 years ago, were sufficient to give rise to towns as distinct from villages. Even though the Neolithic population was more densely settled than the purely hunting or food-gathering peoples, it was nevertheless chiefly engaged in an occupation—agriculture—which requires a large amount of land per person. The Neolithic population density was therefore not a matter of town concentration but rather a matter of tiny villages scattered over the land.

What had to be added to the Neolithic complex to make possible the first towns? Between 6000 and 4000 B.C. certain inventions—such as the ox-drawn plow and wheeled cart, the sailboat, metallurgy, irrigation, and the domestication of new plants—facilitated, when taken together, a more intensive and more productive use of the Neolithic elements themselves. When this enriched technology was utilized in certain unusual regions where climate, soil, water, and topography were most favorable (broad river valleys with alluvial soil not exhausted by successive cropping, with a dry climate that minimized soil leaching, with plenty of sunshine, and with sediment-containing water for irrigation from the river itself), the result was a sufficiently productive economy to make possible the *sine qua non* of urban existence, the concentration in one place of people who do not grow their own food.

But a productive economy, though necessary, was not sufficient: high productivity per acre does not necessarily mean high per capita productivity. Instead of producing a surplus for town dwellers, the cultivators can, theoretically at least, multiply on the land until they end up producing just enough to sustain themselves. The rise of towns and cities therefore required, in addition to highly favorable agricultural conditions, a form of social organization in which certain strata could appropriate for themselves part of the produce grown by the cultivators. Such strata—religious and governing officials, traders, and artisans—could live in towns, because their power over goods did not depend on their presence on the land as such. They could thus realize the advantages of town living, which gave them additional power over the cultivators.

The first cities, doubtless small and hard to distinguish from towns, seem to have appeared in the most favorable places sometime between 6000 and 5000 B.C. From that time on, it can be assumed that some of the inventions which made larger settlements possible were due to towns and cities themselves—viz., writing and accountancy, bronze, the beginnings of science, a solar calendar, bureaucracy. By 3000 B.C., when these innovations were all exercising an influence in Egypt, Mesopotamia, and India, there were in existence what may be called "true" cities. After that there appears to have been, for some 2,000 years, a lull during which the most important innovations, toward the end of the period, were alphabetic writing and the smelting of iron. Curiously, the cities in the regions where city life had originated eventually went into eclipse, and it was not until Greco-Roman times that new principles made possible, in new regions, a marked gain in city existence. The fact that the greatest subsequent cultural developments did not occur primarily in the regions where the first cities arose suggests that cities are not always and everywhere a stimulant of economic and social advance. Childe admits that, if anything, the first cities had a stultifying effect on cultural progress,[3] due perhaps to the unproductive insulation and excessive power of the urban elite. There is no doubt that the religio-magical traditionalism of the early cities was profound.

Why was there so little urbanization in ancient times, and why did it proceed so slowly from that point? The sites of the earliest "cities" themselves show that they were small affairs. The walls of ancient Babylon, for example, embraced an area of very roughly 3.2 square miles,[4] and "Ur, with its canals, harbors, and temples, occupied some 220 acres; the walls of Erech encompass an area of just on two square miles."[5] This suggests that the famous Ur could hardly have boasted more than 5,000 inhabitants and Erech hardly more than 25,000. The mounds of Mohenjo-daro in Sind cover a square mile,[6] and Harappa in the Punjab had a walled area visible in 1853 with a perimeter of two and one-half miles.[7] These were evidently "cities" of 5,000-15,000 inhabitants, yet they were the chief centers for the entire Indus region, an area nearly two-thirds the size of Texas. Less is known about the earliest Egyptian cities, for they were built with mud bricks and have long since disappeared beneath the alluvial soil. Tell el 'Amarna, the temporary capital built much later, about 1400 B.C., perhaps held something like 40,000 people. The wall of Hotep-Sanusert, an earlier capital built about 1900 B.C. on the Fayum, measured 350 by 400 meters[8] and inclosed an area of approximately one-twentieth of a square mile. Thebes, at the height of its splendor as the capital of Egypt about 1600, was described by Greek writers as having a circumference of fourteen miles. By a liberal estimate it may have contained 225,000 inhabitants.

To the questions why even the largest cities prior to 1000 B.C. were small by modern standards, why even the small ones were relatively few, and why the degree of urbanization even in the most advanced regions was very slight, the answer seems as follows: Agriculture was so cumbersome, static, and labor-intensive that it took many cultivators to support one man in the city. The ox-drawn plow, the wooden plowshare, inundation irrigation, stone hoes, sickles, and axes were instruments of production, to be sure, but clumsy ones. Not until iron came into use in Asia Minor about 1300 B.C. could general improvement in agriculture be achieved. The static character of agriculture and of the economy generally was fostered perhaps by the insulation of the religio-political officials from the practical arts and the reduction of the peasant to virtually the status of a beast of burden. The technology of transport was as labor-intensive as that of agriculture. The only means of conveying bulky goods for mass consumption was by boat, and, though sails had been invented, the sailboat was so inefficient that rowing was still necessary. The oxcart, with its solid wheels and rigidly attached axle, the pack animal, and the human burden-bearer were all short-distance means of transport, the only exception being the camel caravan. Long-distance transport was reserved largely for goods which had high value and small bulk—i.e., goods for the elite—which could not maintain a large urban population. The size of the early cities was therefore limited by the amount of food, fibers, and other bulky materials that could be obtained from the immediate hinterland by labor-intensive methods, a severe limitation which the Greek cities of a later period, small as they remained, nevertheless had to escape before they could attain their full size.

There were political limitations as well. The difficulty of communication and transport and the existence of multifarious local tribal cultures made the formation of large national units virtually impossible. The first urban-centered units were city-states, and when so-called "empires" were formed, as in Egypt, in the Sumerian region, and later in Assyria, much local autonomy was left to the subordinated areas, and the constant danger of revolt prevented the extension of the hinterlands of the cities very far or very effectively. It is symptomatic of the weakness of the early cities that they were constantly threatened and frequently conquered not only by neighboring towns but also by non-urban barbarians. Each wave of barbarians tended to rebuild the urban centers and to become agricultural and sedentary, only to be eventually overwhelmed in turn by new invaders. Other limiting factors were the lack of scientific medicine (which made urban living deadly), the fixity of the peasant on the land (which minimized rural-urban migration), the absence of large-scale manufacturing (which would have derived more advantage from urban concentration than did handicraft), the bureaucratic control of the peasantry (which stifled free trade in the hinterland), and the traditionalism and religiosity of all classes (which hampered technological and economic advance).

The limitations explain why we find, when the sites furnish adequate evidence, that the earliest cities were small affairs, usually no more than towns. Whether in the new or in the old world, even the biggest places could scarcely have exceeded 200,000 inhabitants, and the proportion of the total population living in them must have been not more than one or two percent. From fifty to ninety farmers must have been required to support one man in a city.

SUBSEQUENT CITY DEVELOPMENT

If urbanization was to escape its early limitations, it had to do so in a new region, a region more open to innovation and new conceptions. As it turned out, the region that saw a later and greater urban development was farther north, the Greco-Roman world of Europe, flourishing approximately during the period from 600 B.C. to 400 A.D. Iron tools and weapons, alphabetic writing, improved sailboats, cheap coinage, more democratic institutions, systematic colonization—all tended to increase production, stimulate trade, and expand the effective political unit. Towns and cities became more numerous, the degree of urbanization greater. A few cities reached a substantial size. Athens, at its peak in the fifth century B.C., achieved a population of between 120,000 and 180,000. Syracuse and Carthage were perhaps larger.

The full potentialities of the ancient world to support a large city were realized only with the Romans. Through their ability to conquer, organize, and govern an empire, to put the immediate Italian hinterland to fruitful cultivation, to use both force and trade to bring slaves, goods, food, and culture to the imperial capital, they were able to create in Rome (with the possible exception of Constantinople some centuries later) the largest city that was to be known in the world until the rise of London in the nineteenth century. Yet, despite the fact that Rome and Constantinople came to hold populations of several hundred thousand, they were not able to resist conquest by far less urbanized outsiders. The eclipse of cities in Europe was striking. Commerce declined to the barest minimum; each locale became isolated and virtually self-sufficient; the social system congealed into a hereditary system.[9] When finally towns and cities began to revive, they were small, as the following estimates suggest: Florence (1338), 90,000; Venice (1422), 190,000; Antwerp (sixteenth century), 200,000; London (1377), 30,000;[10] Nuremberg (1450), 20,165; Frankfort (1440), 8,719.[11]

Yet it was precisely in western Europe, where cities and urbanization had reached a nadir during the Dark Ages, that the limitations that had characterized the ancient world were finally to be overcome. The cities of Mesopotamia, India, and Egypt, of Persia, Greece, and Rome, had all been tied to an economy that was primarily agricultural, where handicraft played at best a secondary role and where the city was still attempting to supplement its economic weakness with military strength, to command its sustenance rather than to buy it honestly. In western Europe, starting at the zero point, the development of cities not only reached the stage that the ancient world had achieved but kept going after that. It kept going on the basis of improvements in agriculture and transport, the opening of new lands and new trade routes, and, above all, the rise in productive activity, first in highly organized handicraft and eventually in a revolutionary new form of production—the factory run by machinery and fossil fuel. The transformation thus achieved in the nineteenth century was the true urban revolution, for it meant not only the rise of a few scattered towns and cities but the appearance of genuine urbanization, in the sense that a substantial portion of the population lived in towns and cities.

THE WORLD TREND FROM 1800 TO 1950[12]

Urbanization has, in fact, gone ahead much faster and reached proportions far greater during the last century and a half than at any previous time in world history. The tremendous growth in world trade during this period has enabled the urban population to draw its sustenance from an ever wider area. Indeed, it can truly be said that the hinterland of today's cities is the entire world. Contemporary Britain, Holland, and Japan, for example, could not maintain their urban population solely from their own territory. The number of rural inhabitants required to maintain one urban inhabitant is still great—greater than one would imagine from the rural-urban ratio *within* each of the highly urbanized countries. The reason is that much of agriculture around the world is still technologically and economically backward. Yet there can be no doubt that, whether for particular countries or for the entire globe, the ratio of urban dwellers to those who grow their food has risen remarkably. This is shown by the fact that the proportion of people living in cities in 1950 is higher than that found in any particular country prior to modern times and many times higher than that formerly characterizing the earth as a whole.

The rapidity of urbanization in recent times can be seen by looking at the most urbanized country, England. In 1801, although London had already reached nearly the million mark (865,000), England and Wales had less than 10 percent of their population in cities of 100,000 or more. By 1901 no less than 35 percent of the population of England and Wales was living in cities of 100,000 or more, and 58 percent was living in cities of 20,000 or more. By 1951 these two proportions had risen to 38.4 and 69.3 per cent, respectively.

Britain was in the van of urban development. A degree of urbanization equal to that she had attained in 1801 was not achieved by any other country until after 1850. Thereafter the British rate of urbanization began slowly to decline, whereas that of most other countries continued at a high level. By

TABLE 1.
Percentage of World's Population Living in Cities

	Cities of 20,000 or More	Cities of 100,000 or More
1800	2.4	1.7
1850	4.3	2.3
1900	9.2	5.5
1950	20.9	13.1

assembling available data and preparing estimates where data were lacking, we have arrived at figures on urbanization in the world as a whole, beginning with 1800, the earliest date for which anything like a reasonable estimate can be obtained. The percentage of the world's population found living in cities is as shown in Table 1. It can be seen that the proportion has tended to do a bit better than double itself each half-century and that by 1950 the world as a whole was considerably more urbanized than Britain was in 1800. As everyone knows, the earth's total population has grown at an extremely rapid rate since 1800, reaching 2.4 billion by 1950. But the urban population has grown much faster. In 1800 there were about 15.6 million people living in cities of 100,000 or more. By 1950 it was 313.7 million, more than twenty times the earlier figure. Much of this increase has obviously come from rural-urban migration, clearly the most massive migration in modern times.

In 1800 there were apparently less than fifty cities with 100,000 or more inhabitants. This was less than the number in the million class today and less than the number of 100,000-plus cities currently found in many single countries. By 1950 there were close to 900 cities of 100,000 or more people, which is more than the number of towns and cities of 5,000 or more in 1800.

As yet there is no indication of a slackening of the rate of urbanization in the world as a whole. If the present rate should continue, more than a fourth of the earth's people will be living in cities of 100,000 or more in the year 2000, and more than half in the year 2050. For places of 20,000 or more, the proportions at the two dates would be something like 45 percent and 90 percent. Whether such figures prove too low or too high, they nevertheless suggest that the human species is moving rapidly in the direction of an almost exclusively urban existence. We have used the proportion of the population in cities of 20,000 and 100,000 or more as a convenient index of differences and changes in degree of urbanization. Places of less than 20,000 also fit a demographic definition of "urban." When, therefore, more than a third of the population of a country lives in cities of the 100,000 class (38.4 percent in England and Wales in 1951), the country can be described as almost completely urbanized (81 percent being designated as "urban" in the English case in 1951). We thus have today what can be called "urbanized societies," nations in which the great majority of inhabitants live in cities. The prospect is that, as time goes on, a greater and greater proportion of humanity will be members of such societies.

The question may be raised as to how such an extreme degree of world urbanization will prove possible. Who will grow the food and fibers necessary for the enormous urban population? The answer is that agriculture may prove to be an archaic mode of production. Already, one of the great factors giving rise to urbanization is the rather late and as yet very incomplete industrialization of agriculture. As farming becomes increasingly mechanized and rationalized, fewer people are needed on the land. On the average, the more urbanized a country, the lower is its rural density.[13] If, in addition to industrialized agriculture, food and fiber come to be increasingly produced by manufacturing processes using materials that utilize the sun's energy more efficiently than plants do, there is no technological reason why nearly all of mankind could not live in conurbations of large size.

THE REGIONAL PATTERN OF URBANIZATION

The highest levels of urbanization are found today in northwestern Europe and in those new regions where northwest Europeans have settled and extended their industrial civilization. The figures are as shown in Table 2.[14] Oceania is the most urbanized of the world's major regions, because Australia and New Zealand are its principal components. North America is next, if it is defined as including only Canada and the United States. The regions least urbanized are those least affected by northwest European culture, namely, Asia and Africa.

The figures for world regions are less valuable for purposes of analysis than are those for individual countries. The latter show clearly that urbanization has tended to reach its highest point wherever economic productivity has been greatest—that is, where the economy is industrialized and rationalized. This explains why urbanization is so closely associated with northwest Europeans and their culture, since they were mainly responsible for the industrial

TABLE 2.
Percentage of World's Population Living in Cities, By Regions

	In Cities of 20,000 Plus	In Cities of 100,000 Plus
World	21	13
Oceania	47	41
North America (Canada and U.S.A.)	42	29
Europe (except U.S.S.R.)	35	21
U.S.S.R.	31	18
South America	26	18
Middle America and Caribbean	21	12
Asia (except U.S.S.R.)	13	8
Africa	9	5

revolution. Of the fifteen most urbanized countries in the world, all but one, Japan, are European in culture, and all but four derive that culture from the northwest or central part of Europe.

The rate of urbanization in the older industrial countries, however, is slowing down. During the twenty years from 1870 to 1890 Germany's proportion in large cities more than doubled; it nearly doubled again from 1890 to 1910; but from 1910 to 1940 the increase was only 36 percent. In Sweden the gain slowed down noticeably after 1920. In England and Wales the most rapid urbanization occurred between 1811 and 1851. Contrary to popular belief, the fastest rate in the United States occurred between 1861 and 1891. Since, as we noted earlier, there has been no slowing-down of urbanization in the world as a whole, it must be that, as the more established industrial countries have slackened, the less-developed countries have exhibited a faster rate. In fact, such historical evidence as we have for underdeveloped areas seems to show that their rates of urbanization have been rising in recent decades. This has been the case in Egypt, where the rate is higher after 1920 than before; in India, where the fastest urbanization has occurred since 1941; in Mexico, where the speed-up began in 1921; and in Greece, where the fastest period ran from 1900 to 1930. Asia, for example, had only 22 percent of the world's city population in 1900 but 34 per cent of it in 1950, and Africa had 1.5 per cent in 1900 but 3.2 per cent at the later date.

With respect to urbanization, then, the gap between the industrial and the preindustrial nations is beginning to diminish. The less-developed parts of the world will eventually, it seems, begin in their turn to move gradually toward a saturation point. As the degree of urbanization rises, it of course becomes impossible for the rate of gain to continue. The growth in the urban proportion is made possible by the movement of people from rural areas to the cities. As the rural population becomes a progressively smaller percentage of the total, the cities no longer can draw on a noncity population of any size. Yet in no country can it be said that the process of urbanization is yet finished. Although there have been short periods in recent times in England, the United States, and Japan when the city population increased at a slightly slower rate than the rural, these were mere interludes in the ongoing but ever slower progress of urban concentration.

THE TENDENCY TOWARD METROPOLITAN EXPANSION

The continuance of urbanization in the world does not mean the persistence of something that remains the same in detail. A city of a million inhabitants today is not the sort of place that a city of the same number was in 1900 or in 1850. Moreover, with the emergence of giant cities of five to fifteen million, something new has been added. Such cities are creatures of the twentieth century. Their sheer quantitative difference means a qualitative change as well.

One of the most noticeable developments is the ever stronger tendency of cities to expand outward—a development already observed in the nineteenth century. Since 1861, the first date when the comparison can be made, the Outer Ring of Greater London has been growing more rapidly than London itself. French writers prior to 1900 pointed out the dispersive tendency,[15] as did Adna Weber in 1899.[16] There is no doubt, however, that the process of metropolitan dispersion has increased with time. This fact is shown for the United States by comparing the percentage gains in population made by the central cities with those made by their satellite areas in forty-four metropolitan districts for which Thompson could get comparable data going back to 1900. The gains are as shown in Table 3.[17] The difference increases, until in 1930-40 the population outside the central city is growing more than three times as fast as that inside the central city. Furthermore, Thompson has shown that *within the metropolitan area outside the central cities* it was the "rural" parts which gained faster than the urban parts, as the percentage increases per decade shown in Table 4, indicate. Clearly, the metropolitan districts were increasingly dependent on the areas outside the central cities, and especially upon the sparsely settled parts at the periphery of these areas, for their continued growth. Thompson showed that, the greater the distance from the center of the city, the faster the rate of growth.[18]

The same forces which have made extreme urbanization possible have also made metropolitan dispersion possible, and the dispersion itself has contributed to further urbanization by making large conurbations more efficient and more endurable. The outward movement of urban residences, of urban services and commercial establishments, and of light industry—all facilitated by improvements in motor transport and communications—has made it possible for huge agglomerations to keep on growing without the inconveniences of proportionate increases in density. In many ways the metropolis of three million today is an easier place to live and work in than the city of five hundred thousand yesterday. Granted that the economic advantages of urban concentration still continue and still push populations in the direction of urbanization, the effect of metropolitan dispersion is thus to minimize the disadvantages of this continued urban growth.

The new type of metropolitan expansion occurring in the highly industrial countries is not without its repercussions in less-developed lands as well. Most of the rapid urbanization now occurring in Africa and Asia, for example, is affected by direct contact with industrial nations and by a concomitant rise in consumption standards. Although private automobiles may not be available to the urban masses, bicycles and busses generally are. Hence Brazzaville and

TABLE 3.
Percentage Increase in Population in 44 Metropolitan
Districts in the United States, 1900-1940

	Central Cities	Rest of Districts
1900-1910	33.6	38.2
1910-20	23.4	31.3
1920-30	20.5	48.7
1930-40	4.2	13.0

TABLE 4.
Percentage Population Increase Outside Central Cities
in 44 Metropolitan Districts

	Urban Parts	Rural Parts
1900-1910	35.9	43.2
1910-20	30.2	34.5
1920-30	40.6	68.1
1930-40	7.3	28.1

Abidjan, Takoradi and Nairobi, Jamshedpur and New Delhi, Ankara and Colombo, are not evolving in the same manner as did the cities of the eighteenth and nineteenth centuries. Their ecological pattern, their technological base, their economic activity, all reflect the twentieth century, no matter how primitive or backward their hinterlands may be. Thus the fact that their main growth is occurring in the present century is not without significance for the kind of cities they are turning out to be.

FUTURE TRENDS IN WORLD URBANIZATION

Speculation concerning the future of urbanization is as hazardous as that concerning any other aspect of human society. Following the direction of modern trends, however, one may conclude that, with the industrial revolution, for the first time in history urbanization began to reach a stage from which there was no return. The cities of antiquity were vulnerable, and the degree of urbanization reached was so thin in many societies as to be transitory. Today virtually every part of the world is more urbanized than any region was in antiquity. Urbanization is so widespread, so much a part of industrial civilization, and gaining so rapidly, that any return to rurality, even with major catastrophes, appears unlikely. On the contrary, since every city is obsolescent to some degree—more obsolescent the older it is—the massive destruction of many would probably add eventually to the impetus of urban growth.

The fact that the rate of world urbanization has shown no slackening since 1800 suggests that we are far from the end of this process, perhaps not yet at the peak. Although the industrial countries have shown a decline in their rates, these countries, because they embrace only about a fourth of the world's population, have not dampened the world trend. The three-fourths of humanity who live in underdeveloped countries are still in the early stages of an urbanization that promises to be more rapid than that which occurred earlier in the areas of northwest European culture.

How urbanized the world will eventually become is an unanswerable question. As stated earlier, there is no apparent reason why it should not become as urbanized as the most urban countries today—with perhaps 85-90 percent of the population living in cities and towns of 5,000 or more and practicing urban occupations. Our present degree of urbanization in advanced countries is still so new that we have no clear idea of how such complete world urbanization would affect human society; but the chances are that the effects would be profound.

In visualizing the nature and effects of complete urbanization in the future, however, one must guard against assuming that cities will retain their present form. The tendency to form huge metropolitan aggregates which are increasingly decentralized will undoubtedly continue but probably will not go so far as to eliminate the central business district altogether, though it may greatly weaken it. At the periphery, it may well be that the metropolis and the countryside, as the one expands and the other shrinks, will merge together, until the boundaries of one sprawling conurbation will touch those of another, with no intervening pure countryside at all. The world's population doubles itself twice in a century, becoming at the same time highly urbanized, and as new sources of energy are tapped, the possibility of centrifugal metropolitan growth is enormously enhanced. If commuting to work could be done with the speed of sound and cheaply, one would not mind living two hundred miles from work. Almost any technological advance from now on is likely to contribute more to the centrifugal than to the centripetal tendency. It may turn out that urbanization in the sense of emptying the countryside and concentrating huge numbers in little space will reverse itself—not, however, in the direction of returning people to the farm but rather in that of spreading them more evenly over the land for purposes of residence and industrial work. "Rurality" would have disappeared, leaving only a new kind of urban existence.

FOOTNOTES

1. Adna F. Weber, *The Growth of Cities in the Nineteenth Century* (New York: Columbia University Press, 1899).

2. V. Gordon Childe, *Man Makes Himself* (rev. ed.; London: Watts, 1941), chaps. v-vi; *What Happened in History* (London and New York: Penguin Books, 1946 [first printed in 1942]), chaps. iii-iv.

3. *Man Makes Himself,* p. 227.

4. Deduced from data given in Marguerite Rutten, *Babylone* (Paris: Presses Universitaires de France, 1948), p. 34.

5. V. G. Childe, *What Happened in History*, p. 87.

6. Stuart Piggott, *Prehistoric India* (Harmondsworth: Penguin Books, 1950), p. 165.

7. V. G. Childe, *What Happened in History,* p. 118.

8. Pierre Montet, *La Vie quotidienne en Égypte* (Paris: Hachette, 1946), p. 16.

9. Henri Pirenne, *Medieval Cities* (Princeton: Princeton University Press, 1939), pp. 84-85.

10. Pierre Clerget, "Urbanism: A Historic, Geographic, and Economic Study," *Annual Report of the Smithsonian Institution for 1912* (Washington, D.C.: Government Printing Office, 1913), p. 656.

11. Henri Pirenne, *Economic and Social History of Medieval Europe* (London: Routledge & Kegan Paul, 1936), p. 172.

12. The writer acknowledges with pleasure the collaboration of Mrs. Hilda Hertz Golden in the statistical work on which this and succeeding sections are based. Such work has been done as part of a continuing program of comparative urban research in the population division of the Bureau of Applied Social Research, Columbia University.

13. See Kingsley Davis and Hilda Hertz, "Urbanization and the Development of Pre-industrial Areas," *Economic Development and Cultural Change,* III (October, 1954), 6-26. See also the writer's paper, "Population and the Further Spread of Industrial Society," *Proceedings of the American Philosophical Society,* XCV (February, 1951), 10-13.

14. From Kingsley Davis and Hilda Hertz, "The World Distribution of Urbanization," *Bulletin of the International Statistical Institute*, XXXIII, Part IV, 230.

15. Paul Meuriot, *Des agglomérations urbaines dans l'Europe contemporaine* (Paris: Bélin Frères, 1898), pp. 249-78. Literature on the movement of industry and people to the periphery of cities is cited, and a theoretical discussion of the subject given, in René Maunier, *L'Origine et la fonction économique des villes* (Paris: Girard & Brière, 1910), pp. 231-314.

16. *Op. cit.,* pp. 458-75.

17. Warren S. Thompson, *The Growth of Metropolitan Districts in the United States, 1900-1940* (Washington, D.C.: Government Printing Office, 1948), p. 5. The picture is much the same for the rest of the metropolitan districts for decades in which comparability could be established.

18. *Ibid.,* p. 9.

Section E. Some Operational Definitions of Urbanization and the City

THE NATURE AND RISE OF CITIES

Ralph Thomlinson

WHAT IS A CITY?

The initial observation pertinent to defining a city is that neither social scientists nor governing bodies in various countries agree among themselves on a definition. Disagreement often exists even within a nation, as in the United States, where the Bureau of the Census has had to set up a special category for urban places not classified as cities by the relevant state governments—a condition found in several states in the Northeast and a few in the rest of the nation. Although officials and scholars agree in defining a city in contrast to the surrounding countryside, this urban-rural comparison is made by means of many different criteria.[1]

A common approach is to specify a minimum number of inhabitants; above a certain number of residents, a community is called a city. Minimum population has been set by legislative and other bodies at 200 in Denmark; 300 in Iceland; 1,000 in Venezuela and New Zealand; 1,500 in Ireland; 2,000 in France, the Congo, Israel, and Argentina; 2,500 in the United States and Mexico; 5,000 in Belgium, India, Ghana, and the Netherlands; and 10,000 in Greece. In the nineteenth century, the United States favored 8,000. Some countries—Japan, for instance—define two or more "urban" categories with different minimum sizes. Therefore no one can fix an absolute figure that will meet with international unanimity. This definition possesses the further weakness that there are many areas larger than 2,500 (or 10,000) that do not seem urban in character, and smaller communities that we do regard as urban.

A second type of quantitative definition uses density as its criterion. Mark Jefferson said that a density of 10,000 people per square mile is indicative of a city. Other scholars have suggested smaller figures. Although not agreeing with Jefferson in other respects, Hope Tisdale Eldridge wrote that "urbanization is a process of population concentration." The same criticism applies here as to the first kind of definition: It does not always agree with our conception of what a city is.

Historical criteria are used in the third method: A community is a city insofar as its role in the past has conferred this title upon it. We thus refer to earlier times to decide what is a city. But it is just in this way that people accept a number of places as cities. The historical criterion takes us back to a time when city and country were much more distinct than they are today, thus ensuring a less arbitrary definition. Unfortunately, use of this criterion entails the risk of including many now-defunct cities. And how are we to treat newly founded communities?

A fourth kind of definition is based on administrative law: A city has privileges and obligations not possessed by unincorporated rural areas. In this case, a government decision is necessary to place an area on the list of cities. In the United States, state legislatures grant municipal charters, officially declaring that a place is a city, town, borough, or whatever else they choose to call it; this charter provides both rights and duties. In some European countries during the Middle Ages only a city had the right to open a market. To a lawyer a city may be a municipal corporation endowed with a legal existence that enables it to own property, to sue and be sued, and so forth. Juridical factors are central in this definition: A city possesses a charter guaranteeing it certain rights and privileges and imposing upon it certain obligations. But these legal distinctions are breaking down as suburbanization surrounds corporation limits with a juridical haze.

Fifth, the exterior aspect of a community is relevant, for it is by physical impressions that we recognize and classify places. An urban area is built up; a rural area is not. A city is a man-made landscape of buildings, streets, water mains, and other contrived appurtenances. Richard L. Meier defined a city as a place where "artifacts have accumulated to such an extent that they have extinguished most features of the natural environment." But some built-up places are essentially rural, the tall structures being grain elevators and the elongated ones being storage sheds for various agricultural products. Furthermore, say sociologists, cities should be defined in terms of people, not things. And some critics insist that the appearance is only the manifestation of a more profound reality—the way of life—and that phenomena should not be defined by symptoms.

The type of life then supplies a sixth criterion: modes of living and feeling. Some styles and attitudes are appropriate to the city and others to the country. When people contrast the city and the countryside, this difference is usually what they mean. A city is more than just the physical accompaniments of high density—busy streets, skyscrapers, and crowded subways; it is also a style of living and a culturally different manner of regarding life. A stereotypical urbanite talks fast, keeps close track of time, lives in an apartment, and does not know his neighbors. In short, as Louis Wirth said, urbanism is a special way of life. But this way of life is not susceptible to precise definition, which makes it difficult to use as a principle of classification.

A seventh point of view is that the dominant factor determining urban or rural way of life is the occupations of the inhabitants. Stated simply, the urban habitat is made up of workers who do not cultivate the soil. The 1938 Congress of the International Statistical Institute recommended adoption of a definition based on the percentage of the population engaged in agriculture; in a city the most frequent means of subsistence are service, commercial, and industrial occupations. Also, the division of labor is more varied in cities. But by this definition some large towns in Hungary and Bulgaria would have to be labeled "rural," yet a tiny cluster surrounding a railroad coaling stop in Kansas would be called "urban." This criterion also leads to difficulties and ambiguities in the case of mining areas: Extractive activities are not farming, but they are not urban either.

The eighth criterion is insistence on commercial character as defining a city, emphasizing the distributive function of the marketplace. The market element is paramount in Friedrich Ratzel's definition: A city is "a permanent collection of men and habitations which covers a large area and which is found at the crossing of large commercial routes." Arthur Smailes regarded a city as a place having banks and shops. This criterion appears too narrow, for business plays only an accessory part in the activities of many cities.

A ninth approach uses the industrial occupations as the sole criterion: A city is where factories are. But a few factories, or one large one, in a rural area do not constitute an urban enclave worthy of the designation "city." Both this definition and the objections to it are similar to those of the seventh and eighth approaches.

These last three criteria imply a tenth standard: the dependent or even parasitic nature of cities. Werner Sombart spoke of cities as "aggregations of men dependent on products of outside agricultural labor for their subsistence." The daily need to bring in food and other necessities places the city in the position of relying upon rural areas for its existence. Traditionalists often proclaim rural areas as the source of life and cities as parasitic, hypercivilized, and degenerating. In return, these decadent cities usually supply the luxuries of life to rural regions in exchange for foodstuffs, or they may simply exploit the surrounding countryside through military dominance. This view of urban-rural relations often brings forth such virulent criticism as Henri Bordier's "cities represent points of ossification of the social organism." In any case, definition by dependence is not fully satisfactory because, in modern countries, rural and urban areas are interdependent in their industrial, agricultural, military, educational, medical, and artistic needs.

Related to dependence is an eleventh basis for definition: A city is a central place for transportation. Anyone who has traveled the French railroad system knows that nearly all routes lead to Paris and that one often cannot go directly from A to B even though they are only 50 miles apart; rather, he must ride 150 miles to Paris, change trains, and ride 175 miles back out to reach city B. Similar conditions prevail in the hinterlands of New York City: To go from one place in metropolitan New Jersey to another late at night, it is sometimes advisable to cross the Hudson River into New York City, ride the subway, and then recross the Hudson to New Jersey. Rural areas are places that buses pass through; where they stop is usually a town. And if a community is too small to merit a bus station, it hardly deserves to be designated a city. Charles H. Cooley theorized that stops or breaks in transportation provide nuclei for the founding of cities. But, without denying the indispensability of transport to modern city functioning, it is not sufficiently central to urban existence to adopt as the primary defining criterion.

Commuting is becoming common enough to be regarded as the twelfth defining attribute of cities. Most city dwellers commute—but so do many farmers in various parts of the world. Jean Brunhes and Pierre Desfontaines used commuting to distinguish a city from a village: "A city has the majority of its inhabitants employed most of the time inside the agglomeration; a village has the majority of its inhabitants employed most of the time outside the community." Then is a suburb a city or a village—and is a village urban or rural? But this commuting phenomenon may be more closely related to the cost and rapidity of transportation than to the extent of urbanization and therefore is not a fully satisfactory test for urbanism.

A thirteenth criterion is government or religious functions: Cities are essentially church or political centers. In a few countries these two criteria are appropriate now, and in a large number of nations they once were excellent defining criteria. Henri Pirenne described medieval cities as "distinguished by gates, churches, and population density." But this kind of definition is no longer suitable, for religious and government activity are of slight importance in many modern urban communities.

A fourteenth approach is that a city has a central focal point, a place where "things happen." This nucleus, known in Chicago as The Loop and in many cities as Main Street or Downtown, is a markedly congested, massively built-up area in which no one lives but to which many persons come for work, shopping, and entertainment; consequently, the highest property values in the city are found there. Although a central business district is characteristic of many cities, quite a number of old ones have several such districts, and a few very new cities have remarkably little central concentration. The degree of downtown development appears to be largely a result of the type of transportation that prevailed during the formative years of a city's growth: cities that came of age in the automotive era often have highly dispersed businesses, shops, and entertainment facilities.

The fifteenth and final criterion is diversity: Cities are undoubtedly more complex and varied than are rural areas. The variety is evident in the appearances and functions of both buildings and people. Hans Dorries said: "A city is known by its more or less orderly form, closed, grouped around a nucleus which is easy to find; and by its very varied appearance, composed of the most diverse elements." This approach, though containing considerable truth, is not conducive to precise demarcation between urban and rural modes.

The most likely way out of this maze involves a sixteenth possibility: using several of the already-listed criteria. A modern city is

1. A large agglomeration of people living in a contiguously built-up area,

2. Who function to produce nonagricultural goods and services, and more particularly, to distribute all manner of goods and services,

3. And who, as a result of carrying on such functions develop a way of life characterized by anonymity, impersonal and segmentalized contacts with other people, and secondary controls.[2]
Yet even this compromise approach is not without blemish, for it more closely resembles a definition of a complex metropolitan area than of a single city.

Although scholars have failed to agree upon a universal definition of a city, largely because cities themselves differ in different culture areas of the world, their points of disagreement have shed considerable light on the urban dweller and his habitat. Furthermore, a formal definition is probably less valuable, albeit far more succinct, than is this sixteen-part description of the fundamental properties of cities and qualities of city living. A precise definition of the word "city" that would be legitimate and useful in all regions of the world is not possible, but we do know approximately what cities are like.

In sum, cities are built up of large quantities and varieties of edifices offering physical contrasts and requiring transportation facilities to relieve congestion and permit flow of materials and people. Urban centers are characterized by rapidity and fluidity of life, specialization of activities, complex social organization, and intensification of opportunity. Compared with inhabitants of rural areas, city residents are more heterogeneous, often anonymous, and given to impersonal and secondary relationships as a result of their far more numerous recurrent personal contacts.

FOOTNOTES

1. Georges Chabot, "Introduction," *Les villes* (Paris: Colin, 1948).

2. Abram J. Jaffe, "Summary of the Proceedings of the University Seminar on Population," mimeographed (New York: Columbia University, 1951), p. 15.

Section F. The Emergence of
Early Urban Forms

THE URBAN REVOLUTION

V. Gordon Childe

The concept of "city" is notoriously hard to define. The aim of the present essay is to present the city historically—or rather prehistorically—as the resultant and symbol of a "revolution" that initiated a new economic stage in the evolution of society. The word "revolution" must not of course be taken as denoting a sudden violent catastrophe; it is here used for the culmination of a progressive change in the economic structure and social organization of communities that caused, or was accompanied by, a dramatic increase in the population affected—an increase that would appear as an obvious bend in the population graph were vital statistics available. Just such a bend is observable at the time of the Industrial Revolution in England. Though not demonstrable statistically, comparable changes of direction must have occurred at two earlier points in the demographic history of Britain and other regions. Though perhaps less sharp and less durable, these too should indicate equally revolutionary changes in economy. They may then be regarded likewise as marking transitions between stages in economic and social development.

Sociologists and ethnographers last century classified existing preindustrial societies in a hierarchy of three evolutionary stages, denominated respectively "savagery," "barbarism" and "civilization." If they be defined by suitably selected criteria, the logical hierarchy of stages can be transformed into a temporal sequence of ages, proved archeologically to follow one another in the same order wherever they occur. Savagery and barbarism are conveniently recognized and appropriately defined by the methods adopted for procuring

Reprinted from *The Town Planning Review,* Vol. XXI, No. 1 (April 1950). Reprinted by permission of Liverpool University Press.

food. Savages live exclusively on wild food obtained by collecting, hunting, or fishing. Barbarians on the contrary at least supplement these natural resources by cultivating edible plants and—in the Old World north of the Tropics—also by breeding animals for food.

Throughout the Pleistocene Period—the Paleolithic Age of archeologists —all known human societies were savage in the foregoing sense, and a few savage tribes have survived in out of the way parts to the present day. In the archeological record barbarism began less than 10,000 years ago with the Neolithic Age of archeologists. It thus represents a later, as well as a higher stage, than savagery. Civilization cannot be defined in quite such simple terms. Etymologically the word is connected with "city," and sure enough life in cities begins with this stage. But "city" is itself ambiguous so archeologists like to use "writing" as a criterion of civilization; it should be easily recognizable and proves to be a reliable index to more profound characters. Note, however, that, because a people is said to be civilized or literate, it does not follow that all its members can read and write, nor that they all lived in cities. Now there is no recorded instance of a community of savages civilizing themselves, adopting urban life, or inventing a script. Wherever cities have been built, villages of preliterate farmers existed previously (save perhaps where an already civilized people have colonized uninhabited tracts). So civilization, wherever and whenever it arose, succeeded barbarism.

We have seen that a revolution as here defined should be reflected in the population statistics. In the case of the Urban Revolution the increase was mainly accounted for by the multiplication of the numbers of persons living together, i.e., in a single built-up area. The first cities represented settlement units of hitherto unprecedented size. Of course it was not just their size that constituted their distinctive character. We shall find that by modern standards they appeared ridiculously small and we might meet agglomerations of population today to which the name city would have to be refused. Yet a certain size of settlement and density of population is an essential feature of civilization.

Now the density of population is determined by the food supply which in turn is limited by natural resources, the techniques for their exploitation, and the means of transport and food-preservation available. The last factors have proved to be variables in the course of human history, and the technique of obtaining food has already been used to distinguish the consecutive stages termed savagery and barbarism. Under the gathering economy of savagery population was always exceedingly sparse. In aboriginal America the carrying capacity of normal unimproved land seems to have been from .05 to .10 per square mile. Only under exceptionally favorable conditions did the fishing tribes of the Northwest Pacific coast attain densities of over one human to the square mile. As far as we can guess from the extant remains, population densities in Paleolithic and pre-Neolithic Europe were less than the normal American. Moreover such hunters and collectors usually live in small roving bands. At best several bands may come together for quite brief periods on ceremonial occasions such as the Australian corroborrees. Only in exceptionally favored regions can fishing tribes establish anything like villages. Some settlements on the Pacific coasts comprised thirty or so substantial and durable houses, accommodating groups of several hundred persons. But even these villages were only occupied during the winter; for the rest of the year their inhabitants dispersed in smaller groups. Nothing comparable has been found in preneolithic times in the Old World.

The Neolithic Revolution certainly allowed an expansion of population and enormously increased the carrying capacity of suitable land. On the Pacific Islands Neolithic societies today attain a density of thirty or more persons to the square mile. In pre-Columbian North America, however, where the land is not obviously restricted by surrounding seas, the maximum density recorded is just under two to the square mile.

Neolithic farmers could of course, and certainly did, live together in permanent villages, though, owing to the extravagant rural economy generally practised, unless the crops were watered by irrigation, the villages had to be shifted at least every twenty years. But on the whole the growth of population was not reflected so much in the enlargement of the settlement unit as in a multiplication of settlements. In ethnography, Neolithic villages can boast only a few hundred inhabitants (a couple of "pueblos" in New Mexico house over a thousand, but perhaps they cannot be regarded as Neolithic). In prehistoric Europe the largest Neolithic village yet known, Barkaer in Jutland, comprised 52 small, one-roomed dwellings, but 16 to 30 houses was a more normal figure; so the average local group in Neolithic times would average 200 to 400 members.

These low figures are of course the result of technical limitations. In the absence of wheeled vehicles and roads for the transport of bulky crops men had to live within easy walking distance of their cultivations. At the same time the normal rural economy of the Neolithic Age, what is now termed slash-and-burn or jhumming, condemns much more than half the arable land to lie fallow so that the large areas were required. As soon as the population of a settlement rose above the numbers that could be supported from the accessible land, the excess had to hive off and found a new settlement.

The Neolithic Revolution had other consequences beside increasing the population, and their exploitation might in the end help to provide for the surplus increase. The new economy allowed, and indeed required, the farmer to produce every year more food than was needed to keep him and his family alive. In other words it made possible the regular production of a social surplus. Owing to the low efficiency of Neolithic technique, the surplus produced was insignificant at first, but it could be increased till it demanded a reorganization of society.

Now in any Stone Age society, Paleolithic or Neolithic, savage or barbarian, everybody can at least in theory make at home the few indispensable tools, the modest cloths and the simple ornaments everyone requires. But every member of the local community, not disqualified by age, must contribute actively to the communal food supply by personally collecting, hunting, fishing, gardening, or herding. As long as this holds good, there can be no full-time specialists, no persons nor class of persons who depend for their livelihood on food produced by others and secured in exchange for material or immaterial goods or services.

We find indeed today among Stone Age barbarians and even savages expert craftsmen (for instance flint-knappers among the Ona of Tierra del Fuego), men who claim to be experts in magic, and even chiefs. In Paleolithic Europe too there is some evidence for magicians and indications of chieftainship in pre-Neolithic times. But on closer observation we discover that today these experts are not full-time specialists. The Ona flintworker must spend most of his time hunting; he only adds to his diet and his prestige by making arrowheads for clients who reward him with presents. Similarly a pre-Columbian chief, though entitled to customary gifts and services from his followers, must still personally lead hunting and fishing expeditions and indeed could only maintain his authority by his industry and prowess in these pursuits. The same holds good of barbarian societies that are still in the Neolithic stage, like the Polynesians where industry in gardening takes the place of prowess in hunting. The reason is that there simply will not be enough food to go round unless every member of the group contributes to the supply. The social surplus is not big enough to feed idle mouths.

Social division of labor, save those rudiments imposed by age and sex, is thus impossible. On the contrary community of employment, the common absorbtion in obtaining food by similar devices guarantees a certain solidarity to the group. For cooperation is essential to secure food and shelter and for defence against foes, human and subhuman. This identity of economic interests and pursuits is echoed and magnified by identity of language, custom and belief; rigid conformity is enforced as effectively as industry in the common quest for food. But conformity and industrious cooperation need no State organization to maintain them. The local group usually consists either of a single clan (persons who believe themselves descended from a common ancestor or who have earned a mystical claim to such descent by ceremonial adoption) or a group of clans related by habitual intermarriage. And the sentiment of kinship is reinforced or supplemented by common rites focused on some ancestral shrine or sacred place. Archeology can provide no evidence for kinship organization, but shrines occupied the central place in preliterate villages in Mesopotamia, and the long barrow, a collective tomb that overlooks the presumed site of most Neolithic villages in Britain, may well have been also the ancestral shrine on which converged the emotions and ceremonial activities of the villagers below. However, the solidarity thus idealized and concretely symbolized is really based on the same principles as that of a pack of wolves or a herd of sheep; Durkheim has called it "mechanical."

Now among some advanced barbarians (for instance tattooers or woodcarvers among the Maori) still technologically neolithic we find expert craftsmen tending towards the status of full-time professionals, but only at the cost of breaking away from the local community. If no single village can produce a surplus large enough to feed a full-time specialist all the year round, each should produce enough to keep him a week or so. By going round from village to village an expert might thus live entirely from his craft. Such itinerants will lose their membership of the sedentary kinship group. They may in the end form an analogous organization of their own—a craft clan, which, if it remain hereditary, may become a caste, or, if it recruit its members mainly by adoption (apprenticeship through Antiquity and the Middle Age was just temporary adoption), may turn into a guild. But such specialists, by emancipation from kinship ties, have also forfeited the protection of the kinship organization which alone under barbarism, guaranteed to its members security of person and property. Society must be reorganized to accommodate and protect them.

In prehistory specialization of labor presumably began with similar itinerant experts. Archeological proof is hardly to be expected, but in ethnography metal-workers are nearly always full-time specialists. And in Europe at the beginning of the Bronze Age metal seems to have been worked and purveyed by perambulating smiths who seem to have functioned like tinkers and other itinerants of much more recent times. Though there is no such positive evidence, the same probably happened in Asia at the beginning of metallurgy. There must of course have been in addition other specialist craftsmen whom, as the Polynesian example warns us, archeologists could not recognize because they worked in perishable materials. One result of the Urban Revolution will be to rescue such specialists from nomadism and to guarantee them security in a new social organization.

About 5,000 years ago irrigation cultivation (combined with stock-breeding sand fishing) in the valleys of the Nile, the Tigris-Euphrates and the Indus had begun to yield a social surplus, large enough to support a number of resident specialists who were themselves released from food-production. Water-transport, supplemented in Mesopotamia and the Indus valley by wheeled vehicles and even in Egypt by pack animals, made it easy to gather food stuffs at a few centers. At the same time dependence on river water for the irrigation of the crops restricted the cultivable areas while the necessity of canalizing the waters and protecting habitations against annual floods encouraged the aggregation of population. Thus arose the first cities—units of settlement ten times as great as any known Neolithic village. It can be argued that all cities in the old world are offshoots of those of Egypt, Mesopotamia, and the Indus basin. So the latter need not be taken into account if a minimum definition of civilization is to be inferred from a comparison of its independent manifestations.

But some three millennia later cities arose in Central America, and it is impossible to prove that the Mayas owed anything directly to the urban civilizations of the Old World. Their achievements must therefore be taken into account in our comparison, and their inclusion seriously complicates the task of defining the essential preconditions for the Urban Revolution. In the Old World the rural economy which yielded the surplus was based on the cultivation of cereals combined with stock-breeding. But this economy had been made more efficient as a result of the adoption of irrigation (allowing cultivation without prolonged fallow periods) and of important inventions and discoveries—metallurgy, the plough, the sailing boat and the wheel. None of these devices was known to the Mayas; they bred no animals for milk or meat; though they cultivated the cereal maize, they used the same sort of slash-and-burn method as neolithic farmers in prehistoric Europe or in the Pacific Islands today. Hence the minimum definition of a city, the greatest factor common to the Old World and the New will be substantially reduced and impoverished by the inclusion of the Maya. Nevertheless ten rather abstract criteria, all deducible from archeological data, serve to distinguish even the earliest cities from any older or contemporary village.

1. In point of size the first cities must have been more extensive and more densely populated than any previous settlements, although considerably smaller than many villages today. It is indeed only in Mesopotamia and India that the first urban populations can be estimated with any confidence or precision. There excavation has been sufficiently extensive and intensive to reveal both the total area and the density of building in sample quarters and in both respects has disclosed significant agreement with the less industrialized Oriental cities today. The population of Sumerian cities, thus calculated, ranged between 7,000 and 20,000; Harappa and Mohenjo-daro in the Indus valley must have approximated to the higher figure. We can only infer that Egyptian and Maya cities were of comparable magnitude from the scale of public works, presumably executed by urban populations.

2. In composition and function the urban population already differed from that of any village. Very likely indeed most citizens were still also peasants, harvesting the lands and waters adjacent to the city. But all cities must have accommodated in addition classes who did not themselves procure their own food by agriculture, stock-breeding, fishing or collecting—full-time specialist craftsmen, transport workers, merchants, officials and priests. All these were of course supported by the surplus produced by the peasants living in the city and in dependent villages, but they did not secure their share directly by exchanging their products or services for grains or fish with individual peasants.

3. Each primary producer paid over the tiny surplus he could wring from the soil with his still very limited technical equipment as tithe or tax to an imaginary deity or a divine king who thus concentrated the surplus. Without this concentration, owing to the low productivity of the rural economy, no effective capital would have been available.

4. Truly monumental public buildings not only distinguish each known city from any village but also symbolize the concentration of the social surplus. Every Sumerian city was from the first dominated by one or more stately temples, centrally situated on a brick platform raised above the surrounding dwellings and usually connected with an artificial mountain, the staged tower or ziggurat. But attached to the temples were workshops and magazines, and an important appurtenance of each principal temple was a great granary. Harappa, in the Indus basin, was dominated by an artificial citadel, girt with a massive rampart of kiln-baked bricks, containing presumably a palace and immediately overlooking an enormous granary and the

barracks of artisans. No early temples or palaces have been excavated in Egypt, but the whole Nile valley was dominated by the gigantic tombs of the divine pharaohs while royal granaries are attested from the literary record. Finally the Maya cities are known almost exclusively from the temples and pyramids of sculptured stone round which they grew up.

Hence in Sumer the social surplus was first effectively concentrated in the hands of a god and stored in his granary. That was probably true in Central America while in Egypt the pharaoh (king) was himself a god. But of course the imaginary deities were served by quite real priests who, besides celebrating elaborate and often sanguinary rites in their honor, administered their divine masters' earthly estates. In Sumer indeed the god very soon, if not even before the revolution, shared his wealth and power with a mortal vice-regent, the "City-King," who acted as civil ruler and leader in war. The divine pharaoh was naturally assisted by a whole hierarchy of officials.

5. All those not engaged in food-production were of course supported in the first instance by the surplus accumulated in temple or royal granaries and were thus dependent on temple or court. But naturally priests, civil and military leaders, and officials absorbed a major share of the concentrated surplus and thus formed a "ruling class." Unlike a Paleolithic magician or a Neolithic chief, they were, as an Egyptian scribe actually put it, "exempt from all manual tasks." On the other hand, the lower classes were not only guaranteed peace and security, but were relieved from intellectual tasks which many find more irksome than any physical labor. Besides reassuring the masses that the sun was going to rise next day and the river would flood again next year (people who have not 5,000 years of recorded experience of natural uniformities behind them are really worried about such matters!), the ruling classes did confer substantial benefits upon their subjects in the way of planning and organization.

6. They were in fact compelled to invent systems of recording and exact, but practically useful, sciences. The mere administration of the vast revenues of a Sumerian temple or an Egyptian pharaoh by a perpetual corporation of priests or officials obliged its members to devise conventional methods of recording that should be intelligible to all their colleagues and successors, that is, to invent systems of writing and numeral notation. Writing is thus a significant, as well as a convenient, mark of civilization. But while writing is a trait common to Egypt, Mesopotamia, the Indus valley and Central America, the characters themselves were different in each region and so were the normal writing materials—papyrus in Egypt, clay in Mesopotamia. The engraved seals or stele that provide the sole extant evidence for early Indus and Maya writing no more represent the normal vehicles for the scripts than do the comparable documents from Egypt and Sumer.

7. The invention of writing—or shall we say the inventions of scripts— enabled the leisured clerks to proceed to the elaboration of exact and predictive sciences—arithmetic, geometry and astronomy. Obviously beneficial and explicitly attested by the Egyptian and Maya documents was the correct determination of the tropic year and the creation of a calendar. For it enabled

the rulers to regulate successfully the cycle of agricultural operations. But once more the Egyptian, Maya and Babylonian calendars were as different as any systems based on a single natural unit could be. Calendrical and mathematical sciences are common features of the earliest civilizations and they too are corollaries of the archeologists' criterion, writing.

8. Other specialists, supported by the concentrated social surplus, gave a new direction to artistic expression. Savages even in Paleolithic times had tried, sometimes with astonishing success, to depict animals and even men as they saw them—concretely and naturalistically. Neolithic peasants never did that; they hardly ever tried to represent natural objects, but preferred to symbolize them by abstract geometrical patterns which at most may suggest by a few traits a fantastical man or beast or plant. But Egyptian, Sumerian, Indus and Maya artist-craftsmen—full-time sculptors, painters, or seal-engravers—began once more to carve, model or draw likenesses of persons or things, but no longer with the naive naturalism of the hunter, but according to conceptualized and sophisticated styles which differ in each of the four urban centers.

9. A further part of the concentrated social surplus was used to pay for the importation of raw materials, needed for industry or cult and not available locally. Regular "foreign" trade over quite long distances was a feature of all early civilizations and, though common enough among barbarians later, is not certainly attested in the Old World before 3,000 B.C. nor in the New before the Maya "empire." Thereafter regular trade extended from Egypt at least as far as Byblos on the Syrian coast while Mesopotamia was related by commerce with the Indus valley. While the objects of international trade were at first mainly "luxuries," they already included industrial materials, in the Old World notably metal the place of which in the New was perhaps taken by obsidian. To this extent the first cities were dependent for vital materials on long distance trade as no Neolithic village ever was.

10. So in the city, specialist craftsmen were both provided with raw materials needed for the employment of their skill and also guaranteed security in a State organization based now on residence rather than kinship. Itinerancy was no longer obligatory. The city was a community to which a craftsman could belong politically as well as economically.

Yet in return for security they became dependent on temple or court and were relegated to the lower classes. The peasant masses gained even less material advantages; in Egypt for instance metal did not replace the old stone and wood tools for agricultural work. Yet, however imperfectly, even the earliest urban communities must have been held together by a sort of solidarity missing from any Neolithic village. Peasants, craftsmen, priests and rulers form a community, not only by reason of identity of language and belief, but also because each performs mutually complementary functions, needed for the well-being (as redefined under civilization) of the whole. In fact the earliest cities illustrate a first approximation to an organic solidarity based upon a functional complementarity and interdependence between all its members such as subsist between the constituent cells of an organism. Of course this was only a very distant approximation. However necessary the concentration of the surplus really was with the existing forces of production, there seemed a glaring conflict on economic interests between the tiny ruling class, who annexed the bulk of the social surplus, and the vast majority who were left with a bare subsistance and effectively excluded from the spiritual benefits of civilization. So solidarity had still to be maintained by the ideological devices appropriate to the mechanical solidarity of barbarism as expressed in the preeminence of the temple or the sepulchral shrine, and now supplemented by the force of the new State organization. There could be no room for sceptics or sectaries in the oldest cities.

These ten traits exhaust the factors common to the oldest cities that archeology, at best helped out with fragmentary and often ambiguous written sources, can detect. No specific elements of town planning for example can be proved characteristic of all such cities; for on the one hand the Egyptian and Maya cities have not yet been excavated; on the other Neolithic villages were often walled, an elaborate system of sewers drained the Orcadian hamlet of Skara Brae; two-storeyed houses were built in pre-Columbian pueblos, and so on.

The common factors are quite abstract. Concretely Egyptian, Sumerian, Indus, and Maya civilizations were as different as the plans of their temples, the signs of their scripts and their artistic conventions. In view of this divergence and because there is so far no evidence for a temporal priority of one Old World center (for instance, Egypt) over the rest nor yet for contact between Central America and any other urban center, the four revolutions just considered may be regarded as mutually independent. On the contrary, all later civilizations in the Old World may in a sense be regarded as lineal descendants of those of Egypt, Mesopotamia, or the Indus.

But this was not a case of like producing like. The maritime civilizations of Bronze Age Crete or classical Greece for example, to say nothing of our own, differ more from their reputed ancestors than these did among themselves. But the urban revolutions that gave them birth did not start from scratch. They could and probably did draw upon the capital accumulated in the three allegedly primary centers. That is most obvious in the case of cultural capital. Even today we use the Egyptians' calendar and the Sumerians' divisions of the day and the hour. Our European ancestors did not have to invent for themselves these divisions of time nor repeat the observations on which they are based; they took over—and very slightly improved systems elaborated 5,000 years ago! But the same is in a sense true of material capital as well. The Egyptians, the Sumerians, and the Indus people had accumulated vast reserves of surplus food. At the same time they had to import from abroad necessary raw materials like metals and building timber as well as "luxuries." Communities controlling these natural resources could in exchange claim a slice of the urban surplus. They could use it as capital to support full-time specialists—craftsmen or rulers—until the latters' achievement in technique and organization had so enriched barbarian economies that they too could produce a substantial surplus in their turn.

UR AS AN URBAN SYSTEM *CA.* 2800 B.C.

Henry T. Wright

It is not yet possible to describe any early Mesopotamian settlement enclave in detail or to propose and test hypotheses about any urban system as a whole. In this section I will briefly describe the settlement pattern of this enclave as a whole, and present what is known about the organization of activities in the town of Ur. This will provide background for our detailed consideration of the organization of the rural economy.

The enclave of settlement around Ur occupies the northeastern edge of the area surveyed in 1966. The formerly inhabited land to the south around Eridu was largely abandoned alluvial desert, with old canals and depressions filling with water only in spring and with only a few small settlements surviving. Fifteen kilometers to the south were the great dunes and beyond these the stony desert. The southern margin and the upstream end of the enclave are well studied. If the downstream end is considered to be the effective walking limit from Ur, then the enclave was a small one of 9,000 hectares.

Five types of features occur within this enclave: the first is the channel of an ancient water course. At least one of the many channels visible on the air photographs dates to the Early Dynastic period. This comes from the northeast and bifurcated at the town of Sakheri. These two marks then disappear under the silt cover left by later cultivation. The main channel probably curved around the southwest side of Ur, since the site was more built up on this side, and flowed northeast into areas not yet investigated. Evidence of a small canal not definitely visible on the air photos was excavated at the village of Sakheri Sughir. The possible canal ran from west to east. Prior to or

From *The Administration of Rural Production in an Early Mesopotamian Town* in *Anthropological Papers*(38) ©1969, University of Michigan Press. Reprinted by the courtesy of Professor Wright and the Director of the Museum of Anthropology.

during the early stages of the village's occupation, a channel was dug south of the site, but it was allowed to fill with sand and refuse. During the later stages of the site's history, the mound dropped off abruptly to the north. In addition, this slope of the mound received great lenses of clean silt, in volumes out of all proportion to the quantity of mud-brick construction in the area. It seems probable, though not proven, that a small canal ran along this side of the mound. By analogy with the bifurcation at Sakheri and the small canal at Sakheri Sughir, I have shown similar canals branching off the main channel of the Euphrates on the conjectural map of the enclave. The actual pattern was doubtless more complex.

The second type of feature is the town site. The major town, Ur, may have covered about twenty hectares. This is based on the assumption that the southeast end of the mound was not settled until late Early Dynastic times, when much secular housing on the northwest end was replaced by public buildings. There is no direct evidence of this. The site was definitely reveted on the southeast, and may have been completely surrounded by a low wall. Urban land use as revealed by Woolley's excavations, will be discussed below. The minor town, Sakheri, was up the main channel to the northwest of Ur. Surface traces of the period cover eight hectares. Air photos reveal a complete town wall, but its date is unknown. Concentrations of very large jar sherds, kiln wasters, and baked plano-convex bricks suggest storage areas, craft areas, and public buildings, respectively. Little more can be said without excavation.

A third type of feature is the village or hamlet site. The three such sites in this area are less than two hectares in size. As will be discussed in the next chapter, structures were widely scattered on these sites and they rose only slowly, never exceeding a few meters in height. Thus some may be invisible below the later alluvium. One of three in the area under consideration, the site of Shaman, is probably on the main channel halfway between Ur and Sakheri. Though the situation is obscured by much later debris, the village probably covered about one hectare and contained ten dwelling compounds. To the north is Sakheri Sughir, sounded by a joint operation of the University of Chicago Oriental Institute and the Iraq Directorate General of Antiquities in 1966. It covers an area of one and a half hectares in the middle of the first phase of the Early Dynastic period. It could have contained 15 dwelling compounds. To the southwest of Shaman was a small unnamed hamlet site. It is triangular in shape and covered four-tenths of a hectare. It could have contained three compounds. These three sites, one south of the main channel, one north of the main channel, and one on that channel, are roughly halfway between Ur and Sakheri in an area not within convenient walking distance of either town.

A fourth kind of feature can be called a "rural center" in absence of a clear understanding of the activities conducted in it. One of these is known at Tell 'Ubaid. It is located on the north end of the 'Ubaid period village site. It was excavated by Hall and Woolley (1927) and reinvestigated and considerably clarified by Delougaz (1938). Most of the known remains date to the final phase of the Early Dynastic period. Leveled by this later building activity was an earlier oval compound with a series of rooms facing inward to the court. There was a single entrance from the outside. Presumably the later temple platform obliterated some kind of shrine in the center of the court. A few fragments of possible lexical texts suggest that scribes worked here, at least in later times. It is not certain that this oval compound is from the first phase of the Early Dynastic period, but since a cemetery of that phase occurs on the south end of the mound of 'Ubaid, and since the complex was founded no later than the preceding Jemdet Nasr period, such seems reasonable.

A fifth type of feature is cemeteries. Two are known. Both are on natural sandy knolls with evidences of prehistoric occupation. One is at 'Ubaid. . . . Another is southeast of 'Ubaid and southwest of Ur on what must have been the fringes of cultivation. This unnamed and completely eroded site was littered with fine stone bowl fragments more reminiscent of the burials at Ur than those at 'Ubaid. It may have been a cemetery for the town dwellers of Ur.

These various types of features must have occupied much of the 9,000 hectares in the enclave. In addition, it is likely that sites of earlier periods, flooded areas, and salty areas removed more land from cultivation. Assuming one-third to be thus eliminated by analogy with comparable modern situations (Poyck, 1962), 6,000 cultivatable hectares would remain.

It would be difficult to consider the organization of an urban system as a whole without adequate samples of observations on the craft and political centers. In the following paragraphs I will summarize the little that is known about such areas.

Between 1920 and 1932 the site of Ur was extensively investigated by the British Museum and the University of Pennsylvania under the direction of Sir Leonard Woolley. He attempted to reveal the main temple area as it was around 2000 B.C. Only limited areas of the Early Dynastic settlement were revealed. . . . In addition, some of the clay tablets provide information relevant to the organization of activity in the town.

First let us consider urban land use. Four general types of land use can be described. The first is for temple areas. These are elaborately planned complexes often with an outer wall surrounding utility rooms of various kinds and an inner court and shrine or shrines, often on a raised platform. The temple and ziggurat of Nanna at Ur is a particularly large example. When probable storerooms, kitchens, guardrooms, and shrines are eliminated from consideration, there is dwelling room for no more than twenty attendants in this mammoth complex. Since the structure of the first phase of the Early Dynastic was destroyed down to its foundations there is no artifactual debris of this period reported. The debris in the duplicate later Early Dynastic structure is predominantly sealings removed from storage containers, bits of inlay and statuary which probably once decorated the complex, and weapons fragments—clay "sling missiles," spear points, and a bitumen mace head. The latter item is now used on shepherds' staffs. Ceramics are rare. The large size of the possible kitchens suggests that on occasion many people were fed at once.

A second use for town land is for large secular building complexes. Though such buildings must have been the source of the many tablets and container sealings thrown over the southeast revetment, the area southeast of the Nanna temple where they probably stood was not adequately investigated. The better examples of such buildings of the later Early Dynastic period were found above the smaller structures discussed in the next paragraph. These structures show much variation. One complex has massive outer walls and light, irregular, interior partitions leaving small rooms. Another complex has planned, but rather light construction with large courts and a variety of rooms. In these structures, ovens, braziers, and discarded bone suggest some cooking activity. Small ornaments are relatively frequent. Seals, seal impressions, accounting tablets, and a variety of unique finds occur. Small cups and unspouted jars are common. Very large jars seem to be distinctive to this type of structural complex. This type of complex is most poorly understood and probably most crucial to understanding how towns were organized. It is possible that this type of structural complex contained such things as high status dwellings, servants' quarters, storerooms, workshops, and so on.

A third use for town land is for small secular building complexes. Several levels of such architecture were investigated on the southeast side of the mound. Rooms are small and closely packed. Allowing three rooms to a family of six, densities of three hundred people on a hectare would be possible. Grinding stones, braziers, jewelry, and other unique small finds occur. Conical cups and small unspouted jars are common. Medium- and large-sized spouted jars seem distinctive to this type of structural complex. The absence of ovens in these structures is striking. Presumably these are the dwellings of the working population.

A final use of town land is as location for a dump and cemetery. Apparently only the steep edge of the mound outside the town's revetments was used for these purposes.

In the absence of adequate architectural information, 200 people per hectare are assumed for the towns. Ur would have had 4,000 inhabitants. Sakheri would have had 1,600 inhabitants. Having seven people per rural residence unit, about 200 people would have lived in rural settlements. Assuming that some rural settlements were not located in the survey, the Ur enclave would have had about 6,000 inhabitants.

From the artifacts found in these various areas, the practice of the following crafts at Ur can be inferred:

1. throwing and firing of ceramics
2. cutting of stone bowls (the cutting head of a rotary drill for rounding out the inside of stone bowls was found on the dump)
3. smithing of copper vessels
4. hand spinning (spindle whorls were found)
5. seal cutting.

The many other crafts that must have existed can only be directly demonstrated through better samples and better methods.

Some of the texts provide evidence, direct or indirect, of production and administration in the town itself. First, however, a description of the findspot and the character of the tablet sample is necessary.

The tablets were found with the seal impressions in the strata of burned debris on the southeast slope of the town. These strata at times coalesced into one stratum, and fragments of a single tablet sometimes appeared in both strata. Thus the strata seem to result from the clearing away of a single, burned structure or group of structures. Presumably most of the tablets were written in the space of a few years.

The tablets were studied by Burrows (1935). Of the 375 catalogued by him, about 220 are large enough to be useful in a study of content. Very few of these are undamaged. Most are small portions of the original text. The bulk of these involve rural production. They deal with land, grain, animals, reeds, trees, fish, or food allotted to individuals who are connected with these products in some way. . . .

Here we will consider (a) scribal activity itself,* (b) some specialists and officials mentioned in passing in the texts, and (c) some groups of people who apparently had special duties in the town.

The presence of scribes is clearly demonstrated by the existence of texts, however there is no definite reference to the scribal craft in the texts. Nevertheless, certain points are clear. First, the mixture of economic and practice texts suggests that scribes were trained in the place of business. Some texts are merely practice markings. In addition, there are a number of sign lists including the names of statuses, fish, gods, and feasts, which much have been used in training. Second, scribes recorded literary compositions in spite of the simplicity of the writing system. One fragment is from a work about Abzu, the personification of the Deeps, and various birds. This is the oldest reported literary fragment (Biggs, 1966:79). It is possible that such efforts represent a hobby or pastime of the scribes.

There are no texts which explicitly deal with other town specialists or craftsmen in any organized way. Nevertheless, when two individuals having the same name are mentioned in a text, then they are distinguished by some additional appellation. Often this appellation is the name of the man's craft or specialty. Burrows collected the names of eighty of these specialists. Eliminating those referring to administrative or ritual positions and those whose meaning or context are not clear, eight remain:

šidim.gal	chief bricklayer
nagar	carpenter
simug	smith
nu.kir$_x$(SAR)	gardener
muḫaldim	cook

---

*The following modified system is used for transcribing Sumerian: When the reading of a syllable is known, it is written with lower-case letters, when not, it is written with upper-case letters. When the proper order is known then the syllables are separated by a period, when not, they are separated by a colon.

en.giz   kitchen supervisor
MUNU₃.MÚ   maltster
a.zu   physician

Several important buildings are mentioned. The AB was an institution
with a large storehouse and a staff. A temple for Nanna is not mentioned in
the texts, though its archeological remains are clear. It may be that the AB
was the temple of Nanna, but was not given its later name until it was
necessary to distinguish the AB of Ur from that of other towns.

The é-gal, the palace, is also mentioned. Though officials of the lugal,
the resident of the palace, are mentioned; and though a number of personal
names refer to the lugal, there is no convincing direct reference to this per-
sonage. It is possible that at this time Ur had no resident lugal but was
subordinate to that of another town. If the lugal were less important, however, than he later became, it would be difficult to tell his title from his
personal name. This role is poorly understood.

It is likely that many of the texts listing rations of food and other
items, and listing groups of people, in fact refer to the organizing and provisioning of people working in the town. However, in only a few examples is
there any indication on the tablet that such might be so. Four possible cases
are listed below.

The AB. Text 50 records the giving of bread of the AB to various people.
Two loaves go to one individual and five to another. Five or six go to the
female servants of the AB. These people may have cared for the storehouse,
or performed some unknown activity connected with the institution.

Text 95 records the exchange of 73 gur of grain (NINDA₂ x BAP-
PIR.sa₁₀) from the AB and the allotting of 94 gur of grain for eating (še.kú)
to three important people.

The Temple of Inanna. Text 72 records the disposition of bread associated
with the goddess of Innana. Of the thirty loaves, eight of them are actually
offered to the goddess. The rest are apparently given to various people. Perhaps these are the custodians of the temple.

Text 93 records a similar disposition of bread to a number of groups in
addition to Innana and her associates. The É.AN, the house of the god, and
the ki:GEME₂, the place of women, and various individuals and office holders
also received bread.

Several additional texts dealing with the AB and with Innana are known.
The above examples serve to illustrate this type of text relevant to town
activities.

SUMMARY

The context of the rural economy of the enclave around Ur in the first
phase of the Early Dynastic is generally clear: On the southern alluvium there
was a trend toward fewer and larger settlements. Ur was a larger town in a

small cultivated enclave. The town was tied to others up the river in some sort of exchange relations. The town had a few surrounding smaller settlements. There were some central institutions—a storehouse, various temples, and a palace—in some way interrelated. A variety of officials and craftsmen worked in the town. The organization of these statuses and institutions is unclear, and will remain so until more contemporary documentation is available. Nevertheless, the organization of rural production can be studied without complete understanding of town organization.

REFERENCES

Biggs, R. D. "The Abi Salabikh Tablets." *Journal of Cuneiform Studies* 20(2) (1966) 73-89.

Burrows, E. *The Ur Archaic Texts, Ur Excavation Texts,* Vol. II. London: The British Museum and The University Museum of The University of Pennsylvania, 1935.

De Lougaz, P. "A Short Investigation of the Temple at Tell al-'Ubaid." Iraq 5 (1938): 1-11.

Poyck, A. *Farm Studies in Iraq.* Wageningen: Landbouwhogeschool to Wageningen, 1962.

Woolley, L. *The Royal Cemetary, Ur Excavations,* Vol. II. London: Oxford University Press, 1927.

TEOTIHUACAN: COMPLETION OF MAP OF GIANT ANCIENT CITY IN THE VALLEY OF MEXICO

René Millon

Abstract. *The detailed archeological map of Teotihuacán, near Mexico City, demonstrates what the prehistoric city was like from its densely crowded center to its more sparsely settled peripheries. The city's population lived in crowded one-story apartment compounds, grouped into neighborhoods based at least partly on occupation. At its height the city had a minimum population of 75,000, a probable population of 125,000, and a possible population of more than 200,000. Those involved in craft production and associated activities may have numbered in the tens of thousands. The scope and intensity of urbanization at Teotihuacán is not paralleled in other contemporary New World centers. The growth potential of the obsidian and other industries, the rise of Teotihuacán as a market and trade center, and its attraction as a religious center may have combined in a self-generating process that led to the creation of Teotihuacán's unique urban society.*

Teotihuacán, one of the largest preindustrial cities in the world, has been completely mapped in detail. Largescale photogrammetric maps of the ancient Mexican urban center were used in an intensive field reconnaissance of an area of more than 30 km². The first complete map of the entire city may be seen in Figure 1. The scale of Figure 1 is about 1 : 41,500. The scale of the field maps and of the final drawings on which Figure 1 is based is 1 : 2000. Figure 2 covers the same area as Figure 1 and is a reduction of the 1 : 2000 topographic field map on which Figure 1 is based.

The map's grid system of 500-m squares follows the north-south orientation of the ancient city, approximately 15°30′ east of astronomic north. The

From *Science,* Vol. 170, pp. 1077-1082, December, 1970. Copyright © 1970 by The American Association for the Advancement of Science. Reprinted by permission of the author and the publisher.

144

zero point of the grid system is in the center of the city, at the southwest corner of the Ciudadela (Figure 1, No. 3).

In collecting data for the preparation of the map, we looked for any evidence we could find of ancient occupation. We attempted to recognize separate structural units, such as room complexes, platforms, temples, open plazas, walls, thoroughfares, and other architectural features in the city. We termed each such unit a "site." We took into account mounding, including slight changes in elevation, and the density of potsherds and other objects on the surface. By use of these and other criteria, we defined the limits of a site, made a collection of pottery and other objects, and noted the site limits on the map. We noted on one-page site records the most important characteristics of more than 3000 sites, including such features as structural remains, ceramics, and stone tools. Data from such records have been encoded for computer analyses (1).

Figure 3 illustrates how we used our 1 : 2000 photogrammetric maps in our field reconnaissance to help determine the forms and boundaries of ruined, buried buildings, the spatial relations among buildings, and how open space was used in forming the architectural complexes. Figure 3B (scale about 1 : 4300) shows the topography in square N4W1, immediately south and west of the Moon Pyramid, together with the data recorded in the course of the archeological survey. Figure 3A shows our hypothetical reconstructions of buildings, which are based partly on these data and partly on a study of the surface collections we made from each building or other numbered unit and on our written observations and photos relating to these structures. The same kinds of data were collected for the entire city. Figure 3 and 150 other similar pairs of facing drawings for the entire city will be published at the 1 : 2000 scale.

The area shown in Figure 3A extends from the temples and other structures on the west side of the "Street of the Dead" westward to an area of residential room complexes at left, shown as open rectangles. Each of the buildings shown as an open rectangle consisted of rooms, porticos, patios, and access ways similar to, but less elaborate than, the Quetzalpapalotl Palace in the upper right. The reader should bear this in mind when examining Figure 1.

Figure 1. Map of the ancient city of Teotihuacán at its height (about A.D. 600). The city covered about 20 km² (8 square miles). Partially or completely excavated structures, primarily along the Street of the Dead (north-south axis), are shown; also shown are reconstructions based on the Teotihuacán Mapping Project survey of surface remains of unexcavated and partially excavated structures. An undetermined number of structures in various parts of the city have been buried under silt or leveled for agriculture in modern times. Most of the buildings shown were one-story apartment compounds. Note the canalization of most streams within the ancient city.

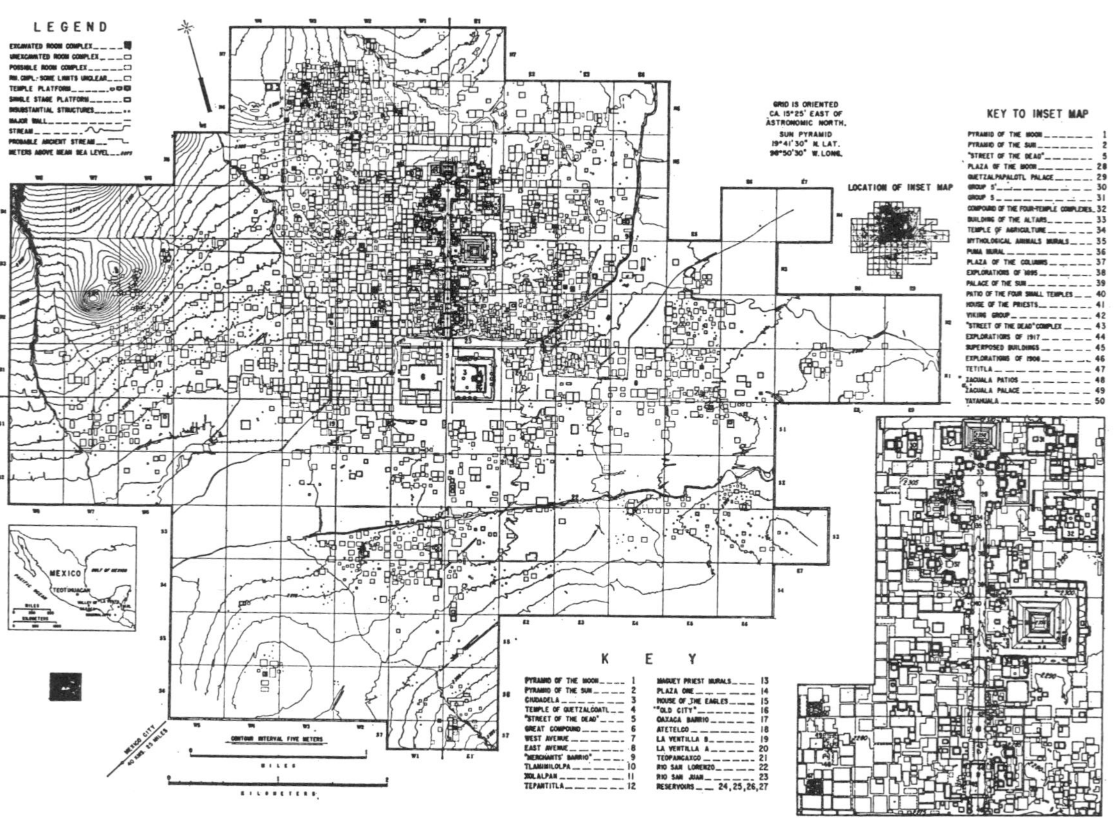
LEGEND
EXCAVATED ROOM COMPLEX
UNEXCAVATED ROOM COMPLEX
POSSIBLE ROOM COMPLEX
RM. CMPL.: SOME LIMITS UNCLEAR
TEMPLE PLATFORM
SINGLE STAGE PLATFORM
INSUBSTANTIAL STRUCTURES
MAJOR WALL
STREAM
PROBABLE ANCIENT STREAM
METERS ABOVE MEAN SEA LEVEL
GRID IS ORIENTED CA. 15°25' EAST OF ASTRONOMIC NORTH.
SUN PYRAMID 19°41'30" N. LAT. 98°50'30" W. LONG.
LOCATION OF INSET MAP
MEXICO
GULF OF MEXICO
TEOTIHUACAN
PACIFIC OCEAN
VALLEY OF MEXICO
CONTOUR INTERVAL FIVE METERS
MILES
KILOMETERS
MEXICO CITY 40 KM. 25 MILES
KEY
PYRAMID OF THE MOON — 1
PYRAMID OF THE SUN — 2
CIUDADELA — 3
TEMPLE OF QUETZALCOATL — 4
"STREET OF THE DEAD" — 5
GREAT COMPOUND — 6
WEST AVENUE — 7
EAST AVENUE — 8
"MERCHANTS' BARRIO" — 9
TLAMIMILOLPA — 10
XOLALPAN — 11
TEPANTITLA — 12
MAGUEY PRIEST MURALS — 13
PLAZA ONE — 14
HOUSE OF THE EAGLES — 15
"OLD CITY" — 16
OAXACA BARRIO — 17
ATETELCO — 18
LA VENTILLA B — 19
LA VENTILLA A — 20
TEOPANCAXCO — 21
RIO SAN LORENZO — 22
RIO SAN JUAN — 23
RESERVOIRS — 24, 25, 26, 27
KEY TO INSET MAP
PYRAMID OF THE MOON — 1
PYRAMID OF THE SUN — 2
"STREET OF THE DEAD" — 5
PLAZA OF THE MOON — 28
QUETZALPAPALOTL PALACE — 29
GROUP 5' — 30
GROUP 5 — 31
COMPOUND OF THE FOUR-TEMPLE COMPLEXES — 32
BUILDING OF THE ALTARS — 33
TEMPLE OF AGRICULTURE — 34
MYTHOLOGICAL ANIMALS MURALS — 35
PUMA MURAL — 36
PLAZA OF THE COLUMNS — 37
EXPLORATIONS OF 1895 — 38
PALACE OF THE SUN — 39
PATIO OF THE FOUR SMALL TEMPLES — 40
HOUSE OF THE PRIESTS — 41
VIKING GROUP — 42
"STREET OF THE DEAD" COMPLEX — 43
EXPLORATIONS OF 1917 — 44
SUPERPOSED BUILDINGS — 45
EXPLORATIONS OF 1908 — 46
TETITLA — 47
ZACUALA PATIOS — 48
ZACUALA PALACE — 49
YAYAHUALA — 50

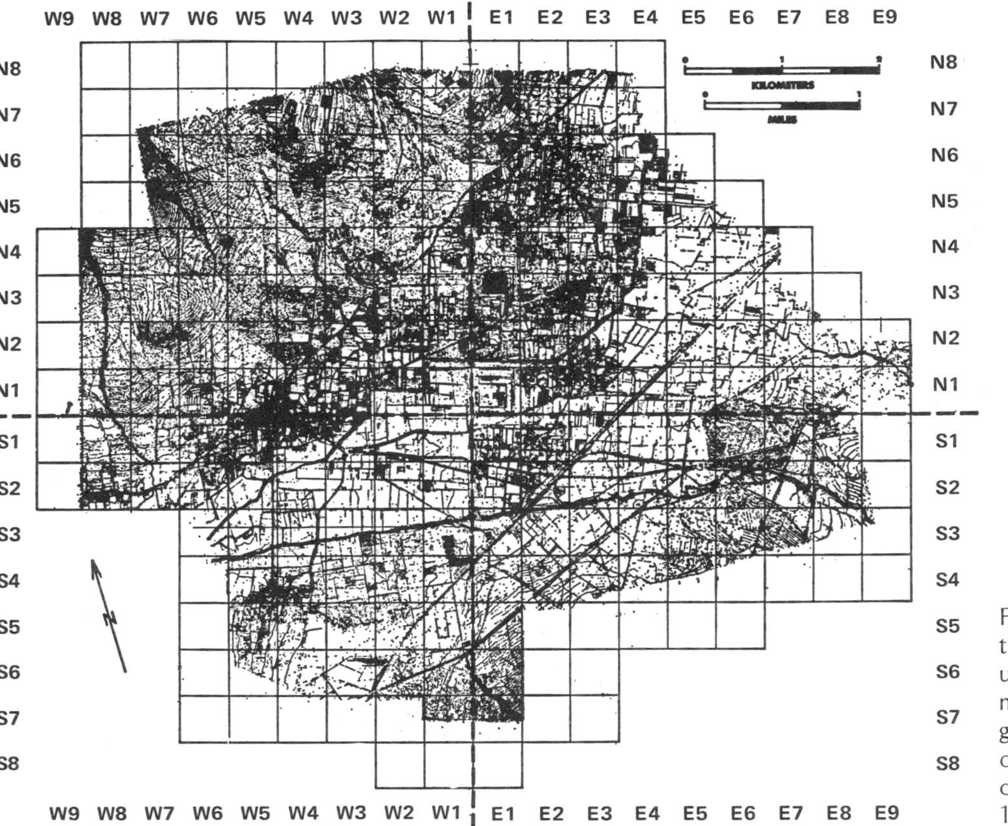

Figure 2. Reduced mosaic of the topographic map sheets used in the field to produce the map shown in Figure 1. The grid system of 500-m squares is oriented to the north-south axis of the ancient city (about 15°30′ east of north).

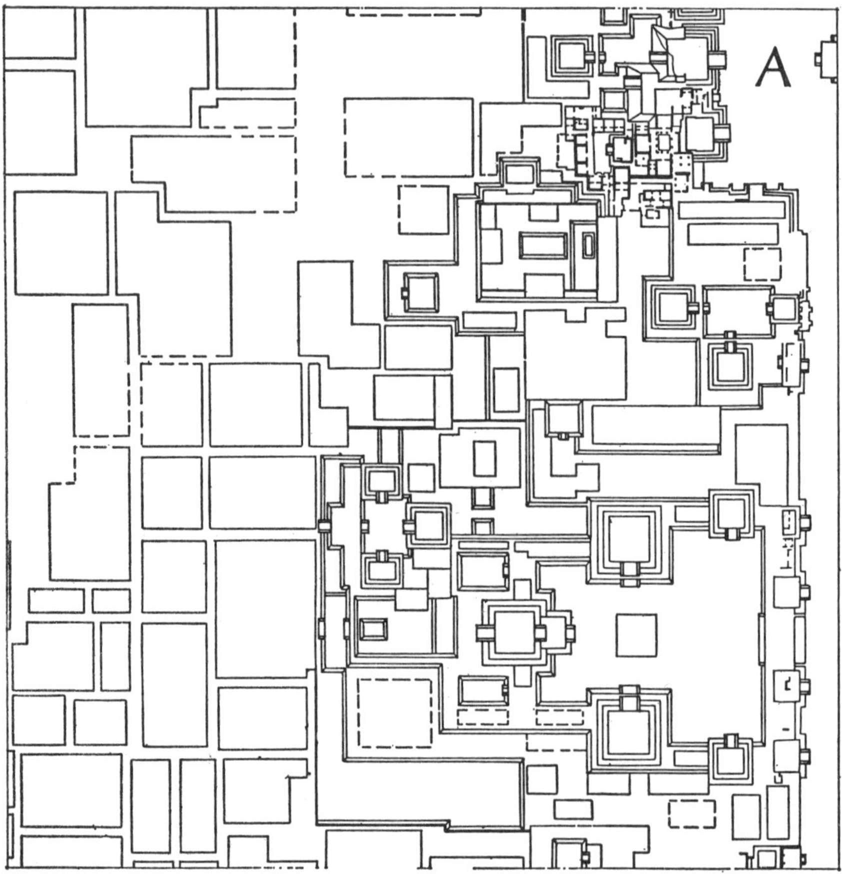

Figure 3. Detailed drawings of N4W1, the 500-m square southwest of the Moon Pyramid (see Figure 1). This pair of drawings is one of 150 such pairs covering the entire ancient city. (A) Drawing showing buildings as we think they would have looked anciently, based on the data shown at right and on written descriptive data and surface collections for each numbered site and subsite shown at right. Buildings shown as open rectangles were apartment compounds—complexes of rooms, patios, access ways, and small temples— similar to but less elaborate than the complex of excavated rooms shown in the northeast part of the drawing. (B) Topographic map with 1-m contours, together with data from the Teotihuacán Mapping Project archeological survey of this square, showing site boundaries and numbers, exposed floors (*F*) and walls (*W*), and wholly or partially excavated structures along the Street of the Dead. Contours were drawn photogrammetrically in 1962 from a flight made in that year. The road that runs north-south in the western part of the drawing is the new road around the archeological zone ("Periferico"). It was built in 1964 after the contours had been drawn and is therefore shown "overriding" them.

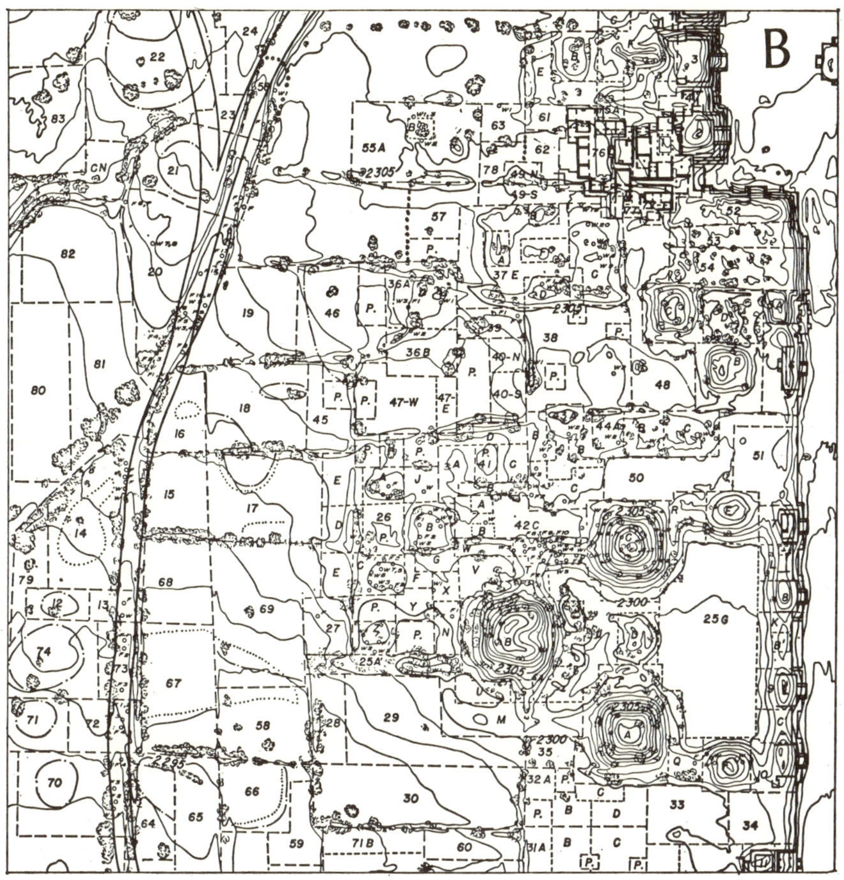

The reconstructions of hypothetical buildings are based on a vast body of information. This information frequently includes exposed floors, walls, and other structural features. There are more than 2600 room complexes, temples, platforms, and other major stone-walled structures shown in Figure 1. Of these structures, more than 1200 (46 percent) had walls, floors, or other structural evidence visible in situ. Our other most reliable indicator of major construction in the survey has been a combination of stone cover and crushed volcanic scoria (*cascajo*), the latter being the preferred major ingredient in the foundations of floors and in the outer coverings of walls. The reliability of the presence of this combination of building materials on a site was tested in seven excavations, and in every case its presence proved reliably to predict the existence of major construction. Conversely, in three cases where *cascajo* was not present and where we did not expect to find any major structures, no major structures were found.

Figure 1 is the first map of the entire city, from its center to its outskirts. I avoid the word "suburbs" because that term most meaningfully applies to parts of a city in which, for the most part, people live but do not work, their place of work being in the city (2). The separation of place of work from place of residence in a city seems largely to be confined to industrialized societies of recent times.

The city was divided into quadrants by its north-south (Street of the Dead) and east-west axes (East Avenue and West Avenue) (Figure 1, Nos. 5, 7, and 8). With some exceptions, buildings in Teotihuacán are oriented to the north-south axis which gives the plan of the city an orderly appearance even in areas of great crowding. Figure 1 represents the city as we think it was late in its history (about A.D. 600) when it covered an area of about 20 km^2 (8 mi^2). If the reader will note the scale of the map, he will have some idea of the great size of the city and of the great number of its apartment compounds. Apartment compounds are one-story rectangular structures designated in the legend of Figure 1 as "excavated" or "unexcavated" room complexes. There are more than 2000 such apartment compounds in the city. Note also the immense size of the Ciudadela and the Great Compound (Figure 1, Nos. 3 and 6; see also cover photograph). We believe that these two enclosures in the geographic center of the city—enclosures that are so similar and yet so different—together formed the city's religious, bureaucratic, and commercial center.

The most sparsely settled section of the city is the extreme southern extension of the Street of the Dead, at the bottom of the map. It forms a continuous and integral part of the city, despite its low density (3, pp. 105-106). The northwest quadrant is by far the most densely settled and presumably the most populous part of the city. It is also the area with the greatest concentration of occupational specialists. The preponderance of residential construction in the northwest may be related to the fact that the southwest quadrant borders the richest cultivable land in the Valley of Teotihuacán and that most of the eastern perimeter also borders cultivable land. In contrast, the northwestern perimeter borders poor cultivable lands. Another and probably related reason for the greater density of settlement in the northwest quadrant is that it was the most densely settled area early in the city's history, around the time of Christ. This area was Teotihuacán's "old city," and it continued to be the most crowded and densely settled section throughout the city's history (square N6W3 and the squares surrounding it; see Figures 1 and 2).

Evidence from surface survey and from excavation indicates that Teotihuacán was divided into *barrios* or neighborhoods. Some groups of buildings are so clearly set off from surrounding structures that they form easily definable spatial units. Other groups of buildings are distinguished by what we find on their surfaces. There are groups of buildings where the same craft seems to have been practiced (obsidian working, pottery making, lapidary work), where foreigners from the same place lived (4) (Figure 1, No. 17), where foreign pottery from different parts of Middle America, principally from the Gulf

Coast, Yucatán, and Guatemala, is found in quantity, and where we think merchants may have lived (Figure 1, No. 9).

The map of Teotihuacán demonstrates that a great deal of planning must have gone into the building of the city. The length of the Street of the Dead shown in Figure 1 (it extends to the very bottom of the map) was apparently decided on early in the city's history, perhaps in the second century A.D., before there were many permanent buildings at Teotihuacán other than pyramids and temples. The decision to extend the Street of the Dead over a distance of 5 km was an audacious one. In staking out a claim for the future growth of the city, the early Teotihuacanos were cutting off the narrow waist of the Teotihuacán valley and effectively blocking from open access the most convenient route for trade and travel between the Valley of Mexico and, to the east, the Valley of Puebla and coastal Veracruz (5).

The fact of planning is evident, but what is not clear is its nature, its extent, and its sequence. Was there ever some kind of master plan which was slowly fulfilled and modified with the passage of time? Or was the building up of the city the result of a series of piecemeal additions to a basic cruciform plan which, when we see it completed, gives us an impression that it was the product of an overall "master plan" although it may not have been so at all (6). The argument that there was no planning outside the city's central core (3, p. 172) is contradicted by the map on the south, the west, and the east.

Population estimates based solely on archeological evidence are difficult to make. Nevertheless, such estimates can now be made with greater accuracy than at any time since the fall of the city, for we have a reasonably good minimum estimate for the entire city of the number of major buildings and their nature and disposition. Only the buildings that we have reason to believe were occupied at the same time are shown in Figure 1. Population estimates are based only on these buildings. We believe that our surface survey techniques make it possible for us to distinguish buildings composed of complexes of rooms from other buildings, such as temples or platforms. We also believe that most, if not all, room complexes were residential, even though most were almost certainly the locus of other activities as well. People who worked in the city seem to have tended to work where they lived. Exceptions or partial exceptions would have been construction workers, marketplace traders, merchants, and some temple workers.

I arrived at the population estimates that follow by examining apartment compounds that have been excavated in various parts of the city (Figure 1). We know that these buildings were lived in, because our own excavations have established unequivocally that there were kitchens in these compounds. [We stress this fact because it has been raised as a false issue (7).] We have postulated that corporate groups of some kind lived in apartment compounds, principally because the prominence within them of one or more temples suggests that compound inhabitants engaged in common ritual activities (8). Inhabitants of compounds may have been linked by ties of kinship, may have engaged in common occupations, or more likely both. But we do not know the size or social composition of the domestic or other groups living in these compounds. For this reason, estimates of populations of apartment compounds must be based on other grounds. Also, it seems probable for several reasons that larger buildings did not necessarily house proportionally larger numbers of people.

What I have tried to do is to determine how many potential sleeping rooms there are in excavated apartment compounds. I have defined a potential sleeping room as one that is completely enclosed—that is, it has four walls and one or more doorways. Excluded from this count were enclosed rooms that appear to have been used for other purposes (rooms on temple platforms) or that seem otherwise exceptional and therefore possibly intended primarily for other uses (for example, since mural paintings are exceptional in interior rooms, rooms with murals were excluded).

Apartment compounds vary extensively in the sizes of their rooms and in the way open space is used (principally patios, porticos, and access ways). The most crowded seem to have one enclosed sleeping room (as defined here) for every 40 to 50 m^2. The most spacious, of which there are few examples, seem to have one enclosed sleeping room for every 150 to 200 m^2. If we take 120 m^2 per sleeping room as a basis for calculation (a conservative estimate), we arrive at a total of thirty such rooms in an apartment complex of 3600 m^2. With the further conservative assumption that such rooms would have provided sleeping space for one to three people, we arrive at a very conservative figure of sixty persons per apartment compound of about 3600 m^2 (Nos. 47, 49, and 50 in Figure 1 are slightly smaller than 3600 m^2). I also made estimates for two apartment compounds of successively smaller size, for which I used slightly higher population densities. For an apartment compound of about 1600 m^2 (No. 11 in Figure 1 is slightly smaller), I estimated a population of thirty. For a compound about 25 by 25 m, I estimated a population of 12. I believe that these are conservative, minimum figures, which more than compensate for rooms included in the count that may not have been used for sleeping. More probable population figures for each of these compound sizes are 100, 50, and 20.

With these two sets of figures, I made population estimates for the entire city, after measuring the sizes of the reconstructed apartment compounds in each of the squares shown in Figure 1. The three building sizes and their estimated populations served as a guide in estimating proportionally the populations of buildings of other sizes. These calculations yielded a minimum population of 75,000 and a probable population of 125,000 for the city at its height. Since the assumptions about the number of persons who lived in apartment compounds of various sizes may be too conservative, it is possible that the city's population was significantly larger, perhaps exceeding 200,000.

The population of Teotihuacán is impressively large for an early city. Not only was its population large, but it was also relatively highly differentiated, with a significant proportion of the population engaged in craft activities. Although most of the city's population probably cultivated land, more than 500 craft workshops have been found in our archeological survey of the ancient city. The vast majority are obsidian workshops, most of which were in use when the population of the city was at its peak (9). There are also well over a hundred other workshops—ceramic, stone, figurine, lapidary, basalt, and slate. To this total must be added an unknown number of workshops where the craftsmen worked in materials and with tools that left no traces or that we have not been able to recognize. In addition, there must have been sizable numbers of craftsmen connected with the building of the city's many structures—masons, plasterers, and carpenters, and perhaps others as well.

A significant proportion of the population of Teitihuacán must have been involved in craft production and craft activities. Perhaps it was twenty-five percent or more, which would mean tens of thousands of people. In addition, an unspecified number of people were engaged in marketplace and long-distance trade. These persons may have been some of the craftsmen themselves or specialized traders or, perhaps more likely, some combination of the two. Did the economic potential represented by the growing obsidian and other industries and the presumed growth of Teotihuacán as a market and trade center, together with the religious attraction that Teotihuacán must have had very early in its history, combine in a self-generating process that led to the creation of Teotihuacán's unique urban society (10)? This appears to be the most promising line of investigation in the present state of our knowledge.

Occupational specialization, proliferating craft industries, high urban density, and a large population are differing manifestations of the same intense process of urbanization. Taken in conjunction with the scope of Teotihuacán's exports and imports, they argue that Teotihuacán society was more complex than recent estimates have suggested. The intensity of the urbanization process appears to set Teotihuacán apart from other contemporary centers in Middle America. At the same time, it makes it more similar to Tenochtitlán, the capital of the Aztecs, which rose 40 km from Teotihuacán on the site of modern Mexico City over 500 years after Teotihuacán's fall. Until equivalent comparative data from other parts of the New World are available, comparisons with early Old World centers may be more useful in trying to understand pre-Hispanic urbanization in the Valley of Mexico.

Teotihuacán stands for the present as the most highly urbanized center of its time in the New World (11). The extraordinary extent and pervasiveness of its influence through so much of Middle America in the early centuries of the Christian era are now more understandable.

FOOTNOTES

1. Computer analyses are being carried out by G. Cowgill.

2. See H. Saalman, *Medieval Cities* (New York: Braziller, 1968), pp. 44-45.

3. See W. Sanders, *The Cultural Ecology of the Teotihuacán Valley* (Dept. of Sociology and Anthropology, Pennsylvania State Univ., State College, 1965).

4. R. Millon, *Bol. Inst. Nac. Antropol. Hist.* 29, 42 (1967); *Gac. Med. Mex.* 93, 339 (1968).

5. R. Millon, *Scientific American* 216 (6), 38 (1967).

6. D. Robertson, *Pre-Columbian Architecture* (New York: Braziller, 1963), pp. 25-27, 35-36; J. E. Hardoy, *Ciudades Precolombinas* (Buenos Aires: Infinito, 1964), pp. 89-93; *Urban Planning in Pre-Columbian America* (New York: Braziller, 1968), pp. 9, 12, 22-23.

7. G. Kubler, *The Art and Architecture of Ancient America* (Baltimore: Penguin, 1962), pp. 29, 328.

8. R. Millon, *37th Int. Congr. Americanists Actas Memorias* 1, 113 (1968).

9. For the past several years M. Spence of Southern Illinois University has been analyzing obsidian, obsidian workshops, the obsidian industry, and specialization within the industry in Teotihuacán on the basis of what was found in our excavations and surface survey.

10. This is suggested in part by the stimulating ideas of J. Jacobs on the economic growth of early cities [*The Economy of Cities* (New York: Random House, 1969)]. See also R. Millon, in *Teotihuacán, XI Mesa Redonda* (Sociedad Mexicana de Antropología, México, 1967), pp. 149-155.

11. Other contemporary Middle American centers, such as Tikal in Guatemala or Dzibilchaltun in Yucatán, seem to have covered larger areas than Teotihuacán [W. Coe, *Tikal* (Philadelphia: University Museum, 1967); W. Haviland, *Amer. Antiquity* 34 (4), 429 (1969); E. Andrews, Map of Dzibilchaltun, Yucatán, México (Middle American Research Institute, Tulane Univ., New Orleans, 1965); *Archeology* 21 (1), 36 (1968)]. But so far as is now known, none seems to have been so highly urbanized as Teotihuacán; that is, none seems to have combined great size, high population density, large populations, foreign enclaves, and thousands of craft specialists in a marketplace and ritual center of immense, monumental proportions. Chan Chan, an immense urban center on the north coast of Peru, is now under intensive study by M. Moseley and others. From what is now known of it, Chan Chan, although of great size, also does not appear to have been so highly urbanized as Teotihuacán [see M. West, *Amer. Antiquity* 35 (1), 74 (1970)].

12. Supported by NSF grants G23800, GS207, GS641, GS1222, and GS2204. Principal participants with R.M. on the project are G. Cowgill (Brandeis University) and R. B. Drewitt (University of Toronto). J. A. Cerda is chief draftsman. I gratefully acknowledge the assistance of P. Baños, W. Barbour, J. Bennyhoff, D. Blucher, H. Castañeda, J. Dow, A. German, E. Ekholm, P. Krotser, G. R. Krotser, D. Massey, E. Rattray, S. Reichlin, S. Shernoff, M. Spence, J. Vidarte, M. Wallrath. I thank I. Bernal, I. Marquina, J. Cortina, J. Acosta, J. L. Lorenzo, P. Salazar, E. Matos, E. Contreras, F. Müller, and E. Taboada of Mexico's Instituto Nacional de Antropología e Historia for their assistance in our work. This report benefited from readings and criticisms by W. Barbour, E. Calnek, G. Cowgill, R. B. Drewitt, A. Green, and C. Millon.

Section G. The City and
Its Environment

CULTURAL ECOLOGY OF NUCLEAR MESOAMERICA

William T. Sanders

The following paper is an attempt to define some of the interrelationships between culture and environment and to demonstrate the value of the concepts of cultural ecology in understanding the process of development of pre-Iron Age civilizations. By cultural ecology I mean simply the study of the interaction of cultural processes with the physical environment. My theoretical position may be stated in the following principles:

1. Each environment offers to human occupation a different set of challenges, and therefore a different set of alternate cultural responses may be expected. There is, of course, some overlapping of both challenges and cultural solutions from environment to environment. One can also say that certain alternative responses are more likely to occur than others. Some of these responses may be technological, others social, and some even religious.

2. In responding to such challenges, cultural response tends to take the path of greatest efficiency in the utilization of the environment.

3. In development of any conceptual scheme in culturology, the environment should be considered as an active, integrated part of the cultural system not as a passive extra-cultural factor.

To most archeologists the term "civilization" has a relatively restricted meaning. Kroeber uses the term more broadly, and even synonymously with "culture," defining it in terms of his pattern concept, and calling it the "total cultural pattern." In this paper I will use the term in the more restricted sense of the archeologist.

A civilization is a particular kind of cultural pattern; as contrasted to

From the *American Anthropologist,* Vol. 64, No. 1, pp. 34-43. Copyright ©1962 by the American Anthropological Association and reprinted with their permission.

cultures as a whole its pattern is broader, less narrowly restricted, and therefore capable of greater elaboration (see Kroeber 1948:311-43). When one views the growth configuration of a civilization one is impressed by its dynamic quality. All cultures change, but in civilizations change is more rapid, more easily measured, and more apparent to the observer. Certain conditions preclude the development of this type of cultural growth; some of them link specifically with the utilization of the environment. These may be enumerated as follows: (1) an effective utilization of natural resources permitting a relatively dense population; (2) the integration of such resources, natural and demographic, into a relatively large society; (3) a system of social stratification, at least on two levels, in which the surplus production of a large majority is systematically accumulated, controlled, and diverted into culturally specified channels by a small dominant minority.

This third condition seems to be an essential one as we have numerous examples of areas of the world with dense populations, relatively large social groupings, but no systematic manipulation of surplus labor and goods. In the earliest civilizations of the New and Old Worlds, this surplus was apparently controlled first by a priestly bureaucracy and directed towards the construction and glorification of buildings dedicated to the gods. Later periods saw the control exercised by, or at least shared by, a secular ruling class. Archeologists recognize civilizations primarily by the tangible results of the "direction of surplus energy," in the form of permanent architecture and an exceptionally high development of skill in other areas of technology. They use technology as a guide for obvious reasons. There is often a striking difference in the quality of the technology of the folk society that produces the surplus and that of the dominant minority that controls it. Furthermore, although few studies have actually been made, we usually find much greater stability and less dynamism on the folk level.

Before the development of the proletarian metal-iron, and the beginnings of the use of metal tools by both levels in the society, this kind of culture had an extremely limited distribution in the Old World. Its primary area was a large, nearly continuous region embracing the Near East, northwest India, northeast Africa, and southeastern Europe. A secondary, historically derived and later development occurred in North China.

Furthermore, the maximal development of the pre-Iron Age civilizations was in four small areas: the Nile valley in Egypt, the Tigris Euphrates valleys in Iraq, the Indus valley in India, and the Hwango Ho valley in China, in all cases associated with a major river valley. Each of these centers was a relatively small, compact, densely populated area; the entire Old Kingdom of Egypt, for example, embraced only about 10,000 square miles of territory.

If we look at the ecological settings of the early civilizations, certain fundamental patterns emerge. The environments can be classed into two major types; (1) nearly rainless deserts with exotic major rivers, or (2), semiarid country with low annual rainfall concentrated in a single season. In the Near East the latter climate falls generally into the type called "Mediterranean" with winter rains; in North China the rainy season falls in the summer. Average annual rainfall in the areas of dense population varies from 200–1,000mm. In the Near Eastern center another significant characteristic is that there is a great deal of ecological diversity based on altitude and micro-variations in climate.

The geographical conditions that seem to be crucial in these centers of the civilizations were: (1) presence of a fertile soil capable of being intensively cultivated and sufficient water for irrigation, and (2), scanty plant cover which could be easily controlled (conditions (1) and (2) permitted an effective and intensive use of the land by a peasant population with an essentially neolithic technology); (3) presence of a major river providing a natural transportation artery, and (4), a general deficiency of natural resources other than good agricultural land (acting as a stimulus to trade).

The situation in an area such as Mesopotamia offers a unique set of problems to a farmer equipped with a Neolithic technology. It is an ecological region of enormous potential, even with a relatively feeble technology. What it does require for successful utilization is a highly organized and cooperative society capable of mass effort in converting swamps and deserts into irrigated cropland. The most effective way to exploit such an environment is the development of a social system of the type we have defined as civilization.

Following V. Gordon Childe's analysis of the spread of civilization from the river valleys into the semiarid highlands and small coastal plains of the rest of the Near East (1951, 1954), it seems to have occurred primarily as a response to ecological condition number (4). The lack of resources in the major river valleys, he argues, led to the establishment of major trade routes, towns grew up at their termini which in turn were the foci of the extended Near Eastern civilization. Furthermore, the expansion occurred into an area where the environmental conditions permitted intensive and/or specialized (olives, dates, grapes, etc.) agriculture, on a small scale.

In the Old World another process developed hand in hand with civilization—urbanization. We have purposefully kept the two processes separate for reasons to be made explicit later.

I define urbanization as a process of evolution of rural communities into urban communities and further define an urban community as possessing the following attributes:

1. Nucleation—in my analysis of modern urban communities in Mexico, all have population densities exceeding 2,000 persons per square kilometer.

2. Relatively large size—in another study, based on modern Mexico (Sanders 1956), I use a specific figure in defining towns and cities, but precise population sizes would not apply to all areas of the world. I would generally state that urban communities would have at least 2,000 to 3,000 inhabitants, and reserve the term city for those with populations exceeding 10,000.

3. Most of the population are nonfood producers, or at least only part-time food producers, and the majority of the population is composed of part and full-time specialists in the production and distribution of technology, regulation of social interaction, or administration of services to the supernatural.

4. A great deal of social differentiation based on occupation, status, control of power, and in some cases, ethnic diversity. In the early development of urban centers in the Near East, the larger communities were political and religious centers, as well as commercial and industrial communities, and the growth of cities was a process directly linked to the growth of the state.

Having set the stage, in terms of basic concepts, definitions, and events in the Old World, I will now attempt to apply these concepts to the New World. As far as present research indicates, the civilizations of the New World developed independently from those of the Old World, from the same kind of folk technological base, thus providing us with a good laboratory test of the above concepts.

Cultures possessing the attributes of civilization occurred in the New World in two regions, the Mesoamerican and the Andean. The fundamental ecological patterns in the Andean region, in terms of the essential factors that permit the development of a civilization comparable to that of the Near East, correspond to a striking degree. In Peru, the heart of the Andean region, there are three primary, parallel, narrow, north-south ecological strips. To the east is a humid, slope and foothill zone with exuberant tropical forest cover. In the center is a high mountainous region with numerous small and large valleys and basins varying in altitude from 5,000 to 13,000 feet above sea level. All over this strip the climatic type is similar to our type (2) in the Near East, light to moderate rainfall concentrated in the summer season. Average rainfall over the area varies from 500–750 mm. a year. To the west is a nearly rainless desert crossed east to west by some twenty-five streams which have their sources in the mountains and flow to the sea, each providing water for a small, compact irrigated plain and isolated from other systems by intervening deserts. The Andean civilization centered in the mountain and desert strip and apparently never penetrated the eastern forest with any degree of success. The ecological principles of the Old World apparently may be applied very successfully to the Andean area, and along the coastal desert, at least, urbanization correlated in its development with civilization.

I will now turn to my primary area of interest and research—Mesoamerica. Here the interrelationships between environment and culture are much more complex. The area is ecologically much more diverse than any other region where pre-Iron Age civilizations have developed. Rainfall varies from 300 mm. in southeastern Puebla to over 5,000 mm. in the northeastern escarpment of Chiapas. Altitude varies from sea level to 2,800 m. (in the area of dense human population) with a corresponding great range of temperature. Vegetation varies from near desert conditions to lush tropical rain forest, soils from siernozems to laterites, hydrography from no surface drainage to small flood season streams, to great rivers with huge tributary basins and extensive flood plains. Within this overall diversity, in terms of problems faced by neolithic farmers, two well-defined ecological patterns emerge: (1) a Lowland pattern with heavy rainfall, exuberant vegetation, lower density and more scattered population, with slash and burn cultivation of basic foodstuffs and orchard cultivation of commercial crops; and (2), a Highland pattern with low rainfall, scanty vegetation, dense population living in larger nucleated communities and practicing intensive agriculture.

In actual fact, parts of the Lowlands have subhumid climates, and parts of the Highlands, humid climates, and any detailed analysis of the area should consider these exceptions.

In 1519, the Mesoamerican variant of civilization occurred over the entire region in all of the various ecological zones, including both Highlands and Lowlands. Urbanism, however, has been demonstrated as a corollary trait only in the Highland province, and in reality only definitely in the Central Plateau or Mesa Central of Mexico. In a more expanded paper, to be published in the projected Handbook about Mesoamerican Indians, I have analyzed in detail the role of this area in the development of urbanism and civilization in Mesoamerica. We will present here some of the results of this analysis and apply our basic concepts from Old World archeology.

Within the plateau is a small, compact, centrally located zone we will call the Nuclear Area because of its cultural dominance in the history of Mesoamerica. It includes the Valley of Mexico, Valley of Morelos, and the upper Atoyac-Nejapa drainage basin in Tlaxcala—Western Puebla, an area of approximately 20,000 km. In 1519, twenty percent of the population of Mesoamerica resided in this demographic heartland, approximately two and one-half million people. Both Pan-Mesoamerican empires, Aztec and Toltec, had their capitals in this area, and earlier Teotihuacán seems to have been the center of a third, similar state. It is also one of the main contenders for the scene of the origins of American Indian agriculture and Mesoamerican civilization.

The annual rainfall in the area of heavy human occupation is everywhere below 1,000 mm., generally ranging from 500–800 mm., most of which falls in the summer months. Vegetation cover is sparse and presents no serious challenge to primitive farmers. Within the fundamental unity is a great deal of diversity based upon altitudes ranging from 800 m. to 2,800 m. above sea level, in some parts of the area over a distance of only 50–60 km. Every agricultural plant in the Mesoamerican complex may be grown in some part of the area, and agricultural specialization has probably always been a distinctive feature. Soils generally are classed by Mexican agronomists as Chestnuts or Chernozems and with relatively simple techniques of soil restoration have sustained nearly continuous cropping for at least 3,500 years. The ecology generally is similar to type (2) in the Near East. There is no single great river system (although most of the area is drained by tributaries of the Balsas river) that could have served a single integrated irrigation system or provided a single transportation artery. In the Valley of Mexico, however, where two-thirds of the population resided in 1519, there was a chain of lakes that played the same role as the rivers in Old World centers of civilization.

Having described the general environmental factors of the area, let us now examine them as operational factors in the evolution of urban civilization. In the discussion we will refer back to our previous definitions of urbanization and civilization, and here, as in the Near East, the two processes were correlative and simultaneous.

1. The ecological conditions noted above are optimal for the development of an intensive system of agriculture. Studies by Palerm (1954, 1955), Wolf (1955), Millon (1957), Armillas (1949, 1950) and myself (ms) have demonstrated conclusively that agriculture in 1519 was as intensive as in the great centers of the Old World civilizations. The combination of low rainfall, easily controlled natural vegetation, fertile soils, water resources (lakes, springs, flood water, melt water from glaciers), and generally limited flat terrain made almost imperative the development of such techniques of soil and water conservation as permanent irrigation, chinampas, flood water irrigation, cajete planting, stone and maguey terracing, and fertilization. In the strip above 2,000 m. the possibilities of early frost and retarded rainy season made irrigation necessary for really effective cultivation, even though 500–800mm. of summer rains would ordinarily be ample. The application of this body of practices resulted in an extremely dense population as contrasted to other areas of Mesoamerica. I have postulated that civilizations with a Neolithic technological base can only develop with a relatively dense population. I furthermore insist that urbanization can develop only under even more demanding demographic conditions, especially in Mesoamerica, with hand tillage. I doubt that the Neolithic farmer with hand tools can produce more than a twenty percent surplus. A city of 100,000 population would require a rural population of 500,000 to support it. In the history of the Nuclear Area, two cities, Tenochtitlan and Teotihuacán reached that size.

2. One of the attributes of an urban community is nucleation. In Gordon Childe's analysis of Mesopotamia (1954), he discusses the process as one of increasing size and social complexity from the Neolithic village to the Copper Age town to the Bronze Age city. In this concept the process begins with a small nucleated community. In terms of the *origin* of urban societies the presence of a rural population living in nucleated as opposed to dispersed communities seems to me a necessary requirement for such a development. Furthermore, in the transition period of growth from village to city, agriculture continued as the primary base, so that intensive agriculture would seem to be a necessary condition for such demographic growth, since the agricultural land still remains relatively accessible even when the population runs into the thousands. My analysis of rural settlement patterns in modern Mesoamerica, and documentary and archeological studies of the pre-Hispanic periods, suggests that the rural settlement pattern in our Nuclear Area from the early pre-Classic to the modern period was basically one of nucleated villages. In the Nuclear Area today the degree of nucleation of the rural community correlates directly with the intensity of agriculture.

3. One of the characteristic features of our Nuclear Area, as was stated previously, is ecological diversity. This is true of most of the Mesoamerican Highlands. At the time of the conquest and in some of the Highlands today we find an intensive development of regional trade and specialization on a rural community level. As Sol Tax (1952) has pointed out, in the Highlands of southwestern Guatemala, rural communities depend as much on trade for their livelihood as do cities. Although geographical diversity is of course not

the only factor involved in this development, certainly it has acted as a powerful stimulus. If we argue that urbanization developed basically out of the agricultural folk society that supported it, and economic specialization is one of the most characteristic traits of urbanization, then the process by which urbanism evolved in Central Mexico seems apparent. Some urban communities grew up at crucial places, in terms of transportation, such as lake shore termini (Chalco) and altitude strips on the border of the Tierra Templada-Tierra Fria. Furthermore, in terms of the origins of cities and towns as centers of trade and craft specialization, the closeness of ecological zoning in Mesoamerica was an important precondition because of the primitiveness of land transportation.

4. One of the major problems in Mesoamerica as a whole in the support of urban communities was the feeble development of transportation technology. By land, all cargo was hauled by human carriers so that only the closeness of ecological zoning permitted a relatively close spacing of markets and a heavy volume of trade. The chain of lakes in the Valley of Mexico provided a powerful stimulus to trade and undoubtedly was one of the crucial factors in the development of urbanism.

5. Palerm, Wolf, Millon and Armillas in various papers have attempted to apply the concept of the Irrigation State to the Nuclear Area, but, thus far, with inconclusive results. One of the major problems in setting up a theoretical construct is purely archeological, the lack of data on the age of irrigation in the area. We know, on the basis of documentary and archeological evidence, that it was of great significance during the Aztec period; but it has not been specifically established for the Teotihuacán period where we have evidence for the first large state and urban community in the area. One important difference between our area and the center of Old World civilization is in the hydrographic pattern. In the Nuclear Area there are a great number of separate systems, each of which during the Aztec period provided water for a small, distinct, integrated irrigated system. Of interest with respect to this is the fact that the city state, made up of a small urban town and its dependent villages, was the largest *stable* political grouping. This is in contrast to Egypt where the normal pattern was political unification of the entire river valley. Supra-city state aggregations did occur several times in the Nuclear Area, but the constituent city states maintained their separate political and social structure and were never integrated into a state of the Egyptian type.

I am not arguing here, of course, that political states of the size of ancient Egypt, or even larger, could not exist in the environment of Central Mexico (the case of the Inca of Peru obviously makes this position untenable). What I am saying is that, in this type of ecology, city-state political integration is the largest level that one can link directly with ecological factors. Palerm and Wolf, in a brilliant essay on the rise of the state of Acolhuacan on the east shore of the lake in the Valley of Mexico, have pointed out the subtle interrelationships between environment, agricultural technology, and sociopolitical systems (Wolf and Palerm, 1955). In this case they postulated the integrative effects of irrigation on the state, but went further and demonstrated, in this area, that the state, once created, regardless of the factors that produced it, acted as a sponsor of extensive irrigation works and as a mechanism of producing a surplus to strengthen its power and further integrate the socioeconomic system.

6. The Nuclear Area is chronically one of overpopulation, a characteristic feature of mountain countries. Population clusters are isolated by high ranges and barren hills into separate compartments. Good flat land is premium land and never abundant so that the topography has always presented serious obstacles to an expanding population. This problem was met by improvement of agricultural technology, but, I suspect, that by Teotihuacán times the basic inventions had all been completed, except probably chinampa agriculture. It could also be met by social techniques, such as a thorough integration of the population by a system of centralized control for the construction of hydraulic works, terraces, and expansion into marginal lands.

Trade itself is one way of meeting the problem, since maguey, a staple food, can grow on even the most barren hillsides, and specialization of crop production would further increase the efficiency of land use. Spanish descriptions of the control of agriculture by the state suggest that, in fact, by 1519 such social techniques were practiced. Another response is, of course, war, conflict, and conquest between the city states and the expropriation of lands or systematic taxation of conquered groups. This in turn would of course strengthen the power of the state and was one of the factors responsible for the growth of towns into cities. Cook, in an article on Mesoamerican demography, considered war as a demographic safety valve along with human sacrifice.

It has only been in relatively recent times that the concepts of Old World culture history have been applied to Mesoamerica, under the leadership of Julian Steward in the United States and Pedro Armillas in Mexico. H. J. Spinden (1928) anticipated this recent development in the 1920s, but he remains a lone pioneer. The lack of such attempts between the years 1930–1950 demands some explanation, since this period was an exceedingly productive one in basic research in Mesoamerican archeology. The primary reason was undoubtedly the development of research in the Maya Lowlands, where archeological exploration revealed the presence of an extraordinarily rich regional variant of Mesoamerican civilization in a humid forested lowland plain. This discouraged attempts to relate the growth of the civilization to environmental factors. Such research developments furthermore tended to obscure the fact that most of Mesoamerica is, in fact, a subhumid area. Excluding most of the Yucatan Peninsula, parts of the Gulf Coast, narrow strips of escarpment, a few small segments of the Pacific coast, and parts of the Guatemala Highlands, rainfall over most of this huge area is either less than 1,000mm. a year, or is so irregular from year to year that some techniques of humidity conservation are necessary for an effective enough system of agriculture to provide the demographic basis of a civilization.

The primary agricultural system in most of Lowland Mesoamerica is one called variously in the literature slash and burn, swidden, shifting cultivation, and, in Mexico, roza. It is a system practiced all over the world in tropical areas and, even where iron tools are used, it tends to be correlated with a low population density and a simple folk rural society residing in small, socially autonomous communities. This generalization is even more valid if we apply it to cultures with Neolithic technologies. A variant of it was apparently practiced by Neolithic societies in humid northern environments as well (northern and central Europe, eastern U.S.) (Childe, 1951).

In the New World, outside of Mesoamerica, this system of farming was practiced all over the lowlands of eastern South America and around the Carribean; and nowhere in this huge area was it the base of a culture of the type we are calling civilization.

The occurrence of Mesoamerican civilization in the tropical lowlands of Mesoamerica, based on slash and burn agriculture, is a unique one and demands further explanation. On the basis of published settlement pattern studies in the Petén and my own studies in northern Yucatan, Tabasco, central Vera Cruz, and the Huasteca, one can say that urbanism was not a correlative trait with civilization in those areas. The density of housemounds at sites such as Tikal, Uaxactún, Chichén Itzá, and the Puuc sites is well within the range of a rural, or at least suburban, population. Bullard (1960), in his survey of a large area of the northern Petén, found a surprising lack of correspondence of house clusters to major ceremonial complexes. Apparently the settlement pattern was composed of two basic social levels: (1) a ceremonial center with a small resident priest-craftsman population as the dominant level, and (2) hundreds of small dependent rural hamlets occurring in a nearly continuous distribution between the ceremonial centers. This demographic and social pattern clearly relates to slash and burn agriculture and the primitiveness of Mesoamerican transportation. Apparently the system will permit a dense enough population to support a civilization of the Mesoamerican type but not urbanism, and the demands of this system for space tend to produce a dispersed agricultural population.

In recent years there has been a gradual crystallization of two opposed theoretical positions in the interpretation of the culture history of Mesoamerica: (1) in one position the area of the birth and early development is thought to have occurred in the humid lowlands based on slash and burn agriculture; (2) in the other, the development of civilization is seen as a corollary process with urbanization and occurring first in some part of the subhumid highlands with intensive agriculture. It is postulated that it then spread into the humid lowlands where, because of the ecological conditions, the development of urbanism was aborted.

Archeological data per se cannot, at the present state of knowledge, resolve the conflict one way or the other. I have, of course, as the previous discussion indicates, accepted this latter approach. Specifically my position may be elaborated in the following points:

1. Mesoamerican civilization developed first in Central Mexico as a corollary process with urbanization.

2. This kind of culture which we are calling civilization must have its roots in the folk society, that was its basal level and required the special kind of folk society that intensive agriculture produces. I see very little in the

character or personality of a slash and burn folk society or economy that would lead to the development of civilization.

3. The spread of Mesoamerican civilization into the lowlands was a process directly related to the regional pattern of specialization and symbiosis we discussed previously. As civilizations expanded in the highlands and immediate lowland strips, then the trade orbits were extended all the way to the coast and all of the lowland province shared in the general civilization. This did not occur in the Andean region, primarily because there was a lowland strip along the Pacific coast which had the proper ecological conditions for intensive agriculture. In Mesoamerica, subhumid lowland areas were more restricted in extent and so the humid areas were incorporated.

4. The spread of Mesoamerican civilization into the humid lowlands was only a partial success, as the spectacular collapse of the Petén Maya civilization demonstrates. The fall of Maya civilization was qualitatively different from the fall of the contemporary Classic civilization of Teotihuacán. In the case of the latter, newer and equally vigorous civilizations replaced it, and the collapse occurred only in the upper, urban level. All of the evidence, archeological and documentary, in the Petén demonstrates that there not only the upper level but the folk agricultural society collapsed as well. There is very little evidence of a post-Classic population in the area, and Spanish records give one the impression that the population in the sixteenth century was nearly as sparse as the modern.

REFERENCES

Armillas, P. "Teotihuacán Tula y los Toltecs." *Runa* 3 (1950): 37-40. Buenos Aires Archivo para las Ciencas del Hombre.

Bullard, W. R. "Maya Settlement Patterns in Northeastern Petén, Guatemala." *American Antiquity* 25 (1960): 355-372.

Childe, V. G. *Social Evolution*. New York: Henry Schuman, Inc., 1951.

Childe, V. G. *What Happened in History*. London: Pelican Books, 1954.

Millon, R. "Irrigation Systems in the Valley of Teotihuacán." *American Antiquity* 23 (1957): 160-166.

Palerm, A. "La distribution del regadio en el area central de Mesoamerica." *Ciencas Sociales, Notas y Informacion*, Union Pan American 5 (1954): 64-74.

Palerm, A. "The Agricultural Bases of Urban Civilization in Mexoamerica." In *Irrigation Civilizations: A Comparative Study*. Pan American Union, Social Science Monographs, 1955.

Kroeber, A. L. *Anthropology*. New York: Harcourt, Brace and Co., 1948.

Sanders, W. T. *The Central Mexican Symbiotic Region: A Study in Prehistoric Settlement Patterns*. Viking Fund Publication No. 23 (1956): 115-128.

Spinden, H. J. *Ancient Civilizations of Mexico and Central America*. American Museum of Natural History. Handbook Series No. 3, 3rd and revised edition, 1927.

Tax, S. *Heritage of Conquest*. Glencoe: The Free Press, 1952.

Wolf, E. R. and Palerm, A. "Irrigation in the Old Acolhua Domain, Mexico." *Southwest Journal of Anthropology* 11 (1955): 265-281.

Section H. The Classic
Pre-Industrial City

Greece

THE POLIS

H. D. F. Kitto

"Polis" is the Greek word which we translate "city-state." It is a bad translation, because the normal polis was not much like a city, and was very much more than a state. But translation, like politics, is the art of the possible; since we have not got the thing which the Greeks called "the polis," we do not possess an equivalent word. From now on, we will avoid the misleading term "city-state," and use the Greek word instead. In this chapter we will first inquire how this political system arose, then we will try to reconstitute the word "polis" and recover its real meaning by watching it in action. It may be a long task, but all the time we shall be improving our acquaintance with the Greeks. Without a clear conception what the polis was, and what it meant to the Greeks, it is quite impossible to understand properly Greek history, the Greek mind, or the Greek achievement.

First then, what was the polis? In the *Iliad* we discern a political structure that seems not unfamiliar—a structure that can be called an advanced or a degenerate form of tribalism, according to taste. There are kings, like Achilles, who rule their people, and there is the great king, Agamemnon, King of Men, who is something like a feudal overlord. He is under obligation, whether of right or of custom, to consult the other kings or chieftains in matters of common interest. They form a regular council, and in its debates the sceptre, symbol of authority, is held by the speaker for the time being. This is recognizably European, not Oriental; Agamemnon is no despot, ruling with the unquestioned authority of a god. There are also signs of a shadowy Assembly of the People, to be consulted on important occasions: though Homer, a

From *The Polis* © 1951, 1957, by H.D.F. Kitto. Reprinted by permission of Penguin Books Ltd.

courtly poet, and in any case not a constitutional historian, says little about it.

Such, in outline, is the tradition about preconquest Greece. When the curtain goes up again after the Dark Age we see a very different picture. No longer is there a "wide-ruling Agamemnon" lording it in Mycenae. In Crete, where Idomeneus had been ruling as sole king, we find over fifty quite independent poleis, fifty small "states" in the place of one. It is a small matter that the kings have disappeared; the important thing is that the kingdoms have gone too. What is true of Crete is true of Greece in general, or at least of those parts which play any considerable part in Greek history—Ionia, the islands, the Peloponnesus except Arcadia, central Greece except the western parts, and south Italy and Sicily when they became Greek. All these were divided into an enormous number of quite independent and autonomous political units.

It is important to realize their size. The modern reader picks up a translation of Plato's *Republic* or Aristotle's *Politics;* he finds Plato ordaining that his ideal city shall have 5,000 citizens, and Aristotle that each citizen should be able to know all the others by sight; and he smiles, perhaps, at such philosophical fantasies. But Plato and Aristotle are not fantasts. Plato is imagining a polis on the normal Hellenic scale; indeed he implies that many existing Greek poleis are too small—for many had less than 5,000 citizens. Aristotle says, in his amusing way—Aristotle sometimes sounds very like a don—that a polis of ten citizens would be impossible, because it could not be self-sufficient, and that a polis of a hundred thousand would be absurd, because it could not govern itself properly. And we are not to think of these "citizens" as a "master-class" owning and dominating thousands of slaves. The ordinary Greek in these early centuries was a farmer, and if he owned a slave he was doing pretty well. Aristotle speaks of a hundred thousand citizens; if we allow each to have a wife and four children, and then add a liberal number of slaves and resident aliens, we shall arrive at something like a million—the population of Birmingham; and to Aristotle an independent "state" as populous as Birmingham is a lecture-room joke. Or we may turn from the philosophers to a practical man, Hippodamas, who laid out the Piraeus in the most up-to-date American style; he said that the ideal number of citizens was ten thousand, which would imply a total population of about 100,000.

In fact, only three poleis had more than 20,000 citizens—Syracuse and Acragas (Girgenti) in Sicily, and Athens. At the outbreak of the Peloponnesian War the population of Attica was probably about 350,000, half Athenian (men, women and children), about a tenth resident aliens, and the rest slaves. Sparta, or Lacedaemon, had a much smaller citizen-body, though it was larger in area. The Spartans had conquered and annexed Messenia, and possessed 3,200 square miles of territory. By Greek standards this was an enormous area: it would take a good walker two days to cross it. The important commercial city of Corinth had a territory of 330 square miles—about the size of Huntingdonshire. The island of Ceos, which is about as big as Bute, was divided into four poleis. It had therefore four armies, four governments, possibly four different calendars, and, it may be, four different currencies and systems of measures—though this is less likely. Mycenae was in historical times a shrunken relic of Agamemnon's capital, but still independent. She sent an army to help the Greek cause against Persia at the battle of Plataea; the army consisted of eighty men. Even by Greek standards this was small, but we do not hear that any jokes were made about an army sharing a cab.

To think on this scale is difficult for us, who regard a state of ten million as small, and are accustomed to states which, like the U.S.A. and the U.S.S.R., are so big that they have to be referred to by their initials; but when the adjustable reader has become accustomed to the scale, he will not commit the vulgar error of confusing size with significance. The modern writer is sometimes heard to speak with splendid scorn of "those petty Greek states, with their interminable quarrels." Quite so; Plataea, Sicyon, Aegina and the rest are petty, compared with modern states. The Earth itself is petty, compared with Jupiter—but then, the atmosphere of Jupiter is mainly ammonia, and that makes a difference. We do not like breathing ammonia—and the Greeks would not much have liked breathing the atmosphere of the vast modern State. They knew of one such, the Persian Empire—and thought it very suitable, for barbarians. Difference of scale, when it is great enough, amounts to difference of kind.

But before we deal with the nature of the polis, the reader might like to know how it happened that the relatively spacious pattern of pre-Dorian Greece became such a mosaic of small fragments. The Classical scholar too would like to know; there are no records, so that all we can do is to suggest plausible reasons. There are historical, geographical and economic reasons; and when these have been duly set forth, we may conclude perhaps that the most important reason of all is simply that this is the way in which the Greeks preferred to live.

The coming of the Dorians was not an attack made by one organized nation upon another. The invaded indeed had their organization, loose though it was; some of the invaders—the main body that conquered Lacedaemon—must have been a coherent force; but others must have been small groups of raiders, profiting from the general turmoil and seizing good land where they could find it. A sign of this is that we find members of the same clan in different states. Pindar, for example, was a citizen of Thebes and a member of the ancient family of the Aegidae. But there were Aegidae too in Aegina and Sparta, quite independent poleis, and Pindar addresses them as kinsmen. This particular clan therefore was split up in the invasions. In a country like Greece this would be very natural.

In a period so unsettled the inhabitants of any valley or island might at a moment's notice be compelled to fight for their fields. Therefore a local strong-point was necessary, normally a defensible hill top somewhere in the plain. This, the "acropolis" ("high-town"), would be fortified, and here would be the residence of the king. It would also be the natural place of assembly, and the religious center.

This is the beginning of the town. What we have to do is to give reasons why the town grew, and why such a small pocket of people remained an independent political unit. The former task is simple. To begin with, natural economic growth made a central market necessary. We saw that the economic system implied by Hesiod and Homer was "close household economy"; the estate, large or small, produced nearly everything that it needed, and what it could not produce it did without. As things became more stable a rather more specialized economy became possible: more goods were produced for sale. Hence the growth of a market.

At this point we may invoke the very sociable habits of the Greeks, ancient or modern. The English farmer likes to build his house on his land, and to come into town when he has to. What little leisure he has he likes to spend on the very satisfying occupation of looking over a gate. The Greek prefers to live in the town or village, to walk out to his work, and to spend his rather ampler leisure talking in the town or village square. Therefore the market becomes a market-town, naturally beneath the Acropolis. This became the center of the communal life of the people—and we shall see presently how important that was.

But why did not such towns form larger units? This is the important question.

There is an economic point. The physical barriers which Greece has so abundantly made the transport of goods difficult, except by sea, and the sea was not yet used with any confidence. Moreover, the variety of which we spoke earlier enabled quite a small area to be reasonably self-sufficient for a people who made such small material demands on life as the Greek. Both of these facts tend in the same direction; there was in Greece no great economic interdependence, no reciprocal pull between the different parts of the country, strong enough to counteract the desire of the Greek to live in small communities.

There is a geographical point. It is sometimes asserted that this system of independent poleis was imposed on Greece by the physical character of the country. The theory is attractive, especially to those who like to have one majestic explanation of any phenomenon, but it does not seem to be true. It is of course obvious that the physical subdivision of the country helped; the system could not have existed, for example, in Egypt, a country which depends entirely on the proper management of the Nile flood, and therefore must have a central government. But there are countries cut up quite as much as Greece—Scotland, for instance—which have never developed the polis-system; and conversely there were in Greece many neighboring poleis, such as Corinth and Sicyon, which remained independent of each other although between them there was no physical barrier that would seriously incommode a modern cyclist. Moreover, it was precisely the most mountainous parts of Greece that never developed poleis, or not until later days—Arcadia and Aetolia, for example, which had something like a canton-system. The polis flourished in those parts where communications were relatively easy. So that we are still looking for our explanation.

Economics and geography helped, but the real explanation is the character of the Greeks—which those determinists may explain who have the necessary faith in their omniscience. As it will take some time to deal with this, we may first clear out of the way an important historical point. How did it come about that so preposterous a system was able to last for more than twenty minutes?

The ironies of history are many and bitter, but at least this must be put to the credit of the gods, that they arranged for the Greeks to have the Eastern Mediterranean almost to themselves long enough to work out what was almost a laboratory experiment to test how far, and in what conditions, human nature is capable of creating and sustaining a civilization. In Asia, the Hittite Empire had collapsed, the Lydian kingdom was not aggressive, and the Persian power, which eventually overthrew Lydia, was still embryonic in the mountainous recesses of the continent; Egypt was in decay; Macedon, destined to make nonsense of the polis-system, was and long remained in a state of ineffective semibarbarism; Rome had not yet been heard of, nor any other power in Italy. There were indeed the Phoenicians, and their western colony, Carthage, but these were traders first and last. Therefore this lively and intelligent Greek people was for some centuries allowed to live under the apparently absurd system which suited and developed its genius instead of becoming absorbed in the dull mass of a large empire, which would have smothered its spiritual growth, and made it what it afterwards became, a race of brilliant individuals and opportunists. Obviously some day somebody would create a strong centralized power in the eastern Mediterranean—a successor to the ancient sea-power of King Minos. Would it be Greek, Oriental, or something else? This question must be the theme of a later chapter, but no history of Greece can be intelligible until one has understood what the polis meant to the Greek; and when we have understood that, we shall also understand why the Greeks developed it, and so obstinately tried to maintain it. Let us then examine the word in action.

It meant at first that which was later called the Acropolis, the stronghold of the whole community and the center of its public life. The town which nearly always grew up around this was designated by another word, "asty." But "polis" very soon meant either the citadel or the whole people which, as it were, "used" this citadel. So we read in Thucydides, "Epidamnus is a polis on the right as you sail into the Ionian gulf." This is not like saying "Bristol is a city on the right as you sail up the Bristol Channel," for Bristol is not an independent state which might be at war with Gloucester, but only an urban area with a purely local administration. Thucydides' words imply that there is a town—though possibly a very small one—called Epidamnus, which is the political centre of the Epidamnians, who live in the territory of which the town is the center—not the "capital"—and are Epidamnians whether they live in the town or in one of the villages in this territory.

Sometimes the territory and the town have different names. Thus, Attica is the territory occupied by the Athenian people; it comprised Athens— the "polis" in the narrower sense—the Piraeus, and many villages; but the people collectively were Athenians, not Attics, and a citizen was an Athenian in whatever part of Attica he might live.

In this sense "polis" is our "state." In Sophocles' *Antigone* Creon comes forward to make his first proclamation as king. He begins, "Gentlemen, as for the polis, the gods have brought it safely through the storm, on even keel." It is the familiar image of the Ship of State, and we think we know where we are. But later in the play he says what we should naturally translate, "Public proclamation has been made . . ." He says in fact, "It has been proclaimed to the polis . . ."—not to the "state," but to the "people." Later in the play he quarrels violently with his son; "What?" he cries, "is anyone but me to rule in this land?" Haemon answers, "It is no polis that is ruled by one man only." The answer brings out another important part of the whole conception of a polis, namely that it is a community, and that its affairs are the affairs of all. The actual business of governing might be entrusted to a monarch, acting in the name of all according to traditional usages, or to the heads of certain noble families, or to a council of citizens owning so much property, or to all the citizens. All these, and many modifications of them, were natural forms of "polity"; all were sharply distinguished by the Greek from Oriental monarchy, in which the monarch is irresponsible, not holding his powers in trust by the grace of god, but being himself a god. If there was irresponsible government there was no polis. Haemon is accusing his father of talking like a "tyrannos"[1] and thereby destroying the polis—but not 'the State'.

To continue our exposition of the word. The chorus in Aristophanes' *Acharnians,* admiring the conduct of the hero, turns to the audience with an appeal which I render literally, "Dost thou see, O whole polis?" The last words are sometimes translated 'thou thronging city', which sounds better, but obscures an essential point, namely that the size of the polis made it possible for a member to appeal to all his fellow-citizens in person, and this he naturally did if he thought that another member of the polis had injured him. It was the common assumption of the Greeks that the polis took its origin in the desire for Justice. Individuals are lawless, but the polis will see to it that wrongs are redressed. But not by an elaborate machinery of state justice, for such a machine could not be operated except by individuals, who may be as unjust as the original wrongdoer. The injured party will be sure of obtaining justice only if he can declare his wrongs to the whole polis. The word therefore now means "people" in actual distinction from "state."

Iocasta, the tragic Queen in the *Oedipus,* will show us a little more of the range of the word. It becomes a question if Oedipus her husband is not after all the accursed man who had killed the previous king Laius. "No, no," cries Iocasta, "it cannot be! The slave said it was 'brigands' who had attacked them, not 'a brigand.' He cannot go back on his word now. The polis heard him, not I alone." Here the word is used without any "political" association at all; it is, as it were, off duty, and signifies "the whole people." This is a shade of meaning which is not always so prominent, but is never entirely absent.

Then Demosthenes the orator talks of a man who, literally, "avoids the city"—a translation which might lead the unwary to suppose that he lived in something corresponding to the Lake District, or Purley. But the phrase "avoids the polis" tells us nothing about his domicile; it means that he took no part in public life—and was therefore something of an oddity. The affairs of the community did not interest him.

We have now learned enough about the word polis to realize that there is no possible English rendering of such a common phrase as, "It is everyone's duty to help the polis." We cannot say "help the state," for that arouses no enthusiasm; it is "the state" that takes half our incomes from us. Not "the community," for with us "the community" is too big and too various to be grasped except theoretically. One's village, one's trade union, one's class, are entities that mean something to us at once, but "work for the community," though an admirable sentiment, is to most of us vague and flabby. In the years before the war, what did most parts of Great Britain know about the depressed areas? How much do bankers, miners and farm-workers understand each other? But the "polis" every Greek knew; there it was, complete, before his eyes. He could see the fields which gave it its sustenance—or did not, if the crops failed; he could see how agriculture, trade and industry dovetailed into one another; he knew the frontiers, where they were strong and where weak; if any malcontents were planning a coup, it was difficult for them to conceal the fact. The entire life of the polis, and the relation between its parts, were much easier to grasp, because of the small scale of things. Therefore to say "It is everyone's duty to help the polis" was not to express a fine sentiment but to speak the plainest and most urgent common sense.[2] Public affairs had an immediacy and a concreteness which they cannot possibly have for us.

One specific example will help. The Athenian democracy taxed the rich with as much disinterested enthusiasm as the British, but this could be done in a much more gracious way, simply because the State was so small and intimate. Among us, the payer of supertax (presumably) pays much as the income-tax payer does: he writes his check and thinks, "There! *That's* gone down the drain!" In Athens, the man whose wealth exceeded a certain sum had, in a yearly rota, to perform certain "liturgies"—literally, "folk-works." He had to keep a warship in commission for one year (with the privilege of commanding it, if he chose), or finance the production of plays at the Festival, or equip a religious procession. It was a heavy burden, and no doubt unwelcome, but at least some fun could be got out of it and some pride taken in it. There was satisfaction and honor to be gained from producing a trilogy worthily before one's fellow citizens. So, in countless other ways, the size of the polis made vivid and immediate, things which to us are only abstractions or wearisome duties. Naturally this cut both ways. For example, an incompetent or unlucky commander was the object not of a diffused and harmless popular indignation, but of direct accusation; he might be tried for his life before an Assembly, many of whose past members he had led to death.

Pericles' Funeral Speech, recorded or recreated by Thucydides, will illustrate this immediacy, and will also take our conception of the polis a little further. Each year, Thucydides tells us, if citizens had died in war—and they had, more often than not—a funeral oration was delivered by "a man chosen by the polis." Today, that would be someone nominated by the Prime

Minister, or the British Academy, or the B.B.C. In Athens it meant that someone was chosen by the Assembly who had often spoken to that Assembly; and on this occasion Pericles spoke from a specially high platform, that his voice might reach as many as possible. Let us consider two phrases that Pericles used in that speech.

He is comparing the Athenian polis with the Spartan, and makes the point that the Spartans admit foreign visitors only grudgingly, and from time to time expel all strangers, "while we make our polis common to all." "Polis" here is not the political unit; there is no question of naturalizing foreigners—which the Greeks did rarely, simply because the polis was so intimate a union. Pericles means here: "We throw open to all our common cultural life," as is shown by the words that follow, difficult though they are to translate: "nor do we deny them any instruction or spectacle"—words that are almost meaningless until we realize that the drama, tragic and comic, the performance of choral hymns, public recitals of Homer, games, were all necessary and normal parts of "political" life. This is the sort of thing Pericles has in mind when he speaks of "instruction and spectacle," and of "making the polis open to all."

But we must go further than this. A perusal of the speech will show that in praising the Athenian polis Pericles is praising more than a state, a nation, or a people: he is praising a way of life; he means no less when, a little later, he calls Athens the "school of Hellas"—And what of that? Do not we praise "the English way of life"? The difference is this; we expect our State to be quite indifferent to "the English way of life"—indeed, the idea that the State should actively try to promote it would fill most of us with alarm. The Greeks thought of the polis as an active, formative thing, training the minds and characters of the citizens; we think of it as a piece of machinery for the production of safety and convenience. The training in virtue, which the medieval state left to the Church, and the polis made its own concern, the modern state leaves to God knows what.

"Polis," then, originally "citadel," may mean as much as "the whole communal life of the people, political, cultural, moral"—even "economic," for how else are we to understand another phrase in this same speech, "the produce of the whole world comes to us, because of the magnitude of our polis"? This must mean "our national wealth."

Religion too was bound up with the polis—though not every form of religion.[3] The Olympian gods were indeed worshipped by Greeks everywhere, but each polis had, if not its own gods, at least its own particular cults of these gods. Thus, Athena of the Brazen House was worshipped at Sparta, but to the Spartans Athena was never what she was to the Athenians, "Athena Polias," Athena guardian of the City. So Hera, in Athens, was a goddess worshipped particularly by women, as the goddess of hearth and home, but in Argos "Argive Hera" was the supreme deity of the people. We have in these gods tribal deities, like Jehovah, who exist as it were on two levels at once, as gods of the individual polis, and gods of the whole Greek race. But beyond these Olympians, each polis had its minor local deities, "heroes" and nymphs, each worshipped with his immemorial rite, and scarcely imagined to exist outside the particular locality where the rite was performed. So that in spite of the panhellenic Olympian system, and in spite of the philosophic spirit which made merely tribal gods impossible for the Greek, there is a sense in which it is true to say that the polis is an independent religious, as well as political, unit. The tragic poets at least could make use of the old belief that the gods desert a city which is about to be captured. The gods are the unseen partners in the city's welfare.

How intimately religious and "political" thinking were connected we can best see from the *Oresteia* of Aeschylus. This trilogy is built around the idea of Justice. It moves from chaos to order, from conflict to reconciliation; and it moves on two planes at once, the human and the divine. In the *Agamemnon* we see one of the moral Laws of the universe, that punishment must follow crime, fulfilled in the crudest possible way; one crime evokes another crime to avenge it, in apparently endless succession—but always with the sanction of Zeus. In the *Choephori* this series of crimes reaches its climax when Orestes avenges his father by killing his mother. He does this with repugnance, but he is commanded to do it by Apollo, the son and the mouthpiece of Zeus—Why? Because in murdering Agamemnon the King and her husband, Clytemnestra has committed a crime which, unpunished, would shatter the very fabric of society. It is the concern of the Olympian gods to defend Order; they are particularly the gods of the Polis. But Orestes' matricide outrages the deepest human instincts; he is therefore implacably pursued by other deities, the Furies. The Furies have no interest in social order, but they cannot permit this outrage on the sacredness of the blood-tie, which it is their office to protect. In the *Eumenides* there is a terrific conflict between the ancient Furies and the younger Olympians over the unhappy Orestes. The solution is that Athena comes with a new dispensation from Zeus. A jury of Athenian citizens is empanelled to try Orestes on the Acropolis where he has fled for protection—this being the first meeting of the Council of the Areopagus. The votes on either side are equal; therefore, as an act of mercy, Orestes is acquitted. The Furies, cheated of their legitimate prey, threaten Attica with destruction, but Athena persuades them to make their home in Athens, with their ancient office not abrogated (as at first they think) but enhanced, since henceforth they will punish violence within the polis, not only within the family.

So, to Aeschylus the mature polis becomes the means by which the Law is satisfied without producing chaos, since public justice supersedes private vengeance; and the claims of authority are reconciled with the instincts of humanity. The trilogy ends with an impressive piece of pageantry. The awful Furies exchange their black robes for red ones, no longer Furies, but "Kindly Ones" (Eumenides); no longer enemies of Zeus, but his willing and honored agents, defenders of his now perfected social order against intestine violence. Before the eyes of the Athenian citizens assembled in the theater just under the Acropolis—and indeed guided by citizen-marshals—they pass out of the theater to their new home on the other side of the Acropolis. Some of the most acute of man's moral and social problems have been solved, and the means of the reconciliation is the Polis.

A few minutes later, on that early spring day of 458 B.C., the citizens too would leave the theater, and by the same exits as the Eumenides. In what mood? Surely no audience has had such an experience since. At the time, the Athenian polis was confidently riding the crest of the wave. In this trilogy there was exaltation, for they had seen their polis emerge as the pattern of Justice, of Order, of what the Greeks called Cosmos; the polis, they saw, was—or could be—the very crown and summit of things. They had seen their goddess herself acting as President of the first judicial tribunal—a steadying and sobering thought. But there was more than this. The rising democracy had recently curtailed the powers of the ancient Court of the Areopagus, and the reforming statesman had been assassinated by his political enemies. What of the Eumenides, the awful inhabitants of the land, the transformed Furies, whose function it was to avenge the shedding of a kinsman's blood? There was warning here, as well as exaltation, in the thought that the polis had its divine as well as its human members. There was Athena, one of those Olympians who had presided over the formation of ordered society, and there were the more primitive deities who had been persuaded by Athena to accept this pattern of civilized life, and were swift to punish any who, by violence from within, threatened its stability.

To such an extent was the religious thought of Aeschylus intertwined with the idea of the polis; and not of Aeschylus alone, but of many other Greek thinkers too—notably of Socrates, Plato, and Aristotle. Aristotle made a remark which we most inadequately translate "Man is a political animal." What Aristotle really said is "Man is a creature who lives in a polis"; and what he goes on to demonstrate, in his *Politics,* is that the polis is the only framework within which man can fully realize his spiritual, moral and intellectual capacities.

Such are some of the implications of this word: we shall meet more later, for I have deliberately said little about its purely "political" side—to emphasize the fact that it is so much more than a form of political organization. The polis was a living community, based on kinship, real or assumed—a kind of extended family, turning as much as possible of life into family life, and of course having its family quarrels, which were the more bitter because they were family quarrels.

This it is that explains not only the polis but also much of what the Greek made and thought, that he was essentially social. In the winning of his livelihood he was essentially individualist: in the filling of his life he was essentially "communist." Religion, art, games, the discussion of things—all these were needs of life that could be fully satisfied only through the polis— not, as with us, through voluntary associations of like-minded people, or through *entrepreneurs* appealing to individuals. (This partly explains the difference between Greek drama and the modern cinema.) Moreover, he wanted to play his own part in running the affairs of the community. When we realize how many of the necessary, interesting and exciting activities of life the Greek enjoyed through the polis, all of them in the open air, within sight of the same acropolis, with the same ring of mountains or of sea visibly enclosing the life of every member of the state—then it becomes possible to understand

Greek history, to understand that in spite of the promptings of common sense the Greek could not bring himself to sacrifice the polis, with its vivid and comprehensive life, to a wider but less interesting unity. We may perhaps record an Imaginary Conversation between an Ancient Greek and a member of the Athenaeum. The member regrets the lack of political sense shown by the Greeks. The Greek replies, "How many clubs are there in London?" The member, at a guess, says about five hundred. The Greek then says, "Now, if all these combined, what splendid premises they could build. They could have a club-house as big as Hyde Park." "But," says the member, "that would no longer be a club." "Precisely," says the Greek, "and a polis as big as yours is no longer a polis."

After all, modern Europe, in spite of its common culture, common interests, and ease of communication, finds it difficult to accept the idea of limiting national sovereignty, though this would increase the security of life without notably adding to its dullness; the Greek had possibly more to gain by watering down the polis—but how much more to lose. It was not common sense that made Achilles great, but certain other qualities.

FOOTNOTES

1. I prefer to use the Greek form of this (apparently) Oriental word. It is the Greek equivalent of "dictator," but does not necessarily have the color of our word "tyrant."

2. It did not, of course, follow that the Greek obeyed common sense any oftener than we do.

3. Not the mystery-religions. . . .

HEALTH AND THE COURSE OF CIVILIZATION
AS SEEN IN ANCIENT GREECE

J. Lawrence Angel

Plato considered the physician a demierge, one who worked for the good of the demos or people, just as did the artists, potters, or engineers of Athens in the fifth century B.C. At the same time patients were receiving priestly cures in the abata or dream-houses of the Asklepieia and other temples of healing deities. (6,10,14) There are no statistics on the number of patients, cures, or relative frequencies of diseases treated by empirical doctors or by priests. But nevertheless the social scientist is intrigued by the possible connection between civilized life and people's concern over disease and public health. Are civilized peoples really less healthy than Rousseau's natural man? What light can researches of the historian and anthropologist direct toward our own problems of health and civilization?

A gigantic multiplication of people has accompanied the colonial expansion and exploitation which both stimulated and profited by the Industrial Revolution (17:73-80). During this expansion and increase in Western wealth the scientists of the later nineteenth century reacted to the crowding, poverty and depressed health of industrial populations as much as to the possibilities for advance in metallurgy or in transport or in warfare. Hence Western peoples have benefited by the amazing advances in control of disease which we have made in the last two generations. This is familiar to every one not only in the lowering of infant mortality and such diseases as typhoid fever and tuberculosis but even more graphically in our longer life expectancy, our increasing

From *The Intern,* Jan.-Feb. 1948. Reprinted by permission of the author.

176

stature, and the steady breaking of athletic records. This is a rosy picture. It is so rosy that we hardly hear the warnings of ecologists and soil experts that we are eating from borrowed land, or the opinions of physicians and anthropologists that we are still disease-bound, increasingly neurotic, and multiplying too fast and thoughtlessly. We are apt to think of our exceptional health and medical achievements as unique and permanent. Hence in planning the world's future it is easy to ignore health, in spite of the famine-haunted state of Asia, and to concentrate on atomic warfare, power politics, and dialectics.

Any scientist is skeptical of such values. He must find out whether similar optimum health was approached in the development of other civilizations. And he must ask if there is any connection between decline in health and schism of civilization. Data to answer these two questions is lacking for ancient Mesopotamia or even for Renaissance Europe, but for ancient Greece we have enough at least for an hypothesis.

Though skeletal remains of ancient Greeks are still scanty, they cover a 4,000 year span and give us several statistically significant trends. (2) Between prehistoric and historic times there was a great increase in body size accompanied by increased "roundness" of shafts of long bones and by various heterogenic changes in proportions (relative lengthening of forearm and of thigh, higher talus, probably deeper pelvis, etc.). Most of this occurred in a few centuries before 500 B.C. (2) And the average length of adult life increased at the same time. (4) Other possible trends are not statistically significant. There is an apparent decrease in incidence of arthritis from ca. twenty-five percent to twelve percent minima, and in diseased teeth from sixteen percent to thirteen percent. (2,3) Osteoporosis occurred only in early prehistoric times (and again in the Middle Ages). Cemetery statistics point to a great decrease in infant mortality. (4) And excavated sites show a great increase in population. (2,3) These observations are enough for us to assume a real improvement in health during the half dozen generations before 500 B.C. parallel to the second and greatest rise of Greek civilization.

Improved health must have made available greater energy than existed in prehistoric Greece. But what improved the people's health?

The diet of the earliest farmers to settle Greece was already very varied, with many fruits, green herbs, wild game, olives, grapes, beans, cheeses, and wheat-bread to supplement the staple barley plus mutton or fish. (2,3,5) But it has always been hard to raise enough good wheat or really large herds of cattle in a country with clayey, calcium-soaked or porous volcanic soils and only twenty to twenty-five percent of the land surface cultivable by the most painstaking methods. (3,9,15) Hence in pre-Greek times population pressure and concomitant below optimum diet and health must have been the norm. After the Greek-speaking invaders had mixed with their predecessors and had taken over Minoan urban civilization in the second millennium B.C. the Mycenaean civilization dominated Greece with a wealthy prince in his little city running each farming valley. The concentration of nonrural population, leisure for specialized officials and craftsmen, and especially the growth of sea enterprise (5) were possible only because of a bigger food supply from such improvements in farming as the oxdrawn plough, presumably also the tribola for threshing, and the use of fertilizer, proper fallowing, terracing, and irrigation. (3) But except for the palaces, Mycenaean Greek houses were cramped and cold, the water supply was still entirely from wells and rain-water reservoirs, there was no regular sewage system, and no state expenditure except for luxuries, chariot-warfare, and possibly marsh-drainage. Thus a major cause of the slump of the paternalistic Mycenaean civilization was overpopulation (which can never be relieved by emigration alone (17)) and the economic competition over a revolutionary new metal, iron (3,5) and not the invasion of the Dorians.

The advances before this decline of 1200–900 B.C. may be background causes for improved general health which we have just observed to accompany the recovery and astonishingly quick further growth of Greek culture from 800–500 B.C. There were no great early Iron Age inventions in farming, though a mass of acute soil, crop, and weather observations had accumulated by the eighth century for Hesiod's "Farmers' Almanac." And with the new and much more efficient iron tools farming technique was accelerated in spite of growth of large estates and slave labor. (7,9) At this time also temperate zone climates were becoming damper and milder (700–300 B.C.) By the sixth century B.C. the more urban parts of Greece were making further improvements in diet. As a reflex of the great trading and colonizing expansion of the immediately preceding generations, wheat for the city bread supply began to be imported in increasing bulk, and such nutritious novelties as the domestic fowl were introduced from the Near East in exchange for olive oil, wine, wool, and silver coins. (3,5,7) It is even possible that the massive introduction of the rich new protein food, hens' eggs, may have had a greater beneficial effect on health and mental energy than a per capita increase in wheat.

Housing also had improved by the fifth century B.C., and new cities were laid out in a grid pattern with underground sewers beginning to supplant open gutter drains and with well-engineered underground aqueducts for public fountains supplementing private wells and cisterns. (7,13) Houses were of several stories around a central court and light well, were oriented to make best use of a southern exposure for warmth, were equipped with wooden couches and beds, and normally had the bathroom placed to use the heat from the open flue leading out of the kitchen. (12) But extra heat in winter came entirely from charcoal braziers (or from olive oil lamps used for light after dark) and there was no adaptation of the draught-drawn potter's furnace for domestic heating even by the fourth century B.C. in snowy Macedonia. Ancient Greeks simply did not have our Northern sealed houses with central heating (except later for public baths). And it is likely that their outdoor life, light clothing, nudity for working, athletics, or fighting, frequent baths, and use of olive oil for skin protection during the open-air months of the year inured them to indoor temperatures of 40 or 45 degrees F. in their winter woolens. Wool was the normal fiber for clothing. In spite of disadvantages from our effete standpoint the average Classical Greek enjoyed a level of diet, housing, and hygiene superior to that of the rulers in Mycenaean or earlier times (and far better than the nineteenth century A.D.). (15)

The same was true of the science of medicine. By the sixth to fourth centuries B.C. empirical physicians (especially the Hippocratic guild) originally from Ionia had largely outstripped the miracle cures of the temple cults and the traditional herb lore dating back past such mythical figures as Chiron. (14,18) The surgical part of such lore had of course remained practical at least since Homeric times and probably from a much earlier period, to judge from setting of fractures in the Bronze Age. In Classical Athens both state and private physicians were treating patients in their homes and Greek doctors had earned the highest reputation in the ancient world, finally reaching a level not passed until the nineteenth century. (14) And free scientific curiosity, observation, and experiment, though often haphazard, were sources of better techniques in farming and city engineering as well as in medicine. (5)

In Greece at least it is quite clear that health improved as a result of the first real growth of civilization and in turn made possible further growth. The civilized Greek of the fifth century B.C. was far healthier than his "primitive" hoe-farming ancestors just as we enjoy better health than our eighteenth century forebears. But was health maintained by civilized life, with its new leisure, its stimuli to all sorts of creative and political activities, its medical and natural science, its warfare, conquests, and depressions, its slavery and its waste? The answer to this question is even more vital to us. It is not an encouraging answer.

Not that a decline in Greek energy is at all obvious. In fact in the fourth and third centuries B.C., after the failure of Athens to unify the Greeks, individual Greek philosophers, scientists, generals, artists, and even mercenaries and slaves provided the most expansive creative force in the ancient world. But decline in energy is increasingly clear in the reduction of the Athenian birthrate in the second century B.C., (16) in Greece's inelastic recovery under Rome's "mild" totalitarianism, and in her inability to repair the material damages of invasions, bubonic plague, earthquakes, and erosion in the first millennium A.D. or to repopulate the countryside. Most of this can be laid to socioeconomic failures of the city state pattern: failure to substitute machines for slaves, to avoid warfare, to conserve natural resources of all sorts (soil, minerals, forests, people), or through either Stoic or Christian sense of brotherhood to take real advantages of the stimulus of mixing populations. (3)

Decline in energy also presupposes decline in health, though this is most subtle. Skeletal remains from the historic period are still too scanty to prove physical deterioration. Though an urban pattern of dental occlusion (more overbites) becomes clear in the Roman period, it is not until the later Middle Ages that dental deterioration reaches the modern low point. There may also be a slight reduction in stature. The best known indication is the plague at Athens in 429 B.C., brought from Africa to a war-wearied population through the port of Piraeus. In spite of Thucydides' meticulous description the disease has not been identified, possibly because it may have been a first and hence atypical response to an exotic disease organism. From this time onward there is a great increase in popular as well as medical interest in all sorts of disease. (14,15) Typhoid fever, dysenteries, and diphtheria are familiar as well as such afflictions as pleurisy and pulmonary tuberculosis. (11,14,15) But the main proof of poorer health is the indentification of malaria as endemic from the end of the fifth century B.C. onward. (1,11) Jones identifies it from the description of intermittent fevers with splenomegaly, bilious complexion, nervousness, and "melancholia" (a new word first found in Aristophanes). Though there are possible hints at malaria in Theognis, (11) in Homer, (11) and even in earlier mythological times (15) the significant thing is the spread of malaria through the whole population of Attica by the fourth century B.C., (1) with such consequences as reduced endurance and fertility, dysgenic social selection, and even increasingly pessimistic philosophy. (11)

It is stimulating to argue that a decline in health starting by 400 B.C. is an illusion resulting from medical advances which led to accurate identification of diseases like malaria, typhoid, or tuberculosis which previously had been unidentified, just as the statistical increase in neoplastic disease in our own society seems largely a result of better identification. Of course this must be one reason for the increase in descriptions of disease. But Greek medical science continued to advance rapidly in the fourth century and in Hellenistic times, with pioneer work in anatomical and physiological details as well as in such techniques as drainage of the pleural cavity or such observations as the distinction between liver induration and jaundice. (14) This advance would seem to reflect increase rather than diminution of therapeutic need. A stronger indication of poorer general health is great increase from the fourth century onward in size and numbers of religious sanctuaries with their abata in which priests supervised sleeping patients who might be healed by dreaming or "incubation." (6,18) Votive offerings of "cured" parts of the body include eyes, ears, tongue, limbs, breasts, and genitals, very realistic though seldom with pathology represented. Jones notes that eye diseases are often described in conjunction with malarial symptoms and quotes Rouse's observation (11) that votive eyes are amazingly common in the fourth century.

This revived temple theurgy was quackery in contrast to the scientific medicine which had outdistanced it in the fifth century B.C. But Epidaurus, Corinth, and other centers of temple healing took on the qualities of modern health resorts with hotels, baths, and theaters. And they served a useful function in giving relaxation to the confused citizens. (14) In fact their rise seems a response to an hypochondriac interest in health which the Greeks began to develop as part of a neurotic reaction to the personal insecurities of the city state political turmoil in the fourth century. Thus the votive tablets of temple cures exactly parallel our magazine and radio advertisements.

This is a complex clue to the fourth century decline in health: it was a response to social conditions before it was a response to disease organisms. The direct causes of increase in such diseases as malaria, typhoid, and tuberculosis must have been: (1) rural dislocation through constant petty warfare with inevitable breakdown of proper swamp drainage and irrigation; (2) urban overcrowding and inadequate expenditure on sewers or sanitary inspectors; (3) wandering of war refugees. And the effect of such diseases must have been greatly increased through fear of disease, a social response. The reduction of population from infanticide, infertility, wars, and social barriers (3,16) likewise shows a combination of biological with social causes. Thus the great developments in the new fields of city planning and public health by Hellenistic times (16) were too late to do more than palliate, just as the attempts to lessen social discrimination (16) and to prevent military and economic waste were too late. (3)

It is fairly clear that the Greeks treated their public health in the same way that they did all questions of conservation (whether of mines, forests, soil potassium, eroding land, or infanticide) as secondary to the more exciting drama of spending themselves on political competition. From Aristophanes and Socrates and Zeno onward, radical thinkers tried in vain to correct these socioeconomic mistakes (just as we try today), but were defeated by the ineradicable military habits of the city states, not by the domination of the Roman Empire. (5) Neither Hellenistic science nor miracle cures could prevent the insidiously slow deterioration which finally made impossible an exuberant revival of Old Greece under the Byzantine emperors.

This scarcely perceptible decline in health was a big factor in the stasis of Greek culture after the time of Christ, though there was a long lag before the full effect of poor health was felt. And as in the case of social growth any single factor is such a dynamic part of a nexus of cause and effect that it is arrogant to find a simple correlated sequence of events beginning, for example, with the social wastefulness of the Peloponnesian War or the Periclean exclusion of metics* from citizenship at Athens. Nevertheless it is worth remembering that the Greeks lost their good health together with other natural resources because they were too busy with power politics and not radical enough in their self-criticism to conserve their assets.

In civilization as we now have it public health is so closely tied up with economic waste, soil erosion, floods, population increase, and social overstratification that we have no time for elaborate intergroup violence if we expect to deal scientifically with our ecological challenges and thus to maintain the health and energy needed for the constant challenge of creative living.

Good health is a feature of growth of civilization, poor health begins with the end of growth. In each case health plays a causal and necessary role, though a superficial one compared to the psychological forces in social interaction. This is oversimplifying the problem of health. But it is far from oversimplifying our own future to conclude that we need far more cooperation between the doctor, public health expert, medical historian, historian, anthropologist, and city planner. We must train more enterprising scientists for research on other societies as well as our own. And we must make recommendations for United Nations insistence on the repair of world health as the first step toward making safe our civilization.

*A metic was an alien resident of an ancient Greek city who had some civil privileges.—Ed.

SUMMARY

Health is one of those things which advances during growth and wastes with stasis and during decline of civilization, though in each case health is only one factor in a network of social and economic causes.

Public health is like other natural resources and its change is a social and ecological as well as medical phenomenon.

Effects of a very slight change in health may be extensive, though apparently subtle and slow to have decisive effect especially after a decline in health.

Maintenance of an optimum level of health is extremely necessary for our survival and consequently we must train more scientists for work on health as a social factor.

REFERENCES

1. Ackernecht, E. H. "The History of Malaria." *CIBA Symposia* 7 (1945): 51-56.

2. Angel, J. L. "Skeletal Change in Ancient Greece." *American Journal of Physical Anthropology* NS4 (1946): 69-97.

3. Angel, J. L. "Social Biology of Greek Culture Growth." *American Anthropologist* 48 (1946): 493-533.

4. Angel, J. L. "The Length of Life in Ancient Greece." *Journal of Gerontology* 2 (1947): 18-24.

5. Childe, V. G. *What Happened in History*. New York: Penguin Books, Inc., 1946.

6. De Waele, F. J. "The Sanctuary of Asklepios and Hygieia at Corinth." *American Journal of Archaeology* 37 (1933): 417-451.

7. Glotz, G. *Ancient Greece at Work*. Translated by M. R. Dobie. New York: Knopf, 1926.

8. Gulick, C. B. *The Life of the Ancient Greeks, with Special Reference to Athens*. New York: D. Appleton and Co., 1902.

9. Jardé, A. *Les céréales dans l'antiquité Grecque*. Paris, 1925.

10. Jayne, W. A. *The Healing Gods of Ancient Civilizations*. New Haven: Yale University Press, 1925.

11. Jones, W. H. S. *Malaria: A Neglected Factor in the History of Greece and Rome*. Cambridge, England: Macmillan and Bowes, 1907.

12. Robinson, D. M. and Graham, J. W. "The Hellenic House. A Study of the Houses Found at Olynthus with a Detailed Account of Those Excavated in 1931 and 1934." *Excavations at Olynthus*, VIII (Johns Hopkins University Studies in Archeology No. 25) Baltimore: Johns Hopkins University Press, 1938.

13. Robinson, D. M. "Domestic and Public Architecture." *Excavations at Olynthus* XII (Johns Hopkins Series in Archeology No. 36) Baltimore: Johns Hopkins University Press, 1946.

14. Singer, Charles. "Greek Biology and Greek Medicine." *Chapters in the History of Science*, ed. C. Singer. Oxford: Clarendon Press, 1922.

15. Stéphanos, Clon. Gréce Géographie Médicale. Dict. encyclopédique des sciences medicales, ed. A. Dechambre. Serie IV, 10, Paris, 1884: 363-581.

16. Tarn, W. W. *Hellenistic Civilization*. London: Arnold, 1930.

17. Thompson, W. S. *Population Problems*. Third Edition. New York: McGraw-Hill, 1942.

18. Withington, E. T. "The Asclepiadae and the Priests of Asclepius." *Studies in the History and Method of Science,* ed. C. Singer. Oxford: Clarendon Press, 1921.

THE SITE OF ROME

Donald R. Dudley

The site of the city—a matter which calls for the most careful consideration of a founder who wishes to set up a state that will long endure—was chosen by Romulus with almost unbelievable foresight. . . . With admirable prudence he realized that maritime sites are by no means the most advantageous for cities founded in the hope of permanence and empire, firstly, because cities so placed are exposed not merely to numerous dangers, but also to those that cannot be foreseen.

How, therefore, could Romulus have combined with more god-like skill the advantages of a maritime position with the avoidance of its drawbacks, than to found his city on the banks of a copious and smooth-flowing river, with a broad estuary on the sea? This river would enable his city to receive from the sea what she needed, and to export by it her own surplus. This same river, too, would make possible not only the import by sea of all that is most necessary for life and civilization, but also those goods carried by it from the land: even at that early date, I believe, Romulus foresaw that this city would provide a visiting place and a home for a world empire: for certainly no city placed in any other part of Italy could more readily have wielded such great authority as Rome.

Again, as to the natural defenses of the city itself, is there anyone so indifferent as not to have surveyed them and to keep them firmly fixed in his mind? The extent and siting of the wall was determined with so much wisdom by Romulus and the other kings, being set on all sides upon steep and precipitous hills, that the one natural approach, between the Esquiline and the

Quirinal, was protected by a huge ditch with an enormous rampart surrounding it. The citadel, too, was so well fortified by its sheer circuit, with the rock, as it were, cut to fit it, that even in that appalling storm of the Gallic invasion it remained secure and impregnable.

Moreover, Romulus chose a site with a good supply of springs, and healthy though in an unhealthy district: for there are hills which themselves catch the breezes and also provide shade for the valleys.

Cicero, On the Republic, II. 3, 5: 5, 10: 6, 11

So much then, for the advantages which the nature of the land conveys on the city: but the Romans have added others by their own foresight. For while the Greeks bore the reputation of being discerning choosers of sites for the foundation of cities, aiming at beauty, defensive siting, harbors, and fertile soil, the Romans showed good discrimination in points neglected by the Greeks, such as the construction of roads and aqueducts, and of sewers that could wash the filth of the city into the Tiber. They have built paved roads throughout the country, leveling ridges and filling up hollows, so as to make possible the movements of heavily loaded wagons. The sewers are vaulted with close-fitting slabs and in some places are wide enough for wagons with a full load of hay to pass through them. And such is the quantity of water brought in by the aqueducts, that veritable rivers flow through the city and its sewers: almost every house has cisterns, waterpipes, and copious fountains. It was Marcus Agrippa who particularly concerned himself with this amenity, though of course he beautified the city with many other benefactions. One may say that the earlier Romans cared little for the beauty of their city, since they were preoccupied with other, more utilitarian measures. But later generations—and especially those of the modern age and our own times, have by no means fallen short on this score, but have filled the city with many and splendid endowments of their munificence. For example, Pompey, the late Julius Caesar, Augustus, his friends and sons, his wife and sister have surpassed all others in their zeal for building and willingness to meet its expenses. The Campus Martius is the site for most of these buildings. It is of impressive size, and allows chariot racing and other equestrian exercises to go on without interfering with the crowds of people exercising themselves with ball games, hoops, and wrestling. The many works of art that surround it, the ground covered throughout the year with grass, the ridges of the hills rising above the river, or sloping down to its edge, all look like the painted backcloth to a stage, and form a spectacle from which it is hard to tear yourself away. . . . There, too, is the Mausoleum, a huge mound near the river on a high base of white marble, covered with evergreen trees to its summit. It bears on the summit a statue of Caesar Augustus, and within the mound are the tombs of himself, his kinsmen, and his friends. Behind it is an enclosed precinct with superb walks, and near the center of the Campus, by the crematorium (ustrinum) of Augustus is a wall, also of white marble, surrounded by a circular fence of iron and planted inside with black poplars.

Again, if one should go to the Old Forum, and see one Forum after

another ranged beside it, with their basilicas and temples, and then see the
Capitol and the great works of art on it, and the Palatine, and the Porticus of
Livia, it would be easy to forget the world outside. Such, then, is Rome.

Strabo, *Geography,* v. 3. 8

SOCIAL AND ECONOMIC DEVELOPMENT OF THE EMPIRE IN THE FIRST TWO CENTURIES

M. Rostovtzeff

The Roman Empire of the first and second centuries was beyond all question a brilliant spectacle. It included in one mighty state all that was civilized in the countries fringing the Mediterranean. Nothing was outside it except the savage tribes of Germans, Slavs, and Finns, the nomads of the desert and the Negroes of central Africa, and the great Iranian and Mongol population of Asia. Even with these the empire kept up regular and constantly improving relations by commerce and diplomacy, though this connection was interrupted from time to time by military operations against frontier tribes. Within the empire no pains were spared to secure constant and unhampered communication between its different parts. The population, except the Eastern serfs bound to the soil, could move at will from place to place.

The state did its utmost to make communication safe and easy. The Mediterranean was a Roman lake: from end to end of it, as also on the Black Sea, the great rivers of western Europe, and the Nile, ships conveyed passengers and goods; and piracy was kept down by fleets at sea and flotillas on the rivers. Communication by sea with India was fairly safe from Egyptian and Arabian ports, and the voyage along the north coast of Europe as far as the Baltic was practicable; but in such enterprises the trader had to rely upon his own resources entirely.

Along the high roads which spread out like a fan from Rome and Italy it was easy to travel to the Atlantic, or the North Sea, or the Dardanelles and the Black Sea coast. A similar network of roads covered Asia Minor, Syria, north Africa, and Britain; and every place resembling a town was linked up with these by branches. Each town kept up the roads connecting it with the main settlements within its territory. The general safety was secured by the armed forces controlled by the representatives of the central power at home and abroad. The self-governing communities and the great landlords, each acting within the limits of their own possessions, organized the local police. The state maintained special detachments of police in Rome, Lyons, and Carthage; and at Rome there was a brigade of firemen as well.

Municipal life throughout the empire was almost entirely free from the irksome control of the central power. The state was satisfied, provided that no clubs or societies of a seditious nature existed within its boundaries, and that the municipal bodies concerned themselves solely with local affairs. But indeed no community within the empire was ambitious to stray beyond that limited sphere. We hear nothing of any political organizations, either at Rome or within the municipalities abroad, which were regarded as dangerous to the state. The Christian communities alone were prosecuted; but we do not know whether they suffered as unlicensed associations (*collegia illicita*), or whether the Christians individually were held to account for their refusal to take part in the cult of the emperor which all the empire practised. There were other societies, some professional and some religious. The latter included an infinite number of burial clubs (*collegia tenuiorum,* literally, "associations of the poor"), whose object was to secure to their members a decent funeral. There were also many other clubs, in which the citizens of the town met according to their ages, and such bodies as philosophic schools, organized like close societies.

Each community lived in accordance with its past traditions, insofar as these traditions were not offensive to the state. In the Greek East, the birthplace of the municipal system, the constitutions or charters of the towns varied greatly both in terms and substance. The Roman government, though indifferent to the details of these charters, supported aristocratic institutions in the larger communities and looked with disfavor on democracy. Hence in most Greek cities the constitution was oligarchical. Alexandria, the capital of Egypt, was treated exceptionally: she had very meager rights and was strictly controlled by the Roman governor. The cities in the West differed less from one another in their rights and privileges. A few Italian towns still retained their ancient charters based upon historic treaties with Rome.

Most communities of Roman citizens in Italy and the provinces possessed charters bestowed on them by the Roman government. In the provinces a regular colony received its rights from its founder, and other towns from the particular emperor who conferred on them the title of *municipium* or *colonia.* All these charters were drawn up on the same plan. They all provided for the creation of the usual municipal institutions—magistrates, a council of elders or of *decuriones* (local senators), and a popular assembly; they all defined the duties and rights of these bodies, and provided law courts. They contained rules for the election of magistrates and *decuriones,* rules for the proceedings in the council, and rules for the management of the popular assembly. In general they resembled copies of the Roman constitution, in the form which it had taken during the centuries that urban institutions had existed at Rome. Most Italian communities in the course of time exchanged their ancient charters for such machine-made constitutions; and it is very probable that they were encouraged to do so by one of Caesar's laws, which prescribed that certain rules should be introduced into the charters of all communities formed of Roman citizens.

Both in the West and in the East the townspeople took a keen interest in their local affairs. Elections to the magistracy or priesthood or council were important events, and there was a lively competition for seats. We see this clearly from the election placards, of which a large number are still extant at Pompeii; these notices were not pasted up on the walls but painted in black or red on the plaster which covered the fronts of the houses. To be elected to the *Augustales,* a corporation consisting mainly of freedmen, was also an honor for which there was keen competition; the *Augustales* had to provide the funds for the worship of the emperor in the country towns. Magistrates and councils were full of local patriotism. In Asia Minor there was an unceasing struggle for primacy among the chief cities, and for the honorable titles of *neocori,* or "keepers of the emperor's temple." In return for honors and offices, for statues in the forum and election to the local priesthood, rich citizens were ready to spend large sums on the adornment of the town or on the needs and entertainment of the inhabitants. Most of the public buildings in Italian, Greek, and provincial towns were built out of the private subscriptions of well-to-do or wealthy individuals.

Life at Rome was more complicated. The immense population of the capital, reckoned at more than a million had no political nor even municipal rights: it was absolutely controlled by the emperor with his ministers and by the Senate. On the other hand, the emperors did all that was possible to make life there convenient and agreeable. I have said already that Augustus made Rome the real capital of the world, and that his successors followed in his footsteps. The city became by degrees the most magnificent in the world, and the pleasantest to live in. Order was secured by the imperial police; the emperor maintained seven regiments of firemen, who rendered aid also in case of inundations or earthquakes; special officials attended to the aqueducts, the drainage, the flow of the Tiber, and the upkeep of public buildings, the open spaces, and streets. The public buildings were remarkable for their size, the beauty of their lines, and the elegance of their appointments. Nowhere were there such noble temples, or such richly adorned forums, with triumphal arches, commemorative columns, and a forest of statues; no city in the empire could show such immense theaters, amphitheaters, and circuses; none had so many public libraries and museums, or such a gallery of statues as Augustus erected in his forum in honour of famous Roman commanders. Peculiar to Rome were the vast and luxurious *thermae*—public baths with athletic-grounds, which served also as clubs and restaurants; and also the noble halls, called basilicas, which were used for law courts. No Hellenistic capital could rival the public parks, hygienic markets, and splendid shops of Rome. Apart from all this, the palace of the emperors rose on the Palatine, and their magnificent tombs on the banks of the Tiber. Life was easy and cheerful in this marvellous city. About 200,000 of the poorest class were maintained by the state, and the rest could find work in abundance, if they wanted it. Nor was there any lack of amusements, especially under such rulers as Nero, Domitian, and Commodus; and occasional presents, either in money or in kind, were distributed among the people.

The towns in the provinces, in proportion to their means, kept pace with Rome. And I do not refer to the ancient capitals of the East—Alexandria, Antioch, Pergamum, Ephesus, Athens, Corinth; nor to the later capitals of the West—Lyons, Carthage, Tarragona, which received from the emperors almost as much consideration and as much generosity as Rome herself. The smaller towns, even the new and unimportant colonies and *municipia* in Africa, Gaul, and Britain were remarkable for careful planning, cleanliness, and good sanitation. The main streets were straight and wide, the side streets straight and clean, and all were paved; the houses were convenient, with drains and a water-supply, with enclosed gardens and conduits. There were large marketplaces, temples, basilicas, covered markets, buildings for the council and magistrates to meet in; public latrines built of stone and abundantly supplied with water; fine public baths with central heating; theaters, amphitheaters, circuses; libraries; hotels and inns. And all this could be found—more or less complete, more or less perfect—in almost every provincial town. The dead were cared for as well as the living. No age in the history of the world comes up to the Roman Empire in the number of beautiful and splendid monuments which it erected in memory of the dead. The roads leading to Pompeii give sufficient proof of this: what variety and what beauty is displayed there! What then were the roads like that led to Rome! And the same is true of the provinces. I might point, for example, to the mausoleum of the Julian family at St. Remy in Gaul, to the Igelsaüle near Trèves, or hundreds of other noble monuments still extant in Africa, Greece, Asia Minor, and Syria. Millions were spent upon the dead, tens and hundreds of millions on the comfort of the living. One may say without exaggeration that never in the history of mankind (except during the nineteenth and twentieth centuries in Europe and America) has a larger number of people enjoyed so much comfort; and that never, not even in the nineteenth century, did men live in such a surrounding of beautiful buildings and monuments as in the first two centuries of the Roman Empire.

Thus, the empire was a worldwide state, consisting of a number of urban districts, each of which had for its center a well-organized town or city. In these towns, and especially in the capital, lived that part of the population which directed the social and economic life of the empire. The chief place among these many millions was held by Italy with a population almost entirely made up of Roman citizens. But the citizen franchise was by no means restricted to Italy. The successors of Augustus grew more and more liberal, and admitted by degrees as citizens the upper class of every city in the empire. The army, which was still recruited, if not in Italy, at least in the Romanized or Hellenized parts of the empire, still represented civilization; and through the ranks many persons of middling or inferior station passed into the class of citizens. So the process went on, by which the body of citizens grew larger and larger, till it included most of the upper and middle classes of the urban population in Italy and the provinces.

Together with this extension there was a radical change in the composition of this body, when compared with the republican age or the reign of Augustus. Above all, the old senatorial nobility had disappeared by the end of the first century, partly in consequence of merciless persecution by the emperors, and partly from natural causes: if they married at all, their marriages were generally childless. Their place was filled by a new imperial nobility, natives either of Italian cities or of the provinces. This change is clearly shown in the case of the emperors themselves: the Julii and Claudii belong to the old patrician aristocracy, the Flavii come from a municipal Italian stock, and most of the Antonines belong to the upper class of the Romanized provinces. The new aristocracy was not much more long-lived than its predecessors: after two or three generations families died out and gave place to others of similar origin. The same indifference to the continuation of the name still led to the same result; and any family which survived for more than two generations was artificially kept alive by the system of adoption.

In the country towns, especially in the upper middle class which aimed at equestrian rank, the same thing is observable—the rapid extinction of families. The equestrian class grows in numbers but is recruited chiefly from without. Here, too, adoption is common, and the adopted son is often a freedman, a former slave of the family. The only class which adds to its numbers is the proletariat in town and country. Of this we have no direct evidence; but it may be inferred from the increasing population of the empire as a whole, which in turn is proved by the steady growth of the cities and increasing area of cultivation in almost all the provinces. It is a marked feature in all the higher classes of the population, that they are unwilling to continue their kind and found a family. Apparently their motive was to secure full enjoyment of their wealth for themselves personally; and they were not willing to hamper their freedom with the cares of a family. Men struggled for wealth in order to secure for themselves a life of peace and comfort, and in order to rise in the social scale. They cared little what became of their riches: they bequeathed them to the emperor, or to their native city, or to some social or religious institution, or to friends and relations, or to flatterers and freedmen.

The senators were still the richest class of the population. But we find in them no desire to increase their wealth by systematic cultivation of their estates. The rich man's object is to receive a safe and steady income with as little personal exertion as possible. Hence money was invested mainly in land. Estates were managed by slaves and freedmen, and were worked by tenants on short or long leases, the latter being preferred. More life and energy was shown by the class of knights and the middle class in the country towns, especially the lower section of it: the higher section, here too, was apt to rest content with what they had got, and preferred spending to acquisition. A stagnation is perceptible throughout the empire, a paralysis even of the desire for gain. Meanwhile, the composition of the highest classes was constantly changing: men of a lower and less refined type replaced the representatives of traditional culture, and then died out themselves before they had time to appropriate entirely the tastes and interests of their predecessors.

How the lower class of the population lived it is difficult to say. In the towns they enjoyed the same advantages of comfort and good order as the rich. At Pompeii or Timgad in Africa there are no houses which one would not care to live in. Things were probably worse in the poor quarters of the capital cities; but their inhabitants could enjoy the splendid squares, gardens, basilicas, and baths. Slaves were, of course, less well off than the free population; but even they, under the empire, attracted more and more the attention and benevolence of the legislator. Of life in the country we unfortunately know nothing. But perhaps this very dumbness is significant. If we hear no paeans of joy, we hear also no complaints. In the troublesome times that followed at the end of the second century and the beginning of the third, the country finds a voice and uses it to complain of its hardships to the emperor. Its silence in the first two centuries is a proof that things were not too bad.

During those centuries the empire was unquestionably rich and, in comparison with other periods, prosperous. What was the source of this wealth? What were the forms assumed by its economic life? These questions are of great importance: in the answer to them lies the explanation of that startling phenomenon in the history of the Roman Empire—the rapid destruction, . . . of its prosperity. The material resources of the state were, beyond doubt, immense. She included the richest parts of Europe, Africa, and Asia, on which the prosperity of modern Europe is based. Besides, she developed the resources of Asia and north Africa more thoroughly than is done at present. She commanded fertile districts for cultivation, extensive pastures for stock-raising on the largest scale, virgin forests, mines and quarries almost unworked, rivers and seas abounding with fish. We must admit in fairness that the Romans found out these resources and did their best to make use of them.

Their prosperity was based on agriculture and stock-raising. It is certain that the empire greatly extended the area of cultivation. In modern Africa, for instance, in Algeria and Tunis, immense districts, which were never reached by Carthaginian civilization and contain no traces of Carthaginian cities or farms, and where now, in spite of French colonizing activity, only scanty flocks of sheep and goats wander over the parched plains, were densely populated and thoroughly tilled in the first two centuries, especially in the second. This is abundantly clear from the ruins, which the traveller meets at almost every step, of prosperous towns and productive farms. The origin of that prosperity is revealed by the remains of imposing Roman buildings, intended to make a systematic use of the rain which falls here in abundance during the winter months.

It is certain that Gaul, Britain, and Spain began under the empire to produce for the first time vast quantities of grain for export, after satisfying the local requirements. In the East the area of cultivation did not at least grow smaller, except perhaps in Greece for a reason which will be explained later. The prosperity of the Western provinces is attested by the ruins of many flourishing towns, whose inhabitants were fed by the country and which did not exist before this period. Even stronger evidence is supplied by the ruins of those large and small farms, which have of late years attracted increasing attention from archeologists. It is surely significant that the soil of Britain is covered, in its level parts, with the ruins of large or small "villas," which were either farms or the central points of large estates. The same is true of France and Belgium and the Rhine country; on the upper Rhine the *decumates agri,* which were included in the province of upper Germany between the reigns of Domitian and Commodus, were covered with a network of substantial farms. In Egypt the extension of the arable area is proved by documents found there, and by our knowledge of large irrigation schemes undertaken by Augustus.

It is certain that stock-raising also was vigorously developed, and special attention was paid to the cultivation of vines and olive trees. For this purpose the empire made use of every suitable district within its boundaries. Modern times can boast of few fresh conquests of this kind. Wine, indeed, is now made in Germany; but on the other hand, the southern part of Tunis, which in ancient times as almost completely covered with olive trees, is now a bare plain. This acclimatization of valuable products is highly characteristic of the empire, and worked remarkable changes in the aspect of the ancient world. The time was past when Greece, and then Italy, supplied the whole world with wine and oil. Under the empire nearly all the provinces grew enough of both commodities to satisfy their own requirements, and even sought to export the excess. This was certainly a serious blow to the agricultural prosperity of Greece and Italy. Having nothing to export in return for the imported grain, they were forced to revert to a more primitive type of agriculture, and once more to grow corn for their own needs.

In spite of the increase in arable area, and the acclimatization of the vine and olive in western Europe, there was no improvement, but rather a falling off, in agricultural skill. Columella, who wrote a handbook on farming in the first century, complains bitterly of the decay of scientific agriculture in Italy; and we may be sure that the same was true of the eastern and western provinces.

The cause of this regression was an extensive development of small farming, which went on together with the growth of great estates. Slave labor applied to the land was no longer of primary importance, even in the East and in Italy. Slaves became dear and free labor cheap, owing to the increasing number of the proletariat. The great landlords were glad to give up the plantation system and let their land to smallholders. The emperors were the first to begin this system on their estates. The East followed suit: the owners of large and middling estates lived in towns and had their land cultivated by smallholders who were in many cases bound to the soil they tilled. These conditions were unfavorable to progressive and scientific cultivation. In spite of more land and more workers on the land, the quality of the work steadily deteriorated.

The same fact is observable in a different department—in the exploitation of natural wealth of other kinds. The number of mines and quarries in working order increased. The knowledge of their mineral wealth was probably the main reason why some new territories were annexed to the empire. We may suppose that this motive, among others, induced Claudius to conquer Britain, and Domitian to annex part of southwest Germany; and at all events the chief attraction of Dacia was its auriferous sand and wealth in other minerals. Here again, beyond question, the sources of the empire's wealth were added to. But the skill of the workers did not keep up with the development of mines. In mining and metallurgy the Romans did not improve upon the methods of the Hellenistic Age, but even lost ground. The treasury, in other words, the emperor, had worked the mines through substantial contractors employing slaves in great numbers; but now a different method was tried: the work was parceled out among petty adventurers who had to rely on their own efforts and the help of a few slaves. Under such conditions technical improvements were of course impossible.

Symptoms of this kind are visible in manufacture as well as in agriculture and mining. Districts which had formerly depended upon imports from the large manufacturing centres now began to take a share in production. Hence, the large centers lost their economic position and grew impoverished. The worst plight of all was that of Greece, whose manufactures disappeared almost entirely from the world's market. A few kinds, indeed, of manufactured articles, some of which cannot be called luxuries, were still produced by special districts and exported thence to the ends of the earth, the vast extent of the Roman Empire being a great furtherance to exportation. Some fabrics were still a specialty exported all over the world by Asia Minor, Italy, and Gaul; the copper vessels of Campania still competed successfully against foreign imitations; and Egypt was supreme in the market for linen stuffs and paper. But these special goods, produced for the sake of export only, became more and more exceptional. They were driven out of the provincial markets by similar wares, sometimes not inferior in quality, produced by the local workshops. Thus, for example, the manufacture of earthenware vessels and lamps and of glass was no longer limited to one center. The first of these products has a history of special interest. Beginning in Greece and Asia Minor the industry passed to Italy: in the second and first centuries B.C. the figured earthenware of north Italy has no rival in the world. In the first century A.D. southern Gaul begins to compete; in the second half of the century the manufacture moves farther north, and reaches the Rhine in the second century. These vessels now conquer not only the northern and northeastern markets but Italy as well; and simultaneously Asia Minor is producing the same article after the same patterns for the southern and southeastern markets. In the second century A.D. all the provinces, both East and West, are turning out in immense numbers the earthenware lamps which had once been almost a monopoly of the workshops in north Italy. Nothing now, except articles of luxury accessible to few, finds a distant market; and indeed local imitations of the products from great centers of industry crop up everywhere. For instance, the famous purple fabrics of Tyre were imitated in Asia Minor. Thus, in manufacture also, production became more and more diffused.

But at the same time the quality grows inferior: there is less both of mechanical skill and beauty. Technique becomes monotonous and somewhat old-fashioned. In jewelery, for instance, it is enough to compare the charming earrings and brooches of the Hellenistic Age with the coarse Roman imitations, and the same may be said of the pottery. It is important also to note this: ruins and tombs have yielded up objects of Roman production by the hundred thousand, and these warrant the assertion that practically no new discovery was made in technique: on the contrary, many earlier discoveries fell into disuse. In point of artistic beauty every one knows that the products of the empire are immeasurably inferior to those of the Eastern monarchies, or Greece, or the Hellenistic Age.

We must seek for the cause of this degeneration in the diffusion of production already mentioned. The provinces had started production to satisfy their own needs, and mass-production at low prices. Thus, the finer and dearer article was driven out of the markets; and the factories and workshops of the purely industrial countries, which found a ready sale in earlier times, now stood idle. At the same time the gradual decline, already mentioned, of culture in the middle classes created a demand for a coarser and less artistic product. This failure of skill and artistic feeling was accompanied by a change in methods of production. The system of large factories, which started at Athens and was developed in the chief Hellenistic centers of industry, had reached some cities in Italy by the first century B.C., but declined steadily after the middle of the second century. In the Italian and provincial towns of the second century A.D., the work was chiefly done by workmen in a small way and in small workshops. A rich manufacturer was a man who owned a number of such establishments; and the hands employed were mainly slaves.

Under the empire, especially during the first two centuries, there was a remarkable development of trade, wholesale and retail, both by land and sea. Regular commercial relations were kept up with the most distant markets—China, India, central and southern Africa, Arabia, central Asia, central and southern Russia, Germany, and even Sweden and Norway. These countries imported manufactured articles in exchange for articles of luxury; or, more precisely, they supplied the raw material to be worked up in the shops of the Greco-Roman world, especially in the East. Africa sent gold, ivory, and precious woods; Arabia sent spices; pearls and precious stones came from India, silk from China, furs from central Asia and Russia, amber from Germany and Scandinavia.

This foreign trade, however, was not really important for the economic development of the empire. The trade carried on within the empire itself, within the different provinces and between them, was of much greater importance. It grew steadily; the class of traders grew larger; and the Semites—Syrians, Jews, and Arameans—became more prominent members of it. Transport between provinces was easy—over the Mediterranean and then along the rivers and highways to the remotest corners. At the end of the third century the Emperor Diocletian published a tariff or list of fixed prices for goods; it was intended for the Eastern provinces, but it includes, together with the manufactures and products of the East, a great number of articles produced by the West, especially by Gaul. Trade was helped also by the moderate amount, varying from two to two and one-half percent., of the customs levied at the frontier of each province. This was a great improvement upon the time when each Greek city or petty Hellenistic kingdom extorted duties from every merchant that entered its territory.

It is certain, however, that the same symptoms which we have already noticed in agriculture and industry were present also in trade. As the provinces became more self-sufficient their need of importation decreased, and the market of every town and village was stocked with local products. In the towns most of the workshops were also shops, and most of the eatables on sale were produced within the territory belonging to the town. This state of things was less pronounced wherever traffic was carried on by river, as in Gaul and Britain, on the Rhine and the Danube with its tributaries, and in Egypt; but more pronounced in Italy, Africa, and Asia Minor, where this cheap means of communication does not exist.

The expense and delay of transport by road isolated the markets and made them aim at being self-supporting. The same causes hindered the development of large capitalistic enterprises in the sphere of local trade, except for wares carried by sea, or caravan, or rivers. It is an interesting fact that the Emperor Hadrian, who favored smallholders in agriculture and petty contractors in the mines, tried to put down the middleman in trade, and to connect the purchaser directly with the producer. In spite of this, capitalistic methods were more successful in trade than in any other department of economic activity during the empire. The merchants, together with the great landowners, were the richest men of the time. They formed important trading companies and associations. The merchants interested in shipping, called *naucleri* or *navicularii,* combined in companies of this kind, and became one of the most powerful economic alliances in the empire.

It appears, therefore, that the empire accomplished a great deal in the sphere of economics. Fresh sources of wealth were discovered. Countries which had previously been content with the most primitive commercial arrangements now became accessible to systematic exploitation. Exchange was facilitated by a better system of roads and protection from pirates at sea. The imposts were not burdensome. In the relation between capital and labor the empire, that is, the government of the empire, remained passive and left the problem to settle itself. Its interposition was rare and governed by no system: at one time it favoured capital and great fortunes, at another it took measures to protect the small proprietor and the working man. The emperors of the second century interfered more than others. I have mentioned already Hadrian's defense of smallholders and tenants. It is right to notice the legislation of all these emperors in order to raise the legal and social level of slaves. It must be remembered, however, that the labor question, as we understand it, was unknown to the ancient world. The existence of slavery and the application of slave labor to industry made it impossible for free laborers to combine and fight the employers. Not only so, but the government frowned on any associations for other than religious purposes and would certainly have suppressed them.

Nevertheless, together with a forward movement we have been forced to notice many disquieting symptoms—the increasing size of landed properties; the change from scientific farming to more primitive methods practiced by small tenants on short or long leases; the decline of intensive agriculture in Greece and Italy, and of science applied to agriculture—Columella, mentioned above, is the last original writer who treats the subject; the deterioration of manufactured objects in technical skill and beauty; and the development of small workshops at the expense of large factories and works.

URBAN VIOLENCE IN IMPERIAL ROME

Thomas W. Africa

Bread, circuses, and an occasional riot—such, we are told, were the main interests of the populace in Imperial Rome: an indolent and debased people, glutted with free food and addicted to spectacles. Tacitus sneered at "the sordid plebs who hang about the Circus and theaters,"[1] and Juvenal impaled them with an epigram: "The people, who once bestowed republican offices, have now only two interests, bread and games."[2] These charges have been echoed by many modern authors, and even authorities of the stature of Rostovtzeff repeat them.[3]

Evidence for the history of the Roman commons is fragmentary, but, even so, the record does not confirm the image of a spoiled, fickle, and irresponsible people.[4] Since Roman history was written by men of the senatorial class, or by those who had attached themselves to its interests, it is not surprising that Roman historians had little sympathy for the lower classes. Tacitus employed an arsenal of invective against the commons: *plebs sordida, vulgus imperitum, inops vulgus*[5] —they were a vile, ignorant, wretched rabble. From his viewpoint, the Roman masses were *canaille, Lumpen,* or, in Burke's words, "a swinish multitude."[6] Impudent and unruly, they seemed an amorphous mass, potentially a mob. Yet even Tacitus made a subjective distinction between the "respectable commons" who rejoiced at the fall of Nero and the "riff-raff" who lamented the tyrant's passing.[7]

Rhetoric should not be confused with historical evidence, and a crowd is not a mob merely because historians label it so when they disapprove of the masses' actions. While Imperial Rome had its share of social scum and

Reprinted from *The Journal of Interdisplinary History,* II (Summer 1971), 3-21, by permission of *The Journal of Interdisciplinary History* and the M.I.T. Press, Cambridge, Mass. Copyright © by the Massachusetts Institute of Technology and the editors of *The Journal of Interdisciplinary History.*

criminals, the people who demonstrated in the Circus, and who sometimes took to the streets in riots, were not the dregs of society. The Roman "mob" was generally composed of shopkeepers, craftsmen, and workers (particularly in transportation and the building trades)[8] who had grievances to air. The Principate had wiped out all but the formalities of republican government. No longer able to effect decisions through republican channels, the Roman commons could only petition the emperor through mass demonstrations, and, if he failed to heed their demands, they sometimes resorted to violence.

In assessing urban violence in Imperial Rome, one must not lose sight of its causes, nor of the grievances and loyalties that prompted humble men to challenge tyrants, and civilians to battle professional soldiers. The environment and values of the Roman masses must be considered, as well as their composition and actions. Clichés about "bread and circuses" throw little light on the lives or aspirations of the urban masses.

Imperial Rome was a city of about one million inhabitants.[9] Filled with palaces, monuments, and slums, it was a city of contrasts where splendor and squalor existed side by side. Short of space, Rome had expanded vertically as well as horizontally, and much of the population lived in multistoried tenements. Most housing was poorly built, and the collapse of apartment houses was not uncommon. Yet, since living space was at a premium, rents were high. Fires were frequent and destructive. Although the city contained many large public baths, sanitation was poor. Congested and noisy, Rome had grown without planning, and its streets were narrow and winding—a factor that aided rioters. Like modern capitals, Rome depended on imported food, and a delay in the arrival of the grain fleet could reduce the city to famine and bread riots.

As the cosmopolitan center of a world state, the population of Rome was mixed, for freedmen of varied ethnic backgrounds were absorbed into the body politic as citizens.[10] The city also included a large number of noncitizens and probably 100,000 slaves. Though upper class Italians were contemptuous of provincials in general, and Eastern peoples in particular, Roman society was not marred by overt racial or ethnic discrimination. Organized in guilds, craftsmen and tradesmen often lived together on the same streets, thus affording them a sense of sodality.

In Imperial Rome, crime was commonplace, and some of it was organized. Domitian broke up a ring of professional murderers who killed their victims with poisoned needles, and who operated both in the city and throughout the empire. Under Commodus, there was a revival of the same gang, but it was soon suppressed.[11] Most criminals at Rome followed more traditional pursuits, and the city was plagued with housebreakers, pickpockets, petty thieves, and muggers. Juvenal gives a vivid description of the many dangers of Rome at night.[12] Yet, despite the inconveniences of life in the great city, Juvenal and a million others found Rome too exciting to leave.

The attractions of Rome included bread for some and circuses for all. Occasionally, the emperors would distribute gifts of cash or grain to the citizenry. In 5 B.C., for example, 320,000 citizens of Rome received a cash gift from Augustus.[13] More important was the monthly dole which the state furnished to a fixed number of citizens, who were issued a square wooden chit redeemable for five *modii* (about one and one-quarter bushels) of grain.[14] A holdover from the Republic, the grain dole was not welfare, or even philanthropy, but was viewed as the hereditary privilege of the descendants of the Romans who had conquered the world and were entitled to its tribute. The privilege was confined to citizens who resided in the city, and only the poor relied on the dole.[15] No man could live on the dole alone, however, much less depend upon it to feed his family, and rent and clothing required money. The Roman masses worked hard for a living, and at the most the dole only supplemented their meager incomes. In all periods, the dole and its recipients have been criticized by well-fed moralists, but the Roman commons were not lazy parasites feeding at the public trough—they were working men who received a food supplement and little else from their imperial masters.

Like all peoples, the Romans enjoyed shows and games, and the more spectacular they were, the better. Much, though not all, of the public entertainment at Rome was free, and holidays were frequent, for the ancients did not subscribe to the Puritan ethic. Under Claudius, ninety-three days per year were devoted to spectacles at government expense; in the third century A.D., the figure almost doubled.[16] How much time a working man could afford to waste on amusement is open to speculation, though common sense suggests some obvious limitations. The city boasted many large theaters which offered pantomimes, ballets, and operas of sorts. However, the main centers of public entertainment were the Circus Maximus and (after Vespasian) the Colosseum. Many Romans were passionately devoted to the races in the Circus, and rivalries were strong between the fans of famous teams of charioteers. Best known are the partisans of the Blues and the Greens, who were also active in Antioch and other cities, especially later at Constantinople. (A comparable phenomenon is the rabid devotion to soccer teams in Latin American countries today.) While not edifying, the races were hardly demoralizing, and even Fronto admits that all classes were fond of them.[17] Originally, the Circus seated 150,000 spectators; later, it accommodated 250,000.[18] When a crowd of this size chanted a grievance to the imperial box, the emperor did well to pay attention. The Colosseum held about 50,000 spectators[19] and featured games with rare beasts from foreign lands. It also provided grislier fare with gladiatorial combats and the staged executions of criminals. Though always bloody, not all gladiatorial fights were to the death, for many gladiators were popular with the crowds, and no impresario would allow the slaughter of a champion who had many fans. Nevertheless, death was part of the scene in the arena. While such sports degraded men, it was an age not squeamish to pain and hand-to-hand combat.[20] In any case, the aristocracy flocked to the arena as eagerly as did the masses, and the Romans have not been the only people in history to enjoy violent sports.

In Roman society, violence was endemic and had been accentuated by the political chaos of the Late Republic.[21] Like other Italians, the Romans were emotional and volatile. Though the state could usually cope with major disorders,[22] personal violence plagued the city. Under the Republic, the police powers of the state had been rudimentary, with a few officials and their limited staffs trying to maintain a semblance of order.[23] Without a police force, Romans traditionally had to rely on relatives and friends when violence entered their lives. While a commoner would call upon his friends and neighbors to assist him, a noble could also summon a throng of clients to do battle for him.[24] In rural areas, the situation was worse, and landowners hired armed bands to protect them and intimidate their foes. In the 50s B.C., Clodius and Milo had headed private armies of thugs at Rome, but such gangs were banned by the Principate. Even when public violence was at a low ebb, the average Roman felt it quite natural to call upon his friends to help him resist an assault—or to commit one.

One of the major achievements of Augustus was the establishment of effective military and paramilitary forces to police Rome. Within or near the city were stationed about 12,000 professional soldiers. Nine cohorts of Praetorian Guards served as the household troops of the emperor, while three urban cohorts policed the city, although they functioned mainly as riot troops.[25] The 3,000 troopers of the urban cohorts were under the command of the urban prefect, who was responsible for public order in the city. A fourth urban cohort was added, probably by Caligula,[26] and a total of seven was reached under Claudius.[27] During the civil wars of A.D. 69 the Praetorians and the urban cohorts gambled in politics, and both units backed Otho against Vitellius. After defeating Otho, Vitellius reduced the urban cohorts to four but increased the Praetorian cohorts to sixteen by adding his own troops. When Vespasian's brother, the urban prefect Sabinus, rose against Vitellius, the urban cohorts supported the prefect, and most died in his abortive attempt to hold the Capitol.[28] In A.D. 70 the victorious Vespasian restored the number of cohorts to four urban and nine Praetorians.[29] His son Domitian added a tenth Praetorian cohort,[30] and the number apparently remained fixed.[31] While available in an emergency, the Praetorian Guards were an elite corps, and the actual policing of the city fell on the urban cohorts.

The "police force" of Rome was augmented by a quasi-military fire brigade, the *vigiles,* who served as both firemen and nightwatchmen and often in a police capacity as well. In A.D. 6 Augustus established seven cohorts of freedmen[32] as *vigiles,* with a strength of about 7,000.[33] In the second century, however, the *vigiles* were largely recruited from freeborn citizens.[34] (Frequently, the office of prefect of the *vigiles* was a stepping-stone to the choice Praetorian prefecture.[35]) When Tiberius engineered the overthrow of the powerful Praetorian prefect Sejanus in A.D. 31, neither the Praetorians nor the urban cohorts could be trusted, so *vigiles* guarded the crucial meeting of the Senate where Sejanus was deposed.[36] Yet, during the great fire of A.D. 64, some *vigiles* behaved unprofessionally, looting and spreading fires themselves.[37] Discounting the Praetorians, the "police force" of Rome, including *vigiles,* numbered about 10,000 in the Augustan age, and later about 11,000.[38] With a third of the population of Chicago, Imperial Rome had a police force of about the same size as that of the modern city. By present standards, Rome was heavily policed in terms of numbers, but much of that force was occupied with fire fighting, and the core of the police were riot troops, not patrolmen. When the average resident of Rome was in difficulty, he stood little chance of aid from a policeman and called upon his neighbors for help. When he had a grievance against the state, he was likely to do the same.

Under an authoritarian regime, it is not easy for a citizen or even a group of citizens to communicate with the head of state. Absorbed in the awesome task of running the empire, the emperor at Rome was generally inaccessible to his subjects. It was equally difficult for him to learn of their needs and wishes, for the ruler was surrounded by secretaries and courtiers. The great exception to the isolation of the emperor was his appearance at the Circus or the theaters. To display their affinity with the people, even rulers who were bored by shows and games made token appearances, although Marcus Aurelius, like Caesar, annoyed the audience by reading and dictating letters.[39] Augustus, on the other hand, frankly enjoyed the shows,[40] and so did most of his successors. When the emperor was present, the crowd took full advantage of the opportunity to attract his attention. In the anonymity of a mass audience, it was safe to be impudent and call out witticisms that bordered on sedition. In the sheer numbers which filled the Circus, there was great power, both in the psychological force of noise itself and in the latent possibility of a riot. Claques organized rhythmic chants and clapping in unison and were often joined by other spectators, who were caught up in the compulsive excitement of a crowd atmosphere. Sometimes the cries and requests were flippant, but often matters of import were brought to the ear of the ruler. Though freedom had long since vanished from Rome, the emperors could not afford to disregard public opinion when it was howled by an immense throng. Even the dour Tiberius, who loathed the games and the crowds, was forced by their cries to grant freedom to a slave comedian and to restore a statue which had been taken from a public building.[41] When the crowds blamed him for high grain prices, however, the emperor ordered the Senate to issue an official censure of the populace for their impudence.[42]

Toward the Circus crowds, the tyrannical Caligula was less forbearing than Tiberius. From a good Roman source (possibly Cluvius Rufus), Josephus preserves an account of a clash between Caligula and the masses in the Circus:

There, the assembled throngs make requests of the emperors according to their own pleasure. Emperors who rule that there can be no question about granting such petitions are by no means unpopular. So in this case, they desperately entreated Gaius to cut down imposts and grant some relief from the burden of taxes. But he had no patience with them, and when they shouted louder and louder, he dispatched agents among them in all directions with orders to arrest any who shouted, to bring them forward at once, and to put them to death. The order was given and . . . carried out. The number of those executed in such summary fashion was very large. The people, when they saw what happened, stopped their shouting.[43]

When faced with a resolute tyrant, Cassius Dio remarks of this episode, the people can only be sullen and mutter.[44] Yet most emperors were receptive to public opinion as represented by the multitude in the Circus. When the masses in the Circus and theaters cried for the death of Nero's hated henchman, Tigellinus, Galba quieted them by announcing that their foe was dying of disease.[45] Later, the crowds in the Circus and theaters—where, Tacitus adds, "they have less restraint"—compelled Otho to order Tigellinus' death.[46] Only foolhardy tyrants like Caligula totally disregarded the voice of the people in the Circus.

When civil war broke out between Septimius Severus and Clodius Albinus in A.D. 196, Dio witnessed an extraordinary display of crowd discipline during a demonstration for peace that took place at the Circus:

While the entire world was disturbed by this situation, we senators remained quiet, at least as many of us as did not, by openly inclining to the one or the other, share their dangers and their hopes. The populace, however, could not restrain itself but indulged in the most open lamentations. It was at the last horse race before the Saturnalia, and a countless throng of people flocked to it. I, too, was present . . . and I heard distinctly everything that was said. . . . They had watched the chariots racing . . . without applauding, as was their custom, any of the contestants at all. But when these races were over and the charioteers were about to begin another event, they first enjoined silence upon one another and then suddenly all clapped their hands at the same moment and also joined in a shout, praying for good fortune for the public welfare. . . . Then, applying the terms "Queen" and "Immortal" to Rome, they shouted: "How long are we to suffer such things?" and "How long are we to be waging war?" And after making some other remarks of this kind, they finally shouted, "So much for that," and turned their attention to the horse race.[47]

Dio adds that divine inspiration must have prompted the demonstration, for how else could so many men have cooperated?[48] It may well be that *vox populi* is *vox dei,* but the senator was not privy to the organizations among the masses that could produce such a disciplined display of peace sentiment from perhaps 250,000 people. Critics of the commons can note with satisfaction that the masses soon turned their attention to the races, but the Roman people had made known their desire for peace in a most impressive manner. Unfortunately, Severus was not swayed by the people's weariness with war, for his throne was at stake.

In Imperial Rome, safety to shout en masse was not an idle thing, for the individual was helpless when confronted with the massive power of the state and its ubiquitous secret police. Originally, the secret police were soldiers in civilian clothes, but they soon became a separate adjunct of the Principate, working closely with the urban cohorts.[49] "Their titles, like those of their twentieth-century equivalents, are the more terrifying for their blandness: *curiosi, frumentarii, agentes in rebus.*"[50] The secret police not only ferreted out subversive courtiers,[51] but also lured common people into making disloyal remarks. Epictetus warns his fellow Romans to beware of strangers who strike up a conversation and begin to criticize the emperor, for they are surely secret agents and, if the unwary victim joins in berating the ruler, he will be arrested for sedition.[52] Historians have preserved accounts of prominent figures who were denounced by informers, but how many more commoners were trapped by the secret police and perished for their indiscretion?

A frequent cause of popular discontent at Rome was food shortages. At best, prices rose, and, at worst, the city was brought to the brink of famine. When the situation became critical, a bread riot could break out. In 41 B.C. the fleets of Sextus Pompeius cut off the food supply for Rome, and the hungry citizenry staged a massive strike, closing all shops and protesting loudly to the government to provide food.[53] Two years later, when the city again faced famine, the entire populace rose to complain of hunger and high taxes. Angry mobs threatened to stone those who did not join them and to burn the houses of those who held aloof. When he tried to calm them in the Forum, Octavian was stoned and wounded by the rioters, who also hurled rocks at Antony when he tried to intercede. Seeing that the mob could not be restrained, Antony summoned a detachment of troops and charged into the crowd to rescue the bloodstained Octavian. The soldiers then began to massacre the civilians and soon cleared the streets. Appian notes that the rioters had included "men of the better class."[54] Though the people of Rome paid a high price in casualties, the riot forced Antony and Octavian to come to terms with Sextus Pompeius in order to relieve the situation that had caused the disorders.[55]

So crucial was the problem of food for the capital that the Principate took great care to ensure prompt and sufficient deliveries of grain for the city.[56] In A.D. 51 a delay in the arrival of the grain fleet caused a serious food shortage, for only a fifteen-day supply was left in Rome. An angry crowd surrounded Claudius in the Forum and pelted him with stale crusts of bread until soldiers rescued the emperor and hurried him away to the palace.[57] Yet Claudius was most conscientious with projects to provide adequate supplies for the city.[58] In A.D. 68 food shortages at Rome helped to topple Nero from his throne.[59] In A.D. 189 the Praetorian prefect Cleander was hoarding grain to raise the price, and his political enemies cut the city's supply even more to bring on famine and riots which could unseat the unpopular prefect. Exasperated by hunger, the masses rose and demanded that Commodus execute Cleander. When the emperor sent out the cavalry to disperse the crowds, heavy street fighting ensued. The Praetorian Guards, however, backed the rioters, and the combined force of infuriated citizens and professional soldiery compelled Commodus to accede to the demands and behead the hated Cleander.[60] In the bread riots, the violence of the mob resulted from impatience with a government that had failed to fulfill one of its major responsibilities.

It is often said that the masses are incapable of acting on behalf of abstract principles, for common men are stupid and crowds are aggregates of the irrational. In his classic study, *The Crowd,* Le Bon pontificates: "The powerlessness of crowds to reason aright prevents them from displaying any trace of the critical spirit, prevents them, that is, from being capable of

discerning truth from error, or of forming a precise judgment on any matter."[61] Such a generality is as worthless as the snobbish quips of ancient
writers on the fickleness and irrationality of the masses.[62] Even Tacitus, who
was no friend to the commons, reports a striking example of the masses
challenging the state on behalf of a very abstract principle—justice for slaves.
In A.D. 61 an unsavory official was murdered by one of his slaves, which by
law required the arbitrary execution of all slaves in the household, innocent
and guilty alike. When it was learned that the full measure of the law was to
be employed, a large crowd gathered to protest and demand that the innocent
slaves be spared. While the matter was being debated in the Senate, the
crowds besieged the building and encouraged those senators who spoke in
favor of moderation and justice. The majority of the Senate voted to carry
out the letter of the law, however, whereupon the crowd armed itself with
stones and torches and tried to prevent the executions. To uphold the authority of the state, Nero dispatched troops and lined with soldiers the route
where the luckless slaves were led to death.[63] The riot had not been a protest
against slavery but against a glaring injustice. Apparently, the Roman masses
cherished the principle of justice more dearly than did most of the haughty
senators. When evaluating clichés about the "debased" Roman commons, this
episode should not be forgotten.

How many comparable episodes went unrecorded or, if recorded, have
been lost, can only be conjectured. A year later, the masses loudly protested
Nero's divorce and degradation of Octavia, and rioters overthrew statues of
her successor, Poppaea.[64] How much of their devotion was inspired by loyalty
to the family of Claudius and how much was due to sympathy for a wronged
and virtuous wife is open to argument, but the masses had already displayed a
fine sense of justice in the affair of the slaves. After the great fire of A.D. 64
Nero blamed the disaster on Christians and executed a number of them as
enemies of society. The emperor invited the public to view the torments
which he inflicted on the unpopular sectarians, but the masses were not
amused: "Compassion arose because they were being sacrificed to the fury of
one man and not for the public good."[65] Admittedly, such examples are rare,
but not because the masses were insensible to the principle of justice. Rather,
the sources for ancient history (especially for social history) are fragmentary
at best, and the historians of antiquity, preoccupied with rulers and the upper
classes, disdained the attitudes of the faceless "mob."

In the early Principate, there was still a residue of republican sentiment
among the common people. In A.D. 19, when news of the death of Tiberius'
heir Germanicus reached the capital, the entire populace closed their shops
and went into mourning before the Senate had time to proclaim a public
display of grief. Part of Germanicus' popularity was based on a belief that he
had intended to "restore the liberties of the Roman people with equal rights
for all."[66] Such egalitarian views were not shared by the conservative "senatorial opposition," who yearned for the oligarchic realities of the Republic,
but among all classes the image of the Republic was still popular. Augustus
had been in his grave for only five years, and the assemblies still functioned at

least as formalities.[67] At any rate, Germanicus had seemed a symbol of egalitarian republicanism to the masses. No doubt, these hopes were ill placed, for Germanicus was a shallow mediocrity and surely no democrat, but nonetheless he represented to many Romans the possibility of a republican restoration.

With the passage of time, the aura of the Republic faded, and the masses became attached to the concept of legitimate emperors and dynastic loyalty. In theory, the emperor was still a republican magistrate, but to the people he was a "just king" who embodied the general will. Dynastic sentiment increased devotion to the ruler. When Caligula was assassinated in A.D. 41, the Senate wished to seize power by "restoring the Republic," and the "restoration" received some support from the urban cohorts, but the masses rallied in support of Caligula's uncle, Claudius, as emperor.[68] Once the commons had accepted the principle of dynastic legitimacy, even a despot could be viewed as a "just king" if he was legitimate and had not offended the masses. Thus Nero, though hated by the aristocracy, was popular with the commons, and many people regretted the overthrow of the last of the Julio-Claudian house. For years his grave was strewn with flowers.[69] In the fierce power struggles of A.D. 69, the masses generally held aloof, for the armies decided who would occupy the throne. Yet Otho took great pains to exploit legitimist sentiment by identifying himself with Nero.[70] After Otho's suicide, Vitellius was viewed as a legitimate emperor, and the masses demanded arms to defend him when the Flavian armies were approaching Rome. Tacitus expresses some surprise at the episode and notes with satisfaction that the support of the people soon melted away.[71] Understandably, the civilian militia hesitated to stand up to legionary veterans in a pitched battle.

At times popular indignation erupted into open violence, and the people of Rome rose against tyrants and usurpers. Ideologically, the masses rallied in the name of a "just king," and the disorders at Rome resemble what Hobsbawm calls "Church and King" riots.[72] According to Rudé, "the target of 'Church and King' is nearly always 'the rich' or the wealthy middle class, and the ideas and institutions that they espouse."[73] Usually, the element of social protest was lacking in the Roman riots, or at least our scanty accounts make little mention of it. In A.D. 193, following the assassination of Commodus, the Senate elected the able and popular Pertinax as emperor, but, after only eighty-seven days, the mutinous Praetorians murdered him and auctioned the throne to a wealthy senator, Didius Julianus. Though the supine Senate accepted the coup, the masses were furious over the murder of Pertinax and the degradation of the imperial office. Denouncing Julianus, the common people spurned his offers of cash gifts and threw stones at him until the soldiers came to his rescue. After some street fighting, the mob seized the Circus Maximus and held it for a night and a day without food or water, calling upon the frontier generals to overthrow Julianus. Since they had no provisions, the crowds then dispersed.[74] The opportunistic generals pretended to heed the voice of the people, though regardless of the disorders at Rome the legionary commanders would not have allowed the Praetorians to impose Julianus on them. However, the popular rising in the capital had added a tone of legitimacy to a new crop of usurpers. Septimius Severus won the scramble for the throne by marching rapidly to Rome, where Julianus was immediately deposed. An astute politician, Severus posed as the avenger of Pertinax and disbanded the guilty Praetorians, replacing them with his own troops.[75] Later, to legitimize his regime, Severus deified the late Commodus and attached himself and his sons to the Antonine family.[76] Whatever his faults, Commodus had been the son of the beloved Marcus Aurelius. By claiming to represent the Antonine dynasty, Severus assumed the aura of the "just king," dear to the hearts of the Roman people. Even without the riot at Rome, the generals would surely have toppled the puppet Julianus, but nevertheless the Roman "mob" had defended the cause of justice and honor while the Senate was groveling before a usurper.

In the third century A.D. there were more incidents of urban violence, though the sources for this period are especially poor. For some obscure reason, the people battled the Praetorians for three days during the reign of Severus Alexander, and the riots ended only when the soldiers threatened to set fire to the city.[77] In A.D. 238 disorders broke out which were true "Church and King" riots with an undertone of attacks on the rich. Rome was languishing under the despotism of Maximinus Thrax, who had overthrown the last of the Severan house. At a false rumor that the tyrant was dead, the Senate elected Gordian as emperor, and mobs swept through Rome overturning statues of Maximinus and lynching his henchmen. Herodian notes that "without warning, men broke into the houses of their creditors and their opponents in lawsuits, indeed into the house of anyone they hated for some trivial reason; after threatening and abusing them as informers, their attackers robbed and killed them."[78] When Gordian was defeated by Maximinus' supporters in Africa, the Senate elected Balbinus and Pupienus as emperors. The latter, however, was unpopular with the Roman masses, who rioted until the two emperors proclaimed Gordian's grandson, Gordian III, as their heir.[79] While Balbinus and Pupienus marched against Maximinus, the Praetorians at Rome were still loyal to him, but the masses were fiercely opposed to Maximinus. After attacking the soldiers with stones in the streets, a large mob seized arms and laid siege to the Praetorian camp.[80] When the rioters cut off the water supply to the barracks, the soldiers made a sally from the camp. Herodian vividly describes the street fighting:

A sharp skirmish resulted and, when the mob fled, the guards pursued and drove them into all parts of the city. Bested in the hand-to-hand fighting, the people climbed to the housetops and rained down upon the Praetorians tiles, stones, and clay pots. In this way, they inflicted severe injuries upon the soldiers, who, being unfamiliar with the houses, did not dare to climb after them, and, of course, the doors of the shops and houses were barred. The soldiers did, however, set fire to houses that had wooden balconies, and there were many of this type in the city. Because a great number of houses were made chiefly of wood, the fire spread very rapidly and without a break throughout most of the city. . . . A great many people died in the fire, unable to escape because the exits had been blocked by the flames. All the property of the wealthy was looted when the criminal and worthless elements in the city joined with the soldiers in plundering. And the part of Rome destroyed by fire was greater in extent than the largest intact city in the empire.[81]

In the conflagration, the riot ended and looters replaced the crowds who had fought against the troops of the "unjust king." However, the masses had once again defended the cause of legitimate government.

Another clash between civilians and Praetorians took place in A.D. 311. While fire swept the Temple of Fortuna, a soldier, possibly a Christian, blasphemed and was promptly lynched by a mob. The Praetorians then attacked the crowd and slew many until they were restrained by the "emperor" Maxentius.[82] In this episode, the masses were not defending a "just king," but the "true gods."

In the fourth century the city of Rome was demilitarized and outbreaks of urban violence increased. Because the troops in the capital had backed his rival, Maxentius, the victorious Constantine disbanded both the Praetorians and the urban cohorts and did not replace them with a military force.[83] The date is uncertain, but it occurred perhaps by A.D. 318 and surely by A.D. 331.[84] "A similar fate must have befallen the *vigiles*,"[85] for they too vanished from the scene, and artisan clubs assumed the duties of fire fighting.[86] Deprived of both professional troops and a police force, the urban prefects had to maintain order with only the aid of their limited staffs. Imperial Rome reverted to the hectic insecurity which had characterized the city under the Late Republic.

The extant books of Ammianus Marcellinus cover only the years 353-378, but they record a number of outbreaks of urban violence. Throughout the century, there were obviously many more riots, for in A.D. 388, Ambrose dryly remarked: "Do you remember, O Emperor, how many homes of prefects at Rome have been burned, and no one exacted punishment?"[87] Some prefects had managed to assert authority by displays of bravado. In A.D. 356, a riot broke out over the arrest of a popular charioteer, and the prefect's aides seized a few of the rioters. A few days later, a major disorder erupted over a wine shortage, but the prefect Leontius drove into the crowd, personally arrested the ringleader, and had him flogged on the spot, whereupon the mob melted away.[88] In A.D. 358 there were more disturbances, but Ammianus provides no details.[89] During a bread riot in the following year, the prefect Tertullus could only calm the mob by offering his own children as hostages. Shamed by the gesture, the crowd dispersed.[90] In A.D. 364 a mob burned down the house of the prefect Symmachus, who had threatened to destroy his stock of wine rather than sell it at reduced prices.[91] A year later, a mob fired the house of the prefect Lampadius, who was vain, high-handed, and hated by the poor. Since there were no police, neighbors drove off the rioters, but the prefect still thought it prudent to flee from the city.[92] During the disputed papal election of A.D. 366, fierce fighting broke out between the followers of Damasus and those of his rival for the bishopric. In one engagement alone, 137 fatalities occurred. Despairing of the strife, the prefect

Viventius withdrew to the suburbs, and order was only slowly restored to Rome.[93] While such outbreaks were detrimental to public order, the contested episcopal elections at Rome and in other cities were rowdy exercises in democracy, one of the few opportunities for the people to make their own decisions under the stifling despotism of the Late Empire.[94] In the absence of police and troops, demonstrations easily degenerated into riots.

Surveying four centuries of urban violence in Imperial Rome, it is obvious that "bread and circuses" played a major role, but not as corruptive factors as the moralists would have it. Since the city depended upon imported food, hungry crowds sometimes engaged in bread riots. While the Circus and theaters may have tempted some Romans to idle amusements, the poor could not afford much absence from work. Though partisanship between the Blues and Greens often grew overheated, the Circus was more important as the principal means for the masses to communicate with the emperor. Often the roar of the crowd was political in tone, protesting high prices and unfair taxes, appealing for justice, and even demonstrating for peace. When the Circus crowds complained about discrimination between social classes in matters of punishment, Diocletian growled to his councillors: "The empty voices of the people are not to be heeded."[95] Less despotic rulers did heed the voices of the people, who, if too long ignored, might resort to violence. When the masses took to the streets, the mobs were largely made up of ordinary citizens, "little people" driven to desperate action, though obviously criminals and social scum readily joined in the violence in hopes of looting. It is too often overlooked that the majority of episodes of urban violence at Rome were either provoked by food shortages or prompted by ideological attachments to abstract justice or the cause of a "just king." Were the sources more complete and less warped by class bias, even more episodes might come to light. Though most ancient (and some modern) writers dismiss the masses as lawless and fickle, the records of even unsympathetic historians tell a different story. To a large extent the history of the Roman Empire is a grim chronicle of military despotism in the name of law and order, cringing servility on the part of the Senate, and irresponsible opportunism by the armies. In defense of justice and legitimate government, the Roman "mob" often acquitted itself better than its social superiors.

FOOTNOTES

1. Tacitus, *Historiae*, I, 4. Cf. *Dialogus*, 29.
2. Juvenal, X, 79-81.
3. Mikhail I. Rostovtzeff, *The Social and Economic History of the Roman Empire* (Oxford, 1957), I, 81-82. For a different view, see Thomas W. Africa, *Rome of the Caesars* (New York, 1965), 14-17, and John P. V. D. Balsdon, *Life and Leisure in Ancient Rome* (New York, 1969), 267-269.
4. Two recent studies which deal with the Imperial period are by Ramsay MacMullen, *Enemies of the Roman Order* (Cambridge, Mass., 1966), 163-191, and Zwy Yavetz, *Plebs and Princeps* (Oxford, 1969). Though both

are valuable, the former is concerned with the empire more than with the city of Rome, and the latter is limited to the period ending in A.D. 68.

5. Tacitus, *Historiae*, I, 4; III, 31; *Annales*, II, 77. See the excellent discussion of the subjectivity of Tacitus' terms by Yavetz, *Plebs and Princeps*, 141-155.

6. Edmund Burke, *Reflections on the Revolution in France* (Chicago, 1955), 115.

7. Tacitus, *Historiae*, I, 4.

8. Peter A. Brunt, "The Roman Mob," *Past and Present*, XXXV (1966), 3-27, esp. 24. Cf. George Rudé, *The Crowd in History* (New York, 1964), 204-205. For the purposes of the present paper, a crowd becomes a mob when it turns to violence. Its social composition is irrelevant, for the mob that lynched Tiberius Gracchus included the Pontifex Maximus and many nobles and equites.

9. Karl J. Beloch, *Die Bevölkerung der griechisch-römischen Welt* (Leipzig, 1886), 392-412, estimated the population of Augustan Rome as about 800,000; in "Die Bevölkerung Italiens im Altertum," *Klio*, III (1903), 489-490, he raised it to about 1,000,000. Whitney J. Oates, "The Population of Rome," *Classical Philology*, XXIX (1934), 101-116, argues for 1,250,000, but see now James E. Packer, "Housing and Population in Imperial Ostia and Rome," *Journal of Roman Studies*, LVII (1967), 80-95, who favors under a million. Tenney Frank, *An Economic Survey of Ancient Rome* (Baltimore, 1940), V, 218, and Jerome Carcopino, *Daily Life in Ancient Rome* (New Haven, 1940), 16-20, agree on about 1,000,000. Henry T. Rowell, *Rome in the Augustan Age* (Norman, Okla., 1962), 102-106, is rightly cautious of ancient statistics and modern calculations.

10. Sepulchral evidence would suggest that freedmen outnumbered freeborn men by three to one, but these statistics ignore the fact that the freeborn poor could not afford epitaphs, and that wealthy freedmen were anxious to boast of their acquired citizen status. See Lily R. Taylor, "Freedmen and Freeborn in the Epitaphs of Imperial Rome," *American Journal of Philology*, LXXXII (1961), 113-132. Susan Treggiari, *Roman Freedmen in the Late Republic* (Oxford, 1969), has an excellent discussion of the ethnic composition (5-11) and numbers of freedmen in Rome (31-36).

11. Cassius Dio, LXVII, 11.6; LXXIII, 14.4.

12. Juvenal, III, 268-308.

13. Augustus, *Res Gestae Divi Augusti*, 15.

14. Suetonius, *Augustus*, 40. Frank, *Economic Survey* (Paterson, N.J., 1959) I, 328-330, assembles the evidence for the dole under the Republic.

15. Though not originally intended as economic aid, the dole made life in a preindustrial city of the size of Rome tenable for the poor. In 2 B.C. a little over 200,000 men were on the dole registers (Augustus, *Res Gestae*, 15). By A.D. 202 the number seems to have dropped by a few thousand (Cassius Dio, LXXVI, 1.1; cf. *Scriptores Historiae Augustae*, "Septimius Severus," 23.2). In the troubled third century, Aurelian substituted baked bread and added a ration of pork and oil (*Scriptores Historiae Augustae*, "Aurelian," 35.1, 48.1-4. See also Rostovtzeff, *Social and Economic History* [Oxford, 1963] II, 735, n. 39). Though the additional items may have been relief measures for refugees, they soon became fixtures in the dole. In A.D. 369 Valentinian substituted six loaves of high quality bread for twenty coarse

loaves (*Codex Theodosianus*, XIV, 17.5). In A.D. 419 the pork ration was five pounds per month for five months out of a year (*Codex Theodosianus*, XIV, 4.10,3). At this time, about 120,000 men were on the dole at Rome, a figure which may reflect a general drop in the city's population (Arnold H. M. Jones, *The Later Roman Empire* [Norman, Okla., 1964], I, 696; II, 1289, n. 35).

16. Carcopino, *Daily Life*, 205-206. See also Balsdon, *Life and Leisure*, 245-248.

17. Fronto, *Principia Historiae*, 17.

18. Dionysius, *Antiquitates Romanae*, III, 68. Pliny the Elder, *Historia Naturalis*, XXXVI, 102.

19. Carcopino, *Daily Life*, 235.

20. Though Seneca, *Epistulae ad Lucilium*, VII, 3-5, considered the gladiatorial games revolting and sadistic, Pliny the Younger, *Panegyricus*, 33, excused them on the grounds that such spectacles conditioned the audience to scorn wounds and death.

21. Andrew W. Lintott's *Violence in Republican Rome* (Oxford, 1968) has been reviewed severely by G. V. Sumner, *Phoenix*, XXIV (1970), 88-92, but enthusiastically by Adrian N. Sherwin-White, *Journal of Roman Studies*, LIX (1969), 286-287.

22. See Tacitus, *Annales*, I, 77, for the government's reaction to the theater riots in A.D. 15.

23. Lintott, *Violence in Republican Rome*, 89-106. Edward C. Echols, "The Roman City Police: Origin and Development," *Classical Journal*, LIII (1958), 377-384, is more sanguine and argues that the Republic had a police force of *custodes urbis*.

24. Lintott, *Violence in Republican Rome*, 6-16, 66. See now his "The Tradition of Violence in the Annals of the Early Roman Republic," *Historia*, XIX (1970), 12-29.

25. Tacitus, *Annales*, IV, 5. Cassius Dio, LIII, 24.6, assigns 10,000 soldiers to guard the emperor and probably includes a corps of personal bodyguards; he also lists four urban cohorts with a strength of 6,000. Echols, "The Roman City Police," 381, would include 3,000 *custodes urbis* in this figure. Dio's statistics may reflect the Severan era. The actual strength of a cohort is controversial. Marcel Durry, "Praetoriae Cohortes," *Realenzyklopädie der klassischen Altertumswissenschaft*, XXII, col. 1613-1614, argues that the figure was 500 before Septimius Severus doubled it. (Thus, Tacitus, *Historiae*, II, 93, deals with an exception.) However, Alfredo Passerini, *Le coorti pretorie* (Roma, 1939), favors a strength of 1,000 from the beginning of the Principate. The latter figure seems more realistic, for it would insure the Princeps the equivalent of two legions at his disposal.

26. Josephus, *Antiquitates Judaicae*, XIX, 188, but he mentions three urban cohorts in *Bellum Judaicum*, II, 205.

27. Echols, "The Roman City Police," 382. Apparently, Claudius also increased the number of Praetorian cohorts to twelve—*Cambridge Ancient History*, X, 232, n.3.

28. Tacitus, *Historiae*, II, 93; III, 57, 69, 73. One cohort deserted to Vespasian; three died with Sabinus. In A.D. 41 the urban cohorts had briefly backed the short-lived "restoration" of the Republic—Josephus, *Antiquitates Judaicae*, XIX, 188.

29. Echols, "The Roman City Police," 383.

30. *Cambridge Ancient History,* XI, 135, n.2.

31. Herodian, III, 13.4, says that Septimius Severus quadrupled the forces at Rome, but this is an unlikely figure even including the legion at Albano and assuming that Severus doubled the numbers in the Praetorian and urban cohorts.

32. Cassius Dio, LV, 26.4-5. Suetonius, *Augustus,* 30. Strabo, V, 3.7.

33. Cassius Dio, LV, 24.6, says 6,000.

34. P. K. Baillie Reynolds, *The Vigiles of Imperial Rome* (London, 1926), 67-68.

35. Note the career of Ofonius Tigellinus—Tacitus, *Historiae,* I, 72.

36. Cassius Dio, LVIII, 9.3-5.

37. Cassius Dio, LXII, 17.1.

38. Mason Hammond, *The Antonine Monarchy* (Roma, 1959), favors a strength of 500 for an urban cohort or one of the *vigiles.* This figure results in a police force of 5,500, equivalent to that of Los Angeles.

39. *Scriptores Historiae Augustae,* "Marcus Aurelius," 15.1.

40. Suetonius, *Augustus,* 45.

41. Suetonius, *Tiberius,* 47. Pliny the Elder, *Historiae Naturalis,* XXXIV, 62.

42. Tacitus, *Annales,* VI, 13.

43. Josephus, *Antiquitates Judaicae,* XIX, 24-26, in (trans. Louis H. Feldman) *The Works of Josephus* (Cambridge, Mass., 1965), IX, 227-229.

44. Cassius Dio, LIX, 13.4.

45. Plutarch, *Galba,* 17.4.

46. Tacitus, *Historiae,* I, 72; Plutarch, *Otho,* 2.2.

47. Cassius Dio, LXXV, 4.2-5, in (trans. Earnest Cary) *Dio's Roman History* (Cambridge, Mass., 1927), IX, 203-205.

48. Cassius Dio, LXXV, 4.5-6. In other cities, the Circus was also the scene of disciplined demonstrations and occasional riots. See, for example, John B. Bury, *History of the Later Roman Empire* (New York, 1953), II, 39-48, 71-74, and Robert Browning, "The Riot of A.D. 387 in Antioch," *Journal of Roman Studies,* XLII (1952), 13-20.

49. William Sinnigen, "The Roman Secret Service," *Classical Journal,* LVII (1961), 65-72, esp. 68.

50. MacMullen, *Enemies of the Roman Order,* 336, n.2.

51. *Scriptores Historiae Augustae,* "Hadrian," 11.4-6.

52. Epictetus, *Dissertationes,* IV, 13.5, specifies that the *agent provocateur* is a soldier in mufti.

53. Appian, *Bella Civilia,* V, 18.

54. Appian, *Bella Civilia,* V, 67-68.

55. Cassius Dio, XLVIII, 31.5-6.

56. Guy E. Chilver, "Princeps and Frumentationes," *American Journal of Philology,* LXX (1949), 7-21.

57. Tacitus, *Annales,* XII, 43; Suetonius, *Claudius,* 18.

58. Frank, *Economic Survey,* V, 41, 268-269.

59. Suetonius, *Nero,* 45.

60. Cassius Dio, LXXII, 13.1-6; Herodian, I, 12-13.

61. Gustave Le Bon, *The Crowd* (London, 1947), 66-67.

62. See, for example, Polybius, VI, 56.11, and the note by Frank W. Walbank, *A Historical Commentary on Polybius* (Oxford, 1957), I, 742.

63. Tacitus, *Annales*, XIV, 42-45.

64. Tacitus, *Annales*, XIV, 59-61. See also the contemporary play, *Octavia*, which is usually included in editions of Seneca's tragedies, though Seneca himself appears as a character in the drama.

65. Tacitus, *Annales*, XV, 44.

66. Tacitus, *Annales*, II, 82; Suetonius, *Caligula*, 5-6. Supposedly, he derived these sentiments from his father, Drusus—Tacitus, *Annales*, I, 33. Suetonius, *Claudius*, I. See Sir Ronald Syme, *Tacitus* (Oxford, 1958), I, 418, on the pro-Germanicus tradition.

67. Arnold H. M. Jones, "The Elections under Augustus," *Journal of Roman Studies*, XLV (1955), 9-21, believes that Augustus allowed considerable freedom to the assemblies; but Peter A. Brunt, "The Lex Valeria Cornelia," *Journal of Roman Studies*, LI (1961), 71-83, is more cautious and rightly so. At any rate, the forms of the Republic were in evidence. For a lively meeting of the *comitia tributa* as late as A.D. 41, see Josephus, *Antiquitates Judaicae*, XIX, 158-159.

68. Josephus, *Antiquitates Judaicae*, XIX, 166-189, 227-228. Suetonius, *Caligula*, 60; *Claudius*, 10. Josephus mentions that the commons feared a revival of the civil wars. With or without their support, Claudius' success was guaranteed by the swords of the Praetorians and the diplomacy of Herod Agrippa.

69. Suetonius, *Nero*, 57. Cf. Tacitus, *Historiae*, I, 4. The false Neros who soon appeared in the East confirm the popularity of the fallen emperor in the provinces. See Tacitus, *Historiae*, I, 2; II, 8; Cassius Dio, LXIV, 9.3; LXVI, 19.3; Suetonius, *Nero*, 57. Despite the "bad press" that he received from senatorial historians and Christian propagandists, Nero became "the once and future king" in the popular mind.

70. Suetonius, *Otho*, 7; Plutarch, *Otho*, 3.1-2. The ambitious Praetorian prefect, Nymphidius Sabinus, had tried to create a claim on the throne by posing as Caligula's bastard—Plutarch, *Galba*, 9.1.

71. Tacitus, *Historiae*, III, 58. See Zwy Yavetz, "Vitellius and the 'Fickleness of the Mob,'" *Historia*, XVIII (1969), 557-569.

72. Eric J. Hobsbawm, *Primitive Rebels* (New York, 1959), 108-125.

73. Rudé, *The Crowd in History*, 138.

74. Cassius Dio, LXXIV, 13.3-5. Cf. Herodian, II, 7.2-3, and *Scriptores Historiae Augustae*, "Didius Julianus," 4.2-5.

75. Cassius Dio, LXXV, 1.1, 4.1. Herodian, II, 10.1. Cassius Dio, LXXV, 1.4-5, witnessed the enthusiasm of the crowds for Severus when he entered the city.

76. Cassius Dio, LXXV, 7.4; LXXVI, 9.4. *Scriptores Historiae Augustae*, "Septimius Severus," 10.3-6. Herodian, III, 10.5.

77. Cassius Dio, LXXX, 2.3.

78. Herodian, VII, 7.3, in (trans. Edward C. Echols) *Herodian of Antioch's History of the Roman Empire* (Berkeley, 1961), 185. Herodian, VII, 3.5, attributes the resentment of the masses to Maximinus' expropriation of public funds earmarked for games and entertainment. Relying on Herodian, VII, 3.1-6, Rostovtzeff, *Social and Economic History*, I, 452-453, views Maximinus as primarily a relentless foe of the *bourgeoisie*. Apparently, the pro-Gordian riot got out of hand when the poor began to attack the homes of the rich.

79. Herodian, VII, 10.5-9.

80. Herodian, VII, 11.6-12.4. Cf. *Scriptores Historiae Augustae*, "Maximini Duo," 22.6; "Gordiani Tres," 22.7-23.1; "Maximus et Balbinus," 9.1-10.8.

81. Herodian, VII, 12.4-7, in (trans. Edward C. Echols) *Herodian*, 196.

82. Zosimus, II, 13. Naturally, Eusebius, *Historia Ecclesiastica*, VIII, 14.3, considers Maxentius responsible for the massacre. Cf. Aurelius Victor, *de Caesaribus*, 40.

83. Aurelius Victor, *de Caesaribus*, 40. Zosimus, II, 17.

84. William Sinnigen, *The Officium of the Urban Prefecture during the Later Roman Empire* (Roma, 1957), 35, n.11; 91, 92, n.21.

85. *Ibid.*, 92-93.

86. Jones, *The Later Roman Empire*, I, 695.

87. Ambrose, *Epistulae*, 40.13, in (trans. Sister Mary Beyenka) *Letters* (Washington D.C., 1954), 11.

88. Ammianus Marcellinus, XV, 7.2-4.

89. Ammianus Marcellinus, XVII, 11.5.

90. Ammianus Marcellinus, XIX, 10.1-4.

91. Ammianus Marcellinus, XXVII, 3.4.

92. Ammianus Marcellinus, XXVII, 3.8-9.

93. Ammianus Marcellinus, XXVII, 3.11-13.

94. At Milan in A.D. 373, the governor, Ambrose, tried to quiet the rowdy electorate and wound up being elected bishop. Paulinus, *vita Ambrosii*, 6-7.

95. *Codex Justinianus*, IX, 47.12.

Section I. the Medieval City

THE MAKING OF A TOWN: NINTH-CENTURY BRUGES

latter ninth century

This account of how the town of Bruges came into existence documents the growth of a commercial center dependent on the needs of courtiers and suitors of the court; it implies that, at least in this case, geographical features and broad social changes affected the rapid development of the town far less than the circumstantial needs of the castle-dwellers.

After this, because of the work or needs of those living in the château,* there began to stream in merchants—that is, dealers in precious goods—who set themselves up in front of the gate, at the château's bridge; then there followed tavern-keepers, then inn-keepers to provide the food and lodging for those who came to do business in the presence of the prince, who was often there. Houses began to be built and inns to be made ready, where those were to be lodged who could not be put up inside the château; and they were accustomed to use this phrase: "Let us go to the bridge." So many dwellings accumulated there that right away it became a large town [*villa magna*] which to this day bears the name "Brugghe," which, in their tongue, means "bridge."

---

*The château of Bruges, built by Baldwin Iron Arm, Count of Flanders, who married Charles the Bald's daughter Judith in 862.

SOURCE Translated from: *Documents relatifs à l'histoire de l'industrie et du commerce en France,* ed. Gustave Fagniez, *Collection de textes pour servir à l'étude et à l'enseignement de l'histoire,* Vol. I (Paris: Alphonse Picard et Fils, 1898), 54-55.

MANORIAL RECORDS

OF THE TENTH AND ELEVENTH CENTURIES

These documents testify, among other things, to the total integration of church-men into manorial society; the imputation of the church's power over the countryside is, however, somewhat exaggerated by the fact that most extant manorial records were kept by monastics and episcopal landlords. The tenth-century charter from Stavelot enumerates the mutual advantages accruing to laymen and the church that could result from a pious donation of lands. Rainulf and his family, assured of a "heavenly reward," enjoy the use of extra lands while they live; the monks of Stavelot acquire all of their possessions upon their deaths. An even greater boon to a monastery was a noble or royal foundation, such as the one described in the founding charter of Boxgrove Priory. The ... eleventh-century document describes a property dispute among vassals of the Count of Blois, who makes a judgment in an impromptu court session. If the lands of a monastery were not sufficiently increased by gifts, they could be augmented by outright purchase, ...

APRIL 25, 943

Whoever should donate something from among his chattel to those who live in community for God's church, can be certain of receiving a heavenly reward. Therefore I, Rainulf, and my wife Huoda, donate jointly our personal possessions to the church of Saint Peter in the monastery of Stavelot, where the body of lord Remaclus lies, whereof the venerable Odilo is both Abbot and guardian, two manses in the village of Navaugle, which lie between [the lands

SOURCE Translated from *Recueil des Chartes de l'Abbaye de Stavelot-Malmedy*, ed. Joseph Halkin and C. G. Roland, Vol. I (Brussels: Kiessling et Cie. P. Imbreghts, 1909), 152-53.

of] Saint Remaclus and Saint Lambert, between the Iwoine and the Vachaux. In return for which we accept from the monastery, with the consent of the aforesaid abbot and all the brethren, boon service in the above-mentioned village of Navaugle and [four manses] in the village of Orgoni. Our agreement is that for as long as we live, I, Rainulf and my wife Huoda and our son Godfrey will pay twelve pennies every year at the feast of Saint Remaclus: so that if we fail to pay or if we should be late in paying, we shall try to collect it as the law provides. And we are not, under this agreement, empowered to sell or trade this property, but are rather to increase it, and after all our deaths both pieces of land, together with all that has accrued to it and all the above-mentioned appurtenances, shall revert to the church of Stavelot without any opposition. In order that this boon-service remain a firm and unchanging agreement, it is supported by this contract.

Done publicly at the monastery of Stavelot on the 17th of the Kalends of May [April 25], in the seventh year of the reign of glorious King Otto. The seal of Abbot Odilo who had this charter drawn up. The seal of Odilardo, his advocate. The seals of Everard Aricus, Engonus, Mannonus, Ermenfindus, Therdericus, Asculfrus, Aricus.

THE CUSTOMS OF NEWCASTLE-UPON-TYNE

These are the laws and customs which the burgesses of Newcastle-upon-Tyne had at the time of Henry [I], king of England . . . :

The burgesses may distrain foreigners within their market and without, and within their houses and without, and within their borough and without, and they may do this without the permission of the reeve, unless the courts are being held within the borough, or unless they are in the field on army service, or are doing castle-guard. But a burgess may not distrain on another burgess without the permission of the reeve.

If a burgess shall lend anything in the borough to someone dwelling outside, the debtor shall pay back the debt if he admit it, or otherwise do right in the court of the borough.

Pleas which arise in the borough shall there be held and concluded except those which belong to the king's crown.

If a burgess shall be sued in respect of any plaint he shall not plead outside the borough except for defect of court; nor need he answer, except at a stated time and place, unless he has already made a foolish answer, or unless the case concerns matters pertaining to the crown.

If a ship comes to the Tyne and wishes to unload, it shall be permitted to the burgesses to purchase what they please. And if a dispute arises between a burgess and a merchant, it shall be settled before the third tide.

Whatever merchandise a ship brings by sea must be brought to the land; except salt and herring which must be sold on board ship.

If anyone has held land in burgage for a year and a day justly and without challenge, he need not answer any claimant, unless the claimant is outside the kingdom of England, or unless he be a boy not having the power of pleading.

If a burgess have a son in his house and at his table, his son shall have the same liberty as his father.

If a villein come to reside in the borough, and shall remain as a burgess in the borough for a year and a day, he shall thereafter always remain there, unless there was a previous agreement between him and his lord for him to remain there for a certain time.

If a burgess sues anyone concerning anything, he cannot force the burgess to trial by battle, but the burgess must defend himself by his oath, except in a charge of treason when the burgess must defend himself by battle. Nor shall a burgess offer battle against a villein unless he has first quitted his burgage.

No merchant except a burgess can buy wool or hides or other merchandise outside the town, nor shall he buy them within the town except from burgesses.

If a burgess incurs forfeiture he shall give 6 oras to the reeve.

In the borough there is no "merchet" nor "heriot" nor "bloodwite" nor "stengesdint" [fines imposed for drawing blood and for striking another].

Any burgess may have his own oven and handmill if he wishes, saving always the rights of the king's oven.

If a woman incur a forfeiture concerning bread or ale, none shall concern himself with it except the reeve. If she offend twice she shall be punished by the forfeiture. If she offend thrice justice shall take its course.

No one except a burgess may buy cloth for dyeing or make or cut it.

A burgess can give or sell his land as he wishes, and go where he will, freely and quietly unless his claim to the land is challenged.

MOHAMMED AND CHARLEMAGNE

Henri Pirenne

GENERAL CONCLUSION

From the foregoing data, it seems, we may draw two essential conclusions:

1. The Germanic invasions destroyed neither the Mediterranean unity of the ancient world, nor what may be regarded as the truly essential features of the Roman culture as it still existed in the fifth century, at a time when there was no longer an Emperor in the West.

Despite the resulting turmoil and destruction, no new principles made their appearance; either in the economic or social order, or in the linguistic situation, or in the existing institutions. Whatever civilization survived was Mediterranean. It was in the regions by the seacoast that culture was preserved, and it was from them that the innovations of the age proceeded: monasticism, the conversion of the Anglo-Saxons, the *ars Barbarica,* etc.

The Orient was the fertilizing factor: Constantinople, the center of the World. In 600 the physiognomy of the world was not different in quality from that which it had revealed in 400.

2. The cause of the break with the tradition of antiquity was the rapid and unexpected advance of Islam. The result of this advance was the final separation of East from West, and the end of Mediterranean unity. Countries like Africa and Spain, which had always been parts of the Western community, gravitated henceforth in the orbit of Baghdad. In these countries another religion made its appearance, and an entirely different culture. The

From *Mohammed and Charlemagne* © 1939 by Henri Pirenne. Reprinted by permission of Harper & Row.

Western Mediterranean, having become a Moslem lake, was no longer the thoroughfare of commerce and of thought which it had always been.

The West was blockaded and forced to live on in isolation. For the first time in history the axis of history was shifted northwards from the Mediterranean. The decadence into which the Merovingian monarchy lapsed as a result of this change gave birth to a new dynasty, the Carolingian, whose original home was in the Germanic North.

With this new dynasty the Pope allied himself, breaking with the Emperor, who, engrossed in his struggle against the Musulmans, could no longer protect him. And so the Church allied itself with the new order of things. In Rome, and in the Empire which it founded, it had no rival. And its power was all the greater inasmuch as the State, being incapable of maintaining its administration, allowed itself to be absorbed by the feudality, the inevitable sequel of the economic regression. All the consequences of this change became glaringly apparent after Charlemagne. Europe, dominated by the Church and the feudality, assumed a new physiognomy, differing slightly in different regions. The Middle Ages—to retain the traditional term—were beginning. The transitional phase was protracted. One may say that it lasted a whole century—from 650 to 750. It was during this period of anarchy that the tradition of antiquity disappeared, while the new elements took control.

This development was completed in 800 by the constitution of the new Empire, which consecrated the break between the West and the East, inasmuch as it gave to the West a new Roman Empire—the manifest proof that it had broken with the old Empire, which continued to exist in Constantinople.

THE PIRENNE THESIS: TOWARDS REFORMULATION

Paul Craig Roberts

In this paper the Pirenne Thesis will be examined in a novel way. Out of this examination will come a strong case for the general validity of Pirenne's thesis that Islam was the most significant of the causative factors in the transition of Roman Gaul to Medieval Europe. This examination will also give us a glimpse of why Pirenne is not guilty of a purely economic interpretation of history as his critics have claimed. And yet at the same time we will see that Pirenne did not fail "for the simple reason that economic factors play a subsidiary role," but because he emphasized the wrong economic factor. . . .

There are two questions to examine. One is whether the advance of Islam is a better causative factor by which to explain the break with Antiquity that gave rise to Medieval Europe than is the German invasions, the pirate fleet of Vandal Carthage, the decadence succeeding the Antonines, or the Atlantic Civilization of the Scandinavians. The other question is whether the economic medium is a better one through which to trace the effectuation of the "barbarization" of Gaul and the rise of medieval civilization (and the revival of trade) than is the political, social or ideological. It is a matter of *finality* in causative factors. It is a matter of the medium through which this conclusiveness was effected.

The validity of the Pirenne Thesis rests upon the answers to the above two questions. It is a matter of qualitative analysis. It has nothing to do with the question of the volume of trade carried on under the Merovingians; it has nothing to do with the question of the presence of professional merchants in Gaul during the Carolingian period; it has nothing to do with the relative

From "The Pirenne Thesis, Economies or Civilizations; Towards Reformulation," by Paul Craig Roberts in *Classica et Mediaevalia* XXV (1964), 297-315. Reprinted by permission of the author.

availabilities of oriental cloths, spices, papyrus, or quantity of gold in circulation in Gaul under the Romans, Merovingians, Carolingians, or during the eleventh century, the twelfth century, or at any time.

The validity of the Pirenne Thesis does not turn on any quantitative measures. It turns on the qualitative analysis of a factor that has been ignored. It is the purpose of this paper to introduce this factor.

The growth of great cities gives rise to demands inflated beyond the possibility of their being locally satisfied. Rome's growth and provisioning was effected only by enlarging the dimensions of the tributary hinterland. Also a required factor for the growth of a city is an efficient means of mass transport. The lack of transport or ease of its disruption constitute a check to a city's growth and a threat to its very existence.

The Roman Empire was the product of a single expanding power center striving (among other things, of course) to extend and protect its claim on resources. It was a vast city-building enterprise which left the imprint of Rome on every part of Europe, Northern Africa, and Asia Minor, altering the way of life in the old cities and establishing by *purposeful design* hundreds of new cities, always following a deliberate policy of dispersal, in subordination to Rome. The conquered towns were often altered, but the new towns were founded in accord with the economic and military needs of the empire.

Economic control was the basis of the Roman Empire, and the widened province of transportation and communication given by the control of the Mediterranean allowed Rome to exercise its command over men and resources in distant areas. By its organization of cities the Roman Empire united the lands of the eastern Mediterranean, from which it drew its chief wealth, with the less developed lands of the western Mediterranean and northern Gaul. The unifying medium was the economic. All economic trade was purposely orientated by Rome towards Rome. Thus, Rome was the concentration into a few square miles of the resources of a whole empire.

Despite the unity, there was a profound difference between Roman civilization in the East and in the West. Roman Gaul was created by Rome and out of Rome. The towns of Gaul were *new* towns; they were Rome's towns; their commerce was Rome's commerce. They received their culture from Rome, the life line of the connection being the economic orientation. Cicero called Narbonne in southern Gaul "a colony of Roman citizens, a watch tower of the Roman people, a bulwark against the wild tribes of Gaul." These towns were founded for military and economic reasons—to mobilize the resources of Gaul for Rome. The institutions and systems of administration reflect this.

Before Rome, Gaul had known only wild tribes. Italy had known the Etruscan and Hellenic cultures. The East had been blessed richly.

In normal times in Gaul or Aquitaine, these "new towns" could draw their food from the surrounding region, so they maintained the urban-rural balance that larger cities of the other provinces, by their very growth, upset. Thus, they usually did not need to be provisioned with essentials (and when they did, they usually needed the legions as well). Consequently, Gaul's commerce was significantly different from that of the other provinces. Gaul was economically self-sufficient. Its surpluses were largely exported to Rome and to the East. This "trade" was one way. Commodities of trade produced in Gaul were either heavy, bulky, or fragile objects, requiring an efficient system of transportation. There was little interregional trade in Gaul of its own products.

The records we have of the earliest cities tell us that in them the functions of the market were undertaken by the temple, though, as in the Soviet Union, a portion of the peasant's production might be privately exchanged, once the collective demand was satisfied. Thus, trade characterized by spontaneous mutual interaction, grew up around the periphery of a hierarchically organized economic order. Should one above substitute "Gaul" for "earliest cities" and "Rome" for "temple," the analogy would not be altogether uninteresting. Gaul's prosperity was based on the exploitation of its own natural resources under the protection of Rome. Its imports of oriental cloths and spices had little significance for its economic organization and well-being or for its civilization.

The cities of the East present a different picture in more ways than one. In the East there was civilization before Rome and civilization after Rome and its independent foundations were retained under Rome. The Romans had an empirical respect for any established order, even when it contradicted their own—a trait that served them well. The commerce of the East was bilateral and extensive; it went in many directions. . . .

THE VINDICATION OF THE PIRENNE THESIS

Under Rome there was economic unity of the Mediterranean, and the general direction of commerce was towards the coasts of the sea—was towards Rome. This had very real significance for the Roman Empire. It was the factor that allowed life to be breathed into its institutions; it made possible its existence. And it was what allowed Gaul to be Roman.

With the founding of Constantinople as the eastern capital, the whole center of gravity in the Empire shifted to the eastern provinces. Yet "Rome" was the Mediterranean and the Mediterranean was "Rome." "A city of the far-flung earth you made."

In Gaul the effect of the Germanic invasions was on the *volume* of trade. They hastened the process of passage from the uniform imperial economic organization to an economy of local production and barter. Hand in hand with this process went the deterioration of Roman society in Gaul. Yet the process was not one of unbroken regression, and it was *not irreversible.*

The effect of the Islamic encirclement of the Mediterranean was on the *orientation* of trade. From the beginning of the eighth century, the whole economic movement of the western Mediterranean was directed towards Baghdad, or that of Gaul confined within itself, later to be directed northward. From this fundamental fact, Roman Gaul *necessarily* breathed its last breath.

Pirenne is wrong when he says commercial activity did not survive the

Saracen mastery of the western Mediterranean. The Mediterranean had long been the great artery of commerce, and it remained so. However, the orientation of Gaulish trade toward the Empire did not survive the Saracens.

Perhaps now we can see why Pirenne's thesis might be true, as well as why he failed to prove it so. He chose to emphasize the role of international trade rather than the qualitative differences in the organization and economic orientation of markets and the significance of this for Roman Gaul. It was not the amount of trade, but the type of trade; not the quality of markets, but the method of organization of markets; not the existence of trade, but the orientation of trade. The Muslim conquest in itself did not transform the money economy of the Merovingians to the natural economy of the Middle Ages. However, it ended forever the orientation of Gaulish trade toward the Empire.

Pirenne recognized the connection between Rome, trade, and the cities of Gaul. However, he misinterpreted the meaning of the connection. Gaul was orientated towards Rome, not towards international trade.

When trade revived in Gaul, it was not orientated toward the provisioning of regal cities. It did not gravitate towards empire. Thus, it did not serve the purpose of empire. Formative economic forces were no longer "Roman." Thus, in what had been Gaul, economic activity, and thereby society, could take a new turn.

The medieval town was born out of local protection. There was no central power. Regionally, the protection offered by the bishops rivalled that of the feudal nobility. In no sense were medieval towns agents of a far-flung institution. Trade could begin to grow to be more and more the result of spontaneous mutual interaction, to be promoted, organized, directed, coordinated, and orientated mainly by the prospect of gain—the means to dignity for those outside the titles of church and nobility. With the Roman power center, which had functionalized things in its interest, passed from the scene, a mostly custom-bound economic system could be modified by continuous stages towards a market system, *with the various intermediate forms offering different combinations of functional and commercial rationality.* For this reason it is justified to study economic history with a view to the presence of different combinations of the functional and commercial methods of organization in order to assess the dominating influence arising out of the conflict between the convivial existence of custom and impersonal commercialism upon social and economic organization (and on intellectual history, i.e., Socialism).

The new trading economy based on individual enterprise and mobile capital was almost from the beginning outside the authority of the domain of both feudal and guild systems. Mobile capital proved to be a powerful force. It tore away the shielding that had protected the medieval town and the powers of the Church and feudal nobility and reached through to break the chains on human action of ritualistic prescription, proving itself to be even more ruthless in the destruction of historic institutions than the most reckless of authoritarian rulers. These institutions were destroyed because their rationality was given to them by their being based on a functional economy. Thus, the administrative and coordinative limitations of this custom-bound system did not permit its institutions to stand in the face of a rising level and rate of change in economic activity. The power of privilege as an organizing and coordinating force was replaced by the power of contract. The functional economy gave way to the commercial economy. The concrete market place of the medieval town was made dynamic by the advent of the abstract market. But this came later. Yet even in the eleventh century Alain of Lille could say "Not Caesar now, but money, is all."

SUMMARY

This paper contains the following main points:

1. The Pirenne Thesis has been side-tracked into irrelevancies.

2. Pirenne justifiably used the economic medium to struggle with a thesis about civilizations which he never clearly presented. I suggest Pirenne can be vindicated by showing that what is now western Europe of what was the Western Empire had no independent social, economic, political, or cultural foundations. Its life line was its economic orientation to Rome which was functionally organized by Rome to serve Rome. When the West was cut off from the Empire by the Moslems and infested with the Germans, Roman civilization simply died. Pirenne was concerned with civilizations, not economies.

CITY-STATE

André Piganiol

The term city-state is applied to an autonomous state composed of a city and its outskirts and revealing a more or less clearly defined distinction between a bourgeois and a peasant class. The outstanding examples of the city-state of antiquity were in Phoenicia, in Greece and in Italy; in the Middle Ages the most typical city-states were in Italy and on the coast of the North Sea.

At first sight the *polis* or ancient city-state seems to have been constructed according to a definite plan; in Rome, for instance, there were three ethnic tribes, thirty curias, three hundred senators. But this superficial uniformity conceals profound social variations. In many cases the tribes or clans, from whose amalgamation the city developed, had widely different customs and religions. This is true of the Albans and the Sabines, two of the constituent elements of Rome. Moreover the centuries of warfare which preceded the foundation of the *polis* left ineffaceable distinctions between victors and vanquished. The institution of helotry and the peculiar form of agrarian organization in Sparta were perhaps survivals of the Doric invasion; and it is not yet determined to what extent the line between patricians and plebeians in Rome indicates an ethnic difference.

The *polis* retained in weakened form many institutions of the larger clans: fraternities of warriors (phratry); large family associations (*genos* in Greek, *gens* in Latin); age groups; communal banquets (*syssity* in Sparta and analogous customs in Carthage and in southern Italy). The ancient division into ethnic tribes of common origin persisted in Athens until the time of

---

Clisthenes and in Rome until the royal epoch, when they were replaced by local tribes organized on the basis of domicile. Another great change made by the *polis* in the course of its development was the liberation of the individual from the tyranny of the *genos.* The *polis* thus destroyed the essential characteristic of primitive law: family solidarity which, in making the family as a whole responsible for the wrongs committed by each member, had been an important source of feuds and internal disturbances. G. Glotz (*La cité grecque*) divides the entire history of the city-state into three periods, determined by the changing relations of the family, the individual and the state: "In the first, the city is composed of families who guard their primordial rights jealously . . . ; in the second, the city suppresses the families with the aid of liberated individuals; in the third, the excesses of individualism ruin the city, making necessary the establishment of more extensive states."

The origin of the ancient city, the force which was responsible for its establishment, has been the subject of much dispute. In the nineteenth century Fustel de Coulanges set forth the theory that the foundation of the city was essentially a religious phenomenon. The nucleus was the family, centering about the hearth, before which the father of the family, who was also a priest, conducted the worship of the ancestors. The union of several families established the hearth of the phratry; and the union of the phratries established the hearth of the tribe. "As soon as the families, the phratries and the tribes had agreed to unite and have the same worship, they immediately founded the city as a sanctuary for this common worship" (Fustel de Coulanges, *La cité antique,* p. 177). In reality the *polis* was the result of an economic evolution. At the foot of a citadel, dating perhaps from the Mycenean age, a market was established and artisans settled. Out of two elements, therefore, the *acropolis* (with which the word *polis* was originally synonymous) and the *astu* (group of business and residence buildings located on the plain), the city developed. The progress of the cities is inseparably bound up with the development of commerce. In Phoenicia and in Greece the regime of city autonomy developed in trading cities near the sea and the achievements of these mercantile cities served as models for the communities which were still mere agricultural markets.

The institutions of a large number of ancient cities show a parallel course of development, the various stages of which may be correlated both with changes in economic structure and with the evolution of the army. At first the city was controlled by the heads of the genos, who composed an oligarchic senate, limiting the action of the king; these were the rich and noble warriors who went to battle in chariots. Later on, with the rise of a class of propertied peasants and with the growth of movable wealth caused by the progress of commerce, a timocratic constitution was established, placing power in the hands of the rich without consideration of nobility; this change coincided with the organization of phalanxes of hoplites. The difficulties involved in the transformation of a state primarily agricultural into a state primarily mercantile explain the appearance of the tyrannies. Partly as a result of the increase in personal wealth (or the lowering of the tax qualification), partly as a result of the organization of a fleet and the growth of a class of sailors, political control was transferred from the tyrants to the people. Then came into existence those direct democratic institutions which constitute the chief political peculiarity of the *polis* in this stage of its evolution and which were made possible by its narrow territorial limits: the drawing of magistrates by lot, rotation in public functions, state bounties to assist citizens in the fulfillment of their public functions, recall constantly threatening magistrates, and the power of the popular assembly both to issue decrees having the force of laws and to act as sovereign judge.

The *polis* has its medieval counterpart in the free commune of Italy and Flanders. While the evolution of the institutions of the commune constitutes a problem in itself the commune and the *polis* show such striking similarities in so many of their characteristics that a comparison throws light upon the inherent tendencies of the city-state. Both developed under essentially the same conditions. Just as the *polis* had its inception after the period of invasions called the "Greek Middle Ages," so the commune appeared after the Carolingian period, springing up like the Ionian and Phoenician cities near the sea or at the centers of traffic networks. Just as the constituent parts of the city-state of antiquity were the *acropolis* and the *astu,* so the commune was the product of the castle-fortress (*burgus*) and the market (*portus*) and in both cases the sanctuary was in the heart of the city. Geographical conditions played their part in the liberation of the commune from the feudal lord as they had in the protection of the autonomy of the *polis.* It was not by accident that the *polis* flourished in mountainous Greece and in the island or cape settlements of the Phoenicians; or that the free communes were usually located on strategic sites, around canals as in Flanders or on an archipelago as in Venice.

The mediaeval commune, like the city of old, was a liberal force: as the *polis* had released the individual from the tyranny of the genos, so the commune destroyed the monopoly of freedom which the nobility had formerly enjoyed. Both ancient and medieval cities engendered a rigorous patriotism. The class of hereditary citizens constituted a kind of nobility, united by a strong feeling of solidarity, which found practical expression in social legislation, stipends for children orphaned by war and pensions for invalids. Such celebrations as the Panathenean festival or the worship of St. Mark at Venice were not merely religious but patriotic. There were, however, powerful elements of disintegration, important among which was the conflict between the military and the commercial interests, resulting usually in the victory of the latter and eventuating in the replacement of the soldier citizens by mercenaries. The rival free cities were constantly in arms against one another, while family feuds were a cause of frequent civil wars. As a result of the impetus toward economic and social legislation the poorer classes tended toward communism. Abolition of debts and division of land became part of the program of the most radical groups. The social conflict was more serious in the medieval cities, where the artisans were organized in guilds. Another source of internal disturbance arose from the attempt to subordinate the city to the country. The struggle between the urban class and the farmers, which was developing during the autonomy of Athens and was perceptible in Carthage, became acute in the medieval cities.

The free commune of the Middle Ages, like some of the mercantile cities of antiquity, was not a self-sufficient organism. Because of excessive population resulting from the growth of industry and commerce the city was obliged to import most of its necessities. The state met this problem by seeking to gain control of certain imported commodities. The Athenians were permitted to load ships with wheat for Athens only and the Venetians were compelled to transport commodities exclusively to Venice. The foreign policy of the ancient and medieval cities was dominated by the desire to open markets for trade; their efforts were directed toward establishing fortified trading posts in foreign lands, multiplying their colonies and founding empires by levying tribute on foreign cities. Thus the commercial city became consciously imperialistic.

The city was so constituted as to render its development into a large state very difficult. Even Rome did not altogether succeed in adapting her municipal institutions to the administration of an empire. The Greek cities sought to solve the problem through the instrument of confederation. The reason for their failure is well illustrated by the case of the Boeotian cities, which in trying to extend the institutions of direct democracy outside the city-state rendered the central authority almost powerless. No less serious than these political difficulties was the weakening effect of the restrictive economic policy, which finally resulted in curbing progress and in fettering exchange. The free city, unable to withstand the accumulated strain, declined and finally disappeared.

Ancient political theorists described the city-state as agrarian rather than mercantile, and thus seriously misunderstood its essential nature. Plato subordinated the producing class to warriors and philosophers; he regarded proximity to the sea as dangerous and desired to abolish private property and even money. Aristotle considered virtue and not wealth to be the true goal of the city. As their model city-state both Plato and Aristotle unreservedly accepted Sparta, which was no more than a camp piously preserving the customs of prehistoric times and hardly deserves to be classed as a city-state. Only in modern times has the true nature of the city-state been understood. It is the modern theorists who have recognized and appreciated the importance of the merchants in the organization of the mediaeval communes. The economic factors in the development of the *polis* are more difficult to determine because of the nature of the sources available, but there is no doubt that the merchants exercised a determining influence in the growth of the cities of Phoenicia and of many of those of Greece, while in Rome the enfranchisement of the people was perhaps due in part to the activity of the merchant colony established in Aventine.

$$\text{THE TOWNS}$$

Henri Pirenne

THE REVIVAL OF URBAN LIFE

As long as Mediterranean commerce continued to draw Western Europe into its orbit, urban life went on in Gaul as well as in Italy, Spain and Africa. But when the Islamic invasion had bottled up the ports of the Tyrrhenian Sea after bringing the coasts of Africa and Spain under its control, municipal activity rapidly died out. Save in southern Italy and in Venice, where it was maintained thanks to Byzantine trade, it disappeared everywhere. The towns continued in existence, but they lost their population of artisans and merchants and with it all that had survived of the municipal organization of the Roman Empire.

The "cities," in each of which there resided a bishop, now became no more than centers of the ecclesiastical administration of their dioceses. Thus they preserved considerable importance, no doubt, from the religious point of view, but from the economic point of view none. At most, a small local market, supplied by the peasants round about, provided for the daily needs of the numerous clergy of the cathedral and of the churches or monasteries grouped around it and those of the serfs employed in their service. At the big annual festivals the diocesan population and pilgrims flocking into the city kept up a certain activity, but in none of this are any signs of a revival visible. In reality these episcopal cities were merely living on the country. The bishops and abbots within their walls lived on the rents and dues which they obtained from their estates, and their existence thus rested essentially on agriculture.

From *Economic and Social History of Medieval Europe* ©1933 by Henri Pirenne. Reprinted by permission of Harcourt Brace Jovanovich, Inc.

The cities were the centers not only of religious but also of manorial administration.

In time of war their old walls furnished a refuge to the surrounding population. But during the period of insecurity which set in with the dissolution of the Carolingian Empire, the need for protection became the first necessity of a people threatened in the South by the Saracen incursions and in the North and West by those of the Normans, to which were added, at the beginning of the tenth century, the terrible cavalry raids of the Hungarians. These invasions led on all sides to the construction of new places of refuge. In this period Western Europe became covered with fortified castles, erected by the feudal princes to serve as a shelter for their men. These castles, or, to use the term by which they were customarily designated, these *bourgs* or *burgs,* were usually composed of a rampart of earth or stones, surrounded by a moat and pierced with gates. The *vilains* from round about were requisitioned to construct and maintain them. A garrison of knights resided inside; a donjon served as the lord's dwelling-place; a church of canons looked after the needs of religion; and barns and granaries were set up to receive the grain, smoked meats and dues of all kinds levied on the manorial peasants, which served to feed the garrison and the people who, in times of peril, came huddling into the fortress with their cattle. Thus the lay burg, like the ecclesiastical city, lived on the land. Neither had any real economic life of its own. They were perfectly compatible with an agricultural civilization, for, far from opposing it, they may be said to have served in its defense.

But the revival of commerce soon completely altered their character. The first symptoms of its action are observable in the course of the second half of the tenth century. The wandering life of the merchants, the risks of every sort to which they were exposed, in an age when pillage formed one of the means of existence of the smaller nobility, caused them from the very beginning to seek the protection of the walled towns and burgs, which stood at intervals along the rivers or natural routes by which they traveled. During the summer these served as halting-places, during the bad season as wintering-places. The most favorably situated, whether at the foot of an estuary or in a creek, at the confluence of two rivers, or at a spot where the river ceased to be navigable and cargoes had to be unloaded before they could proceed farther, thus became places of passage and of sojourn for merchants and merchandise.

Soon the space that cities and burgs had to offer these newcomers, who became more and more numerous and embarrassing in proportion as trade increased, was no longer sufficient. They were driven to settle outside the walls and to build beside the old burg a new burg, or, to use the term which exactly describes it, a *faubourg (forisburgus),* i.e., an outside burg. Thus, close to ecclesiastical towns or feudal fortresses there sprang up mercantile agglomerations, whose denizens devoted themselves to a kind of life which was in complete contrast to that led by the people of the inside town. The word *portus,* often applied in documents of the tenth and eleventh centuries to these settlements, exactly describes their nature. It did not, in fact, signify a port in the modern sense, but a place through which merchandise was carried, and thus a particularly active place of transit. It was from it that in England and in Flanders the inhabitants of the *port* themselves received the name of *poorters* or *portmen,* which was long synonymous with *bourgeois* or *burgess* and indeed described them rather better than the latter, for the primitive bourgeoisie was exclusively composed of men living by trade. The reason why they came, before the end of the eleventh century, to be known by the word *bourgeois,* which was really much better suited to the inhabitants of the old burgs, at the foot of which they settled, is to be found in the fact that very early the mercantile group too surrounded itself by a wall or palisade for the sake of security, and thus became a burg in its turn. This extension of meaning is all the more easily comprehensible, since the new burg very soon overshadowed the old. In the most active centres of commercial life, such as Bruges, it was already at the beginning of the twelfth century surrounding the fortress, which had been its nucleus, on all sides. The accessory had become the essential, the newcomers had triumphed over the old inhabitants. In this sense it is strictly true to say that the medieval town, and consequently the modern town, had its birth in the faubourg of the city, or of the bourg which determined its site.

The collection of merchants in favorable spots soon caused artisans also to collect there. Industrial concentration is as old as commercial concentration. We can observe it with particular plainness in Flanders. Cloth-making, which had at first been carried on in the country, emigrated of itself to places which offered a sale for its products. There weavers found wool imported by the merchants, fullers' and dyers' soap and dye-stuffs. A real industrial revolution, of which we do not, unfortunately, know the details, accompanied this transformation of a rural industry into an urban one. Weaving, which had up to then been an occupation carried on by women, passed into the hands of men, and at the same time the old small *pallia* were replaced by pieces of cloth of great length, which were better suited for export and have remained the stock size used in the cloth manufacture up to the present day. There is good reason also for supposing that a change took place at this time in the looms used by the weavers, if only to allow a warp measuring from twenty to sixty ells to be fitted to the beam.

In the metallurgical industry of the Meuse valley an evolution analogous to that which took place in the Flemish cloth industry may also be observed. Copper-working, which perhaps dates back to the bronze-working which was actively developed there at the time of the Roman occupation, received a powerful impetus when the revival of navigation on the river gave it the chance to produce for export. At the same time, it became concentrated at Namur, Huy, and above all at Dinant, towns whose *marchands batteurs* went to the mines of Saxony for their copper in the eleventh century. Similarly, the excellent stone in which the region of Tournai abounded was worked in that town, and the manufacture of baptismal fonts became so active that we meet with them as far away as Southampton and Winchester. In Italy, the story is the same. Silk-weaving, introduced by sea from the East, became concentrated at Lucca, while Milan and the Lombard towns, soon imitated by Tuscany, devoted themselves to the manufacture of fustians.

THE MERCHANTS AND THE BOURGEOISIE

The essential difference between the merchants and artisans of the nascent towns and the agricultural society in the midst of which they appeared, was that their kind of life was no longer determined by their relations with the land. In this respect they formed, in every sense of the word, a class of *déracinés.* Commerce and industry, which up till then had been merely the adventitious or intermittent occupations of manorial agents, whose existence was assured by the great landowners who employed them, now became independent professions. Those who practised them were incontestably "new men." Attempts have often been made to derive them from the servile personnel attached to the domestic workshops of the manor, or the serfs who were charged with feeding the household in times of scarcity and in time of plenty disposed of their surplus production outside. But such an evolution is neither supported by the sources nor probable. There is no doubt that territorial lords here and there preserved economic prerogatives in the nascent towns for a fairly long time, such prerogatives, for instance, as the obligation of the burgesses to use the lord's oven and mill, the monopoly of sale enjoyed by his wine for several days after the vintage, or even certain dues levied from the craft gilds. But the local survival of these rights is no proof of the manorial origin of urban economy. On the contrary, what we note everywhere is that from the moment that it appears, it appears in a condition of freedom.

But the question immediately occurs, how are we to explain the formation of a class of free merchants and artisans in the midst of an exclusively rural society, where serfdom was the normal condition of the people? Scarcity of information prevents us from replying with that precision which the importance of the problem demands, but it is at least possible to indicate the chief factors. First, it is incontestable that commerce and industry were originally recruited from among landless men, who lived, so to speak, on the margin of a society where land alone was the basis of existence. Now these men were very numerous. Apart altogether from those, who in times of famine or war left their native soil to seek a livelihood elsewhere and returned no more, we have to remember all the individuals whom the manorial organization itself was unable to support. The peasants' holdings were of such a size as to secure the regular payment of the dues assessed upon them. Thus the younger sons of a man overburdened with children were often forced to leave their father in order to enable him to make his payments to the lord. Thenceforth they swelled the crowd of vagabonds who roamed through the country, going from abbey to abbey taking their share of alms reserved for the poor, hiring themselves out to the peasants at harvest time or at the vintage, and enlisting as mercenaries in the feudal troops in times of war.

These men were quick to profit by the new means of livelihood offered them by the arrival of ships and merchants along the coasts and in the river estuaries. Many of the more adventurous certainly hired themselves to the Venetian and Scandinavian boats as sailors; others joined the merchant caravans which took their way more and more frequently to the "ports." With luck, the best among them could not fail to seize the many opportunities of making a fortune, which commercial life offered to the vagabonds and adventurers who threw themselves into it with energy and intelligence. Strong probability would suffice to support such a reconstruction of the facts, even if we did not possess, in the story of St. Godric of Finchale, a valuable example of the way in which the *nouveaux riches* were then formed. Godric was born towards the end of the eleventh century in Lincolnshire of poor peasant stock and, forced, no doubt, to leave his parents' holding, he must have had to use all his wits to get a living. Like many other unfortunates in every age he became a beachcomber, on the lookout for wreckage thrown up by the waves. Shipwrecks were numerous and one fine day a lucky chance furnished him with a windfall which enabled him to get together a pedlar's pack. He had amassed a little store of money, when he met with and joined a band of merchants. Their business prospered and he soon made enough profit to enable him to form a partnership with others, in common with whom he loaded a ship and engaged in coastal trade along the shores of England, Scotland, Flanders and Denmark. The partnership prospered. Its operations consisted in taking abroad goods which were known to be scarce there and bringing back a return cargo, which was then exported to places where the demand was greatest and where, in consequence, the largest profits could be realized.

The story of Godric was certainly that of many others. In an age when local famines were continual, one had only to buy a very small quantity of grain cheaply in regions where it was abundant, to realize fabulous profits, which could then be increased by the same methods. Thus speculation, which is the starting point in this kind of business, largely contributed to the foundation of the first commercial fortunes. The savings of a little pedlar, a sailor, a boatman, or a docker, furnished him with quite enough capital, if only he knew how to use it. It might also happen that a landowner would invest a part of his income in maritime commerce. It is almost certain that the nobles on the Ligurian coast advanced the necessary funds to build the Genoese ships and shared in the profits from the sale of cargoes in the Mediterranean ports. The same thing must have happened in other Italian cities; at least we are tempted to assume so when we observe that in Italy a large proportion of the nobility always lived in the cities, in contrast to their brothers north of the Alps. It is only natural to suppose that a certain number of them were in some way interested in the economic revival which was developing around them. In these cases landed capital unquestionably contributed to the formation of liquid capital. However, their share was secondary, and though they profited by the recovery of trade, it was certainly not they who revived it.

The first impetus started from outside, in the South with Venetian and in the North with Scandinavian navigation. Western Europe, crystallized in its agricultural civilization, could not of itself have become so rapidly acquainted with a new sort of life, in the absence of external stimulus and example. The attitude of the Church, the most powerful landowner of the time, towards commerce, an attitude not merely passive but actively hostile, is quite enough proof of that. If the first beginnings of commercial capitalism partly evade our notice, it is much easier to follow its evolution during the course of the twelfth century. In the vigor and relative rapidity of its development it may, without exaggeration, be compared with the industrial revolution of the nineteenth century. The new kind of life which offered itself to the roving masses of landless men had an irresistible attraction for them, by reason of the promise of gain which it offered. The result was a real emigration from the country to the nascent towns. Soon, it was not only vagabonds of the type of Godric who bent their steps thither. The temptation was too great not to cause a number of serfs to run away from the manors where they were born and settle in the towns, either as artisans or as employees of the rich merchants whose reputation spread through the land. The lords pursued them and brought them back to their holdings, when they succeeded in laying hands on them. But many eluded their search, and as the city population increased, it became dangerous to try to seize the fugitives under its protection.

By concentrating in the towns industry was able to supply their export trade more and more largely. Thus the number of merchants steadily increased and with it the importance and the profits of their business. At that time of commercial growth, it was not difficult for young men to find employment as assistants to some rich master, to share in his business and in the end to make their own fortunes. The *Gesta* of the bishops of Cambrai relate in detail the story of a certain Werimbold, who, in the time of Bishop Burchard (1114-30), entered the service of a wealthy merchant, married his daughter and developed his business to such a degree that he himself became rich. He purchased a great deal of land in the town, built a magnificent house, bought off the toll collected at one of the gates, constructed a bridge at his own expense and in the end left the greater part of his property to the Church.

The foundation of large fortunes was certainly at this period a common phenomenon in all centers where an export trade was developing. Just as landowners had in the past showered gifts of land on the monasteries, so now merchants used their fortunes to found parish churches, hospitals, almshouses, in short, to spend themselves in religious or charitable works for the benefit of their fellow-citizens and the good of their own souls. Indeed, religion may well have spurred many of them on to win a fortune, which they intended to dedicate to the service of God. It should not be forgotten that Peter Waldo, the founder in 1173 of the Poor Men of Lyons, which shortly gave rise to the sect of the Waldenses, was a merchant and that, almost at the same date, St. Francis was born at Assisi in the house of another merchant. Other *nouveaux riches,* more bitten with worldly ambition, sought to raise themselves in the social hierarchy by giving their daughters in marriage to knights; and their fortune must have been very large to have stifled the aristocratic reluctance of the latter.

These great merchants, or rather *nouveaux riches,* were naturally the leaders of the bourgeoisie, since the bourgeoisie itself was a creation of the commercial revival and in the beginning the words *mercator* and *burgensis* were synonymous. But while it developed as a social class this bourgeoisie was also forming itself into a legal class of a highly original nature, which we must now consider.

URBAN INSTITUTIONS AND LAW

The needs and tendencies of the bourgeoisie were so incompatible with the traditional organization of Western Europe that they immediately aroused violent opposition. They ran counter to all the interests and ideas of a society dominated materially by the owners of large landed property and spiritually by the Church, whose aversion to trade was unconquerable. It would be unfair to attribute to "feudal tyranny" or "sacerdotal arrogance" an opposition which explains itself, although the attribution has often been made. As always, those who were the beneficiaries of the established order defended it obstinately, not only because it guaranteed their interests, but because it seemed to them indispensable to the preservation of society. Moreover, the bourgeois themselves were far from taking up a revolutionary attitude towards this society. They took for granted the authority of the territorial princes, the privileges of the nobility and, above all, those of the Church. They even professed an ascetic morality, which was plainly contradicted by their mode of life. They merely desired a place in the sun, and their claims were confined to their most indispensable needs.

Of the latter, the most indispensable was personal liberty. Without liberty, that is to say, without the power to come and go, to do business, to sell goods, a power not enjoyed by serfdom, trade would be impossible. Thus they claimed it, simply for the advantages which it conferred, and nothing was further from the mind of the bourgeoisie than any idea of freedom as a natural right; in their eyes it was merely a useful one. Besides, many of them possessed it *de facto;* they were immigrants, who had come from too far off for their lord to be traced and who, since their serfdom could not be presumed, necessarily passed for free, although born of unfree parents. But the fact had to be transformed into a right. It was essential that the villeins, who came to settle in the towns to seek a new livelihood, should feel safe and should not have to fear being taken back by force to the manors from which they had escaped. They must be delivered from labor services and from all the hated dues by which the servile population was burdened, such as the obligation to marry only a woman of their own class and to leave to the lord part of their inheritance. Willy-nilly, in the course of the twelfth century these claims, backed up as they often were by dangerous revolts, had to be granted. The most obstinate conservatives, such as Guibert de Nogent, in 1115, were reduced to a wordy revenge, speaking of those "detestable communes" which the serfs had set up to escape from their lord's authority and to do away with his most lawful rights. Freedom became the legal status of the bourgeoisie, so much so that it was no longer a personal privilege only, but a territorial one, inherent in urban soil just as serfdom was in manorial soil. In order to obtain it, it was enough to have resided for a year and a day within the walls of the town. "City air makes a man free" (*Stadtluft macht frei*), says the German proverb.

But if liberty was the first need of the burgess, there were many others besides. Traditional law with its narrow, formal procedure, its ordeals, its judicial duels, its judges recruited from among the rural population, and knowing no other custom than that which had been gradually elaborated to regulate the relations of men living by the cultivation or the ownership of the land, was inadequate for a population whose existence was based on commerce and industry. A more expeditious law was necessary, means of proof more rapid and more independent of chance, and judges who were themselves acquainted with the professional occupations of those who came under their jurisdiction, and could cut short their arguments by a knowledge of the case at issue. Very early, and at latest at the beginning of the eleventh century, the pressure of circumstances led to the creation of a *jus mercatorum,* i.e., an embryonic commercial code. It was a collection of usages born of business experience, a sort of international custom, which the merchants used among themselves in their transactions. Devoid of all legal validity, it was impossible to invoke it in the existing law courts, so the merchants agreed to choose among themselves arbitrators who had the necessary competence to understand their disputes and to settle them promptly. It is here undoubtedly that we must seek the origin of those law courts, which in England received the picturesque name of courts of *piepowder (pied poudré),* because the feet of the merchants who resorted to them were still dusty from the roads. Soon this *ad hoc* jurisdiction became permanent and was recognised by public authority. At Ypres, in 1116, the Count of Flanders abolished the judicial duel, and it is certain that about the same date he instituted in most of his towns local courts of *échevins,* chosen from among the burgesses and alone competent to judge them. Sooner or later the same thing happened in all countries. In Italy, France, Germany and England the towns obtained judicial autonomy, which made them islands of independent jurisdiction, lying outside the territorial custom.

This jurisdictional autonomy was accompanied by administrative autonomy. The formation of urban agglomerations entailed a number of arrangements for convenience of defense, which they had to provide for themselves in the absence of the traditional authorities, who had neither the means nor the wish to help them. It is a strong testimony to the energy and the initiative of the bourgeoisie that it succeeded by its own efforts in setting on foot the municipal organization, of which the first outlines appear in the eleventh century, and which was already in possession of all its essential organs in the twelfth. The work thus accomplished is all the more admirable because it was an original creation. There was nothing in the existing order of things to serve it as a model, since the needs it was designed to meet were new.

The most pressing was the need for defense. The merchants and their merchandise were, indeed, such a tempting prey that it was essential to protect them from pillagers by a strong wall. The construction of ramparts was thus the first public work undertaken by the towns and one which, down to the end of the Middle Ages, was their heaviest financial burden. Indeed, it may be truly said to have been the starting point of their financial organization, whence, for example, the name of *firmitas*, by which the communal tax was always known at Liége, and the appropriation in a number of cities *ad opus castri* (i.e., for the improvement of the fortifications) of a part of the fines imposed by the borough court. The fact that today municipal coats of arms are surrounded by a walled crown shows the importance accorded to the ramparts. There were no unfortified towns in the Middle Ages.

Money had to be raised to provide for the expenses occasioned by the permanent need for fortifications, and it could be raised most easily from the burgesses themselves. All were interested in the common defense and all were obliged to meet the cost. The quota payable by each was calculated on the basis of his fortune. This was a great innovation. For the arbitrary seigneurial tallage, collected in the sole interest of the lord, it substituted a payment proportionate to the means of the taxpayer and set apart for an object of general utility. Thus taxation recovered its public character, which had disappeared during the feudal era. To assess and collect this tax, as well as to provide for the ordinary necessities whose numbers grew with the constant increase of the town population, the establishment of quays and markets, the building of bridges and parish churches, the regulation of crafts and the supervision of food supplies, it soon became necessary to elect or allow the setting up of a council of magistrates, consuls in Italy and Provence, *jurés* in France and aldermen in England. In the eleventh century they appeared in the Lombard cities, where the consuls of Lucca are mentioned as early as 1080. In the following century, they became everywhere an institution ratified by public authority and inherent in every municipal constitution. In many towns, as in those of the Low Countries, the *échevins* were at once the judges and administrators of the townsfolk.

The lay princes soon discovered how advantageous the growth of the cities was to themselves. For in proportion as their trade grew on road and river and their increasing business transactions required a corresponding increase of currency, the revenues from every kind of toll and from the mints likewise flowed in increasing quantities into the lord's treasury. Thus it is not surprising that the lords assumed on the whole a benevolent attitude towards the townsfolk. Moreover, living as a rule in their country castles, they did not come in contact with the town population and thus many causes of conflict were avoided. It was quite otherwise with the ecclesiastical princes. Almost to a man they offered a resistance to the municipal movement, which at times developed into an open struggle. The fact that the bishops were obliged to reside in their cities, the centers of diocesan administration, necessarily impelled them to preserve their authority and to oppose the ambitions of the bourgeoisie all the more resolutely because they were roused and directed by the merchants, ever suspect in the eyes of the Church. In the second half of the eleventh century the quarrel of the Empire and the Papacy gave the city populations of Lombardy a chance to rise against their simoniacal prelates. Thence the movement spread through the Rhine valley to Cologne. In 1077, the town of Cambrai rose in revolt against Bishop Gerard II and formed the oldest of the "communes" that we meet with north of the Alps. In the diocese of Liége the same thing happened. In 1066 Bishop Théoduin was forced to grant the burgesses of Huy a charter of liberties which is several years earlier than those whose text has been preserved in the rest of the Empire. In France, municipal insurrections are mentioned at Beauvais about 1099, at Noyon in 1108-9, and at Laon in 1115.

Thus, by fair means or foul, the towns gained peaceably or by force, some at the beginning, others in the course of the twelfth century, municipal constitutions suitable to the life of their inhabitants. Originating in the "new burgs," in the *portus,* where the merchants and artisans were grouped, they were soon developed to include the population of the "old burgs" and the "cities," whose ancient walls, surrounded on all sides by the new quarters, were falling into ruin like the old law itself. Henceforth, all who resided within the city wall, with the sole exception of the clergy, shared the privileges of the burgesses.

The essential characteristics of the bourgeoisie was, indeed, the fact that it formed a privileged class in the midst of the rest of the population. From this point of view the medieval town offers a striking contrast both to the ancient town and to the town of today, which are differentiated only by the density of their population and their complex administration; apart from this, neither in public nor in private law do their inhabitants occupy a peculiar position in the State. The medieval burgess, on the contrary, was a different kind of person from all who lived outside the town walls. Once outside the gates and the moat we are in another world, or more exactly, in the domain of another law. The acquisition of citizenship brought with it results analogous to those which followed when a man was dubbed knight or a clerk tonsured, in the sense that they conferred a peculiar legal status. Like the clerk or the noble, the burgess escaped from the common law; like them, he belonged to a particular estate (*status*), which was later to be known as the "third estate."

The territory of the town was as privileged as its inhabitants. It was a sanctuary, an "immunity," which protected the man who took refuge there from exterior authority, as if he had sought sanctuary in a church. In short, the bourgeoisie was in every sense an exceptional class. Each town formed, so to speak, a little state to itself, jealous of its prerogatives and hostile to all its neighbors. Very rarely was a common danger or a common end able to impose on its municipal particularism the need for alliances or leagues such, for example, as the German Hanse. In general, urban politics were determined by the same sacred egoism which was later to inspire State politics. For the burgesses the country population existed only to be exploited. Far from allowing it to enjoy their franchises, they always obstinately refused it all share in them. Nothing could be further removed from the spirit of modern democracy than the exclusiveness with which the medieval towns continued to defend their privileges, even, and indeed above all, in those periods when they were governed by the crafts.

THE GHETTO

Louis Wirth

For the past five hundred years the Jewish settlements in the Western world have been known as ghettos. The modern ghetto, some evidence of which is found in every city of even moderate size, traces its ancestry back to the medieval European urban institution by means of which the Jews were segregated from the rest of the population. In the East, until recently, the ghetto took the form of the "pale" of settlement, which represents a ghetto within a ghetto. The ghetto is no longer the place of officially regulated settlement of the Jews, but rather a local cultural area which has arisen quite informally. In the American cities the name "ghetto" applies particularly to those areas where the poorest and most backward groups of the Jewish population, usually the recently arrived immigrants, find their home.

From the standpoint of the sociologist the ghetto as an institution is of interest first of all because it represents a prolonged case study in isolation. It may be regarded as a form of accommodation through which a minority has effectually been subordinated to a dominant group. The ghetto exhibits at least one historical form of dealing with a dissenting minority within a larger population, and as such has served as an instrument of control. At the same time the ghetto represents a form of toleration through which a *modus vivendi* is established between groups that are in conflict with each other on fundamental issues. Some of these functions are still served by the modern ghetto, which, in other respects, has a character quite distinct from that of the medieval institution. In Western Europe and America, however, it is of primary interest because it shows the actual processes of distribution and

From the *American Journal of Sociology* Vol. XXXIII, pp. 57-65, July, 1927-May, 1928. Reprinted by permission of The University of Chicago Press.

grouping of the population in urban communities. It indicates the ways in which cultural groups give expression to their heritages when transplanted to a strange habitat; it evidences the constant sifting and resifting that goes on in a population, the factors that are operative in assigning locations to each section, and the forces through which the community maintains its integrity and continuity. Finally, it demonstrates the subtle ways in which this cultural community is transformed by degrees until it blends with the larger community about it, meanwhile reappearing in various altered guises of its old and unmistakable atmosphere.

This paper concerns itself, not with the history of the ghetto, but with its natural history. Viewed from this angle the study of the ghetto is likely to throw light on a number of related phenomena, such as the origin of segregated areas and the development of local communities in general; for, while the ghetto is, strictly speaking, a Jewish institution, there are forms of ghettos that concern not merely Jews. Our cities contain Little Sicilies, Little Polands, Chinatowns, and Black Belts. There are Bohemias and Hobohemias, slums and Gold Coasts, vice areas and Rialtos in every metropolitan community. The forces that underlie the formation and development of these areas bear a close resemblance to those at work in the ghetto. These forms of community life are likely to become more intelligible if we know something of the Jewish ghetto.

The concentration of the Jews into segregated local areas in the medieval cities did not originate with any formal edict of church or state. The ghetto was not, as is sometimes mistakenly believed, the arbitrary creation of the authorities, designed to deal with an alien people. The ghetto was not the product of design on the part of anyone, but rather the unwitting crystallization of needs and practices rooted in the customs and heritages, religious and secular, of the Jews themselves. Long before it was made compulsory the Jews lived in separate parts of the cities in the Western lands of their own accord. The Jews drifted into separate cultural areas, not by external pressure or by deliberate design. The factors that operated toward the founding of locally separated communities by the Jews are to be sought in the character of Jewish traditions, in the habits and customs, not only of the Jews themselves, but of the medieval town-dweller in general. To the Jews the spatially separated and socially isolated community seemed to offer the best opportunity for following their religious precepts, their established ritual and diet, and the numerous functions which tied the individual to familial and communal institutions. In some instances it was the fear of the remainder of the population, no doubt, which induced them to seek each other's company, or the ruler under whose protection they stood found it desirable, for purposes of revenue and control, to grant them a separate quarter. The general tenor of medieval life no doubt played an important role, for it was customary for members of the same occupational group to live in the same locality, and the Jews, forming, as a whole, a separate vocational class and having a distinct economic status, were merely falling in line, therefore, with the framework of medieval society, in which everyone was tied to some locality. In addition, there were the numerous ties of kinship and acquaintanceship which developed an *esprit de corps* as a significant factor in community life. There was the item of a common language, of community of ideas and interests, and the mere congeniality that arises even between strangers who, coming from the same locality, meet in a strange place. Finally, the segregation of the Jews in ghettos is identical in many respects with the development of segregated areas in general. The tolerance that strange modes of life need and find in immigrant settlements, in Latin quarters, in vice districts, and in racial colonies is a powerful factor in the sifting of the urban population and its allocation in separate local areas where one obtains freedom from hostile criticism and the backing of a group of kindred spirits.

Corresponding to the local separateness of the Jew from his Christian neighbors there is to be noted the functional separation of the two groups. Just as the world beyond the ghetto wall was external to the life within the ghetto, so the personal relationships between Jews and non-Jews were those of externality and utility. The Jews supplemented the economic complex of medieval European life. They served a number of functions which the inhabitants of the town were incapable of exercising. The Jews were allowed to trade and engage in exchange, occupations which the church did not permit Christians to engage in. Besides, the Jews were valuable taxable property and could be relied on to furnish much needed revenue. On the other hand, the Jews, too, regarded the Christian population as a means to an end, as a utility. The Christians could perform functions such as eating the hind quarter of beef, and could purchase the commodities that the Jews had for sale; they could borrow money from the Jew, and pay interest; they could perform innumerable services for him which he could not perform himself. In the rigid structure of medieval life the Jews found a strategic place. The attitude of the medieval church had coupled trade and finance with sin. The Jews were free from this taboo, which made the occupation of merchant and banker seem undesirable to the Christian population. The Christian churchmen were not troubled about the "perils of the Jewish soul," for, so far as they knew, he had no soul to be saved. What made the trade relation possible, however, was not merely the fact that it was mutually advantageous, but the fact that trade relationships are possible when no other form of contact between two peoples can take place. The Jew, being a stranger, and belonging, as he did, to a separate and distinct class, was admirably fitted to become the merchant and banker. He drifted to the towns and cities where trade was possible and profitable. Here he could utilize all the distant contacts that he had developed in the course of his wandering. His attachment to the community at large was slight, and when necessity demanded it he could migrate to a locality where opportunities were greater. He owned no real property to which he was tied, nor was he the serf of a feudal lord. His mobility in turn developed versatility. He saw opportunities in places where no native could see them. While the ghetto was never more than a temporary stopping place, the Jew was never a hobo, for he had an aim, a destination, and his community went with him in his migrations.

While the Jew's contacts with the outside world were categorical and abstract, within his own community he was at home. Here he could relax from etiquette and formalism. His contacts with his fellow Jews were warm, intimate, and free. Especially was this true of his family life, within the inner circle of which he received that appreciation and sympathetic understanding which the larger world could not offer. In his own community, which was based upon the solidarity of the families that composed it, he was a person with status. Whenever he returned from a journey to a distant market, or from his daily work, he came back to the family fold, there to be recreated and reaffirmed as a man and as a Jew. Even when he was far removed from his kin, he lived his real inner life in his dreams and hopes with them. He could converse with his own kind in that familiar tongue which the rest of the world could not understand. He was bound by common troubles, by numerous ceremonies and sentiments to his small group that lived its own life oblivious of the world beyond the confines of the ghetto. Without the backing of his group, without the security that he enjoyed in his inner circle of friends and countrymen, life would have been intolerable.

Through the instrumentality of the ghetto there gradually developed that social distance which effectually isolated the Jew from the remainder of the population. These barriers did not completely inhibit contact, but they reduced it to the type of relationships which were of a secondary and formal nature. As these barriers crystallized and his life was lived more and more removed from the rest of the world, the solidarity of his own little community was enhanced until it became strictly divorced from the larger world without.

The forms of community life that had arisen naturally and spontaneously in the course of the attempt of the Jews to adapt themselves to their surroundings gradually became formalized in custom and precedent, and finally crystallized into legal enactment. What the Jews had sought as a privilege was soon to be imposed upon them by law. As the Jews had come to occupy a more important position in medieval economy, and as the church at about the time of the Crusades became more militant, there set in a period of active regulation. The ghetto became compulsory. But the institution of the ghetto had by this time become firmly rooted in the habits and attitudes of the Jews. The historians of the ghetto are usually inclined to overemphasize the confining effect of the barriers that were set up around the Jew, and the provincial and stagnant character of ghetto existence. They forget that there was nevertheless a teeming life within the ghetto which was probably more active than life outside.

The laws that came to regulate the conduct of the Jews and Christians were merely the formal expressions of social distances that had already been ingrained in the people. While on the one hand the Jew was coming to be more and more a member of a class—an abstraction—on the other hand there persisted the tendency to react to him as a human being. The ghetto made the Jew self-conscious. Life in the ghetto was bearable only because there was a larger world outside, of which many Jews often got more than a passing glimpse. As a result they often lived on the fringe of two worlds. There was always some movement to get out of the ghetto on the part of those who were attracted by the wide world that lay beyond the horizon of the ghetto walls and who were cramped by the seemingly narrow life within. Sometimes a Jew would leave the ghetto and become converted; and sometimes these converts, broken and humiliated, would return to the ghetto to taste again of the warm, intimate, tribal life that was to be found nowhere but among their people. On such occasions the romance of the renegade would be told in the ghetto streets, and the whole community would thereby be welded into a solid mass amid the solemn ceremonies by which the stray member was re-incorporated into the community.

The inner solidarity of the ghetto community always lay in the ties of family life, and through the organization in the synagogue these families gained status within a community. Confined as the province of the ghetto was, there was ample opportunity for the display of capacity for leadership. The ghetto community was minutely specialized and highly integrated. There were probably more distinct types of personality and institutions within the narrow ghetto streets than in the larger world outside.

The typical ghetto is a densely populated, walled-in area usually found near the arteries of commerce or in the vicinity of a market. The Jewish quarter, even before the days of the compulsory ghetto, seems to have grown up round the synagogue, which was the center of Jewish life, locally as well as religiously. A common feature of all ghettos was also the cemetery, which was a communal responsibility and to which unusual sentimental interest was attached. There were a number of educational, recreational, and hygienic institutions, such as a school for the young, a bath, a slaughter house, a bakehouse, and a dance hall. In the close life within the ghetto walls almost nothing was left to the devices of the individual. Life was well organized, and custom and ritual played an institutionalizing role which still accounts for the high degree of organization of Jewish communities, often verging on over-organization. These institutions did not arise ready made. They represent what life always is, an adaptation to the physical and social needs of a people. In this case particularly, those institutions that had to deal with the conflict and disorder within the group and the pressure from without were the character-istic form of accommodation to the isolation which the ghetto symbolized and enforced. This holds good not merely for the institutions of the ghetto, but for the functionaries and personalities that center around them. The Jews as a race as we know them today are themselves a product of the ghetto.

The ghetto, from the standpoint of biology, was a closely inbreeding, self-perpetuating group to such an extent that it may properly be called a closed community. Not that there was no intermarriage, but these mixed marriages as a rule were lost to the ghetto. The Jews have frequently and rightly been pointed out as the classic example of the great force of religious and racial prejudices, of segregation and isolation, in giving rise to distinct physical and social types. These types persist roughly to the extent that ghetto life and its effects have continued relatively unchanged, which is most true of Eastern Europe and the Orient. The difference in community life accounts in large part for the differences between various local groupings within the Jewish population.

The Russian, Polish, and in part the Roumanian, Jews differ from those of Western Europe—the German, French, Dutch, and English Jews—in several fundamental respects. For a long period the Jews of the East were merely a cultural dependency—an outpost—of Western Jewry. When an independent cultural life did develop in Russia, Poland, and Lithuania, it was self-sufficient and self-contained, set apart from the larger world. Not so with the Jews of Western Europe. They were never quite impervious to the currents of thought and the social changes that characterized the life of Europe since the Renaissance. While the Jews of the East lived in large part in rural communities, in a village world, those of the West were predominantly a city people, in touch with the centers of trade and finance near and far, and in touch at least for some time with the pulsating intellectual life of the world. While the Jews of the Rhine cities were associating with men of thought and of affairs, their brethren in Russia were dealing with peasants and an uncultured, decadent, feudal nobility. When the Jewries of the West were already seething with modernist religious, political, and social movements, those of the East were still steeped in mysticism and medieval ritual. While the Western Jews were moving along with the tide of progress, those of the East were still sharing the backwardness and isolation of the gentile world of villagers and peasants. Although until the middle of the last century the Jews of the East were never quite so confined in their physical movements as were the ghetto Jews of the West, the former lived in a smaller world, a world characterized by rigidity and stability; and when they were herded into cities, in which they constituted the preponderant bulk of the total population, they merely turned these cities into large villages that had little in common with the urban centers of the West. Many features of local life in the modern Jewish community bear the imprint of the successive waves of immigrants first from the West and then from the East.

The formal enactments that made the ghetto the legal dwelling place of the Jews were abolished toward the middle of the last century in most of the countries of the world. Strangely enough, the abolition of the legal ghetto was opposed by a great portion of Jews as late as a hundred years ago, for they had a premonition that the leveling of the ghetto walls would mean the wiping out of separate community life, which the formal ghetto rules merely symbolized. Those who saw in the new freedom the waning influence of the Jewish religion and the ultimate dissolution of Jewish life in separate communities had two things left to console them: (1) the formal equality decreed by law did not at once gain for the Jew ready acceptance and a parallel social status among his fellow citizens; and (2) although Western Jewry seemed to be crumbling, there were approximately six millions of Jews left on the other side of the Vistula who were still clinging to the old bonds that exclusion and oppression had fashioned. But since that time even Russia has been revolutionized, and the so-called "last bulwark" of Judaism threatens to disappear.

THE INFLUENCES OF THE CHURCH
ON MEDIEVAL CULTURE

Caroline D. Eckhardt

The early Christian church consisted of small and isolated groups of the faithful, a persecuted subculture outlawed by the rulers of imperial Rome. Gradually, as the powers of Rome receded, the new religion gathered strength, became organized and institutionalized, and eventually not only replaced the pagan religions of the Empire but also acquired many of the social, political, and intellectual functions of the Empire itself. In the Middle Ages Christianity was always part religion and part governmental institution, which means that its influence on medieval people extended to categories of human existence which are not considered, in the modern world, as the province of religion: politics and economics; demography and social structure; language, law, education; philosophy, architecture, music, art, and literature. Like any institution attempting to do nearly everything (here, to guide man's complete spiritual and worldly existence), the medieval Church did nothing perfectly, and many things not even creditably. But it was the major institution that held Western civilization together for a thousand years.

DEVELOPMENT OF THE CHURCH: INSTITUTIONAL STRUCTURE

The Christian church evolved in response to a variety of environmental needs and opportunities. The development of its institutional structure resembles the growth of a modern city without urban planning: locations, relationships and functions were worked out pragmatically, with more attention paid to immediate needs than to ultimate effects; there were periodic consolidations, regularizations, revisions; some accidental or opportunistic solutions to specific problems found their way into the "establishment" and became inviolable, while others served their temporary purposes and disappeared. The complex, changing, and only partially logical pattern that resulted should surprise us no more in the structure of the medieval Church than it does in the design of New York City.

The earliest Church, consisting of scattered groups of converts to the new religion, had no unified structure at all. Individual groups in separate cities (primitive Christianity was urban) had their own leaders—inspired teachers, people with courage and charisma, the wise or experienced—the same variety of leaders we see in minority movements now. But as the new religion which believed in *one* God, *one* truth, and *one* Messiah grew, the need to coordinate the faithful and prevent fragmentation of the faith was recognized. A regional overseer, a bishop, governed the Christian groups within a city, then in rural areas also. The bishop's territory, including his "city" where he had his church, was called a diocese, a number of these together a province, the preeminent bishop of the province an archbishop or metropolitan. The tendency of the Church to reflect the Roman administration it superseded is evident from these names: *diocesis, civitas, provincia,* are Roman territorial units; a *metropolis* was a mother-city from which others were colonized, hence the central or preeminent city among a group. The archbishop in the metropolis was thus in charge of a number of bishops who in turn governed the priests, deacons, subdeacons, and others who ministered to the local churches.

The bishop of Rome gradually came to occupy a unique position, signified by the title Pope, "father," as head of the whole Church. Spiritually, the bishop of Rome was regarded as the direct successor of St. Peter, to whom Christ had entrusted the Church. Politically, the bishop at Rome was at the center of the Roman Empire, which recognized Christianity as its official religion in the fourth century A.D. The supremacy of the Papacy in church government was long contested, and under individual popes who were weak leaders it was more theory than fact, but this principle, with its twin supports in Scripture and in practical politics, became dominant, and provided the Church with a single central authority at the top of the hierarchical organization that included, at its base, the parish priest and his assistants.

This structure was complicated subsequently by the addition of various types of churchmen beyond the basic plan, and by the proliferation of the huge bureaucracy necessary to staff the Church in all its functions. The most socially influential of these accretions were the monasteries and the mendicant orders. Responsible not to the "secular" hierarchy of priest, bishop, and archbishop, but to the Papacy alone, the monastic foundations developed as a response to the desire among intense Christians to live in solitude (*monachus* is one who lives alone), away from the distractions and obligations of normal society, so that they could devote themselves wholly to God. In the early Christian centuries it was not uncommon for idealistic believers to live as isolated hermits, but the less extreme custom of living in communal groups set apart from society became, from the fifth century onward, the dominant expression of this urge to reject the world. The monastery was seen as part of the Church but not of ordinary society: monks were to live communally, sharing the few material items necessary for survival (owning no private property), working the monastery's farmlands for a minimal subsistence, spending much of their time in the contemplation and adoration of God according to the pattern of prayers and rituals set forth in their house's Rule (Latin *regula,* which gave the monks their name of "regular" clergy). Monks and nuns lived in separate houses, since monastic asceticism included absolute chastity, enforced by segregation of the sexes.

The monastic ideal, like most idealisms, surpassed the ability of its followers to fulfill it. The history of the medieval Church is partly a repeating cycle of idealism, deterioration, protest and reform, and so on again. The monasteries acquired property. Many monks ceased to labor or to observe their vows of poverty, chastity, and obedience. External authorities such as feudal lords viewed the monasteries' farmlands as real estate, and used their revenues for worldly purposes. When abuses became notorious, protest movements arose and founded new kinds of communities. For example, the reform movement of the thirteenth century created the new orders of Franciscan and Dominican friars, who rejected the concept of living apart from the world (it had not prevented worldliness) and undertook to fulfill the ideal of poverty, chastity, and holiness by preaching and working among the common people in imitation of the life of Christ. The friars were to own no property, and to beg for subsistence (which is why they are called the "mendicant," begging, orders). The most remarkable leader of the friars was St. Francis, whose overwhelming love for God's creatures included the whole natural world. He praised the Lord in gratitude for our brother the sun, our sister the moon, our mother the earth; he was reluctant to put out a flame because his brother, the fire, was God's creature too. The Dominican friars, strongly concerned with orthodoxy, became the main agents of the Inquisition which was organized to combat heresy. The orders of friars founded sister groups for nuns, who did not wander through the world but made clothing for the poor, taught children, copied manuscripts, nursed the sick in hospitals.

By the fourteenth century the mendicant orders too had lost their first idealism and were widely accused of every kind of corruption.

One factor which has not yet been discussed is the decline of Roman imperial authority in precisely the period which saw the rise of the Church as an institution. The disintegration of Roman government left Europe without centralized civil authority. More and more the Church, as the one strong social institution which persisted, absorbed the functions of those that had disappeared. The bishop of Rome became the acknowledged ruler of that city and its environs, and ultimately the Papacy asserted its claim as the secular, as well as spiritual, ruler of all of Christendom. This claim depended on the concept that the Pope was God's representative assigned to govern Christian society in every sense. As secular government reemerged in Europe, the conflicting political claims of Pope and King repeatedly clashed. The origin of this conflict lies in the fact that in the early Middle Ages, the Church had indeed often functioned as government, not simply because of a desire for secular power (which not surprisingly did motivate some clerics) but more basically because a functional vacuum existed—certain fundamental social needs were not being met by other institutions—and the Church filled that vacuum. Once having done so, it resisted being supplanted, and attempted instead to consolidate and expand the political authority which primitive Christianity, scattered groups of people practicing an outlawed faith in the cities of the Empire, would scarcely have comprehended.

This survey of the structure of the medieval Church is intended to indicate, as major characteristics, its basically hierarchical organization reaching from the Pope in Rome to the simplest parish priest in England, in France, in Italy, anywhere in the Western world; and the gradual nature of its growth. Most aspects of this structure, including the Papacy itself, resulted from particular needs and opportunities, not abstract plans, and the structure continued to be amplified as new needs arose, both bureaucratic and spiritual. It should always be remembered that the Church as an institution, far from being static, was subject to continuing change, to internal shifts of power (ranging from subtle adjustments of the balance of forces to open crisis and schism), and to external pressure both from the secular factors of life in Christian Europe and from the presence of the non-Christian cultures. Throughout the Middle Ages, Islam presented a very real ideological and political threat to Christendom. Spain, for example, which had been conquered by the Moslems in the eighth century, was not completely in Christian hands until the end of the fifteenth; when the two cultures faced each other decisively in the Middle East, in the great contest of the Crusades, it was Islam which emerged the victor. And within the cities of European Christendom there were the Jews, who lived in uneasy coexistence with Christian church and state, sometimes welcomed, sometimes oppressed, sometimes permitted to exist with minimal interference, always an alien presence which implicitly suggested the limits of the Church's theoretically universal domain.

POLITICS AND ECONOMICS

The medieval Church, as a form of government, became involved with other forms of government—its allies and its rivals—on every level, and the history of medieval politics records the activities of churchmen and laymen alike. Every section of Europe was submitted to at least two authorities, one representing the Church, the other, whatever secular government existed. This situation seemed ready-made for conflict, increasingly so as secular authority centralized and produced strong rulers who could challenge the Church's position effectively.

The fundamental political question behind all the medieval church-and-state conflicts was whether the Church was ordained by God to supervise human affairs only spiritually, or also temporally. Either of the two extreme viewpoints, the Church's claim to be supreme in the world and include secular government as one of its own functions, and the secular rulers' claim that the Church's power extended only to religious matters, would on occasion be advocated by those who saw it in their interests to do so, but the actual situation was much more complicated. There were churchmen appalled at the Church's worldliness who saw its participation in secular politics as a corrupting influence, and felt it could refrain from sin only by withdrawing from all temporal affairs, owning no property, and discarding the business of this world to pursue its proper concern of preparing men for the next. And there were some secular rulers who favored the Church's participation in government, either because they were religious and accepted the Church's own claims as valid, or because it was pragmatically advantageous for them to have the Church as a political factor to offset rival lords or alliances of the middle classes.

The ideological question about power—whom did God appoint to rule the world?—was settled by power, not ideology. Let us consider a few of the innumerable kinds of conflicts, ranging from Church's political influence on local affairs such as the selection of bishops, to her part in the international wars of the Crusades.

An individual bishopric was, in terms of Church structure, a subdivision of Christendom, a collection of parishes under the administration of a bishop; but politically, a bishopric was a territory composed of certain real properties, and the person to whom it was entrusted therefore formed part of secular administration also. From this double function developed what is known as the "lay investiture" controversy. Secular authorities such as kings and feudal lords (who were laymen) wanted to bestow bishoprics, exactly as they bestowed other properties, on their political allies; to them a bishop was a feudal vassal, and they claimed the right to choose him. Even his difference from other feudal vassals—the fact that he would leave no heirs, so that at the death of a bishop the bishopric would again be available for the secular authority to use as a reward for services—was not an undesirable factor. The Church, on the other hand, claimed that since a bishop was part of ecclesiastical hierarchy, no layman could appoint him or invest him with his symbols of office. The Papacy wanted its bishops responsible to the Church, not to secular governments. Eventually compromises were worked out. Only churchmen would choose and invest bishops, but secular authorities kept a measure of control, for example the right to decide a disputed election, and the crucial right to receive feudal obligations from bishops holding lands from kings. Such typical theoretical arrangements did not prevent individual conflicts over the question of where a bishop's primary loyalty lay. This is evident in the case of one of the most interesting medieval churchmen, Thomas of Becket, at first a worldly prelate and companion of England's Henry II, who approved Becket's appointment as Archbishop of Canterbury.

Becket underwent a peculiar conversion, and became an ascetic and a strict defender of the Church's prerogatives against his former friend Henry. In retaliation Henry had him declared guilty of feudal disobedience to his overlord the King. Becket appealed to the Pope, who threatened to forbid all religious services in Henry's domain if he did not restore Becket to his position of Archbishop—which Henry did, but shortly thereafter a group of Henry's followers, acting upon his fury at Becket's excommunication of bishops who had supported the king, assassinated the Archbishop in his cathedral at Canterbury. The central ambiguity of a propertied churchman's situation—was he responsible to secular rule, insofar as he held worldly possessions, or was he responsible to the Church?—is implied by the events of Becket's career. Henry approved his appointment on the assumption that the Archbishop would be his servant, not Rome's, and attempted to enforce this concept of primary responsibility by trying Becket for feudal disobedience, while Becket in appealing from Henry's court to the Papacy demonstrated that he considered his primary responsibility lay there. This power struggle was of course atypical, as most bishops and archbishops served both masters more or less satisfactorily. The long-range outcome was that laymen eventually lost all power over Church appointments, but churchmen lost their power over temporal affairs.

On a larger scale than individual appointments, the Church contested temporal supremacy in Europe with the kings who are called the Holy Roman Emperors (successors of the Roman emperors, ruling now a Christian world). The Holy Roman Empire began with Pope Leo III's crowning of Charlemagne, in 800 A.D., as a new Augustus. Europe was never again united under an emperor as it had been in Roman times, but the title continued, particularly among German princes, and in theory the Holy Roman Emperor was the temporal counterpart to the Pope. Periodically a German prince calling himself the Emperor would attempt to assert an actual military authority over Rome, which necessarily brought him into direct opposition with the Papacy's political claims, and Europe saw a number of wars resulting from this power struggle. Ultimately the rivalry between the Popes and the Emperors for European supremacy lost its meaning, and the course of history shows that real political strength lay elsewhere—with the commercial cities, strong because of their wealth—and with the centralized nations of England, France, and Spain.

The most famous, or infamous, example of the Church's participation in international politics is its sponsorship of the Crusades, which involved not only all of European Christendom but much of the rest of the Mediterranean world too. The impulses behind the Crusades reflect, not surprisingly, the multiple interests of the Church. The religious justification for the wars was that the Holy Land should not remain in the hands of people whom Christians regarded as infidels (in fact Moslems had long ruled Palestine, but towards the end of the eleventh century Turkish rule there restricted Christian access to holy places). Secondly, Islam itself was felt to be a growing threat to Christianity as the Christian Byzantine Empire was increasingly weakened by Turkish attacks. Insofar as the Crusades were undertaken to oust the Moslems from the Holy Land and, as a longer-range goal, to protect Christian Europe from Islam, they were wars of ideology. But further motives were involved. Like all wars of conquest, the Crusades were fought for profit and for power.

The Italian commercial cities wanted the eastern Mediterranean to be in European hands so they could establish trading ports there. European nobles and adventurers went on crusade in hopes of acquiring kingdoms and wealth, or for the mere love of war. The Church which preached the Crusades was aware of all these motives, accepted them and at times exploited them.

Each Crusade consisted not of a unified military organization (the Papacy itself led no armies), but of individual secular leaders and their forces. Sometimes the various armies failed to cooperate; sometimes they fought one another; the Fourth Crusade attacked the Christian Byzantine Empire instead of Moslem strongholds. The Crusades as a whole accomplished none of their goals. The Church had demonstrated its political capacity to summon Christendom to war, however, and the crusade as a technique was used by the Papacy even within Europe—for example, the crusade preached against the Emperor Frederick II, himself a Jerusalem crusader, and the crusades carried out against heresies, notably the Albigensian or Cathar heresy in southern France. In this case the Papacy promised the lands and wealth of the heretic South to the feudal leaders of northern France and anyone who would join them, and succeeded here in doing what it failed to do in Jerusalem, using the political weapon of war to enforce obedience to Christianity as a religion and to the Church as an institution.

All in all, the Church's record in politics is comparable to that of most governments in human history: it governed sometimes wisely, sometimes well, sometimes with inexcusable cruelty, and it used its power to protect its own interests.

Like other institutions, the Church needed funds, and so became a major factor in medieval economics. It had two basic sources of revenue: its own properties, which were immense (the Church was the largest landowner in Europe), and the properties and incomes of its members, which could be taxed. The Church acquired its own real estate usually by bequest, as it was customary for people to leave the Church something in their wills, from a minor sum of money, to funds or materials to build a chapel or maintain a monastery, to huge grants of property of all kinds. Early in the twelfth century, the Countess of Tuscany left a will in which she gave all of her possessions not directly held from the Emperor to the Papacy—had this will been honored, the Church would have received much of central and northern Italy. Property given to the Church belonged to it as an institution, not to one member of it, and therefore did not revert to secular hands when individual churchmen died, so that the Church's estate always became cumulatively greater.

Taxes levied on secular property and incomes included the tithe (one-tenth of gross income, or its equivalent in goods), which was collected in the local parish; a portion of this tax went to the bishop, and a portion of the bishop's revenue to Rome. In addition, special donations could be requested to meet urgent needs, such as the expenses of the Crusades, and there were a number of lesser sources of income, from fees charged for various services to the gifts that pilgrims left at shrines, or the price sinners paid for indulgences (pardons which forgave penitents the punishment in Purgatory which they would otherwise have deserved).

The Church used its revenues to pay the costs of all of its enterprises, from the daily needs of churchmen themselves to the requirements of waging war. Again and again the Church's critics deplored its wealth and luxury, but a picture of the Church as simply economically wasteful, squandering a major part of the income of medieval Europe on gorgeous robes, fine foods, palatial residences, and so forth, would not be accurate: These abuses existed, as they always do in any institution with power, but much of the Church's wealth was spent on such activities as the education of children, the performance of routine religious duties, the care of the poor and sick, and the building and maintenance of churches. An enterprise such as the construction of a cathedral required huge sums of money, and gave employment to many workers and pride to a whole city. It is not possible to make a fair assessment of the Church's economic influence without remembering that it fulfilled functions now assigned to secular government, and was a producer as well as a consumer.

DEMOGRAPHY AND SOCIAL STRUCTURE

Christianity as an institution and as an ideology affected the demography of medieval Europe in a number of ways. All of our statements about medieval population are, at best, rough estimates, as the era of regular and scientific census-taking had not arrived, and the data are always scanty, irregular, and of questionable accuracy. But we can at least suggest the kinds of demographic influence that presumably were operating.

Insofar as men and women who joined the Church were celibate, and therefore did not reproduce, their genetic contribution to the succeeding generation would have been nil, and the potential size of the succeeding generation would have been reduced by the number of children they did not beget. If ten percent of the population at a given date were celibate, the potential size of the subsequent generation should be reduced by ten percent, and celibacy, a matter of ideology and church law, would constitute an effective means of population control.

However, such a theoretical model is far too simple to be correct. Until the twelfth century, the marriage of priests was not necessarily forbidden, and there were always some monks, nuns, and priests who broke their vows of celibacy and left illegitimate offspring. In addition, the number of children produced by one generation is no adequate indication of the next generation's size at adulthood, since other factors are involved. The size of a population at any given time is determined not only by how many people have been born, but also by how many are still living. Such factors as disease, malnutrition, starvation, and war affected medieval population size. This means that the implication of our theoretical model (clerical celibacy causing a ten percent decrease in the next generation) could be completely cancelled in the full context of the many factors influencing population size. If, for example, the limiting factor in a given community was the availability of food, and clerical celibacy reduced the number of infants born to one generation of 800 parents from a hypothetical figure of 2,000 to 1,800, while food as the limiting factor permitted only 800 to survive (no population increase), the final demographic effect of clerical celibacy itself has been nil.

In all likelihood, although we do not have good data on the proportion of medieval people who entered the Church before reproducing, and remained celibate (the ten percent figure above is probably two or three times too high), it should be accurate to say that the doctrine of celibacy caused a small but definite reduction from the potential medieval birth rate, but that this effect would have been extraneous in times of difficulty since even the smaller number of children produced could not all survive. In times of possible population growth, however, the slightly reduced number of children would have slightly slowed the rate of population increase, so that celibacy would have been a real, although small, factor in population control.

In terms of statistics, estimated population size varies so greatly from place to place and time to time that no statement of one overall trend could be valid. The estimated population of England, for example, was well over three million in 1348, and slightly over one million (less by two-thirds) in 1444, about a century later.[1] This extraordinary loss is attributable largely to the plague.

Clerical celibacy may have had a qualitative effect on medieval population, an effect still more difficult to estimate than the quantitative effect because it involves assumptions about the degree to which personality and intelligence are inherited. If we were to postulate the common characteristics of the people who chose to devote their lives to the Church, we would probably see them as having higher than average intelligence, in view of the Church's emphasis on learning, and as having higher than average commitment to long-range goals. It has been suggested that any religion which requires celibacy of its priesthood is disgenic, in excluding such people from reproduction, but too many other problems are involved here to permit any clear conclusion. We do not really know exactly what level of intelligence is most advantageous to the human species, and the contrary suggestion has been made that the type of person who commits himself to a celibate priesthood, while he may be of high intelligence and self-discipline, also may be prone to fanaticism and extremism, so that (insofar as these too might have a biologically heritable component) his failure to leave children is no net loss to society.

Aspects of Christianity other than clerical celibacy must have influenced population trends. In contrast to celibacy was the concept that God intended mankind to "be fruitful and multiply," so that the function of sexual intercourse was not pleasure but progeny. This attitude, along with the absolute prohibition of infanticide, would have counteracted celibacy and tended to raise the birth and infant survival rates, as it precluded or diminished two of the means of population control theoretically available: the avoidance of conception, and the killing of unwanted infants, both of which were practiced in non-Christian societies.

Finally, the Church's position on warfare can be seen as both decreasing and increasing mortality rates, depending on whether the Church exerted its considerable political leverage to stop, or to promote, a particular war. In general the Church discouraged local warfare. Violence against one's neighbor could be punished in the ecclesiastical courts, and in the earlier Middle Ages the Church tried to limit fighting among Christians by forbidding all local combat on certain days of the week (Wednesday to Monday), in certain seasons of the year, and on certain additional holy days; this regular truce between enemies was called the Truce of God. The practical effect of this result of peace movements within the Church is difficult to estimate. Some people obeyed, others did not, and private warfare gradually declined in the later Middle Ages as the result of other factors also.

When the Church chose to sponsor war, the demographic effect was of course not lives saved but lives lost. It was partly to relieve Europe itself of the belligerence of its armed men that Pope Urban II preached the First Crusade at the end of the eleventh century, and, interestingly enough, he associated the phenomenon of local warfare with population pressure, thinking to bring Europe internal peace and decreased population (as well as the glory of God) by redirecting her excess to the East. The Crusades continued for two centuries, at a vast but imprecisely known cost in human life.

Social structure, as well as demography, was influenced by the Church in more than one way. In general, the Church strengthened the feudal pattern according to which one man was the vassal of another, with the serf at the bottom of this structure and the king or highest overlord at the top, because the Church had a similar hierarchical internal structure and theologically accepted the concept of hierarchy as right and natural, and also because she was in fact part of the feudal pattern herself—bishops and abbots were also feudal lords and vassals, and the Papacy was the feudal overlord of those areas in Italy called the Papal States. The Church thus had a considerable vested interest in feudalism.

On the other hand, she also saw it in her interest to cooperate at times with European kings in their struggles against their feudal nobility; when Church and King were allies, the nobles could be controlled, and central government strengthened. The Church also took a position in fundamental opposition to the psychological implications of feudal hierarchy in her doctrine that each individual soul was equal in importance and responsibility in the eyes of God, so that King and serf would finally be judged by the same criteria. This egalitarian concept postponed any actual leveling until after death, and the Church made it clear that in this life hierarchy, not democracy, ruled, but the emphasis on each individual's intrinsic worth cut across all of the established distinctions of rank, wealth, and power—and sex, for theologically as well as legally woman (in this world) was man's inferior.

The Church as an institution offered social mobility in permitting the rise of individuals on the basis of ability. Among the Popes who came from the lower classes were Gregory VII (eleventh century), to whom an emperor came barefoot in the winter as a penitent, and Hadrian IV (the only English Pope, twelfth century), who made a recalcitrant emperor kiss his feet in submission. But such extreme examples of social mobility as members of the lower classes gaining positions where they ruled emperors were not common. Peasants did not often become Popes. More frequent was the rise of a man of middle-class origin to an appointment of high, although not highest, status. Thomas of Becket, the Archbishop of Canterbury who defended clerical prerogatives against King Henry II of England, and whose murder made him a martyr and gave him the victory in their quarrel, came from a middle-class family. Churchmen, being men, were often corruptible, and many preferments were awarded for illegitimate reasons, but the Church did provide medieval people with an alternative to the feudal hierarchy or the social system of the towns, an alternative in which individual intelligence and integrity might receive quick recognition and reward.

LANGUAGE, LAW, EDUCATION

During the five centuries of the Empire, the Latin language of Rome was the official language of the Western world, from Roman England in the North to Roman Africa in the South. After the fifth century A.D., when the political unity of the Empire disintegrated, its linguistic unity disintegrated also since the natural processes of language evolution were no longer retarded by official imperial Latin as a standard stabilizing tongue (the way the language of Washington, D.C., heard and read all over the U.S.A., now acts to standardize the many dialects of American English).

Under the Empire there had already existed a considerable distance between the literary language of the educated élite, and the daily language of ordinary people. This popular tongue gave rise to the various modern Romance languages—French, Spanish, Italian, Portuguese, Romanian, Romansh —each of which represents the separate linguistic development of the Roman language as spoken by the inhabitants of the different regions at the time of the Empire's decline. In addition, the Germanic invaders brought their own languages, for example Anglo-Saxon (Old English) which displaced Latin in England. Medieval Europe was characterized by great linguistic variety, a greater variety than exists now, for some more powerful European tongues have absorbed weaker neighbors, but even now the barriers to international communication are significant and people wish for a universal language, Esperanto or another.

The medieval Church provided the equivalent of Esperanto by perpetuating the use of Latin as an international language, a medium of communication for all men serving the Church or educated in her schools, and a language heard, if not fully understood, by every Christian man everywhere. The Latin words of the Mass were the same wherever they were spoken. The medieval churchman knew his Bible in Latin, in the "Vulgate" version of St. Jerome (c. 345-420 A.D.), so called because it was commonly used (*vulgus* means the common people). The official language of the Church was always Latin—in Latin she chastised kings, baptized babies, commented on the Scriptures, kept lists of the livestock owned by her monasteries, and prayed to the Lord.

Churchmen throughout Christendom could correspond in a language which was to them a second mother tongue.

The Latin language as a factor promoting cultural unity extended beyond the direct functions of Christianity. As a result of the fact that education was usually conducted by the Church, most educated people used Latin as a means of communication in secular affairs also. The ambassadors of kings drew up treaties in Latin; poets wrote love poems and blasphemous parodies of religious lyrics in Latin; the lives of kings, as well as of saints, were recorded in Latin; scientists composed treatises in Latin; people left one another their worldly goods in Latin. It was the universal language of educated people in Western Europe for some thousand years after it ceased to be the spoken language of the Empire. Even today we carry it on our coins.

The Church, like any institution, had its own laws, but unlike most institutions she developed a complete system of courts through which to administer those laws. Ecclesiastical and secular court systems existed side by side in the Middle Ages, with areas of claimed jurisdiction which were not absolutely separate. The two legal systems sometimes conflicted and the power of the Church courts eventually receded.

The laws of the Church at first consisted of Scripture itself, plus the accumulated decisions of councils of churchmen and of individual authorities, principles adapted from Roman law, and so forth. Codification of these materials began in the sixth century, the most important single compilation being the twelfth-century *Decretum* (decree) of the monk Gratian, which underwent further revision and became the basis of the Church's canon law (*canon* means rule) until the twentieth century. This body of laws regulated not only matters of internal Church governance but also almost every area of human life, since Christianity supervised a man's existence from his birth through his death. The ecclesiastical courts handled all cases involving churchmen, who were immune to civil prosecution, and also cases involving laymen accused of an immense variety of offenses ranging from heresy, a matter of improper belief, to swearing, or seducing one's neighbor's wife, matters of improper conduct. They inflicted penalties as the civil courts did (but not capital punishment) and in addition used the punishment of excommunication, exclusion from the Christian community, which meant that the accused person could not participate in religious services or receive the sacraments—he was in effect an outlaw—and therefore should expect to go to hell if he died before reconciliation to the Church. When excommunication was abused, and overused, it ceased to terrify; some Italian cities, repeatedly put under excommunication for largely political reasons, came to ignore it, but to many people this weapon of ecclesiastical law was a very real threat, and it occasionally brought even kings to obedience.

Although there were always some secular schools and private teachers, and practical skills were taught by one person to another, education through most of the Middle Ages was largely a service provided by the Church. Any career in the Church assumed literacy, so that a basic education at least in reading, writing, and the Latin language had to be provided for those who planned to enter holy orders, and there were repeated attempts to extend instruction to the children of laymen without regard to their possible entry into Church careers. The degree to which this goal of providing general elementary education was realized varies greatly across medieval space and time. There was no "school system" separate from other institutions; children went to school at the monasteries, convents, cathedrals, and parish churchs. While the orientation of such schools was naturally religious, and the study of Latin underlay all, the medieval student learned more than basic literacy, Christian doctrine, and the Latin language. Studies were traditionally divided into the seven liberal arts which were thought to train the intellect: grammar, rhetoric, and logic; then arithmetic, geometry, music, and astronomy. Grammar was a very wide and what we would call interdisciplinary area, as it could include history and literature; rhetoric also involved the study of literature. Monasteries copied and preserved classical literature; cathedral schools too collected manuscripts; the Papacy had its own library, as did some individual churchmen who loved books. So synonymous did literacy and the Church become that anyone who could read and write was considered a "cleric" in the wide sense of the word (someone associated with the Church). As late as 1598, the English playwright Ben Jonson, who had killed a man in a duel, successfully claimed "benefit of clergy"—immunity from civil prosecution—on the grounds that he was literate, and so escaped execution. The medieval Church saw education as one of its routine functions, although this never meant educating the entire populace (an ideal rarely realized in the modern world), and although contemporary criticisms that churchmen scarcely understood the Latin they babbled show that she did not always succeed even in educating her own.

From the twelfth century onward there was an increase in secular schools in the commercial cities, where the primary impetus towards literacy was not the need to read religious texts but the need to keep business records. The twelfth and thirteenth centuries also saw the founding of universities, which were essentially communities of students and teachers, not adjuncts to religious foundations like the monastic, cathedral, or parish schools. However, the universities too had many ties to the Church. Teachers and students were usually clerics, theology was a major subject of study, the Papacy itself founded some universities while others grew out of cathedral schools. And the universities, like everything else in Christendom, were under Church jurisdiction, although they sometimes took the part of secular authorities in power struggles between Church and State.

INTELLECT AND IMAGINATION: PHILOSOPHY, LITERATURE, THE ARTS

The influence of the Church on the mind of medieval man was pervasive, and everywhere the products of his intellect and imagination reflect the Christian world view and the Christian religion. Works of philosophy, literature, music, art and architecture, all characteristically marked with the

Christian imprint, were often produced by churchmen (since they were typically the educated class), or sponsored by the Church for its own adornment and instruction. It is impossible here to survey all the indebtedness of medieval art and thought to the Church, but some of the ways in which the Church made its influence felt can be indicated.

Every age has its dominant philosophy, its rarely questioned pattern of basic assumptions along which human thought and activity align themselves. Ours is scientific materialism. We assume the primary importance, independent validity, and inherent orderliness of the material world, and devote a great deal of our individual and collective energies to elucidating the principles by which its many systems work, and then using this knowledge to make the world work to our advantage. The central preoccupation of our civilization is ourselves and the world we live in, which (we assume) the scientific method of investigation permits us to comprehend.

Medieval assumptions were different. The medieval mind assumed that the material world is not the result of accident or evolution but of creation, and that the Mind which created it so far surpasses human comprehension that no conclusion to which our reasoning leads is necessarily valid. The Creator, whose purpose in making this world and giving it life was that it should love Him, offers us a partial compensation for our essential insufficiency by revealing His will directly to us. Whenever reason and revelation conflict, it is evidently reason, as a merely human activity, which is in error. God has revealed Himself in two primary reflections of His will—the natural world itself, and Scripture (Nature and Scripture are God's "Two Books"), which rightly understood are complementary, not contradictory. Both illustrate His overwhelming love for mankind, and tell us that the reason for our existence is to love Him also. Our preoccupation should be God, not mankind or the material world, except insofar as our activities with reference to one another and the world help us to fulfill our true function of loving God, and so enable us to earn the privilege of being eternally in His presence after our earthly deaths.

The difference between this dominant set of assumptions and our own may help explain some aspects of medieval culture. To us, an emphasis on science and rationalism seems only natural. When we want to understand something we collect data about it and interpret the data by the rational patterns of induction, deduction, analogy. We then formulate a hypothesis, test our hypothesis against the data, and if it passes this test with reproducible results and does not conflict with other scientific principles, we accept it as a conclusion, and are satisfied that we "know." When medieval man wanted to understand something he followed this process also, but saw its conclusions as subsidiary to the kind of knowledge which religion offered, because of his assumption that human reason is imperfect while the Divine Mind, to which we have access through the Two Books and through prayer, is perfect and omniscient. The reason why the Middle Ages were not a major period of scientific advancement is that man's search for knowledge was differently oriented. His accepted priorities required that Scripture take precedence over

Science, so that he generally believed the description of human origins presented in Genesis, for example, and the geocentric concept of the universe. This belief does not mean that he was intellectually naive, however. It derived not from an unexamined impression, but from his complete network of philosophical assumptions, exactly as our culture's beliefs that man evolved naturally from earlier primates and that the sun is the center of the solar system derive from our general acceptance of science. Each civilization and each thinking individual accepts some set of philosophical assumptions by an act of faith through which the consequent activities of human reason are controlled.

Medieval philosophers looked critically at assumptions, wrestled with the problems of how we know truth (what is the relationship between what our reason tells us, and what divine revelation says?), what kinds of things concepts are (do such universal categories as justice exist, or are they only names we apply to individual cases? does Man exist, or only men?), whether the human mind can rationally understand God, or must accept Him as an act of faith. Anselm of Canterbury struggled with his need to prove God, and did so: God is the most perfect being we can conceive, but if He were only an idea in our minds He would lack one aspect of perfection—existence; therefore He exists. (Others pointed out that this argument could prove the existence of a "most perfect" anything.) Peter Abélard tried to make faith comprehensible, amenable to rational explanation, and found some of his writings condemned as heretical. Thomas Aquinas used Aristotelian methods to explain Christianity, and although some of his contemporaries thought he overemphasized rational philosophy, his *Summa theologica* is official Church philosophy today. William of Occam rejected the usefulness of rationalism in theology; no reasoning will finally prove the existence of God or the validity of Christian doctrines, so we must rely upon faith. That medieval philosophy produced no wholly satisfactory answer to such problems is not surprising. Even in our society, where rationalist assumptions predominate, the relationship between reason and faith continues to be questioned.

The Christian religion asserted the existence of one Truth, which stated that man had been created to serve and adore God. Life in this world was to function as a testing-time that determined a man's destination in the next, and nothing in this world was of intrinsic value. It is easy to see that this world view, rigorously pursued, would have stifled all joy in life in favor of a harsh asceticism, and strangled artistic impulses in its requirement for absolute adherence to a single Truth. Some repression occurred, both in the open condemnation of particular ideas as unacceptable, and in the more subtle and more constant pressure towards a general conformity with established viewpoints. But the doctrine of this world's insignificance was not rigorously pursued in all times and places, and its severity was mitigated by two gentler concepts, those of God's infinite mercy and of His infinite love, which might compensate for human weakness. There were always tendencies towards extreme other-worldliness and rejection of the works of man, but the Church itself, as an institution of this world, attempted to focus art and thought on religious subjects rather than to destroy them. In fact, she relied heavily on visual images to express her doctrines to a largely illiterate public, and many an artist who in another time would have painted portraits of rich men's families for his living, then created Madonnas and angels and gods and demons to decorate medieval churches and convey the importance of the next world by means of the artistic possibilities of this world's stone and colors. All medieval religious art embodies this tension between the implied meaning of its chosen shapes and forms, that this material world is insignificant compared to the world of the spirit, and the impact of the beauty of its shapes and forms, which inevitably suggests the value of this material world nevertheless. The innumerable Madonnas simultaneously assert and deny the flesh.

Art was an intrinsic part of medieval worship, serving as a visible bridge between the two worlds. The crowning works of the medieval artistic imagination, unifying mind and matter, were the great Gothic cathedrals, with their primarily vertical lines leading the worshipper's eyes always upward towards the heavens. Every form of artistic expression contributed: the architect's knowledge of materials produced the design, with its rising shapes made possible by careful buttressing; the sculptor's skill adorned the building itself, carving majestic gods and comic gargoyles; the painter or mosaicist decorated interior surfaces; the art of the illuminator (the illustrator of manuscripts) would be seen in the cathedral's books; the gold-worker made the chalice a work of art in itself; the metal-worker produced iron grilles with intricate designs; the makers of fabrics embroidered and bejeweled the priest's robes, and wove fine cloths for the altar. The windows of the cathedral transmitted simultaneously light, beauty, and ideology through their stained-glass images. The ear as well as the eye would be pleased, for music was part of religious services. In the medieval period, church music evolved from monody (in which all voices sing the same tune) to polyphony (a harmony of multiple tunes). All of the arts combined to form the complex art of the adoration of God.

Much of medieval literature is secular—perhaps Christian in its vocabulary or its setting, but not fundamentally religious in its impact—but what is probably the finest single literary work between classical antiquity and Shakespeare, Dante's *Divine Comedy*, demonstrates how beautifully Christianity could become poetry. Written in Italian at the beginning of the fourteenth century, when Dante was exiled from his native Florence, this visionary poem records Dante's journey through hell, purgatory, and heaven, a symbolic journey representative of the progress of the soul through sin and suffering, to repentance, and finally to the sublime presence of God. There are a great many other works inspired by Christianity which seem lesser partly by comparison to Dante's, among them hymns and prayers, biographies of saints, tales of the miracles which the Virgin Mary worked for the faithful, like the tender story of the poor man who wanted to bring Mary a gift, but had no earthly goods to offer her, and so gave her the only proof of his love he could: in the empty church he danced before her statue, and when his performance was finished the statue of the Virgin smiled. During the medieval centuries the drama, having virtually disappeared after classical times, was reborn from within the Church as events of Christian history (the Creation, the Fall, through the Crucifixion and Resurrection, to Judgment Day) were acted out, first as small additions to Church services and later as fully developed cycles of plays.

Christianity's emphasis on the importance of the next world led people to look at objects around them in terms of possible other-worldly meanings, and to symbolize and allegorize as natural habits of mind. Thus a writer of a bestiary (a book about animals) would describe each animal as a modern scientist might, and then offer also a Christian significance. The fox, because it is wily, ought to remind us of the Devil; the phoenix, because it is said to be reborn from its own ashes, ought to make us think of Christ, who was resurrected. Nearly everything in the natural world acquired religious associations. The color white represented purity, blue, faith; the sun stood for divine wisdom which enlightened man's mind; a garden, for Paradise. This habit of mind provided the medieval poet or artist with a variety of words or images which had multiple meanings, and permitted him to create works of the imagination which, whether sacred or secular, were pregnant with simultaneous implications. A poem in praise of springtime could suggest also the poet's praise of Christ, who was resurrected, like the year, in the springtime. Medieval man was led by his theology to think metaphorically, and his art was thereby enriched.

SYNTHESIS: FLORENCE, 1300

The multiform impact of the Church on medieval society can perhaps now be suggested by a brief sketch of her activities in one city at a particular time. Let us choose the Italian commune of Florence at the beginning of the fourteenth century.[2]

In 1296 the citizens of Florence agreed to rebuild their main church, and taxed themselves to provide funds. They secured the services of a famous architect, and in 1300 work on the new cathedral began (it was shortly discontinued because of civil war in the city, and not resumed until 1330). In addition to this cathedral, Santa Maria de Fiore, Florence took pride in the church of San Giovanni, which had been given an outer covering of marble just before 1300. The diocese of Florence, divided into fifty-seven parishes, contained many lesser churches also, and was the seat of Dominican and Franciscan houses. In Florence, as everywhere in Europe, the daily work of the Church went on, and 1300 would have found churchmen saying Mass, baptising the newborn, burying the dead, preaching, teaching, hearing confession, collecting taxes, and dispensing charity. Florentine children went to church schools (or to the schools run by the middle classes); towards the end of the century Florence would establish its university.

The year 1300 was proclaimed by Pope Boniface VIII to be a great jubilee year with special celebrations in Rome, as the center of western Christendom. This brought a temporary truce in the complicated factional disputes of Florentine politics, as the Pope wanted peace within Italy for that year so that pilgrims could safely converge on Rome. Nevertheless, Boniface was himself one of the main political factors in Florence. Believing in the supreme political authority of the Papacy, and having a particular desire to control Florence and the other cities of Tuscany, Boniface had given his support to one Florentine faction, who came to be called the "Blacks," in contrast to another, the "Whites." Boniface had requested military aid from the King of France, who agreed to send his brother, Charles of Valois, to Rome (ostensibly for an expedition against Sicily). In 1301, the jubilee truce over, Charles led the papal forces into Florence, and permitted the Black leader to dismiss the White government, to plunder and burn as he wished, and to set up a Black court which summoned the White leaders to trial. Among the Whites who fled the city and thus escaped death sentences was the poet Dante, who had served briefly in the White government during the summer of 1300. Had Dante not been forced into exile, the poem by which his name is remembered might not have been written.

In 1300, then, the Church asserted her presence in Florence in various ways. Her normal continuing functions were carried out, as they were throughout the medieval centuries, by the parish churches, and Franciscan and Dominican friars were preaching to the people. Artists and builders would have been working on the new cathedral. Poet and Pope, temporarily at truce, would have awaited the end of the jubilee year and the beginning of the political turmoil which both must have known would ensue.

FOOTNOTES

1. T. H. Hollingsworth, *Historical Demography* (Ithaca: Cornell Univ. Press, 1969), p. 386.
2. This section is indebted to Ferdinand Schevill, *Medieval and Renaissance Florence* (New York: Harper, 1963), I and II.

Section J. The Transformation
to
the Industrial City

The Change in Demographic patterns

THE CITY

Werner Sombart

SOURCES AND LITERATURE

I am unacquainted with any literature on the history of the city, which could be used in connection with our study. A great many writings dealing with the history of individual cities are at best mere histories of municipal law or of monuments. The economic and cultural points of view are almost never taken into consideration. It would hardly be of use, then, to cite these books here.

The material presented in the following pages on the origin and the organization of the early capitalistic city has been compiled almost entirely from original sources. Travel books and descriptions of other kinds take first place among the sources used. Needless to say that Mercier's *Tableau de Paris* (1781), 12 vols., has no counterpart for any city. Still, we find reasonably accurate information about London in the seventeenth and eighteenth centuries in the descriptions by Defoe-Richardson, Miege-Bolton, Archenholtz, etc.

The sources for Naples in the sixteenth century are to be found in E. Gothein, *Culturentwicklung Süd-Italiens* (Breslau, 1886); Naples in the eighteenth century is described in *Essai sur la société et les moeurs des Italiens* (1782), Letter LV, *et seq.*

With regard to Madrid in the seventeenth century, some travel journals and the memoirs of Mme d'Aulnoy[1] are adequate for our purposes. (Cf also, Karl Justi, *Diego Velasquez und sein Jahrhundert* [Bonn, 1888]; English tr., *David Velasquez and His Time* [London, 1889].)

THE CITIES IN THE SIXTEENTH, SEVENTEENTH,
AND EIGHTEENTH CENTURIES

One of the most significant events in the whole history of our civilization . . . is the rapid increase in population of a number of towns at the
beginning of the sixteenth century. The product of this development is the
city with a population running to six figures. Toward the end of the eighteenth century this type of city, exemplified by London and Paris, comes close
to the modern metropolis.

During the sixteenth century the number of cities with 100,000 inhabitants and over, increased to thirteen or fourteen.[2]

The first group to be considered are the Italian cities: Venice (1563:
168,627; 1575-77: 195,863), Naples (240,000), Milan (about 200,000), Palermo (1600: about 100,000), and Rome (1600: about 100,000). On the other
hand, Florence, in 1530, had a population of only 60,000.

The next are the Spanish-Portuguese cities: Lisbon (1629: 110,800) and
Seville (at the end of the sixteenth century had 18,000 households repre-
senting a population of about 100,000), and the cities of the Netherlands:
Antwerp (1560: 104,972) and Amsterdam (1622: 104,961).

Let us finally consider Paris and London. Paris, against whose expansion
royal edicts had already been issued by the middle of the sixteenth century (I
shall revert to them presently) obviously decreased in population because of
the religious wars; in 1594 the population of Paris was about 180,000. London grew rapidly and by the end of the sixteenth century exhibited all the
signs of an overpopulated city, as we may gather from a decree by Queen
Elizabeth in 1602.[3] We must place its population for that period at about
250,000.

During the seventeenth century a few of the formerly large cities decreased in population. Lisbon and Antwerp fell below the 100,000 mark, and
the population of Milan and Venice likewise shrank considerably. On the
other hand, Vienna (1720: 130,000) and Madrid grew into big cities.

Rome, Amsterdam, Paris, and London continued to expand. Rome had
a population of 140,000 at the end of the seventeenth century; Amsterdam,
one of 200,000. At the same time, Paris reached half a million, while London,
in 1700, exceeded this mark with 674,350.

While London grew only gradually during that century, Paris developed
more rapidly, particularly in the reign of the first two Bourbons. Now we
frequently meet with those odd edicts, to which I have referred above, forbidding the erection of new houses with a view to checking the growth of the
city. They usually begin with phrases like "Whereas the increase in size of our
good city of Paris is highly prejudicial," or "Whereas it has been the intention
of His Majesty that the city of Paris be of a fixed and limited size. . . ."
(These prohibitory edicts express a spirit kindred to that of the guilds of the
Middle Ages: opposition to an unrestrained growth of an organic structure,
opposition to the tendency to unrestrained expansion and quantification

inherent in the capitalistic system, opposition of the old frugality, and conservatism to the boundless urge to expand inherent in the commercial spirit.)

As might have been expected, these prohibitions proved useless. In spite of their reiteration (1627, 1637), Paris kept on growing mightily during these very decades. Baudrillart, a judicious historian, holds that there is a greater difference between the Paris of Louis XIII and that of the League than between the Paris of the League and that of the Third Republic. The awareness of contemporaries of this change is expressed by Corneille in his comedy, *Le Menteur,* written in 1642 (II:5):

> *Tout un ville entière, avec pompe bâtie*
> *Semble d'un vieux fossé par miracle sortie*
> *Et nous fait présumer, à ses superbes toits,*
> *Que tous ses habitants sort des dieux ou des rois.*

The eighteenth century brought the following changes: The 200,000 mark in population was passed by Moscow, St. Petersburg, Vienna, *Palermo (1795: 200,162), with Dublin not far behind (1798: 182,370, as against 8,159 in 1644 and 128,870 in 1753).

The 100,000 mark was reached by Hamburg, Copenhagen, Warsaw; Berlin and *Lyon grew to 141,283 (1783) and 135,207 (1787), respectively.

*Naples approached the half-million mark (1796: 435,930), London the million mark (864,845 according to the census of 1801), while *Paris had a population of between 640,000 and 670,000 at the outbreak of the Revolution.

ORIGIN AND INNER STRUCTURE OF THE CITIES

When we inquire into the reasons for the gigantic growth of these cities we discover the same kind of city-building factors at work which we have found in the growth of the towns in the Middle Ages. Moreover, this is worth noting—the large cities of the early capitalistic epoch are basically consumer cities. The most important consumers are familiar to us; the princes, prelates, and nobles, who are now joined by a new group, "haute finance" (which may be regarded as a class of consumers without disparaging its "productive" function in the politico-economic organization). The largest cities have attained that degree of expansion because they were the residence of the largest number of great consumers. Hence, the expansion of the cities is essentially due to a concentration of consumption in the urban centers of a given country.

The correctness of this view can be proved negatively by pointing out that the "producers," commerce and industry, were unable to develop the cities in which they were situated beyond mere middle size.

Purely commercial cities as, for example, Bristol, which a traveler, about

---

*An asterisk before the name of a city in the text indicates that the relevant figures are taken from the article by Inama-Sternegg in *Handwörterbuch der Staatswissenschaften.*

the middle of the eighteenth century, called the "largest, most populous and flourishing place in the island, and one of the principal cities in Europe,"[4] or the other flourishing commercial cities of England at that period, Exeter, Lynn, Norwich, Yarmouth, etc., numbered no more than 30,000 to 40,000 inhabitants when London had long passed the half-million mark. In general, industry had no inherent ability to develop large cities. The industrial centers of the eighteenth century, the mining cities or the centers of the household industries, like Newcastle, Glasgow, Leeds, Manchester, and Birmingham in England; Iserlohn, Paderborn, Jauer, and Hirschberg in Germany, are middle-sized or smaller cities. Neither Great Britain nor Germany, with the exception of their capitals, could boast of a city with a larger population than 100,000, before the end of the eighteenth century.

When we closely examine the so-called commercial cities, for instance, Amsterdam or Hamburg, it is not long before we discover that they owe their rise to city status to forces other than trade. Hence, we can name but one commercial town which, prior to the nineteenth century, had risen to the rank of a city: Lyon, the site of the greatest luxury industry of the early capitalistic epoch. And even in the case of Lyon, banking activities probably have played an important part in the growth of the city.

It will now be easy to show conclusively that it was the concentration of consumption which brought about the early development of the cities. Such a development occurred everywhere under the pressure of a germinating capitalistic system, irrespective of the peculiar character of the country.

Using the most important cities of the seventeenth and eighteenth centuries as illustrations, I shall proceed now to test my assertion.

1. Berlin is the model of the purely residential city, in which only the court, the government official, and the military appear as urbanizing factors. The first signs of an accelerated rate of growth appeared in the latter half of the eighteenth century; it was not until the beginning of the 1760s that its population passed the 100,000 mark. But even at the end of the eighteenth century, Berlin was almost exclusively a city of soldiers and officials and, consequently, of necessity a poor city. In 1783 the garrison, including the families of officers and soldiers, numbered no less than 33,088 people, or 23 percent of the total population of 141,283. (In 1895 this same group comprised 29,448 persons, or 1.8 percent of the entire population.) The state and municipal officials totaled 3,433 or, with their dependents, about 13,000. In addition to these two groups there was an extraordinarily large number of servants (10,074). These three sections of the population, and the section depending directly on the court, formed a group totaling 56,000 persons, or two-fifths of the entire population of the capital.[5] How poor these salaried employees of the king of Prussia were is evidenced by the fact that they, in turn, could give employment and homes to a group no more numerous than their own. During that period, 50,000 salaried employees in London or Paris would have fed a population from 200,000 to 300,000 at least.

2. Amsterdam, too, began as the residence of a prince. We gather this from the fact that the departure of the court toward the end of the seven-

teenth century resulted in great losses in every direction.[6] The gap was soon bridged, however. Amsterdam became the home of the creditors of all European states, a city which consumed the surplus of the wealthiest colonial empire of the world.

3. Venice is similar in character to Amsterdam. The extensive possessions acquired in the early colonial days of the Republic produced in due course a smug, over-wealthy class with incomes from abroad, which swelled the substantial group of land owners. A writer of the fifteenth century informs us with respect to the colonial families of Crete: "A number had accumulated large fortunes and lived in Venice on their income."[7] Nor should it be overlooked that Venice, prior to the loss of her colonies, was the capital of the third largest state in Europe. The great wealth spent in Venice was conducive to a rich, lavish life of pleasure which attracted many foreign visitors. Next to Rome, Venice was the most celebrated city in the sixteenth century: *sede principalissima del piacere* (principal pleasure resort), as it is described in a letter of the year 1565; *paradisus delitiarum* (paradise of delights), as it is called in Hentzner's *Itinerarium* (1617).[8] The greatest attractions of Venice were amusements and women.

4. Rome, in the opinion of Gregorovius, "the only metropolis" because of its physical extent, combined a multitude of important consumers of various kinds:

a. The pope, with the numerous court attendants, who relied on Peter's pence and, in most cases, on a very considerable private income.

b. The pilgrims. Two hundred thousand are said to have been in Rome in 1500.

c. The cardinals and the prelates. Cartesius de Cardinalatu estimates[9] that as early as the fifteenth century a cardinal had to have an income of 12,000 gold florins and a staff of about 140 persons. Some of the cardinals had incomes of 30,000 ducats, and more.[10]

d. The relatives of the popes on whom riches were lavished. Pietro Riario, the son of Sixtus IV, drew an annuity of 60,000 gold florins.

e. The great noble families, the Orsini, Colonna, etc., who had huge estates and a correspondingly great income from ground rents.

In the period when the popes resided in Avignon, Rome threatened to decay. Cardinal Napoleone Orsini assured the French king after the death of Clement V that, through the departure of the popes, Rome was brought to the verge of ruin. In 1347, Cola di Rienzi held that Rome resembled a robbers' den rather than a habitation fit for respectable people.[11]

5. Madrid. What Rome and Venice meant to the fifteenth and sixteenth centuries, Madrid became in the seventeenth century—*the* Metropolis. The mightiest king on earth held court in Madrid; it was the center of the greatest empire in the world, and to it flowed all the silver treasures of America. No wonder, then, that Madrid attracted all who represented power and riches in Spain. Nothing was more keenly coveted than the honor of being received in the king's household. The court offices bestowed by the king were the especial goal of the younger sons of the nobility. It is fairly easy to trace the

growing importance of Madrid to the congregation of the great of the country in that city, particularly since the accession of Philip III. "The rural districts," so we learn from a contemporary, "are being abandoned by the rich notables."[12] It also seems that Madrid, next to Rome, was the first modern city to have an appreciable influx of pleasure-bent foreign visitors. For this reason Madrid was called "the noble inn of foreigners."[13]

6. Naples. If Madrid, in the seventeenth century, was the third, or perhaps the second, largest city in Europe (it is estimated to have had 400,000 inhabitants at the height of its glory), Naples now grew so rapidly that during the following century it ranked immediately behind London and Paris.

Naples is a textbook example of the vindication of the thesis advanced in this work, namely, that the early development of the cities is based on the concentration of consumption in them. Naples was never anything but the residence of a prince. It owes its status as a city to this circumstance and to the fact that it was the capital of Italy's first unified state, possessing a centralized administration and judiciary.

The greatness and wealth of Naples flowed from two sources: the royal court and the church. These facts were well recognized in their time. *"Regis servitum nostra mercatura est"* (Serving the king is our business), says Caracciolo, in whose writings we see mirrored the social structure of Naples. Indeed, the number of offices in Naples was infinitely large, for centralization led to hypertrophy of offices. The payment of fees was worked out as a system, which was likewise recognized by contemporaries as an essential source of income. An observer moving in the higher strata of Naples' society must have gained the impression that there was hardly anything besides the "unlimited number of jurists, lawers and clerks." (Folieta). With the definite establishment of Spanish rule, Caracciolo at once notes the wane of that influence which had been exerted by the court. The king is now far away, he says, and the city is declining. The barons have given up their large retinues, and, in consequence, public life has lost rhythm and brilliance. No longer does anyone here display princely splendor. The city loses its population, rents are falling, and all merely because Naples has ceased to be the residence of the king.

Later, everything changes again. Naples had another period of prosperity under Spanish rule. When the nobility resumed its lavish mode of life, Naples witnessed a greater pomp than ever before and the population again increased rapidly.[14]

7. Paris. When Lavoisier, the founder of modern chemistry, dedicated his not inconsiderable faculties to the "public good" and fought in the National Assembly for the fiscal reform of France, he made an extremely interesting calculation in order to ascertain the quantity and value of the goods brought into Paris for local consumption. His very accurate computations disclose that every year the people of Paris bought necessities worth 260,000,000 livres for themselves, and feed worth 10,000,000 livres for their horses. Of course, all this had to be paid for. The answer which Lavoisier gives to the question as to the sources from which the 250,000,000 livres were

paid, interests us because it contains a remarkable estimate of the composition of the population of Paris at the outbreak of the Revolution. The answer, after eliminating certain obviously erroneous statements which crept into Lavoisier's computations, presents the following picture.[15]

Export industries and trade brought in about 20,000,000 livres, 140,000,000 livres constituted the share of Paris in the interest paid on the public debt (*revenu des intérêts et dépenses payé par la trésor public*); 100,000,000 livres represented ground rents and profits from industries outside of Paris spent in the city (*revenu des propriétaires de terre, de biens ruraux et de manufactures*). Brilliant indeed! What depth of insight and comprehension! Paris, with a negligible exception, is revealed as purely a consumers' city which drew its livelihood from the court, the officials, the public creditors, and the receivers of ground rents.

The same idea is advanced by all well-informed contemporaries. And in the absence of statistical material we must, to our regret, depend on their statement for the correctness of our opinion.

Mirabeau the Elder, the author of *L'Ami des hommes*, estimated that the population of Paris would be reduced by about 200,000 if, in conformity with his proposal, the following persons were to be ordered back to the provinces: (1) the court officers who are drawing large salaries; (2) all the large landowners who have come to Paris to carry on their litigations before the courts. They should be made to understand that the cases could best be handled in their own rural districts, where they would enjoy greater consideration and more ease; (3) mischievous litigants.[16]

In his opinion, and that of all physiocrats, there is "a false distribution of population and wealth," for, "all the gentlemen, all the rich people, all those who have independent incomes or pensions which enable them to live comfortably, install themselves in Paris or some other large city where they spend almost the entire interest from the bonds of the state. This spending of money attracts a host of merchants, artisans, servants and laborers."[17] These wealthy rentiers, with whom the "financiers who maintain a direct connection with the royal treasury..."[18] and others were associated, stimulate the growth of a highly developed and, in the opinion of the physiocrats, an overrefined luxury industry. "The landowner, a rustic when on his estate, becomes in Paris an *arbiter elegantiarum* and gives new ideas to the artisan who, thus lifted above routine work, becomes eminent in his line...."[19]

To what extent all industries and businesses thrived only on the expenditures of the wealthy, who thus become the founders of the city in the sense which we have given to this term, is again told by Mercier, in his usual incisive manner:

How are we to help this mass of needy who have no other guarantee of livelihood than the depraved luxury of the great . . .
We see in this capital men spending their whole life making toys for children; varnishing, gilding, and tufting occupies a whole army of workers; a hundred thousand are busy day and night mixing sweetmeats or making ornamental pastries. Fifty thousand other men, comb in hand, wait for the moment of

awakening of those idlers who vegetate under the impression that they are alive and who make their toilet twice a day to overcome the boredom which weighs them down.[20]

In most cases the physiocrats forget to stress in their discourses the fact that a not inconsiderable portion of the population of Paris lived on the income of the Church and her servants. It is Mercier again who serves as the most valuable source on this point also:

Paris is filled with abbés, tonsured clerics, serving neither Church nor State, who live in continuous idleness, whiling away their time with futilities and inanities. . . . In many a house we find an abbé who is called "friend of the family" but is only a simple valet in charge of servants. . . . Then come the tutors who are also abbés. . . .[21]
The bishops violate without much concern the residence laws and leave the posts assigned to them by the holy canons. Boredom drives them from their dioceses which they look upon as places of exile. Most of them come to Paris to enjoy their wealth.[22]

We are indebted to the same authority for the only reliable account of the various strata which made up the population of Paris at the end of the early capitalistic period. In conclusion, I shall present the survey furnished by Mercier. In order to bring out the picture in sharper relief, and also for the sake of greater clarity, I shall reproduce the survey in schematic form.

Paris has eight distinct classes of inhabitants:
1. Princes and nobles
2. Gentlemen of the robe
   a. bar
   b. church
   c. medical profession
3. Financiers, from the farmer-general to those who lent money on estates; the stockbrokers, those new vultures, occupying the center of this predatory brotherhood, despicable and despised
4. Business men or merchants, living exclusively on the great, who, being gentlemen, never buy anything for cash, and are obliged to humiliate themselves daily before them or their servants
5. Artists
   Painters
   Architects   } inferior rank
   Sculptors
   Music composers, ranking high
   Men of letters, ranking highest, the *nobilitas literata*
6. Artisans, wealthy artisans deriving their comfort exclusively from the work performed for the wealthy (as I have shown elsewhere)
7. Laborers
8. Servants
9. Populace
(There are nine classes after all?!)

Above all there are also a great number of unproductive people, such as the monks performing religious services in private chapels; and so many nobles, court clerks, bailiffs, constables, attorneys' clerks, armed guards, beadles, rentiers, coachmen, postilions, grooms, and, moreover, the foreigners who come to Paris in droves.[23]

8. London. A great royal court, surrounded since the end of the sixteenth century by a circle of feudal lords spending their income there, is still the core of London when we enter the seventeenth century. We sense the power of attraction of the capital for the nobility and gentry in the seventeenth century from the numerous decrees issued—strangely enough, by the first two Stuarts—against the tendency of country gentlemen to reside in London. One of these decrees, from the year 1632, runs as follows:

The King's Most Excellent Majesty hath observed, That of late yeares a great number of the Nobility and Gentry, and abler sort of his People with their Families have resorted to the Citties of London and Westminster, and places adjoyning, and there made their Residence more then in former tymes . . . by their Residence in the said Citties and Parts adjoyning, they have not imployment but live without doing any Service to his Majesty or his People, a great part of their Money and Substance is drawn from the severall Countries whence it ariseth, and is spent in the Citty in excess of Apparell provided from forraigne parts . . . and of the great Numbers of loose and idle People, that follow them and live in and about the said Citties, the disorder there groweth so great. . . .[24]

However, these residence prohibitions suffered the fate of all decrees that purport to drive the river upstream; they were simply disregarded. During that century the migration of landowners to London must have taken place with increasing frequency. This movement was the chief factor in the growth of London in the seventeenth century, for at the turn of the following century, London was described as "the mighty Rendez-vous of Nobility, Gentry, Courtiers, Divines, Lawyers, Physicians, Merchants, Seamen and all kind of excellent Artificers of the most refined Wits and the most excellent Beauties."[25]

Since the end of the seventeenth century and the beginning of the eighteenth century, a new element appeared as a city builder, the creditors of the state and the big financiers. As early as the seventeenth century, London had a well-established banking business. What great amounts of cash could be mobilized on short notice is demonstrated, for instance, by the fact that the subscription of the capital stock of the Bank of England (£1,200,900) was completed between June 21 and July 2, 1694. D. Hume recognizes, with profound acumen, the power of the state debts to promote the growth of the city: ". . . [Our] national debts cause a mighty confluence of the people and riches to the capital, by the great sums levied in the provinces to pay the interest [on these debts]."[26]

In the middle of the seventeenth century we find society still living in the city, as evidenced by the complaints of city ladies with sensitive olfactory nerves about the nuisance of coal smoke (coal was then beginning to be widely used): "O Husband wee shall never bee well, wee nor our children while wee live in the smell of this Cities Seacoale smoke."[27]

This period inaugurates the transfer of the mansions of the nobility to the suburbs. Bolton, who continued the work of Guy Miege, has left us a vivid picture of this process of transformation which the city of London underwent in the middle of the eighteenth century. "The Nobility and chief among the Gentry are at this time much better accommodated in fine Squares and Streets where they breath a good Air and have Houses built after the modern way." He lists a great number of these new houses. We also conclude from his descriptions that the character of elegant London was, in his time, still determined by the establishments of the gentry.[28] The nobility was living at that time in the immediate vicinity of London. Defoe counts seventeen localities in the outskirts of London, "all crowded and surrounded with fine houses or rather palaces of the nobility and gentry of England."[29]

In attempting statistically to ascertain the part played by the several urbanizing elements of the population in the development of London in the eighteenth century, I have sought to do for that city what Lavoisier has similarly done for Paris, although by quite a different method. The conclusions arrived at by me naturally make no claim to absolute accuracy. Undoubtedly, however, they gain considerably in credibility by the fact that the components calculated closely approximate those given for Paris by Lavoisier. The apparent disparity exists only insofar as the turnover of trade in London exceeded that of Paris.

We can readily understand why descriptions of London, as the one by Chamberlayne, for instance, place such great emphasis on the importance of trade as a city-forming element. Trade impressed all observers as the most prominent feature of English life. Statistics, however, plainly show that trade could have supported only a small part of the population of London. In 1700, the imports and exports of England amounted to about RM 214,000,000, (about £10,500,000), a figure reached by the trade of the city of Bremen around the middle of the nineteenth century. The tonnage of incoming and outgoing vessels in all harbors of England in 1688 totaled 285,000 tons, equaling Hamburg's traffic about the year 1800, or one-fiftieth of its present volume.[30] With all due respect to the commercial greatness of London in that day, we should not uncritically accept the extravagant statements of contemporary writers who speak of the "infinite number of ships, which by their masts resemble a Forest, as they lie along this Stream" (Thames), or of the "infinite number of great wellfurnished Shops." (Chamberlayne). In order to appreciate the true part that trade shared in the development of London, we should present the following calculation.

In 1700, the imports and exports of all England amounted to not quite £11,000,000. Assuming a net profit of ten percent, which is high enough even for that period, this will give us a profit of £1,100,000. Assuming London's share to be two-thirds of the total English trade, which is certainly ample, we arrive at the round sum of £750,000 as the yearly profit of the London merchants. Considering, as King does, that in 1688 the average income of an artisan's family was £40, and that of a laborer's family £15 a year, the foregoing sum could have furnished an income for only about 7000 artisans' families and 24,000 workers' families, or 12,000 families in each category. King holds that the average number of persons in these families was three and a half or four. Hence, it is unlikely that trade could have supported much more than a population of 100,000 souls, i.e., from one-seventh to one-sixth of the total population of London at that period.

Moreover, we must not lose sight of the fact that trade transacted in London could be a factor in the promotion of the growth of the city only insofar as it was not engaged in merely supplying the needs of the population of London itself. When we deduct that portion from the total trade, the part which was operative in the growth of the city is considerably reduced.

The civil lists of the English kings of that period may serve as a basis of comparison. In 1696 Parliament granted William III a civil list of £700,000. Queen Anne received the same sum. Under George I the civil list was increased to £800,000 and under George II to £900,000, (£100,000 for the separate household of the queen). In addition to this, the prince of Wales had a private income of £100,000. Thus, the king, the queen-mother, and the heir apparent disposed of a combined income of approximately the same amount as that of all the merchants of the realm together and consequently, constituted a source of income for as large a population as that supported by the merchant class. The figures here are taken from the above-mentioned work by Miege-Bolton.[31] This work offers in an appendix ("A regular collection of series of lists containing all the offices and the whole establishment civil, military and ecclesiastical in Great Britain and Ireland"), a nearly complete roll of the salaries of the military and civil officers of the kingdom, which reveals salaries of almost incredible size, especially in the upper brackets. Not infrequently these salaries rise to £1000, £1500, and even £2000. Continuing our calculation, we find that if £2000 had to be earned as profit, such a profit, even assuming a rate of twenty percent and two complete capital turnovers a year, would have necessitated an investment of £200,000 or one-fortieth of the yearly turnover of all goods in London. If we assign the various portions, by their source of income, to the several city-forming strata, we may effect the following distribution: two-sixths of the population derive their livelihood from the king and his court, one-sixth from the officials, two-sixths from the landed rentiers and the indirect rentiers of the state (high finance), and one-sixth from trade and industrial activities.

THEORIES OF THE CITY IN THE EIGHTEENTH CENTURY

The sketch of the social structure of the city in the early capitalistic epoch, which I have attempted to draw in the preceding pages, finds unequivocal corroboration in the numerous "city theories" of the eighteenth century, from which we may infer the character of the city at that time. For, although most authors believed they were describing the origin and the conditions promoting the development of the city or the metropolis, their theories are in reality only generalizations regarding the actual municipal structures accessible to their observation. For this reason I shall now, in conclusion, quote some of the most widely read and respected contemporary authorities on the theory of city growth.

Cantillon, as far as I can see, is the pioneer in this field as in so many other fields of political economy in the eighteenth century. He assigns the origin of the city to the following causes:

If a Prince or Nobleman . . . fixes his residence in some pleasant spot, and several other Noblemen come to live there to be within reach of seeing each other frequently and enjoying agreeable society, this place will become a City. Great houses will be built there for the Noblemen in question, and an infinity of others for the Merchants, Artisans, and people of all sorts of professions whom the residence of these Noblemen will attract thither. For the service of these Noblemen, Bakers, Butchers, Brewers, Wine Merchants, Manufacturers of all kinds, will be needed. These will build houses in the locality or will rent houses built by others . . . all the little houses in a City such as we have described depend upon and subsist at the expense of the great houses. . . . The City in question will increase still further if the King or the Government establish in it Law Courts. . . . A Capital City is formed in the same way as a Provincial City. . . . Thus, all the Lands in the State contribute more or less to maintain those who dwell in the Capital.[32]

A similar train of reasoning is found with minor modifications in almost all contemporary treatises on the formation of the city. This concept was developed with particular emphasis by the physiocrats, who made it the foundation of their theory, but it was also taken up by many nonorthodox physiocratic writers.

The politico-economic literature of the eighteenth century is devoted to the discussion of the most desirable way of spending incomes from ground rent. This subject is the theme of a host of pamphlets and treatises dealing with luxury, which are as characteristic of the politico-economic literature of the eighteenth century as the treatises on the subject of population.

Since this economically important portion of the national income is expended in towns and, especially, in the large cities, the problems posited by luxury and the cities soon coalesced. In almost every instance the discussions of luxury are extended to an examination of what caused the cities to become populous, to the very composition of this population, to the specific items and the distribution of the expenditures of the rich, with the resulting economic effects.

In order to ascertain the connection between theories of luxury and the city, one need only refer to Quesnay's "Questions intéressantes sur la population, l'agriculture et le commerce,"[33] which deals, in the twenty questions set forth in the section "Ville," with the nexus between city formation and economic circulation. Question XV,[34] for instance, propounds: "Are the great fortunes forming in the city not prejudicial to agriculture . . . does their existence not prove that they accumulate in the cities and do not return to the country?" Then in Question XVIII: "Does the restoration of the income from landed property permit the proprietors and all other people, who are able to spend lavishly, to live in the country?"[35] etc. Or, in the section "Richesse," article VI: "Ever since the great and rich have gone to the capital, have their expenses not augmented enormously, and would one not judge therefrom that luxury has increased? Has luxury not always been a measure of the wealth of a nation?"[36] etc. Quesnay, too, bases his argumentation on Cantillon, whose brilliant treatise, in its first part, is concerned with many of the same problems. See, for example, chapter XIV,[37] the title of which constitutes a whole program.

For comparison with the theory of Cantillon, I quote the following passage from Helvétius: "The wealth of the city has attracted pleasure seekers. The rich landowners who want to enjoy themselves leave their estates and spend several months in the city where they have mansions built for themselves. The city will grow with every day.... Eventually it will become a capital."[38] We have already seen a similar view expressed by Quesnay. Wholly kindred in spirit are the arguments of Count Mirabeau.[39]

Of Italian writers, Beccaria and Filangieri should be mentioned. "The big landowners, with their greater needs and a life more refined than the lowly and simple customs of the common people, became victims of ennui—the plague of the rich. In order to distinguish themselves from others and to assert their superiority over the working classes, which are just as good as they are, they eventually had to congregate and live near one another at the sources of the law, near the highest courts of the land where, while extending the sphere of their pleasures, they extended their powers as well. This is the origin of the large cities and, in consequence, of the capitals."[40] Filangieri, likewise, attributes the formation of the city to the rich landowner: "In that place (the city), in order to display his luxury he (the landowner) prostitutes the canvas of the painter, the chisel of the sculptor, the talent of the architect, the imagination of the poet, and all sorts of artisans. In the city he also maintains a band of idlers, more for the sake of display than for his own convenience. In the city, he eats up finally his own income as well as that of future generations."[41]

The English theory of Stuart is but a restatement of Cantillon's ideas with only this modification. Stuart recognizes as free, city-forming elements not only the landlords ("to whom this surplus [of food] directly belongs") but also the new class of financiers, i.e., people with a vested claim to the nation's income ("with a revenue in money already acquired") around whom are grouped tradesmen and artisans ("those who purchase it [their food] with their daily labor or personal service").[42]

FOOTNOTES

Sources and Literature
1. Marie d'Aulnoy, *La Cour et la ville de Madrid* (Paris, 1874).
The Cities in the Sixteenth, Seventeenth, and Eighteenth Centuries
2. The figures are taken from the painstaking inquiry by F. Beloch,

"Die Entwicklung der Grosstädte in Europa," published in *Comptes rendus du VIIIᵉ Congrès International d'Hygiène et de Démographie*, pp. 55 *et seq*. The census figures of Dublin have been taken from A. Moreau de Jonnès, *Statistique de la Grande-Bretagne*, . . . (Paris, 1837), 1, p. 88. The last figure for London is that of the census of 1801; the figures given for Berlin are those in the compilation of Normann, cited by H.G.R. Mirabeau, *De la Monarchie prusienne* (London, 1788), 1, pp. 395 *et seq*.

3. The edict is cited in T. Rymer's *Foedera*, . . . (London, 1726-35), 16, p. 448.

Origin and Inner Structure of the Cities

4. Daniel Defoe, *A Tour Through the Islands of Great Britain*, . . . (London, 1778), 2, p. 253.

5. H.G.R. Mirabeau, *op.cit.*

6. W.E.J. Berg, *De Refugiés in de Nederlande*, . . . (Amsterdam, 1845), 1, pp. 269, *et seq*.

7. E. Gerland, "Kreta als venetianische Kolonie" (1204-1669), in *Historisches Jahrbuch* (München, 1899), 20, p. 22.

8. Cf. the descriptions of Venice in H. Simonsfeld, *Der Fondaco dei Tedeschi in Venedig*, . . . (Stuttgart, 1887), 2, pp. 265 *et seq*.

9. F. Gregorovius, *Geschichte der Stadt Rom im Mittelalter* (Stuttgart, 1859-72), 7, p. 236; English tr. by Annie Hamilton, *City of Rome in the Middle Ages* (London, 1900), 7, p. 247, note.

10. *Ibid.*, 8, p. 287; English tr., 8, p. 302.

11. Ludwig Pastor, *Geschichte der Päpste*, . . . (Freiburg, i.B., 1901), 1, pp. 78 *et seq*.

12. "Conservación de monarquías y discursos." Discurso XIV, cited in L. Ranke, *Fürsten und Völker von Südeuropa* (Berlin 1837-45), 1, p. 458. Cf. K. Haebler, *Wirtschaftliche Blüte Spaniens*, . . . (Leipzig, 1888), pp. 53, 153, 155, and *passim*.

13. Cf. the interesting description of Madrid in her Golden Age, based on good sources, which W. F. von Gleichen-Russwurm gives in *Das galante Europa*, . . . (Stuttgart, 1910), p. 19.

14. The descriptions in E. Gothein, *op.cit.*, pp. 317 *et seq.*, pp. 342 *et seq.*, make pleasant reading. Cf. J. Burckhardt, *Die Cultur der Renaissance* (Leipzig, 1878), 2, pp. 106, 166; English tr. by S.G.C. Middlemore, *The Civilization of the Renaissance* (London, 1909), p. 371. Hippolyte a Collibus, *Incrementa urbium*, . . . (Helmestadii, 1665), 1, p. 207.

15. A. L. Lavoisier, "Essai sur la population de la ville de Paris, sur sa richesse et ses consommations," in *Mélanges d'école politique*, ed. Daire (Paris, 1847), 1, pp. 601 *et seq*.

16. V. R. Mirabeau, *op. cit.* (Avignon, 1756), 2, p. 408.

17. F. Quesnay, "Fermiers," in *Encyclopédie*, ed. Oncken (Frankfort and Paris, 1888), p. 189. Authors speak of the unnaturally large size of Paris as early as the sixteenth century. Cf. V. R. Mirabeau, *op.cit.*, 2, p. 408. The same applies to London in the seventeenth century. John Graunt, *Natural and Political Observations*, . . . (London, 1662), *passim*.

18. V. R. Mirabeau, *op.cit.*, 2, p. 442.

19. *Ibid.*, p. 412. Cf. H. Taine, *Les Origines de la France contemporaine* (Paris, 1885), 1, p. 52, for figures on the enormous incomes of the high church and secular dignitaries. Strangely enough, the authority from whom

Taine derives his information on the absenteeism of the French nobility and its gathering in Paris is none other than Arthur Young who speaks of French conditions as if conditions in England were different.

20. L. S. Mercier, *op.cit.*, 1, pp. 67-68.

21. *Ibid.*, Chapter XC.

22. *Ibid.*, Chapter XCI.

23. *Ibid.*, 2, pp. 39 *et seq.*, 44 *et seq.*

24. T. Rymer, *op.cit.*, 19, p. 374.

25. E. Chamberlayne, *Angliae Notitia: The Present State of England* (London, 1687), p. 200.

26. David Hume, *Essays* (London, 1882), 3, p. 364.

27. "Artificial Fire" (1644). Ms. in the British Museum, cited in W. Cunningham, *The Growth of English Industry and Commerce* (Cambridge, 1907), 2, p. 319.

28. Guy Miege, *The Present State of Great Britain and Ireland*, ed. by Bolton (London, 1745), p. 101.

29. Daniel Defoe, *A Tour, . . .* 2, pp. 135-36.

30. See the figures in J. Goldstein, *Berufsgliederung und Reichtum* (Stuttgart, 1897), p. 143, quoting Chalmers and Price Williams.

31. *Op.cit.*, p. 236.

Theories of the City in the Eighteenth Century

32. Richard Cantillon, *Essai sur la nature du commerce en général* (London, 1755), pp. 17 *et seq;* English tr. by Henry Higgs (London, 1931), pp. 16-17.

33. In: *Oeuvres économiques et philosophiques,* ed. Oncken (Frankfort and Paris, 1888), pp. 250 *et seq.*

34. *Ibid.*, p. 297.

35. *Ibid.*, p. 298.

36. *Ibid.*, p. 302.

37. Cantillon, *op.cit.*

38. "De l'Homme," *Oeuvres*, 2, p. 360.

39. H.G.R. Mirabeau, *op.cit.*, pp. 403 *et seq.*

40. C. Beccaria, *Economia pubblica* (1771) Paragraph 30. Custodi, P. M. 11, pp. 58-59. See also p. 86, where the author deals with the origin of luxury industries in the great cities.

41. Gaetano Filangieri, *Leggi politiche e leggi economiche* (1780). Custodi, P. M. 32, pp. 185-86.

42. Sir James Stuart, *Inquiry, . . .* (London, 1767), 1, p. 48.

MIDDLE-CLASS WEALTH

Werner Sombart

Elsewhere, I have described in detail how during the Middle Ages and the subsequent centuries new wealth poured forth from a thousand sources. This new wealth may be designated middle-class, as opposed to feudal, wealth. The insight gained there may assist us here in studying the vital modifications in the social structure of the old society as a result of this newly created wealth which led to a shift in the composition of that upper stratum as between the princes and the *misera contribuens plebs.* For this purpose we need only arrange the previously systematized facts in chronological order and consider the abstract possibilities of the growth of fortunes (which we know) in their actual social context. We then perceive approximately the following picture of this change in the upper social stratum.

The fortunes of the early Middle Ages were composed almost exclusively of landed property, and it was the big landowners (the Church being excluded) who formed the nobility. At that time rich burghers were practically nonexistent. Like that Poinlane of whom we hear again and again, they were rare exceptions.

This situation changes in the thirteenth and fourteenth centuries. During that period we observe the rapid multiplication of great fortunes which did not originate in the feudal nexus, so that we may now speak of capital fortunes. This process was most conspicuous in Italy. It was the time when Europe began to despoil the Orient, when, probably, rich mines of precious metals were discovered in Africa and when the profits from money lending at usurious interest rates to big landowners and, particularly, to rich princes reached large figures.

What is true of Italy in the thirteenth and fourteenth centuries applies also to Germany in the fifteenth and sixteenth centuries. In that period great wealth began to accumulate in the south German cities in consequence of the opening of the Bohemian and Hungarian gold and silver mines and, later, of the arrival of the American silver treasures, which stimulated the great finance operations of that era, the "Era of the Fuggers."

Holland followed in the seventeenth century, participating in the plunder of Spain and Portugal and developing new sources of wealth in the Far East, where she exacted tribute from the peoples by means of forced trade, robbery, and slavery.

In the seventeenth century the growth of wealth sets in also in France and England. However, middle-class wealth in both countries apparently remained within relatively narrow limits until the end of the seventeenth century. Financial enterprises, which almost exclusively form the foundation of the great capital fortunes, were not extensively engaged in until the end of the reign of Louis XIV and after the Glorious Revolution.

This situation is clearly illustrated by the only estimate of incomes that has come down to us from those days. The well-known calculation of Gregory King[1] for the year 1688 estimates the average income of a "big merchant and overseas trader" at not more than £400, that of a "big merchant and inland trader" at only £200. King places the number of the former at 2000, of the latter at 8000. Opposed to this middle-class element stand the following representatives of landed property:

	Average Income in Pounds
160 secular lords	2800
26 ecclesiastical lords	1300
800 baronets	880
600 knights	650
300 esquires	450
12000 gentlemen	280

Among those listed above there must have been some representatives of new wealth. But I am certain that, had Gregory King made his tabulation thirty years later, he would have also mentioned the rapidly acquired wealth of the stock-exchange speculators and the promoters of the South Sea Bubble, who, during the second decade of the new century, had created an entirely new type of wealth. When the fortunes of the South Sea Company were confiscated, two were over £200,000 (£243,000 each), five from £100,000 to £200,000, five between £50,000 and £100,000, and ten between £25,000 and £50,000.[2]

The figures for income and fortunes which we find in Defoe begin to show an entirely different aspect. Guy Miege[3] places the average income of a gentleman at £500.

The causes of this great change are obvious: Brazilian gold and the wars of Louis XIV with their large-scale financing operations and army contracts, all of which stimulated speculation. These are the three most important sources of great fortunes in more recent times. (What enormous wealth must have been acquired through the issuance of shares by such companies as the Hudson Bay Company or the African Company—whose shares soared within a short time from one hundred to four hundred, to drop later to two—not to speak of the profits made in the South Sea Bubble!)

It was then that middle-class fortunes (i.e., mobile fortunes), which would not suffer by comparison with fortunes of our own days, sprang up in great numbers. With the advent of Brazilian gold, the silver era of modern capitalism ended, and the era of gold began.

As in England, so we observe in France, at the turn of the seventeenth century, the sudden development of great fortunes. Because of the existence of accurate records in France we are able to trace the change even more definitely than in England. I offer a series of data, taken at random, on the wealth of French financiers (i.e., possessors of new fortunes), which I have completed by the addition of some relevant figures.

A country squire has drawn up a list of the amounts which were the subject of marriage contracts in his family[4]:

	Florins
1433	300
1477	1,000
1534	1,200
	Écus d'or
1582	1,200
	Livres
1613	7,500
1644	16,000
1677	15,000
1707	44,000
1734	360,000
1765	150,000

The following figures give us an idea of the dowries which the rich Turcarets[5] of the eighteenth century used to give their daughters:

La Live de Bellegarde: for each daughter 300,000 livres in cash and 10,000 livres in diamonds.

La Masson: 1,700,000 livres.

Antoine Crozat: 1,500,000 livres (plus a "gratuity" of 50,000 livres for the mother-in-law, the duchess of Bouillon).

Sam. Bernard: 800,000 livres.

Olivier, comte de Senozan (He himself had dealt in rabbit skins): 1,100,000 livres in cash and 100,000 livres in furniture.

Haudry: 400,000 livres.

La Reynière: 600,000 livres in cash and 200,000 livres in install-
ments to fall due in quick succession.

Such figures do not surprise use when we learn the extent of the profits
and wealth of these nouveaux riches.

	Livres
Vincent Le Blanc (profits)	17,000,000
M. de Saint-Fargeau	28,000,000
Marquis de la Faye	20,000,000
Mme de Chaumont	127,000,000
S. Bernard	over 100,000,000
Crozat	over 100,000,000
Fillon de Villemur (died in 1753) left an estate of	40,000,000
Peirenc de Moras left an estate of	12-15,000,000
Dangé left an estate of	13,000,000
Tournehem (the foster-father of Mme de Pompadour) left an estate of	20,000,000

The financier Paris profited by 63,000,000 livres from the floating of a
single issue. (I have drawn these data from the above-mentioned book of
Thirion.)[6]

Most of the amounts are probably exaggerated (as, for instance, are also
most of the statements concerning the wealth of modern American billion-
aires). However, they leave no doubt that huge fortunes had begun to accumulate. This inference is borne out by many other indications of which we shall
speak later. Moreover, we find a corroboration of our assumption in the
accounts of the best informed contemporaries:

We speak nowadays of a million as people used to speak about a thousand
louis d'or a hundred years ago. We count by millions, hear only of millions in
every enterprise, and millions dance before our eyes whether it be a question
of a ship, a voyage (!), or a court pageant....[7]

FOOTNOTES

1. Reprinted in German and thoroughly annotated by J. Goldstein,
Berufsgliederung und Reichtum (Stuttgart, 1897).

2. Cf. the schedule in M. Postlethwayt, *Universal Dictionary of Trade
and Commerce* (n.p., 1758), 2, pp. 746-47.

3. *The Present State of Great Britain and Ireland,* ed. by Bolton (London, 1745), p. 157.

4. From a "Livre de raison," cited in C. de Ribbe, *Les Familles* (Paris,
1874), 2, p. 125.

5. Turcaret, the figure of the newly rich financier, created by Lesage
(1688-1747) in the comedy of the same name presented in Paris in 1709.
(Translator's note.)

6. Henri Thirion, *La Vie priveé des financiers au XVIII*^e *siècle* (Paris,
1895).

7. L. S. Mercier, *Tableau de Paris* (Amsterdam, 1783-88) X, p. 248.

THE CLASS STRUGGLE AND THE CHANGE FROM
FEUDALISM TO CAPITALISM

Karl Marx and Friedrich Engels

The history of all hitherto existing society[1] is the history of class struggles.

Freeman and slave, patrician and plebeian, lord and serf, guild-master[2] and journeyman, in a word, oppressor and oppressed, stood in constant opposition to one another, carried on an uninterrupted, now hidden, now open fight, a fight that each time ended, either in a revolutionary reconstitution of society at large, or in the common ruin of the contending classes.

In the earlier epochs of history, we find almost everywhere a complicated arrangement of society into various orders, a manifold gradation of social rank. In ancient Rome we have patricians, knights, plebeians, slaves; in the middle ages, feudal lords, vassals, guild-masters, journeymen, apprentices, serfs; in almost all of these classes, again, subordinate gradations.

The modern bourgeois[3] society that has sprouted from the ruins of feudal society has not done away with class antagonisms. It has but established new classes, new conditions of oppression, new forms of struggle in place of the old ones.

Our epoch, the epoch of the bourgeoisie, possesses, however, this distinctive feature; it has simplified the class antagonisms. Society as a whole is more and more splitting up into two great hostile camps, into two great classes directly facing each other: Bourgeoisie and Proletariat.

From the serfs of the Middle Ages sprang the chartered burghers of the earliest towns. From these burgesses the first elements of the bourgeoisie were developed.

284

The discovery of America, the rounding of the Cape, opened up fresh ground for the rising bourgeoisie. The East Indian and Chinese markets, the colonization of America, trade with colonies, the increase in the means of exchange and in commodities generally, gave to commerce, to navigation, to industry, an impulse never before known, and thereby, to the revolutionary element in the tottering feudal society, a rapid development.

The feudal system of industry, under which industrial production was monopolized by closed guilds, now no longer sufficed for the growing wants of the new markets. The manufacturing system took its place. The guild-masters were pushed on one side by the manufacturing middle-class; division of labor between different corporate guilds vanished in the face of division of labor in each single workshop.

Meantime the markets kept ever growing, the demand, ever rising. Even manufacture no longer sufficed. Thereupon, steam and machinery revolutionized industrial production. The place of manufacture was taken by the giant, Modern Industry, the place of the industrial middle-class, by industrial millionaires, the leaders of whole industrial armies, the modern bourgeois.

Modern industry has established the world market, for which the discovery of America paved the way. This market has given an immense development to commerce, to navigation, to communication by land. This development has, in its turn, reacted on the extension of industry; and in proportion as industry, commerce, navigation, railways extended, in the same proportion the bourgeoisie developed, increased its capital, and pushed into the background every class handed down from the Middle Ages.

We see, therefore, how the modern bourgeoisie is itself the product of a long course of development, of a series of revolutions in the modes of production and of exchange.

Each step in the development of the bourgeoisie was accompanied by a corresponding political advance of that class. An oppressed class under the sway of the feudal nobility, an armed and self-governing association in the medieval commune,[4] here independent urban republic (as in Italy and Germany), there taxable "third estate" of the monarchy (as in France), afterwards, in the period of manufacture proper, serving either the semifeudal or the absolute monarchy as a counterpoise against the nobility, and, in fact, cornerstone of the great monarchies in general, the bourgeoisie has at last, since the establishment of Modern Industry and of the world market, conquered for itself, in the modern representative State, exclusive political sway. The executive of the modern State is but a committee for managing the common affairs of the whole bourgeoisie.

The bourgeoisie, historically, has played a most revolutionary part.

The bourgeoisie, wherever it has got the upper hand, has put an end to all feudal patriarchal, idyllic relations. It has pitilessly torn asunder the motley feudal ties that bound man to his "natural superiors," and has left remaining no other nexus between man and man than naked self-interest, than callous "cash payment." It has drowned the most heavenly ecstacies of religious fervor, of chivalrous enthusiasm, of philistine sentimentalism in the icy water of egotistical calculation. It has resolved personal worth into exchange value, and in place of the numberless indefeasible chartered freedoms, has set us that single unconscionable freedom—Free Trade. In one word, for political exploitation, veiled by religious and political illusions, it has substituted naked, shameless, direct, brutal exploitation.

The bourgeoisie has stripped of its halo every occupation hitherto honored and looked up to with reverent awe. It has converted the physician, the lawyer, the priest, the poet, the man of science, into its paid wage-laborers.

The bourgeoisie has torn away from the family its sentimental veil, and has reduced the family relation to a mere money relation.

The bourgeoisie has disclosed how it came to pass that the brutal display of vigor in the Middle Ages, which Reactionists so much admire, found its fitting complement in the most slothful indolence. It has been the first to show what man's activity can bring about. It has accomplished wonders far surpassing Egyptian pyramids, Roman aqueducts, and Gothic cathedrals; it has conducted expeditions that put in the shade all former Exoduses of nations and crusades.

The bourgeoisie cannot exist without constantly revolutionizing the instruments of production, and thereby the relations of production, and with them the whole relations of society. Conservation of the old modes of production in unaltered form, was, on the contrary, the first condition of existence for all earlier industrial classes. Constant revolutionizing of production, uninterrupted disturbance of all social conditions, everlasting uncertainty and agitation distinguish the bourgeois epoch from all earlier ones. All fixed, fast-frozen relations, with their train of ancient and venerable prejudices and opinions, are swept away, all new-formed ones become antiquated before they can ossify. All that is solid melts into air, all that is holy is profaned, and man is at last compelled to face with sober senses, his real conditions of life, and his relations with his kind.

The need of a constantly expanding market for its products chases the bourgeoisie over the whole surface of the globe. It must nestle everywhere, settle everywhere, establish connections everywhere.

The bourgeoisie has through its exploitation of the world market given a cosmopolitan character to production and consumption in every country. To the great chagrin of Reactionists, it has drawn from under the feet of industry the national ground on which it stood. All old-established national industries have been destroyed or are daily being destroyed. They are dislodged by new industries, whose introduction becomes a life and death question for all civilized nations, by industries that no longer work up indigenous raw material, but raw material drawn from the remotest zones; industries whose products are consumed, not only at home, but in every quarter of the globe. In place of the old wants, satisfied by the productions of the country, we find new wants, requiring for their satisfaction the products of distant lands and climes. In place of the old local and national seclusion and self-sufficiency, we have intercourse in every direction, universal interdependence of nations. And as in material, so also in intellectual production. The intellectual creations of individual nations become common property. National one-sidedness and narrowmindedness become more and more impossible, and from the numerous national and local literatures there arises a world literature.

The bourgeoisie, by the rapid improvement of all instruments of production, by the immensely facilitated means of communication, draws all, even the most barbarian, nations into civilization. The cheap prices of its commodities are the heavy artillery with which it batters down all Chinese walls, with which it forces the barbarians' intensely obstinate hatred of foreigners to capitulate. It compels all nations, on pain of extinction, to adopt the bourgeois mode of production; it compels them to introduce what it calls civilization into their midst, i.e., to become bourgeois themselves. In a word, it creates a world after its own image.

The bourgeoisie has subjected the country to the rule of the towns. It has created enormous cities, has greatly increased the urban population as compared with the rural, and has thus rescued a considerable part of the population from the idiocy of rural life. Just as it has made the country dependent on the towns, so it has made barbarian and semi-barbarian countries dependent on the civilized ones, nations of peasants on nations of bourgeois, the East on the West.

The bourgeoisie keeps more and more doing away with the scattered state of the population, of the means of production, and of property. It has agglomerated population, centralized means of production, and has concentrated property in a few hands. The necessary consequence of this was political centralization. Independent, or but loosely connected provinces, with separate interests, laws, governments and systems of taxation, became lumped together in one nation, with one government, one code of laws, one national class-interest, one frontier and one customs-tariff.

The bourgeoisie, during its rule of scarce one hundred years, has created more massive and more colossal productive forces than have all preceding generations together. Subjection of Nature's forces to man, machinery, application of chemistry to industry and agriculture, steam-navigation, railways, electric telegraphs, clearing of whole continents for cultivation, canalization of rivers, whole populations conjured out of the ground—what earlier century had even a presentiment that such productive forces slumbered in the lap of social labor?

We see then: the means of production and of exchange on whose foundation the bourgeoisie built itself up, were generated in feudal society. At a certain stage in the development of these means of production and of exchange, the conditions under which feudal society produced and exchanged, the feudal organization of agriculture and manufacturing industry, in one word, the feudal relations of property became no longer compatible with the already developed productive forces; they became so many fetters. They had to burst asunder; they were burst asunder.

Into their places stepped free competition, accompanied by a social and political constitution adapted to it, and by the economical and political sway of the bourgeois class.

The weapons with which the bourgeoisie felled feudalism to the ground are now turned against the bourgeoisie itself.

But not only has the bourgeoisie forged the weapons that bring death to itself; it has also called into existence the men who are to wield those weapons—the modern working-class—the proletarians.

In proportion as the bourgeoisie, i.e., capital, is developed, in the same proportion is the proletariat, the modern working-class, developed, a class of laborers, who live only so long as they find work, and who find work only so long as their labor increases capital. These laborers, who must sell themselves piecemeal, are a commodity, like every other article of commerce, and are consequently exposed to all the vicissitudes of competition, to all the fluctuations of the market.

Owing to the extensive use of machinery and to division of labor, the work of the proletarians has lost all individual character, and, consequently, all charm for the workman. He becomes an appendage of the machine, and it is only the most simple, most monotonous, and most easily acquired knack that is required of him. Hence, the cost of production of a workman is restricted, almost entirely, to the means of subsistence that he requires for his maintenance, and for the propagation of his race. But the price of a commodity, and also of labor, is equal to its cost of production. In proportion, therefore, as the repulsiveness of the work increases, the wage decreases. Nay more, in proportion as the use of machinery and division of labor increases, in the same proportion the burden of toil also increases, whether by prolongation of the working hours, by increase of the work enacted in a given time, or by increased speed of the machinery, etc.

Modern industry has converted the little workshop of the patriarchal master into the great factory of the industrial capitalist. Masses of laborers crowded into the factory, are organized like soldiers. As privates of the industrial army they are placed under the command of a perfect hierarchy of officers and sergeants. Not only are they the slaves of the bourgeois class, and of the bourgeois State, they are daily and hourly enslaved by the machine, by the overlooker, and, above all, by the individual bourgeois manufacturer himself. The more openly this despotism proclaims gain to be its end and aim, the more petty, the more hateful and the more embittering it is. . . .

But with the development of industry the proletariat not only increases in number; it becomes concentrated in greater masses, its strength grows, and it feels that strength more. The various interests and conditions of life within the ranks of the proletariat are more and more equalized, in proportion as machinery obliterates all distinctions of labor, and nearly everywhere reduces wages to the same low level. The growing competition among the bourgeois, and the resulting commercial crises, make the wages of the workers even more fluctuating. The unceasing improvement of machinery, ever more rapidly developing, makes their livelihood more and more precarious; the collisions between individual workmen and individual bourgeois take more and more the character of collisions between two classes. Thereupon the workers begin to form combinations (Trades' Unions) against the bourgeois; they club together in order to keep up the rate of wages; they found permanent associations in order to make provisions beforehand for these occasional revolts. Here and there the contest breaks out into riots.

Now and then the workers are victorious, but only for a time. The real fruit of their battles lies, not in the immediate result, but in the ever expanding union of the workers. This union is helped on by the improved means of communication that are created by modern industry, and that place the workers of different localities in contact with one another. It was just this contact that was needed to centralize the numerous local struggles, all of the same character, into one national struggle between classes. But every class struggle is a political struggle. And that union, to attain which the burghers of the Middle Ages, with their miserable highways, required centuries, the modern proletarians, thanks to railways, achieve in a few years. . . .

Of all the classes that stand face to face with the bourgeoisie today, the proletariat alone is a really revolutionary class. The other classes decay and finally disappear in the face of modern industry; the proletariat is its special and essential product.

The lower middle-class, the small manufacturer, the shopkeeper, the artisan, the peasant, all these fight against the bourgeoisie, to save from extinction their existence as fractions of the middle class. They are therefore not revolutionary, but conservative. Nay more, they are reactionary, for they try to roll back the wheel of history. If by chance they are revolutionary, they are so, only in view of their impending transfer into the proletariat, they thus defend not their present, but their future interests, they desert their own standpoint to place themselves at that of the proletariat.

The "dangerous class," the social scum, that passively rotting mass thrown off by the lowest layers of old society, may, here and there, be swept into the movement by a proletarian revolution; its conditions of life, however, prepare it far more for the part of a bribed tool of reactionary intrigue.

In the conditions of the proletariat, those of old society at large are already virtually swamped. The proletarian is without property; his relation to his wife and children has no longer anything in common with the bourgeois family-relations; modern industrial labor, modern subjection to capital, the same in England as in France, in America as in Germany, has stripped him of every trace of national character. Law, morality, religion, are to him so many bourgeois prejudices, behind which lurk in ambush just as many bourgeois interests.

All the preceding classes that got the upper hand sought to fortify their already acquired status by subjecting society at large to their conditions of appropriation. The proletarians cannot become masters of the productive forces of society, except by abolishing their own previous mode of appropriation, and thereby also every other previous mode of appropriation. They have nothing of their own to secure and to fortify; their mission is to destroy all previous securities for, and insurances of, individual property.

All previous historical movements were movements of minorities, or in the interest of minorities. The proletarian movement is the self-conscious independent movement of the immense majority in the interest of the immense majority. The proletariat, the lowest stratum of our present society, cannot stir, cannot raise itself up, without the whole superincumbent strata of official society being sprung into the air.

Though not in substance, yet in form, the struggle of the proletariat with the bourgeoisie is at first a national struggle. The proletariat of each country must, of course, first of all settle matters with its own bourgeoisie.

In depicting the most general phases of the development of the proletariat, we traced the more or less veiled civil war, raging within existing society, up to the point where that war breaks out into open revolution, and where the violent overthrow of the bourgeoisie, lays the foundation for the sway of the proletariat.

Hitherto, every form of society has been based, as we have already seen, on the antagonism of oppressing and oppressed classes. But in order to oppress a class, certain conditions must be assured to it under which it can, at least, continue its slavish existence. The serf, in the period of serfdom, raised himself to membership in the commune, just as the petty bourgeois, under the yoke of feudal absolutism, managed to develop into bourgeois. The modern laborer, on the contrary, instead of rising with the progress of industry, sinks deeper and deeper below the conditions of existence of his own class. He becomes a pauper, and pauperism develops more rapidly than population and wealth. And here it becomes evident, that the bourgeoisie is unfit any longer to be the ruling class in society, and to impose its conditions of existence upon society as an overriding law. It is unfit to rule, because it is incompetent to assure an existence to its slave within his slavery, because it cannot help letting him sink into such a state, that it has to feed him, instead of being fed by him. Society can no longer live under this bourgeoisie, in other words, its existence is no longer compatible with society.

The essential condition for the existence, and for the sway of the bourgeois class, is the formation and augmentation of capital; the condition for capital is wage-labor. Wage-labor rests exclusively on competition between the laborers. The advance of industry, whose involuntary promoter is the bourgeoisie, replaces the isolation of the laborers, due to competition, by their involuntary combination, due to association. The development of Modern Industry, therefore, cuts from under its feet the very foundation on which the bourgeoisie produces and appropriates products. What the bourgeoisie therefore produces, above all, are its own gravediggers. Its fall and the victory of the proletariat are equally inevitable.

FOOTNOTES

1. That is, all written history. In 1847, the prehistory of society, the social organization existing previous to recorded history, was all but unknown. Since then Haxthausen discovered common ownership of land in Russia, Maurer proved it to be the social foundation from which all Teutonic races

started in history, and by and by village communities were found to be, or to have been, the primitive form of society everywhere from India to Ireland. The inner organization of this primitive Communistic society was laid bare, in its typical form, by Morgan's crowning discovery of the true nature of the gens and its relation to tribe. With the dissolution of these primeval communities society begins to be differentiated into separate and finally antagonistic classes. I have attempted to retrace this process of dissolution in "Der Ursprung der Familie des Privateigenthums und des Staats," 2nd edit., Stuttgart 1886.

2. Guild-master, that is a full member of a guild, a master within, not a head of, a guild.

3. By bourgeoisie is meant the class of modern Capitalists, owners of the means of social production and employers of wage-labor. By proletariat, the class of modern wage-laborers who, having no means of production of their own, are reduced to selling their labor-power in order to live.

4. "Commune" was the name, taken in France, by the nascent towns even before they had conquered from their feudal lords and masters, local self-government; and political rights as "the Third Estate." Generally speaking for the economical development of the bourgeoisie, England is here taken as the typical country, for its political development, France.

THE MODERN STATE

Robert Bierstedt, Eugene J. Meehan and Paul A. Samuelson

The transition from medieval feudalism to the modern state system did not occur overnight. In fact, it is very difficult to mark either the beginning or the end of the transition period. People did not awaken early one morning and shout, "Huzzah, the Middle Ages are ended!" Yet the transition was marked by a major social, political, and economic upheaval—perhaps the greatest in the history of mankind. It proceeded slowly, but it ran deep. Very often the people were hardly aware of changes taking place around them; when they were aware, they often decried or lamented the changes. The pace varied from one society to the next, and the final result—the modern state— was seldom the same in detail, though the rough outlines of the state appeared everywhere in due course. Each region remained to some extent unique, and these distinctions are with us still in most of Europe. Thus northern Italy was "modern" as early as the fourteenth century; Russia remained medieval until the nineteenth century; England and France effected their transition in the fifteenth and sixteenth centuries. By the age of the Tudor kings, England was a modern state, as was France. We shall deal mainly with these two countries in our discussion of the change from medieval to modern life, for they set the pattern for those who came later, and their experience is a significant part of our own social heritage.

THE SCOPE OF THE UPHEAVAL

Few periods in human history can match the impact of the transition from medieval to modern times. The changing pattern of politics was only a small part of a total social upheaval and the political structure engendered by the change was much affected by developments occurring in nonpolitical aspects of social and economic life. The whole foundation of Western society was overturned in a few short centuries, and a way of life that stretched back to the classic age disappeared. We may almost say that man has yet to completely adjust to the new conditions—social, economic, and political—that appeared in the early modern era. The economic basis of human life was overturned, and this undermined the political structure that had taken shape on the basis of the older economic system. The family, education, religious institutions, and the vocations and avocations of men—all shared in the general reshaping of human culture, generating a new system of human values and a new attitude of mind. An intellectual revolution of the first order accompanied, and perhaps led at times, the social transition, and this in turn had repercussions in every other phase of human life. The soaring architecture of medieval Gothic gave way to a new mode of artistic expression; painting found new life in the use of perspective, which freed the painter from the conventional symbolism of medieval art. The medieval allegories of Dante were replaced by the stark realism of Machiavelli and the lusty naturalism of Boccaccio and Cellini. Medieval Latin was replaced by national languages, and a vernacular literature appeared which appealed to more than the tiny fraction of the population competent in the classic tongues. The printing press made possible a wider public than ever before. Modern science, with its new conception of man and the universe made its first hesitant appearance, then speedily found its own special niche in Western society. The pessimism and morbidity of the Middle Ages gave way to optimism, humanism, and curiosity about the world in which man lived and about man himself. Fearful concern about the life hereafter was replaced by a sunnier attitude, by more concern with the nature of life on earth. The stylized and formal routines of the medieval court were superseded by a more individualistic, a more capricious and personal set of human relations. The catalog of fundamental changes could be extended almost indefinitely.

An age in which the foundations of an old social order are being laid to rest and a new set of primary beliefs are being established is at once a stimulating and a challenging period in which to live. It forces some men to retreat to the shelter and safety of past tradition; others it stimulates to new creativity, idiosyncrasy, and experimentation. Some men refuse to question anything in the existing order; others question everything. The fifteenth and sixteenth centuries are for the most part alive and teeming with activity— economic, political, intellectual, and religious. Europeans shook free the medieval shackles and began casting about for new worlds to conquer, new walls to storm. The men and women of the Middle Ages scarcely come alive, perhaps because we lack information about them and their lives; they are preperspective drawings on the fabric of history and they lack flesh. The men and women who lived through the age of transition are creatures of flesh and blood; they live, they sparkle, whether as rogues or saints. We can understand them, appreciate their problems, and if occasionally we see flashes of an age which is strange and incomprehensible, they are for the most part people like ourselves—they are modern. . . .

POLITICAL TRANSITION

The appearance of the modern, unified, national state as a coherent social entity is without question the most significant consequence of the demise of medieval feudalism. In the process of transition, the scattered personal loyalties of the feudal system were replaced by a single loyalty to a centralized political system, personified by the king. Personal loyalty to the feudal lord was replaced by loyalty to the king, and then by loyalty to the state. National sentiment and national pride and arrogance developed rapidly. The modern parallel can be found in the changing pattern of loyalty in the American Colonies following the Revolution; loyalty to the nation as a whole eventually overshadowed allegiance to the individual state—the Virginian became an American, and the psychology of the change is quite complex. In Europe, a similar process, working perhaps more slowly, made Frenchmen of the men of Burgundy and Touraine and Picardy, and made Englishmen of Yorkshiremen, Londoners, and Lancastershiremen. The consolidation was nearly completed in England by the time of the first Tudor King, in France by the age of Louis XI, and in Spain by the early sixteenth century, when the marriage of Ferdinand and Isabella (1469) united the two largest political units in that country. National sentiment was carefully nurtured by the royal houses of Europe, and we may judge the success of the effort by the virulent nationalism that appears in Elizabethan drama. A new political institution, the national state, came into being; it also brought a new type of ruler, the absolute monarch, ruling, in some cases, by "divine right."

THE CHARACTER OF THE POLITICAL SYSTEM

Let us look more closely at the political changes that occurred as Europe passed from medieval to modern times. We find that they affected every facet of politics, from the theoretical to the practical, from the mundane to the fundamental and basic. Europeans produced a new justification of political authority, a new concept of law, a new political process, a new locus of political power, and so on through a long list of fundamentals.

Political Authority

The usual medieval conception of political authority was drastically modified in the transition to modern society; indeed, it is hard to see how the modern state could emerge on any other basis. Medieval writers accepted government as a divine remedy for sin, took for granted the kingly form of government, and severely inhibited the right of the population to protest against misrule. Most people believed that a political society was impossible outside the true religion and that one of the prime functions of the state was the protection and expansion of the church. The authority of the ruler was limited by law and custom, and by the natural or divine law, as well as by incipient representative institutions. Legislation, as a deliberate exercise of authority, was rare, and national political institutions were almost nonexistent.

Modernization altered the entire pattern of thinking about political authority, extending its scope enormously, reintroducing the concept of legislation as a deliberate act of will, and amending the fundamental justification of political authority. The influence of Greek political writings, particularly the *Politics* of Aristotle, helped turn men to the belief that society was a natural form of human association and not a divinely inspired creation. This created a serious theoretical problem, for if political associations were natural, how was the authority to rule others to be justified? The question puzzled political theorists in the early modern period no end. One school of thought, bent on supporting the absolute authority of the king, turned to a religious foundation for political authority, arguing that the king was divinely appointed to rule. One ardent royalist, Sir Robert Filmer, even managed to trace the authority of the King of England to the parental authority of Adam over his children, and John Locke devoted the whole of his first *Essay on Government* to the demolition of this vapid proposal.

In the long run, the view that political associations were natural won out, though not before a fairly extensive period in which the divine right of kings was widely accepted. In consequence, some very complex, and unnecessary, explanations of the foundations of political authority appeared in the seventeenth and eighteenth centuries. Some held that government was needed to restrain the inherently evil impulses in men. Others held that men were good and political institutions made them evil; hence government was the devil's work. In time, most Western political thinkers came to agree that the best possible source of political authority, and perhaps the only legitimate source, was the consent of those over whom authority was exercised—that just government must rest on the consent of the governed. There remained the question how consent was to be given, and hòw often it was needed. . . .

The concept of law, and law making or legislation, also underwent a substantial revision during the transition period. In the medieval view, law was the custom of the community, augmented and justified by the will of God as expressed by reason and embodied in the law of nature. Customary law had been adequate in a static society where fundamental institutions changed but little over the centuries. In a period of social upheaval, customary law proved a serious handicap to society, and the older practice of direct positive legislation was revived. Again, this produced difficult theoretical problems. Who had the right to make law? Under what conditions? What laws might be made? Must the law be obeyed at all times? What if law and custom were in conflict? Was the king bound by the law? Could the king be deposed if he made harsh laws? Could he be put to death? Such questions were of great moment in the early stages of modern history, however academic they may now appear.

They were answered in various ways. The supporters of loyal absolutism argued simply that the king was *legibus solutus,* as the Roman Emperor had been; hence he was the sole source of law. Others held that legislation was only valid if it reflected the will of the community; hence the consent of the community, through representatives, was required. Some believed the king bound by all laws, and others felt that he was bound only to the law of God. Some felt that natural law could be enforced only by God himself; others were willing to hasten judgment and make applications of natural law by a trial of peers.

Natural law in fact proved to be an immensely powerful weapon against the absolutist kings. The Middle Ages had regarded natural law as synonymous with the law of God and used it mainly to support customary practices; it was essentially a conservative force in society. But the concept of natural law also held a latent capacity to work in a more radical manner, and from the early eighteenth century onward it became a weapon of radicalism in the attack upon royal prerogative. The concept was reshaped into a demand for the right to select the rulers of society, for the right to certain basic personal freedoms and rights, for limits on the power and authority of government, and for the right to participate fully and meaningfully in the political process. The medieval use of natural law to preserve existing rights was transmuted into a demand for the creation of new rights. Natural law had been an instrument used to protect the many against their masters; it now became a device which the new propertied classes could use to justify their demand for freedom of enterprise and a partnership in the political system. Most Americans are familiar with a number of illustrations of the modern conception of natural law, for the Declaration of Independence is almost a classic statement of the eighteenth-century tradition. A still more radical concept of natural law appeared in France, asserting the brotherhood of men and their natural equality, as in the French Declaration of the Rights of Man (1791).

The Changing Political Process

In virtually every case, the termination of feudalism marked the beginning of a period of royal absolutism, the accumulation of political authority in the hands of the king. The political process under the absolutists was little more than a continuation of the medieval practice of household rule over a personal domain. The key to political authority, in such conditions, was family connections, together with access to the king's person. The peculiarities of the system are well illustrated by Shakespeare's treatment of Falstaff, who expected great things when his princely drinking companion mounted the throne, though in this case Henry V failed to live up to expectations. This is still fundamentally a medieval conception of political action. From that point, the political systems of Western Europe tended to develop in one of two directions: first, toward democratic or open societies in which the population participated actively and meaningfully in the political process; second, toward totalitarian or closed political organizations in which the general population was excluded from political activity as far as possible. We may take Britain as a prime example of the first of these trends and the Soviet Union as an exemplar of the second. In general, British political institutions evolved slowly and gradually without excessive turmoil, perhaps because the fundamental revolution came early in British history. The transition in Russia and in France came differently and much later, bringing violence, bloodshed, and a massive disruption of society. These distinctions have left their mark on the present political structure in these countries, as we shall see in a moment.

The first step in the transition to a modern political system in Britain was the depersonalization and institutionalization of government. The bureaus and agencies of government, though still responsible to the king, became *national* institutions; they were removed from the king's personal household. The transition has been well documented by British historians. In the reign of Henry VIII, while Thomas Cromwell was in control of the political administration (between 1530 and 1542), the machinery of government was thoroughly overhauled. Cromwell produced a well-defined bureaucracy, still responsible to the king, of course, but of a different character than before. Offices that had been part of the king's personal retine for centuries were transformed into national institutions, leaving Britain with a government, and not only a king.[1] The king remained absolute, but in another century, most of the political authority of the ruler was transferred to the two houses of Parliament.

The second step in the process of creating modern politics was the overthrow of the absolute monarchy. Here England took the lead, for the Revolution of 1640 virtually ended absolutism in England, and the Glorious Revolution of 1688, in which William and Mary were brought to the throne by Parliament, clearly inaugurated a limited constitutional government. In other parts of Europe, the process was slower. The French royal house remained absolute until the Revolution of 1789. World War I terminated absolutism in some countries, such as Russia; World War II brought it to an end in still others. In a few, it remains active today. Of course, many of the countries were liberated from one form of absolutism only to be imprisoned in another; we cannot assume that the overthrow of absolutism automatically leads to the development of an open, democratic society. Even today many of the so-called underdeveloped areas of the world are learning the bitter lesson that one absolutism can lead to another as overthrown colonial regimes are replaced by domestic tyrannies.

Once political authority in Britain was centered in Parliament, that body became the locus of political struggle. In the seventeenth century, both the House of Lords and the House of Commons were controlled by a combination of church leaders, landed aristocrats, and wealthy merchants. The landed gentry, were, in effect, substituted for the absolute monarchy, though the latter still retained some measure of political power.

The new economic class thrown up by the Industrial Revolution in the late eighteenth century was much strengthened by the economic impact of the Napoleonic wars, and a struggle for political power began early in the nineteenth century between the landed aristocracy and this new economic group. Faced with the possibility of revolution, the aristocracy capitulated, in stages, beginning with the Reform Bill of 1832. This opened the House of Commons to the new economic leaders, though it did nothing to enfranchise the masses, and the House of Lords remained a bastion of the landed groups until 1911.

The final stage in the evolution of British democracy came in the twentieth century. Between 1850 and 1920, a new force—the mass organization—appeared on the economic scene. Trade unions were formed early in the nineteenth century and expanded rapidly after 1880 into large mass unions. By 1914, organized labor was a powerful economic force and a political force of some consequence. As new legislation opened the franchise to all persons, a combination of political and trade union leaders, acting through the newly formed Labor party, managed to organize and direct the voting power of the masses into a coherent political force. In 1924, Labor was strong enough to form a minority government with Liberal support, and in 1929 it made the same attempt, only to founder disastrously under the impact of the Great Depression. Not until 1945 did Labor win a decisive victory at the polls and produce a majority government. In a sense, the general election of 1945 marked the coming of age of mass politics in Britain. The system is open, in the sense that there are no restrictions on political action which differentiate the population on a class or economic basis.

The French experience was quite different. When the Bourbons were overthrown late in the eighteenth century, France did not follow Britain into moderate and gradual channels. Violence and extremism flourished to the general disrepute of the entire structure. It is difficult now to recapture the turbulence, the violent and passionate hatred, and the vengeful spirit of the revolution, yet no adequate conception of the political problems of modern France is possible that does not probe the currents of this tumultuous age. The demise of moderation, the terrors of Jacobin rule, the monstrous bloodletting under Robespierre, the impotence of the Directorate, and the final *coup d'etat* by Napoleon led to an expansive, dictatorial, nationalistic, and even chauvinistic tradition that is quite at odds with the British temper. Since Napoleon's downfall, France has literally been torn by irreconcilable forces, often equally potent, and where factions have not been strong enough to rule, they have managed to prevent others from ruling. The precarious balance of forces has not always been maintained, as the brief regime of Napoleon III demonstrates. The spirit of the "man on the white horse," the great leader who can once again carry France to the heights of glory and eminence sits above French politics almost like a vengeful spirit. Democracy lives a precarious existence in such surroundings, as France has turned now in one direction and now in another seeking a solution to her political difficulties.

By comparison, the direction of politics in Russia or China has been simple, clear, and decisive. When the despotic Russian Tsar was overthrown in 1917, a period of absolutism extending deep into Russian history was brought to an end. The moderate Kerensky regime was speedily undermined by a determined and ruthless faction led by Lenin and Trotsky. Whatever the theoretical ambitions of the group that seized power in the October Revolution, the political system they established has been closed and dictatorial from its very inception. Only a small part of the population has any political significance, and the real locus of power has remained the tiny oligarchy that controls the party mechanism. No one may aspire to rule in the U.S.S.R. with impunity; political activity is expressly forbidden and the machinery which makes popular government possible simply does not exist. This is a closed system par excellence. The procedures by which political authority is acquired and exercised in Russia and China are even today relatively obscure in detail, though the broad outlines of the system are known, for the process is cloaked with secrecy, and the information needed to understand the operation of the system is not allowed to circulate.

The modern state, then, has developed along two quite different lines. On the one hand, there has been a movement toward mass political systems in which political rights are widely dispersed, and individual freedom is maximized; on the other hand, many modern states have moved in the direction of authoritarian and dictatorial rule, severely limiting participation in politics. The conflict between these two concepts of political activity is one of the dominant themes in contemporary politics, and the issue is as yet far from resolved. What is involved is two different sets of political values, justified by two quite different explanations of the role of politics in the life of man. The issue cannot always be set forth in black and white terms, but the overall relationship is clear. . . .

The State and the Individual

When we turn our attention to the relations between the individual and the state we find a third major area in which there have been drastic changes in the transition from medieval to modern politics. Medieval man had virtually no political rights, and his personal rights were in many cases severely limited. Yet the nature of the feudal system offered some guarantee of a man's customary and traditional privileges, and if his freedom to change his position was limited, he did retain a definite status in society and that status was in some respects protected and guaranteed. This social protection was gradually stripped away, leaving man to shift for himself in a competitive social and economic system. But if man is to be responsible for his own welfare yet does not have the power and authority to provide for that welfare, he is left in the most frustrating of social conditions. What is to be done in this case? The modern state has produced two basic solutions to the problem. In closed societies, the state has deprived man of responsibility and vested it in the community, producing a situation which is very much like medieval life. In open societies, responsibility remains with the individual, but the society has attempted to create a set of conditions which make the self-realization of man possible. By treating all men as equals, particularly in the vital areas of political rights, freedom of association, and freedom of personal choice, and by accepting the desires of men as a limit on the activities of collective society, open societies have moved in the direction of a social system which makes it possible for man truly to be master of his own destiny. The ideal has not yet been achieved in practice, of course, but some states have gone far toward creating a society in which men are accepted as equals—in politics, in economics, and in all other areas of human life; others have simply accepted human inequality and institutionalized it.

In most cases, the key to differentiating between open and closed societies is the extent of the political rights granted to the citizenry. Where political rights are equal and meaningful, where the activity of the state is subject to the direction and control of its citizens, the basic instrument needed to create an open society is available. For it is society—the state—which controls the conditions of human life within its borders. If the activity of the state is to be carried on by a select group in utter disregard of the wishes or desires of the body of citizens, then man can hardly be held responsible for his own condition, and the basic premise of medieval life has been recreated. Political rights, in other words, offer man a means of rationalizing his own freedom and responsibility, a means of creating the conditions in which the satisfactory life may be pursued. Meaningful political rights, vigorously exercised, can create the conditions under which the social, economic, and individual life of man can move in the direction which man himself desires. The one major difficulty here, which we shall examine later, is the possibility that the intent and purpose of some other society may render it impossible for open societies to maintain internal conditions as they might wish. The maximization of political rights may be incompatible with the maintenance of the security of the society. This is a problem which every open society in modern times must face.

The open society, then, is predicated upon equality of members and maximization of the political rights of members; the closed society presumes inequality and a severe reduction of the political rights of members. There is a further distinction to be made. The open society begins with a conception of society that is individualistic, that sees society as a collection of individual parts. While the society may have interests which conflict with the interests of the individual member, it is assumed by those who accept this conception of society that the function of the state is to promote the best interests of the individuals who form the state. On the other hand, it is possible to view the state as an organic entity, to make an analogy between the state and the living organism, and to postulate for the state a life, a will, and a set of goals which may be quite indifferent to the desires and interests of the individual members of the association. Thus Jean Jacques Rousseau, an eighteenth century French philosopher, argued in *The Social Contract* that there was a "general will," which desired the "true" best interests of the whole society, and that society ought to be directed by this general will, even though it might differ from the particular wills of the members of society. The organic view of society, and any social theory that exalts the interests of the collective above individual interests, requires the subordination of individual desires to the interests of the whole. That the organic analogy is false we need hardly repeat. But a very large part of the world's population today accepts the view that certain collective interests are desirable enough to sacrifice the welfare and even the life of particular individuals, and the degree to which this view is compatible with a belief in sovereign, responsible individuals needs careful examination.

Living in a society in which freedom of association is more or less taken for granted, we are apt to overlook its immense importance to man. In a world that is large and complex, the voice of the individual is likely to be very small and perhaps overlooked. If the individual is to be heard, he must have the right to associate with others of like mind, to create an association which will further his interests. It is not surprising that closed societies tend invariably to restrict free association and deliberately eliminate competing organizations, while open societies have recognized, though imperfectly, that competing organizations are a necessary feature of large complex modern societies. A recent text in political science begins with a chapter dealing with "The Alleged Mischiefs of Faction," in which a strong argument in favor of faction and group interests is presented.[2] The extent to which freedom of association is present in society is a vital matter, and to ask whether the state controls economic, recreational, religious, social, and political associations is to ask a crucial question.

Finally, we need to be aware of the great importance of individual freedom of choice in personal affairs when we examine the structure of society. The difference between open and closed society, between a free society and a totalitarian society, appears most clearly in the delineation of areas where free choice by the individual is permitted. No state can allow absolute freedom of choice, of course, and remain viable; no state can eliminate all freedom of choice, for if nothing else remains, the individual may choose between life and death. But the spectrum between these extremes is quite clearly marked. In one case, the state determines the choice of occupation, residence, living standard, clothing, amusements, and even basic thinking (by controlling education, economics, information, and social organization). Such a society is rightly called totalitarian, for it seeks "total" control over individual thought and action. At the other extreme is the social life envisioned by the anarchist, in which no individual is coerced into any activity to which he does not agree willingly. A careful examination of those areas in which the will of the individual is sovereign and final can provide us with an extremely useful index to the character of a political system and a practical guide to the manner of life which that society encourages.

Government and Economics

The relationship we find between government and economics is a part of the overall relationship between the state and the individual, but it is so important in human life that it deserves separate treatment. Economic activity affects the life of man in a direct and immediate fashion, and the relationship between economics and politics is almost organic. One need not be a Marxist to realize that regulation and control of economic affairs is one of the most important functions of political government. . . . The distribution of economic power in society may have important political repercussions, while the use of political power may have a substantial influence on the operation of the economic system. Here we are concerned only to trace briefly the development of political-economic relations in the period following the demise of feudalism.

We have already noted that the transition to modern times involved an economic revolution of massive proportions. The economy of Western Europe was converted to capitalism: the means of production became privately owned and economic activity came to be based upon the pursuit of profit. The distinction here lies with the private profit factor, for the state may own an enterprise which shows a handsome profit, and other enterprises, such as cooperatives, may be owned privately and yet not operated on a profit-seeking basis. In many parts of the world, both private and public profit-seeking enterprises appear, as in the United States, where state-owned liquor stores operate at a profit alongside private business in other fields. In the early modern period, the king, who was usually the wealthiest person in the kingdom, often became an entrepreneur in both his private and public capacity. Louis XIV of France, for example, owned nearly one hundred different manufacturing establishments in the early part of the eighteenth century, and other royal rulers were involved in economic matters on an equally large scale. At the beginning of the modern period, then, the economic policies of the political ruler played a vital part in the development of the economic system.

Mercantilism, which we have already mentioned, aimed at the development of national power and economic self-sufficiency through control of imports and exports and manipulation of commercial relations. Thus some domestic industries were repressed, while others were fostered by state subsidies and protective tariffs or by state purchases. Jean Baptiste Colbert, finance minister for Louis XIV of France, was one of the most famous advocates of mercantilist theory, and we can see the effects of mercantilism very clearly in his policies. Roads and transport were improved at state expense, certain types of goods needed internally could not be exported, certain classes of skilled workers were not allowed to emigrate to other countries, high tariffs were deliberately imposed to exclude foreign goods from French markets, and many industries were heavily subsidized. Overseas colonies also had a part to play in the economic process both as planned sources of supply and as means of achieving a favorable balance of trade—an excess of exports over imports which would cause gold to flow into the country. And all of this activity forced the French to maintain a large navy at considerable expense to protect overseas trading interests. This is almost a classic illustration of mercantilism in action.

Obviously, mercantilism could produce some galling and obnoxious restrictions on private economic activity. When mercantilist policies were combined with the remnants of feudal rights and privileges, the result could be highly complex and confusing. In France, an elaborate system of internal tariffs made domestic commerce a tiresome and expensive matter. And for the

Colonies, as Americans know only too well, mercantilism placed an aggravating body of restrictions on free economic activity, many of which seem to defy common sense—for example, the requirement that goods intended for the West Indies be first shipped to London and then reshipped to the nearby islands.

Early in the eighteenth century, the precepts of mercantilism were challenged by a group of French economists who became known as the *physiocrats*. The group, which included Jacques Turgot, the finance minister to Louis XV, and Francois Quesnay, denied that the wealth of a nation depended on trade and an influx of gold bullion into the country. Wealth, they asserted, came from the land, from farming and agriculture. The best way to increase national wealth was to eliminate all restrictions on trade and commerce, particularly within the national borders, and permit the individual free access to markets and goods. One of the physiocrats, Jean Claude Gournay, coined the phrase, *Laissez faire, laissez passer* (in effect, "let us alone"), which became a slogan for the physiocratic movement. They believed that economic activity was subject to natural laws which government ought not to alter; that government was best when it governed least. The physiocrats were very influential, particularly in the eighteenth and nineteenth centuries, for they were the progenitors of Jeffersonian democracy and of the classical school of economists in Britain.

The physiocrats' demand for *laissez faire* was taken up by a Scottish professor, Adam Smith, in a very famous book entitled *The Wealth of Nations*. Smith argued that economic activity was regulated by an "invisible hand" which guided and directed affairs so long as free competition existed. Each man, by pursuing his own good, was thus led to further the common good of all. Although Smith placed some limits on laissez-faire theory, his followers tended to disregard them and Smith's book became a bible for those who advocated a "hands-off" policy in economic matters. Free trade, free competition, and the inviolability of private property became the guiding principles of the new school of economic thought—what is usually called "economic liberalism."

Economic liberalism was peculiarly well suited to the economic needs of Western Europe and the United States in the early nineteenth century. It emphasized the importance of individual competition, freedom to exploit natural resources, freedom of contract, free trade, and a free market; thus it fitted the individualistic temper of the age. These ideals were seldom if ever achieved in practice, but as theoretical goals they proved satisfactory for an era in which rapid industrialization was the general rule. However, the application of laissez-faire policies in America and Europe produced social abuses that aroused a storm of protest from humanitarian elements in society and led to a wide variety of reform activity, ranging from political control of economic actions sufficient to prevent gross abuse through complete state ownership of the means of production. We treat the proposals for reform in another chapter; hence we can leave the development of economic-political relations at this point and turn to the problems arising out of interstate relations.

FOOTNOTES

1. See G. R. Elton, *The Tudor Revolution in Government* (London: Cambridge University Press, 1953).

2. David B. Truman, *The Governmental Process* (New York: Alfred A. Knopf, Inc., 1951).

THE AUTHOR DEFINES HIS PURPOSE

Max Weber

A product of modern European civilization, studying any problem of universal history, is bound to ask himself to what combination of circumstances the fact should be attributed that in Western civilization, and in Western civilization only, cultural phenomena have appeared which (as we like to think) lie in a line of development having *universal* significance and value.

Only in the West does science exist at a stage of development which we recognize today as valid. Empirical knowledge, reflection on problems of the cosmos and of life, philosophical and theological wisdom of the most profound sort, are not confined to it, though in the case of the last the full development of a systematic theology must be credited to Christianity under the influence of Hellenism, since there were only fragments in Islam and in a few Indian sects. In short, knowledge and observation of great refinement have existed elsewhere, above all in India, China, Babylonia, Egypt. But in Babylonia and elsewhere astronomy lacked—which makes its development all the more astounding—the mathematical foundation which it first received from the Greeks. The Indian geometry had no rational proof; that was another product of the Greek intellect, also the creator of mechanics and physics. The Indian natural sciences, though well developed in observation, lacked the method of experiment, which was, apart from beginnings in antiquity, essentially a product of the Renaissance, as was the modern laboratory. Hence medicine, especially in India, though highly developed in empirical technique, lacked a biological and particularly a biochemical foundation. A rational chemistry has been absent from all areas of culture except the West. . . .

From *The Protestant Ethic and the Spirit of Capitalism* by Max Weber. Copyright © 1930. By permission of Charles Scribner's Sons.

And the same is true of the most fateful force in our modern life, capitalism. The impulse to acquisition, pursuit of gain, of money, of the greatest possible amount of money, has in itself nothing to do with capitalism. This impulse exists and has existed among waiters, physicians, coachmen, artists, prostitutes, dishonest officials, soldiers, nobles, crusaders, gamblers, and beggars. One may say that it has been common to all sorts and conditions of men at all times and in all countries of the earth, wherever the objective possibility of it is or has been given. It should be taught in the kindergarten of cultural history that this naive idea of capitalism must be given up once and for all. Unlimited greed for gain is not in the least identical with capitalism, and is still less its spirit. Capitalism *may* even be identical with the restraint, or at least a rational tempering, of this irrational impulse. But capitalism is identical with the pursuit of profit, and forever *renewed* profit, by means of continuous, rational, capitalistic enterprise. For it must be so: in a wholly capitalistic order of society, an individual capitalistic enterprise which did not take advantage of its opportunities for profit-making would be doomed to extinction.

Let us now define our terms somewhat more carefully than is generally done. We will define a capitalistic economic action as one which rests on the expectation of profit by the utilization of opportunities for exchange, that is on (formally) peaceful chances of profit. Acquisition by force (formally and actually) follows its own particular laws, and it is not expedient, however little one can forbid this, to place it in the same category with action which is, in the last analysis, oriented to profits from exchange. Where capitalistic acquisition is rationally pursued, the corresponding action is adjusted to calculations in terms of capital. This means that the action is adapted to a systematic utilization of goods or personal services as means of acquisition in such a way that, at the close of a business period, the balance of the enterprise in money assets (or, in the case of a continuous enterprise, the periodically estimated money value of assets) exceeds the capital, i.e., the estimated value of the material means of production used for acquisition in exchange. It makes no difference whether it involves a quantity of goods entrusted *in natura* [in kind] to a travelling merchant, the proceeds of which may consist in other goods *in natura* acquired by trade, or whether it involves a manufacturing enterprise, the assets of which consist of buildings, machinery, cash, raw materials, partly and wholly manufactured goods, which are balanced against liabilities. The important fact is always that a calculation of capital in terms of money is made, whether by modern book-keeping methods or in any other way, however primitive and crude. Everything is done in terms of balances: at the beginning of the enterprise an initial balance, before every individual decision a calculation to ascertain its probable profitableness, and at the end a final balance to ascertain how much profit has been made. For instance, the initial balance of a *commenda*[1] transaction would determine an agreed money value of the assets put into it (so far as they were not in money form already), and a final balance would form the estimate on which to base the distribution of profit and loss at the end. So far as the transactions are rational, calculation underlies every single action of the partners. That a really accurate calculation or estimate may not exist, that the procedure is pure guesswork, or simply traditional and conventional, happens even today in every form of capitalistic enterprise where the circumstances do not demand strict accuracy. But these are points affecting only the *degree* of rationality of capitalistic acquisition.

For the purpose of this conception all that matters is that an actual adaptation of economic action to a comparison of money income with money expenses takes place, no matter how primitive the form. Now in this sense capitalism and capitalistic enterprises, even with a considerable rationalization of capitalistic calculation, have existed in all civilized countries of the earth, so far as economic documents permit us to judge—in China, India, Babylon, Egypt, Mediterranean antiquity, and the Middle Ages, as well as in modern times. These were not merely isolated ventures, but economic enterprises which were entirely dependent on the continual renewal of capitalistic undertakings, and even continuous operations. However, trade especially was for a long time not continuous like our own, but consisted essentially in a series of individual undertakings. Only gradually did the activities of even the large merchants acquire an inner cohesion (with branch organizations, etc.). In any case, the capitalistic enterprise and the capitalistic entrepreneur, not only as occasional but as regular entrepreneurs, are very old and were very widespread.

Now, however, the Occident has developed capitalism both to a quantitative extent, and (carrying this quantitative development) in types, forms, and directions which have never existed elsewhere. All over the world there have been merchants, wholesale and retail, local and engaged in foreign trade. Loans of all kinds have been made, and there have been banks with the most various functions, at least comparable to ours of, say, the sixteenth century. Sea loans,[2] *commenda,* and transactions and associations similar to the *Kommanditgesellschaft,*[3] have all been widespread, even as continuous businesses. Whenever money finances of public bodies have existed, money lenders have appeared, as in Babylon, Hellas, India, China, Rome. They have financed wars and piracy, contracts and building operations of all sorts. In overseas policy they have functioned as colonial entrepreneurs, as planters with slaves, or directly or indirectly forced labor, and have farmed domains, offices, and, above all, taxes. They have financed party leaders in elections and *condottieri* in civil wars. And, finally, they have been speculators in chances for pecuniary gain of all kinds. This kind of entrepreneur, the capitalistic adventurer, has existed everywhere. With the exception of trade and credit and banking transactions, their activities were predominantly of an irrational and speculative character, or directed to acquisition by force, above all the acquisition of booty, whether directly in war or in the form of continuous fiscal booty by exploitation of subjects.

The capitalism of promoters, large-scale speculators, concession hunters, and much modern financial capitalism even in peace time, but, above all, the capitalism especially concerned with exploiting wars, bears this stamp even in modern Western countries, and some, but only some, parts of large-scale inter-national trade are closely related to it, today as always.

But in modern times the Occident has developed, in addition to this, a very different form of capitalism which has appeared nowhere else: the ra-tional capitalistic organization of (formally) free labor. Only suggestions of it are found elsewhere. . . . Even real domestic industries with free labor have definitely been proved to have existed in only a few isolated cases outside the Occident. The frequent use of day laborers led in a very few cases—especially State monopolies, which are, however, very different from modern industrial organization—to manufacturing organizations, but never to a rational organiza-tion of apprenticeship in the handicrafts like that of our Middle Ages. . . .

And just as, or rather because, the world has known no rational organi-zation of labor outside the modern Occident, it has known no rational social-ism. Of course, there has been civic economy, a civic food-supply policy, mercantilism and welfare policies of princes, rationing, regulation of economic life, protectionism, and *laissez-faire* theories (as in China). The world has also known socialistic and communistic experiments of various sorts: family, reli-gious, or military communism, State socialism (in Egypt), monopolistic cartels, and consumers' organizations. But although there have everywhere been civic market privileges, companies, guilds, and all sorts of legal differences between town and country, the concept of the citizen has not existed outside the Occident, and that of the bourgeoisie outside the modern Occident. Similarly, the proletariat as a class could not exist, because there was no rational organi-zation of free labor under regular discipline. Class struggles between creditor and debtor classes; landowners and the landless, serfs, or tenants; trading interests and consumers or landlords, have existed everywhere in various com-binations. But even the Western medieval struggles between putters-out and their workers exist elsewhere only in beginnings. The modern conflict of the large-scale industrial entrepreneur and free-wage laborers was entirely lacking. And thus there could be no such problems as those of socialism.

Hence in a universal history of culture the central problem for us is not, in the last analysis, even from a purely economic viewpoint, the development of capitalistic activity as such, differing in different cultures only in form: the adventurer type, or capitalism in trade, war, politics, or administration as sources of gain. It is rather the origin of this sober bourgeois capitalism with its rational organization of free labor. Or in terms of cultural history, the problem is that of the origin of the Western bourgeois class and of its peculi-arities, a problem which is certainly closely connected with that of the origin of the capitalistic organization of labor, but is not quite the same thing. For the bourgeois as a class existed prior to the development of the peculiar modern form of capitalism, though, it is true, only in the Western hemisphere.

Now the peculiar modern Western form of capitalism has been, at first sight, strongly influenced by the development of technical possibilities. Its rationality is today essentially dependent on the calculability of the most important technical factors. But this means fundamentally that it is dependent on the peculiarities of modern science, especially the natural sciences based on mathematics and exact and rational experiment. On the other hand, the development of these sciences and of the technique resting upon them now receives important stimulation from these capitalistic interests in its practical economic application. It is true that the origin of Western science cannot be attributed to such interests. Calculation, even with decimals, and algebra have been carried on in India, where the decimal system was invented. But it was only made use of by developing capitalism in the West, while in India it led to no modern arithmetic or bookkeeping. Neither was the origin of mathematics and mechanics determined by capitalistic interests. But the *technical* utilization of scientific knowledge, so important for the living conditions of the mass of people, was certainly encouraged by economic considerations, which were extremely favorable to it in the Occident. But this encouragement was derived from the peculiarities of the social structure of the Occident. We must hence ask, from *what* parts of that structure was it derived, since not all of them have been of equal importance?

Among those of undoubted importance are the rational structures of law and of administration. For modern rational capitalism has need, not only of the technical means of production, but of a calculable legal system and of administration in terms of formal rules. Without it adventurous and speculative trading capitalism and all sorts of politically determined capitalisms are possible, but no rational enterprise under individual initiative, with fixed capital and certainty of calculations. Such a legal system and such administration have been available for economic activity in a comparative state of legal and formalistic perfection only in the Occident. We must hence inquire where that law came from. Among other circumstances, capitalistic interests have in turn undoubtedly also helped, but by no means alone nor even principally, to prepare the way for the predominance in law and administration of a class of jurists specially trained in rational law. But these interests did not themselves create that law. Quite different forces were at work in this development. And why did not the capitalistic interests do the same in China or India? Why did not the scientific, the artistic, the political, or the economic development there enter upon that path of rationalization which is peculiar to the Occident?

For in all the above cases it is a question of the specific and peculiar rationalism of Western culture. Now by this term very different things may be understood, as the following discussion will repeatedly show. There is, for example, rationalization of mystical contemplation, that is of an attitude which, viewed from other departments of life, is specifically irrational, just as much as there are rationalizations of economic life, of technique, of scientific research, of military training, of law and administration. Furthermore, each one of these fields may be rationalized in terms of very different ultimate values and ends, and what is rational from one point of view may well be irrational from another. Hence rationalizations of the most varied character have existed in various departments of life and in all areas of culture. To characterize their differences from the viewpoint of cultural history it is necessary to know what departments are rationalized, and in what direction. It is hence our first concern to work out and to explain genetically the special peculiarity of Occidental rationalism, and within this field that of the modern Occidental form. Every such attempt at explanation must, recognizing the fundamental importance of the economic factor, above all take account of the economic conditions. But at the same time the opposite correlation must not be left out of consideration. For though the development of economic rationalism is partly dependent on rational technique and law, it is at the same time determined by the ability and disposition of men to adopt certain types of practical rational conduct. When these types have been obstructed by spiritual obstacles, the development of rational economic conduct has also met serious inner resistance. The magical and religious forces, and the ethical ideas of duty based upon them, have in the past always been among the most important formative influences on conduct. . . .

FOOTNOTES

1. A *commenda* was a form of medieval trading association which usually was organized to carry out one sea voyage; when that voyage was completed, the profits were divided among the partners. [Editor's note]

2. A method used in the Middle Ages to insure against loss at sea without violating regulations concerning usury. [Editor's note]

3. A form of company between the partnership and the limited liability corporation. At least one of the participants is made liable without limit, while the others enjoy limitation of liability to the amount of their investment. [Translator's note]

A CONTRIBUTION TO THE CRITIQUE OF POLITICAL ECONOMY

Karl Marx

The general conclusion at which I arrived and which, once obtained, served to guide me in my studies, may be summarized as follows. In the social production which men carry on they enter into definite relations that are indispensable and independent of their will; these relations of production correspond to a definite stage of development of their material powers of production. The sum total of these relations of production constitutes the economic structure of society—the real foundation on which rise legal and political superstructures and to which correspond definite forms of social consciousness. The mode of production in material life determines the general character of the social, political and spiritual processes of life. It is not the consciousness of men that determines their existence, but, on the contrary, their social existence determines their consciousness. At a certain stage of their development, the material forces of production in society come into conflict with the existing relations of production, or—what is but a legal expression for the same thing—with the property relations within which they had been at work. From forms of development of the forces of production, these relations turn into their fetters. Then comes the period of social revolution. With the change of the economic foundation the entire immense superstructure is more or less rapidly transformed. In considering such transformation the distinction should always be made between the material transformation of the economic conditions of production which can be determined with the precision of natural science, and the legal, political, religious, esthetic or philosophic—in short ideological—forms in which men become conscious of this conflict and fight it out. Just as our opinion of an individual is not based on what he thinks of himself, so we cannot judge of such a period of transformation by its own consciousness; on the contrary, this consciousness must rather be explained

from the contradictions of material life, from the existing conflict between
the social forces of production and the relations of production. No social
order ever disappears before all the productive forces, for which there is room
in it, have been developed; and the new higher relations of production never
appear before the material conditions of their existence have matured in the
womb of the old society. Therefore, mankind always takes up only such
problems as it can solve; since, looking at the matter more closely, we will
always find that the problem itself arises only when the material conditions
necessary for its solution already exist or are at least in the process of formation. In broad outlines we can designate the Asiatic, the ancient, the feudal,
and the modern bourgeois methods of production as so many epochs in the
progress of the economic formation of society. The bourgeois relations of
production are the last antagonistic form of the social process of production—
antagonistic not in the sense of individual antagonism, but of one arising from
conditions surrounding the life of individuals in society; at the same time the
productive forces develing in the womb of bourgeois society create the material conditions for the solution of that antagonism. This social formation
constitutes, therefore, the closing chapter of the prehistoric stage of human
society.

THE HISTORY OF A CONTROVERSY

Ephraim Fischoff

Weber's original intention in *The Protestant Ethic* must be seen against the background of his time. An heir of the historical school (he regarded himself as one of the epigoni of Schmoller) and of the Marxist tradition, both of which had combatted the isolative treatment of the economic process and the *homo economicus* by abstract classical economics, he probed the history of culture to determine the decisive interconnections of economics with the totality of culture. The whole historical work of Weber has ultimately one primary object, the understanding of contemporary European culture, especially modern capitalism. It presses forward to the underlying morale (*Geist*) of capitalism and its pervasive attitudes to life; and beyond this to modern Occidental rationalism as such, which he came to regard as the crucial characteristic of the modern world.

The discussion of problems raised by Marx, who gave the subject of capitalism its large importance in modern social theory, resulted in a great literature on this theme. Certain German scholars had already begun to assimilate Marx's theoretical work into the conceptual framework developed by the German historical school, among them some of the *Kathedersozialisten,* principally Toennies and Sombart. These bourgeois economists and social theorists were much concerned with the problem of the psychological foundations of capitalism, and suggested certain corrections of the Marxist hypotheses under the general rubric of "the spirit of capitalism." Weber paid the highest tribute to Marx's genius and recognized the enormous usefulness of the materialistic method as a heuristic device, but he resisted all efforts to absolutize it into

From *Social Research,* Vol. II, 1944 pp. 61-77. Reprinted by permission of the publisher.

the sole method of social science, much less into a *Weltanschauung*. The truth value of this method, as indeed of all intellectual schemata, he regarded as only "ideal-typical." As against the Marxian doctrine of the economic determinism of social change, Weber propounded a pluralistic interactional theory.

It is necessary to be clear as to the limited character of Weber's goal and the cautious manner of his procedure in this essay. In this first work inquiring into the influence of religious doctrine on economic behavior, he had not the slightest intention of producing a complete theory of capitalism, a social theory of religion, or even a complete treatment of the relation between religion and the rise of capitalism. The essay was intended as a tentative effort at understanding one of the basic and distinctive aspects of the modern ethos, its professional, specialized character and its sense of calling or vocation. Already he was impressed by the dominantly rational character of modern life; and he was concerned to demonstrate that there were various types of rationalization, a fact generally overlooked by technological theories of history.

Defining capitalism from his historistic view as a unique system characterized by the general trends of antitraditionalism, dynamism, rationalism and calculated long-range industrial production, he was principally concerned to analyze and trace the genesis of the character-structure adequate to and congruent with it. In his view, modern capitalism was not the automatic product of technological development but of many objective factors, including climate —which influences the conduct of life and labor costs—and many social-political factors, such as the character of the medieval inland city and its citizenry. But he insisted that there was one factor which could not be ignored: the emergence of a rational, antitraditional spirit in the human agents involved. The two main aspects of this are the evolution of modern science and its comparatively modern relationship to economics, and the growth of the modern organization of individual life (*Lebensführung*), particularly in its practical consequences for economic activity. Weber's limited thesis was merely that in the formation of this pattern of rationally ordered life, with its energetic and unremitting pursuit of a goal and eschewal of all magical escapes, the religious component must be considered as an important factor. How important he was unable to say, and indeed he felt that in historical imputation such quantification is impossible. Consequently his view was that no one can tell how the capitalist economic system would have evolved had the specifically modern elements of the capitalistic spirit been lacking.

In tracing the affinity between the bourgeois life pattern and certain components of the religious stylization of life, as shown most consistently by ascetic Protestantism, Weber emphasized the gradual genesis of a psychological habit which enabled men to meet the requirements of early modern capitalism. That is, instead of the entrepreneur feeling that his gaining of wealth was at best tolerated by God, or that his *usuraria pravitas* had to be atoned for (as did the native Hindu trader), he went about his business with sturdy confidence that Providence purposely enabled him to prosper for God's glory, that this success was construable as a visible sign of God and, when achieved by legal means, as a measure of his value before God as well as man. On the other hand, the handworker or laborer, with his willingness to work, derived his sense of a religious state of grace from his conscientiousness in his calling. Finally, because of the abomination of the generic sin of idolatry or apotheosis of created things (*Kreaturvergötterung*), as manifested in hoarding possessions, indulgence and frivolous consumption, the money accumulated in the exercise of a calling was turned back into the business enterprise, or saved.

Weber strongly emphasized the importance to bourgeois accumulation of planned this-worldly asceticism (*innerweltliche Askese*), as distinguished from other-worldly asceticism, and of the emotional type of pietism. He insisted that Protestant sects, especially the Quakers and Baptists, engendered a methodical regulation of life, in striking contrast to Catholicism, Lutheranism and Anglicanism. His crucial point was that ascetic Protestantism created for capitalism the appropriate spirit, so that the vocational man (*Berufsmenschen*) in his acquisition of wealth no longer suffered from the deep inner lesions characteristic of the more earnest individuals of an earlier day, no matter what their apparent solidity and exemplary power. One example of this inner uncertainty regarding economic activity was the practice of restoring at death goods obtained by usury; another was the establishment of religious institutions to atone for financial success. There were innumerable theoretical and practical compromises between conscience and economic activity, between the ideal of *Deo placere non potest,* accepted even by Luther, and the acquisitive careers entered into by many earnest Catholics. In Weber's view the noteworthy degree of congruence or affinity between the modern capitalistic system and the set of attitudes toward it made for a high inner integration, which was of great importance for the subsequent development of capitalism. It was this integration which was the central concern of his essay (*Archiv,* vol. 30, p. 200).

Weber made it clear that it was his intention to analyze just one component of the generic *Lebensstil* of our rationalized civilization, among the many which stood at the cradle of modern capitalism, and to trace its changes and its ultimate disappearance. He warned against exclusive concentration on the religious factor, as exerted through the inner psychological motivations and the powerful educational force and discipline provided by the Protestant sects. It was, he insisted, only one factor, and he rejected all attempts to identify it with the spirit of capitalism, or to derive capitalism from it. Taking the religious ethic of Protestantism as a constant, and assuming temporarily that it was predominantly a religious product, he proposed to trace the congruence between it and the characterological type requisite for capitalism. It was his intention, however, to return to the problem and investigate the nonreligious components of the religious ethic.

As to the insistence by some of his critics, such as Fischer and Rachfahl, that the problem required a statistical-historical approach, Weber recognized the need of research on the development of particular areas in order to determine the numbers and strength of the various religious groups involved, and the importance of the vocational ethics in comparison with other factors. But he insisted that his was a study in the sociology of cultures, investigating the convergence of religious and economic factors in the production of modern "rational" man, and that for his type of study the statistical method was not indicated. His concern was to ascertain the specific direction in which a given religion might operate, the diverse effects of a specific system of religious ethics on the style of life. This problem, he felt, could be approached only by the "understanding" method of motivational analysis which he employed. In this first essay, therefore, he concentrated on tracing the complex ramifications leading from articles of faith to practical conduct, in an acute and learned examination of the psychological motivations issuing out of Reformed Protestantism and leading to methodical rationalization of activity and the consequent encouragement of capitalist behavior and attitudes. This thesis is carried through all the varieties of Reformed Christianity with a subtle and insightful *dogmengeschichtliche* analysis.

The Protestant essay was not regarded by Weber as a final or dogmatic formulation of a theory of the genesis or evolution of the Reformation, but as a preliminary investigation of the influence of certain religious ideas on the development of an economic spirit or the ethos of an economic system. He was not producing an idealistic (or as he preferred to term it, a spiritual) interpretation of capitalism, deriving it from religious factors. Much nonsense has been written on this point because of his alleged rejection of Marxism. Actually, he was an admirer of the Marxian hypothesis, only objecting that it should not be made absolute and universal, a summary philosophy; but then he rejected all absolutes and all monisms. Hence he rejected at least as forcibly any idealistic monism, and in the essay and its supplements he explicitly disavowed the foolish attribution to him of any spiritualistic hypothesis.

He sought no "psychological determination of economic events," but rather emphasized the "fundamental importance of the economic factor." He recognized clearly that economic changes arise in response to economic needs, and are conditioned by a wide variety of factors, including the demagogic, geographic, technological and monetary. He recognized that capitalism would have arisen without Protestantism, in fact that it had done so in many culture complexes; and that it would not and did not come about where the objective conditions were not ripe for it. He admitted that several other systems of religious ethics had developed approaches to the religious ethic of Reformed Protestantism, but he insisted that the psychological motivations involved were necessarily different; what was decisive was the ethos engendered, not preachments or theological compendia, and this, he argued, was unique in Reformed Protestanism for a variety of reasons. He recognized that there are constant functional interactions between the realms of religion and economics, but in this study he concentrated on the influences emanating from the side of religion. He not only indicated his awareness of the other side, but demonstrated how by an irony of fate the very fulfillment of religious injunctions had induced changes in the economic structure, which in turn engendered the massive irreligion of a capitalist order. He admitted that the religious ethic itself is not determined exclusively by religion, and he clearly urged the necessity of investigating the influence of the social milieu, especially economic conditions, upon the character and development of religious attitudes.

Yet he held that the religious revelation of the founder of a sect is an autonomous experience and not a mere reflection of accommodation to economic or other needs. It was his feeling that it is no solution to the problem of the distinctiveness of the Calvinist religious form to say that it is an adjustment to capitalistic practices already in existence; the question then arises as to why Catholicism did not show the same results after making the accommodation. But when a religious revelation has become a social phenomenon and has given rise to a community, a process of social selection sets in and class stratification supervenes in the originally homogeneous religious group, causing the formation of distinctive, socially determined differences within the religion. Weber was going to study this side of the problem, but he never returned to the task. In *The Protestant Ethic* he concentrated on the religious factor alone, considering it as though it were exclusively a religious entity. He was, however, well aware of the tentative nature of his contribution, and he sketched the mammoth and indeed unrealizable program of studies necessary before the project could be regarded as complete.

By no means all the criticisms leveled against Weber were due to bias or failure to heed his cautions regarding the intention of his essay. First, there is the indubitable fact that as the essay stands it has certain elementary defects of structure, particularly because of the incompleteness which exposes it to misunderstandings by a careless reader, although Weber protested that an academic critic should never be guilty of such malfeasance. Writing in the *Archiv* in 1908, Weber explained again the reasons for the noncompletion of the essay—partly personal factors, partly the pressure of other work and partly the fact that Troeltsch had begun to treat in the "most felicitous manner a whole series of problems that lay on Weber's route," which the latter was loath to duplicate; and he expressed the hope that in the coming year he might work on the essay and issue it separately. He admitted that critics had a right to charge that the original essay was incomplete, and he recognized the danger that the hasty reader might overlook this fact, but he insisted that it could scarcely be construed as an idealistic construction of history.

Replying to Fischer's criticism, Weber insisted that in the Protestant essay he had expressed himself with utter clarity on the relationship between religion and economics generally, but he none the less admitted that misunderstanding might possibly have arisen from certain turns of phrase. Accordingly he promised to remove in a future reissue all expressions which seemed to suggest the derivation of institutions from religious motives; and he expressed his intention of clarifying the fact that it was the spirit of a "methodical" *Lebensführung* which he was deriving from Protestant asceticism, and which is related to economic forms only through congruence (*Adäquanz*). In a later anticritical article, adverting with regret to the incompleteness of the essay, Weber suggests ironically that had he completed it as promised by tracing the influence of economic conditions on the formation of reformed Protestantism, he would probably have been accused of having capitulated to historical materialism, even as he was now charged with an overemphasis on the religious or ideological factor. Hence, he insisted, his essay should properly be regarded only as a fraction of an investigation into the history of the development of the idea of vocation and its infusion into certain callings.

Apart from its incompleteness this essay betrays the other faults so characteristic of most of Weber's writing—a great carelessness of the reader's requirements, evinced in the plethora of detail in the text and above all in the ocean of footnotes, inundating the reader and frequently sweeping him far from the mainland. His wife speaks of "die montströse Form dieser Abhandlung," which was aggravated in the second edition when the "Fussnotengeschwulst" increased enormously. She sought, however, to justify this flood by pointing out that since Weber was using "careful causal imputation of intuitively apprehended connections," he wished to provide all possible proof in this extensive scholarly apparatus, and "to guard himself against any misunderstanding of his cautious relativizations."

The essay may be justly criticized for various errors of fact and interpretation. Weber himself later corrected some erroneous statements appearing in the original essay, as by indicating that when he had said that Calvinism shows the juxtaposition of intensive piety and capitalism, wherever found, he had meant only Diaspora Calvinism.

Another justifiable line of attack on Weber's thesis is based on concrete researches into the economic history of the continent, principally Holland and the Rhineland. Both Weber and Troeltsch had based their work on inadequate study of sources, and had quoted Anglo-Saxon writers to demonstrate the effect of German and Netherland Calvinists on the economic development of the Rhineland. On the basis of investigations into the history of Holland—and it must be recalled that this republic was probably the first country in which capitalism developed on a large scale—recent Netherland historians like DeJong, Knappert and de Pater find no proof to sustain such a theory of a connection between Calvinism and capitalism among the Netherlanders. Further, Beins' researches into the economic ethic of the Calvinist church in the Netherlands between 1565 and 1650 lead him to raise serious objections to Weber's thesis. A similar view is expressed in the important economic history of the Netherlands by Baasch, who stresses the secular factors in the evolution of capitalism in Holland which made the Netherlanders the chief bankers of the seventeenth century and by the end of the eighteenth made the colony of Jews in Amsterdam the largest in Europe. The same adverse conclusion is reached by Koch's investigation of the economic development of the lower Rhine area and Andrew Sayous' study of the Genevans; Hashagen's essay on the relation between Calvinism and capitalism in the German Rhineland comes to similar conclusions. Evidence has also accumulated that Calvinism did not have any necessary effect on the rise of capitalism in Hungary, Scotland or France.

These researches militate against Weber's hypothesis that the Calvinist belief buttressed capitalism or even favored its emergence. But this line of criticism readily degenerates into the oversimplification referred to above, that Weber was intent on establishing the causal primary of the Protestant ethic in the genesis of capitalism and the necessary determination of the latter by the former wherever it appeared. The tendency toward such an oversimplification vitiates most of the arguments of Robertson and of Hyma, who closely follows him. In so far as all these writers, among whom may be included Brentano, Sée, Pirenne, Brodnitz and von Schulze-Gävernitz, construe Weber's thesis as implying a necessary causal influence exerted by Calvinism on the evolution of capitalism, they have misread Weber.

Most animadversions on his thesis, even in works composed during the last decade, spring from a misunderstanding or oversimplification of his theory, for which he is only slightly to blame. Surely Weber, one of the foremost historians of jursiprudence and economics in his generation, needed no reminder that the origins of capitalism are complex and diverse, and are due to changes in economic process as well as in spiritual outlook. By and large most of his critics have simply not perceived the direction of his interest, the moderation of his purpose and the caution of his procedure.

Only a very few of his critics rose to the level of his argument and recognized that his errors or shortcomings were inherent in his particular method. And the handful who did attack Weber's method, such as Sée, Robertson, Walker and Borkenau, did so in ignorance of his writings on the nature of social science and the method appropriate to it. Weber's shortcomings were not due to ignorance, naivete or partisanship; on the contrary, he had a considered and subtle approach. An acquaintance with Weber's views as to the nature and goal of the social sciences—his view of theory as only ideal-typical, and his peculiar method of historical research committed to the interpretative understanding of historical atoms, of particular emergents chosen on the basis of their cultural significance and understood by means of a controlled intuitive method—might have clarified the reason for a whole range of errors or inadequacies in his *Protestant Ethic.* Certainly no validation of his method is here projected: clearly it has shortcomings; its usefulness has very plain limitations; and its employment is fraught with particular occupational hazards. But any essay avowedly composed under that method should be evaluated on its own terms, as an essay in interpretative understanding. From this view not a few of the strictures here listed would lose their point, or would at least appear in their proper perspective as the inevitable consequences of Weber's atomistic method.

His employment of the ideal-type method leads to various distortions, as in his overemphasis of the concepts of vocation and predestination. Here a bias in the choice of the historical atom to be interpreted and in the definition of its character and influence makes itself strongly felt. The oversimplification induced by the method also extends to his construction of the Protestant ethic as a component of Calvinism, Puritanism, Pietism, Methodism and the Anabaptist sects, and to his treatment of Puritanism. Another instance is his definition of modern capitalism, accentuating its novelty, rationality and ascetic character. Once he had so defined it he did not have much difficulty in discovering elements of congruity with the schematic construction of the Protestant ethic slanted in the same direction. To the empirical historian the whole procedure necessarily appears suffused by a tendency to idealization, with a comparative neglect of secular factors, economic, political and technological.

Weber's method of atomistic isolation necessarily leads to oversimplification of a complex historical entity through the accentuation and isolation of a particular component factor regarded as significant from a certain point of view; its tracing of alleged influences on the further course of historical evolution; and its tendency toward reifying the particular component factors of a given historical entity. In the nature of the case this method cannot serve for the illumination of a total historical problem, or the interpretation of a whole epoch or movement.

His pluralistic agnosticism, manifested in his refusal to pledge allegiance to any exclusive viewpoint lest it do injustice to the unique individuality of historical entities and the perpetual shift of cultural horizons, was laudable in intention. It seemed to be pointing the way to the functionalization of research and interpretation in the social sciences. Actually, however, Weber's isolative treatment led to inevitable distortions. His method entailed the breakdown of any complex phenomenon into its components, and then choosing each one seriatim as a constant, tracing its effects on the other variables. At the end of the process, he indicated, there would have to be a return to assess the varying force of each component in the actual historical composite, and to determine how closely the empirical phenomena approached the ideal types he had formulated. This he had planned to do for his problem of the relationship between the Protestant ethic and the spirit of capitalism, but he must have felt the infinite and impossible nature of the task. Moreover, his approach offers no method for determining the interrelation of factors, the degree of influence pertaining to each, or their temporal variations, thereby leaving room for the play of personal evaluation in the choice and characterization of the particular historical atoms.

For the historian concerned with determining the causes of a particular historical datum, the problem of timing historical phenomena and tracing temporal variations is one of the crucial difficulties arising out of the impossibility, inherent in Weber's method, of determining the degree of influence to be assigned to the various factors involved. The ideal-type method neglects the time coefficient, or at any rate impairs the possibility of establishing time sequences, because it involves a telescoping of data. Granted, for instance, that Weber's interpretation of Calvinist theology is correct and that it was of the type that would result in activism, dynamism, industry, etc., the question still remains whether these influences did not begin to exert a significant effect only after capitalism had already reached a dominant position.

Consequently, while there is readiness enough to accept the congruity between Calvinism and capitalism, it has been suggested that a consideration of the crucial question of timing will show that Calvinism emerged later than capitalism where the latter became decisively powerful. Hence the conclusion that Calvinism could not have causally influenced capitalism, and that its subsequent favorable disposition to capitalist practice and ethics is rather to be construed as an adaptation.

The development of the Weberian thesis by Troeltsch, and his American disciple, Reinhold Niebuhr, meets this criticism by tracing the modifications induced in later Calvinism by the various social factors impinging upon it after the first appearance of the original doctrine, such as religious wars, political pressures and the exigencies of acquisitive life. His rich analysis reveals how the social ethic was the net result of the particular religious and ethical peculiarities of Calvinism, which showed a marked individuality in its doctrine of predestination, its activism and its ethic, aiming at achieving what was possible and practical. On the other hand, Troeltsch emphasizes the importance in the evolution of the ethic of the republican tendency in politics, the capitalistic tendency in economics and the diplomatic and militaristic tendencies in international affairs. All these tendencies radiated from Geneva, at first in a very limited way; then they united with similar elements within the Calvinist religion and ethic, and in this union they became stronger and stronger, until in connection with the political, social and ecclesiastical history of individual countries they received that particular character of the religious morality of the middle classes (or bourgeois world) which differs from the early Calvinism of Geneva and France.

In the light of all this, Weber's thesis must be construed not according to the usual interpretation, as an effort to trace the causative influence of the Protestant ethic upon the emergence of capitalism, but as an exposition of the rich congruency of such diverse aspects of a culture as religion and economics. The essay should be considered as a stimulating project of hermeneutics, a demonstration of interesting correlations between diverse cultural factors. Although at the time of the republication of the essay Weber insisted that he had not changed his views on this matter at all, the whole intent of his later work does show an implicit shift of view, or at any rate of emphasis. No longer laying the basic stress on the causal factors in the economic ethic of radical Protestantism as related to the capitalist spirit, his later researches, culminating in the systematic sociology of religion, accepted rather the congruency of these diverse aspects of our culture, and their subsumption under the comprehensive process of rationalization. It is important to emphasize that some of the distortions involved in Weber's ideal-type method are neutralized in his later sociological studies of the non-Christian religions, to which all too little attention has been paid. In these mighty studies, which are cultural sociologies of the *Weltreligionen,* Weber traces the influence of material, geographic and economic circumstances on the religious and ethical ideas of different cultures. Yet though he treated religious norms, institutions and practices with cold detachment, he never denied the historical reality and power of the religious complex. His general view remained that human affairs are infinitely complicated, with numerous elements interacting; and it was his unshakable conviction that to attribute causal primacy is to be guilty of oversimplification.

In view of Weber's limited intention and the cautious demarcation of his task (including the frequently expressed indication of its incompleteness), his idiosyncratic method which would not permit statistical proof or disproof, and his later supplementation of the original effort by systematic studies in the sociology of religion, it must be concluded that his task was justified by its results. Although the discussion of his problem has not in itself promoted our knowledge of past economic life in proportion to the considerable effort it has evoked, it has greatly sharpened our appreciation of Catholic and Protestant doctrinal history; and it has also paved the way for the formulation of an adequate social theory of religion. Weber's essay on *The Protestant Ethic* is also in a peculiar sense an introduction to his massive system of sociology and his philosophy of history, and exemplifies in striking fashion the anfractuosities of his intellect and temper. As an illuminating tentative approach to a great problem, as an introduction to the domain of the sociology of religion which it served to stake out, as the stimulus to a generation of researchers in this new discipline, and finally, as the precursor of functional analysis in culture history, Weber's essay deserves a better fate than it has thus far enjoyed.

The Change in Economic Systems and Technology

THE CAUSES OF THE INDUSTRIAL REVOLUTION:
AN ESSAY IN METHODOLOGY

R. M. Hartwell

J. H. Clapham wrote in 1910 that, "Even if . . . the history of 'the' industrial revolution is a 'thrice squeezed orange', there remains an astonishing amount of juice in it".[1,2] Indeed, half a century later interest in the industrial revolution is increasing, not waning, and, as a topic for research it seems still to be strangely unworked. The gaps in the literature—for example, the history of any major industry for the years 1760 to 1860—are more obvious than the achievements. The twentieth century has been remarkable for historical productivity, for the increasing quantity and range of source materials available, for the growing sophistication of techniques, and for the large-scale growth in numbers of *professional* economic historians, with their own societies, journals, university departments and degrees, but there still is relative ignorance about many major problems of the industrial revolution, and in lieu of detailed investigation into their solutions, inevitably much speculation. It is, of course, easier to speculate than to do research, and although speculation is a good guide for research, too many insights established speculatively have tended to become dogma, and their acceptance as revealed truth has often inhibited that very research which alone could establish their validity.[3] Nevertheless, historians of the industrial revolution have ranged widely, from inquiries into the first use of the term and the dating of the upswing, through local, business and industrial histories, to inconclusive and often confused discussion about causes and consequences. The most lively literature has been concerned with the way of life and the standard of living during industrialization, i.e., with the consequences of the industrial revolution, and the important problem of determining why the revolution occurred at all, and why it

From *The Economic History Review,* Vol. XVIII, Nos. 1, 2, and 3, 1965, pp. 164-182.

323

occurred in England, i.e., with the causes of the industrial revolution, has not received its warranted attention. Indeed, on the origins of the industrial revolution, the historians have been neither very illuminating nor particularly argumentative, being seemingly happy to accept simultaneously a number of suggested solutions without testing their mutual consistency, either deductively or empirically. This is surprising. On any historical accounting, the industrial revolution is one of the great discontinuities of history; it would not be implausible indeed, to claim that it has been the greatest.[4] The transition, first in England and then throughout Europe and increasingly throughout the world, from stable subsistence or low *per capita* real incomes to sustained increases in *per capita* real incomes, and the revolution in industrial technology and organization, and the radical change in the structure of national economies, and the massive growth of population, represent a fundamental discontinuity in world economic development. But perhaps failure to explain does not indicate lack of interest or effort? Perhaps the problem of *explaining* the origins of the industrial revolution in England is too complex for even the most talented historian to disentangle. Or, making the problem equally insoluble, perhaps the meagerness of data, particularly statistical data, makes causal analysis and the measurement of the relative importance of "causes" impossible. Indeed, the understanding of economic growth has also been found impossible by the economists, who have been unable to formulate satisfactory theories of growth and to relate them to practical policies for growth. Alfred Marshall failed to produce his projected fourth volume, "Progress: its Economic Conditions"[5]; no economist since has been more successful. However, the historians at least have long had their eyes on what today is admitted by the economists to be a major problem; the economists, in contrast, ignored the problems of growth for more than a century. Only since 1945 have the economists again been interested in what was the major theme of Adam Smith's foundation text of the study of economics, first published in 1776: "an inquiry into the nature and causes of the wealth of nations."

The economists' renewed interest in history has been the result, partly of the Keynesian revolution (the logical outcome of which have been the growth models, attempts to define the relationship between inputs of capital, labor and technical knowledge and rates of growth of output), and partly of the need to understand, for practical reasons, the problems of the underdeveloped economies of the world. The results for economic history have been important. History now seems useful to the economist because it provides (or should provide) a large source of information about past economic growth, bountiful facts for processing into practical generalizations for growth.[6] These empiricists of growth have revived, to some extent, an historical school in economics. At the same time they are beginning to stimulate a more theoretical school in economic history, especially in the United States of America. Economic history has always been concerned largely with the documentation, description and explanation of what the economists call economic growth, and with so much empirical and theoretical literature on growth by the economists now available, some historians are turning towards the economists for guidance. The main result should be to make the historian aware of the unsystematic nature of many of his explanations of growth, of how often his inferences have been outrageous extrapolations from inadequate data, often, indeed, *"a priori* assumptions made specious by an unsystematic and unscientific marshalling of unreliable data."[7]

Thus, for example, "explanations" of the industrial revolution have consisted mainly of suggesting a large number of variables, sometimes relationships between variables, and usually of attributing the crucial discontinuity to the aggregate effects of the autonomous variation of *one* important variable. The most popular explanation has taken the form of a simple capital accumulation model. It is fair to say that the historians, in their detailed analyses, have suggested *many* "causal factors," yet nearly all have sought "a main cause" and have elevated *one* variable, explicit or implicitly, to the role of *chief cause.* The student, faced with a shelf of authorities, each with a different cause, or a different combination of causes of the industrial revolution, may well be excused for this confusion. Recently, for example, a meeting of economic historians, arranged by *Past and Present,* to discuss the origins of the industrial revolution, agreed that they had no answer to that problem, and called for more research "to clarify the problems of capital formation . . . and of effective demand"; on neither of these problems, nor on two others—the problems of "social structure" and of "why the revolution occurred first in Britain"—was there any general agreement, or, if the printed account is an accurate guide, much useful discussion.[8]

The most important general accounts of the industrial revolution have been those of Toynbee,[9] Mantoux[10] and Ashton,[11] with significant contributions also by Bowden,[12] Fay,[13] Beales[14] and Heaton.[15] Beard's slender volume on the industrial revolution is worth mentioning only because it was written so early.[16] Since the time when economic history began to develop as a formal discipline in the last quarter of the nineteenth century, however, most of Britain's best-known economic historians have written, at one time or another, about the industrial revolution; for example, Cunningham, Ashley, Unwin, the Hammonds, Clapham, Clark, Redford, Lipson, Court, Chambers and John.[17] Recent contributions have been made by Rostow, Deane and Cole, and Habakkuk and Deane.[18] All these, and many others too numerous to mention, have attempted to give some explanation of the conditions which first gave rise to English industrialization. While most of these historians have stressed technological change, and nearly all have given primary importance to capital accumulation, some also have stressed laissez faire, and most have said something about the importance of market expansion (usually abroad). In addition to economic variables, however, the industrial revolution has been attributed to the protestant ethic, to the commercial bias of English science and law and to the flexibility of the English social structure. To some, English leadership was no more than an accident of geography, the combination of a fortunate site for trading and favorable factor endowments. The following table lists the factors which the historians have used to explain the acceleration of growth in the eighteenth century.

Table: Forces Making for Growth

1. *Capital Accumulation:* increased savings (from commerce and agriculture), low interest rates, increased investment (e.g. in transport); ploughing-back of high proportion of increased industrial profits; increased investment from profit inflation; better mobilizing of savings because of improved financial institutions; economy of savings (e.g., inventories) because of improved transport.
2. *Innovations—Changes in the Technology and Organization of Agriculture and Industry:* new and improved machinery; new sources of power; more roundabout and larger-scale production (e.g., enclosures and factories) with greater division of labor; industrial localization (external economies).
3. *Fortunate Factor Endowments:* coal, iron ore and other minerals necessary for industrialization; favorable size of the economy (short hauls); favorable trading site for growth markets (America and Asia); skilled labor force; increasing labor inputs (because of absolute increase in population, and a relatively larger industrial labour force, the result of greater agricultural productivity); entrepreneurial and inventing talent in good supply.
4. *Laissez Faire:* long-term changes in philosophy, religion, science and law, culminating in the eighteenth century in secularism, rationalism and economic individualism; propagandists for free enterprise and receptive statesmen; Adam Smith; social mobility.
5. *Market Expansion:* increasing foreign trade; increasing domestic consumption because of (a) increasing population and (b) rising real incomes; urbanization; improved transport which (a) lowered costs and prices, stimulating demand and (b) unified and increased the market; relatively lower prices of industrial goods, increasing demand.
6. *Miscellaneous:* Continental wars which favored English and discouraged continental development; 'the bounty of God' (the decline of plague and the good harvests of the 1730s and 1740s); the autonomous growth of knowledge; "the English genius."

Not all historians have listed all these "forces making for growth"; and, moreover however long the list of any particular historian, there has been an almost irresistible urge for that same historian to stress *one* force above all others, and to assume, at least implicitly, that growth was the result of variations in that factor operating in an aggregate fashion on the whole economy to produce a clearly recognizable discontinuity in English economic history; in other words, to produce both a turning-point and also a take-off.

Modern discussion of the causes of the industrial revolution dates from 1884 when Arnold Toynbee's lectures were published. Toynbee had a turning-point—"Previously to 1760 the old industrial system obtained in England"—

and a simple explanation—"The essence of the Industrial Revolution is the substitution of competition for the medieval regulations which had previously controlled the production and distribution of wealth"—but he gave no clear chronology or analysis of the events leading up to 1760. To Toynbee the change in economic policy, from mercantilism to *laissez faire,* was the cause of industrialization, and Adam Smith was largely responsible. *"The Wealth of Nations* and the steam engine destroyed the old world and built a new one," he wrote, underlining the importance of technical change while making it quite clear that freedom of enterprise was the prime mover. "Without competition, no progress could be possible," he argued.[19] Writing at the same time as Toynbee, W. Cunningham in his *The Growth of English Industry and Commerce in Modern Times* also labelled the section of his history on the eighteenth and nineteenth centuries "Laissez Faire," and began it with an account of the industrial revolution. After noting the magnitude of the social and economic changes that followed from industrialization, Cunningham generalized: "The introduction of expensive implements, or processes, involves a large outlay; it is not worth while for any man, however energetic, to make an attempt, unless he has a considerable command of capital, and has access to large markets. In the eighteenth century these conditions were being more and more realized'.[20] To Cunningham, then, the conjuncture of increasing capital accumulation and expanding markets were the strategic factors in England's economic advance. Another pioneer economic historian W. J. Ashley, in his *The Economic Organization of England,* included a chapter on "The Industrial Revolution and Freedom of Contract," and dated change from the agricultural revolution which led to "a vast increase in the production of food, and this increase rendered possible the expansion of our population, which was stimulated by the growth of factory industries, offering employment to children."[21] To Ashley the increasing productivity of agriculture was both the prerequisite and the promotor of industrialization.

The most detailed study of the industrial revolution remains today that of Paul Mantoux, published in 1906. To Mantoux, the industrial revolution was "essentially a commercial phenomenon, and was connected with the gradual hold obtained by merchants over industry. Not only was it accompanied, but it was prepared, by the expansion of trade and credit." The advent of machinery was "an inevitable result of the extension of trade." But Mantoux also stressed the importance of agriculture, classing agricultural improvement with commercial expansion as necessary "preparatory changes." "The growth of great industrial centers would have been impossible if agricultural production had not been so organized as to provide for the needs of a large industrial population." To Mantoux the industrial revolution was caused by the expansion of trade and credit reacting on the organization and technology of industry. "Division of labor," he wrote, "varies with the size of the market."[22] That market expansion forced development was also the view of A. Redford, who wrote that "the fundamental stimulus to industrial change and technological innovation in England during the seventeenth and eighteenth centuries arose almost certainly from the effects of that progressive widening of the world's markets which followed the geographical discoveries . . . acting upon the highly specialized economy of a country rich in coal and metallic ores, and endowed with an enterprising and adaptable people.'[23]

Similar views, but more explicitly stressing the expansion of *demand,* were expressed by W. Bowden and E. W. Gilboy. Witt Bowden argued that increasing wealth at home and abroad had increased demand beyond the limits which the traditional forms of industry could supply. "It was in respect to the demand for English goods," he wrote, "that the eighteenth century differed most radically from earlier periods. Pressure for goods was felt alike by the manufacturer, the trader and the farmer." "So large was the demand at home, and so extensive were the overseas markets controlled by Englishmen, that without new methods of production, 'no exertions of the manufacturers could have answered the demands of trade.' "[24] E. W. Gilboy saw the main stimulus in increasing home demand: "Changing consumption standards, the increase of population and shifting of individuals from class to class, and a rise in real income provided a stimulus to the expansion of industry which must not be underestimated."[25]

More eclectic explanations of the origins of the industrial revolution have been given by E. Lipson and T. S. Ashton. Lipson accepted that "the explanation is commonly found in the expansion of . . . overseas trade with a far-flung commercial empire in America, India and Africa, which together with the Continent of Europe supplied markets for . . . manufactures," and added five other factors: capital accumulation, entrepreneurial ability, population growth, the early exploitation of coal, and a home market "where property was widely diffused and whose standard of comfort was substantial without being luxurious."[26] Ashton's introduction to his *The Industrial Revolution* summarized the great changes that occurred in England after 1760, and sought their origins in a fortunate combination of favorable factors. "The conjuncture of growing supplies of land, labor, and capital made possible the expansion of industry; coal and steam provided the fuel and power for large-scale manufacture; low rates of interest, rising prices, and high expectations of profit offered the incentive. But behind and beyond these material and economic factors lay something more. Trade with foreign parts had widened men's views of the world, and science their conception of the universe: the industrial revolution was also a revolution in ideas." In particular, *The Wealth of Nations* inspired new attitudes: "It was under its influence that the idea of a more or less fixed volume of trade and employment, directed and regulated by the State, gave way—gradually and with many setbacks—to thoughts of unlimited progress in a free and expanding economy." But Ashton too sought a main cause, reckoning that, "If we seek—it would be wrong to do so—for a single reason why the pace of economic development quickened about the middle of the eighteenth century, it is to this [the lower rate at which capital could be obtained] we must look."[27]

This list by no means exhausts the historical writing about the origins of the industrial revolution; it is meant to be representative rather than comprehensive. Some recent contributions are now added, to demonstrate that the method in this historical inquiry has not changed, particularly the *penchant* for a simple explanation. H. J. Habakkuk and P. Deane, for example, after considering and rejecting the possibility of population growth, technical improvements or increasing investment effecting the breakthrough, come down in favor of international trade.[28] P. Deane and W. A. Cole, however, reject increasing international trade as the promoter of growth, and find rather that agricultural change and population growth play the vital roles in the "mechanics of eighteenth century growth."[29] A. H. John finds the key to change in agriculture,[30] while J. D. Chambers sees industrialization as the response to an autonomous increase in population.[31] Finally, there is W. W. Rostow, to whom the industrial revolution was the result of a rise in the rate of productive investment, and the development of a narrow range of substantial manufacturing sectors operating in favorable institutional environment which quickly transmitted change throughout the economy.[32]

The mainspring of the industrial revolution may lie deep in the long history of European civilization, the only civilization (Japan excepted) yet to achieve industrialization, but a shorter-term process of economic change in eighteenth century England also has to be analyzed. In the historians' accounts of the industrial revolution there has been little attempt to determine the strategic variables of the economy of England and their functional relationships, less attempt to distinguish and weight exogenous and endogenous factors causing change, and no attempt to construct a dynamic model of the economy which could explain the process of growth. A satisfactory account of the industrial revolution would describe the economy before industrialization, analyze its structural relationships, and identify its external constraints. The rate of growth of output, in a mechanical sense, was determined by the rate of growth of population, by the rate of capital accumulation, and by changes in the technology and organization of agriculture and industry. However, there are no accurate and few plausible estimates of these variables: some attempts to determine population growth,[33] one attempt to estimate capital growth,[34] and no serious attempt at all to measure technical change.[35] A major problem is to determine to what extent growth was the result of endogenous or exogenous forces; to what extent, for example, independent variables like an autonomous growth of foreign trade or an increase in population growth for noneconomic reasons promoted economic growth is not known. Certainly a force, or forces for change—whether internal and/or external—were sufficiently great over the course of half a century to alter the structure of the economy and to increase and sustain the rate of growth. The historians have identified an impressive range of forces making for growth, but they have been unable to reach any agreement on the relative importance of those forces, or how they operated in a process of economic change. In particular, they have not demonstrated how their favored endogenous one variable model of eighteenth century growth could have worked. Indeed, the historians have no agreed definition of the industrial revolution (in terms of rate of growth of output, or changing economic structure, or technical change, etc.), have not explained the turning-point,[36] and have not analyzed "the mechanics of eighteenth century growth."

Economists also may not have succeeded in their analyses of economic growth, but at least their efforts have been systematic; they have attempted to relate functionally the appropriate variables of growth, and although there is still no set of principles that can be labelled "the theory of economic growth," there are rigorous if simple models of growth which are continually being made more complicated (i.e., more realistic). The economists also have collected an enormous amount of statistical data, particularly time-series, to illustrate the long-term behavior of economies and whose systematic analysis has provided insights and generalizations about historic growth.[37] Can the economists, therefore, help the historians? After all, the factors which interest the economist are just those which have featured prominently in the writings of the historian; particularly the increasing accumulation of capital, the progress of technology, the change in social environment, and the growth of demand (for example, through population growth). Can a wedding of economic and historical thinking on the roles of these variables help to explain the origins of the industrial revolution?

CAPITAL ACCUMULATION

To Adam Smith the fundamental determinant of growth was the rate of capital formation, and this rate was proportional to the rate of investment. "The annual produce of the land and labor of any nation," he wrote, "can be increased in its value by no other means, but by increasing either the numbers of its productive laborers, or the productive powers of those laborers who had before been employed. The number of its productive laborers, it is evident, can never be much increased, but in consequence of an increase of capital, or of the funds destined for maintaining them. The productive powers of the same number of laborers cannot be increased, but in consequence either of some addition and improvement to those machines and instruments which facilitate and abridge labor; or of a more proper division and distribution of employment. In either case an additional capital is almost always required.[38] The importance of capital formation for growth has been largely accepted by all economists and historians[39] since Adam Smith, and it has been argued recently that the industrial revolution was no more than an acceleration in the rate of capital formation. A. Lewis has written, for example, that, "All countries which are now relatively developed have at some time in the past gone through a period of rapid acceleration, in the course of which the rate of annual net investment has moved from five percent or less to twelve percent or more. This is what we mean by an Industrial Revolution."[40] But the idea (even if true) of growth as a result of the savings rate and the aggregate capital-output ratio conceals more problems that it solves for a rapidly changing economy.[41] Moreover, there is scepticism that capital accumulation *per se* will necessarily produce growth; indeed the fundamental question—the extent to which capital is indispensable for growth—has not yet been answered, and certainly postwar experience in underdeveloped countries has provided no answer. The relationship between investment and the growth of output is not uniform; there have been wide varieties of experience, both between nations, and also in the same nation over time.[42] And even when growth has followed capital accumulation, the important problem remains of determining how complementary inputs (for example, labor and raw material supplies) adjusted smoothly to the requirements of growth. However, perhaps the most damaging argument against this conception of growth concerns the propensity to save. Rather than increased savings and investment causing growth, both are more likely to be the result of growth. In eighteenth century England, for example, a main source of capital for industry was reinvested profit; other sources were banks and merchants, who grew with industry;[43] in other words, the rate of investment was dependent on the rate of growth, the ability to save was not autonomous and accompanied rather than preceded growth. The amount of capital needed is debated; S. Pollard claims, for example, that a substantial diversion of resources was necessary for capital formation,[44] while M. Postan that "by the beginning of the eighteenth century there were enough rich people in the country to finance an economic effort far in excess of the modest activities of the leaders of the Industrial Revolution."[45] Unfortunately reliable evidence about the rate of aggregate capital accumulation in the eighteenth century is meager, although Deane and Cole have tried to demonstrate that the rate of *per capita* capital accumulation in England did not increase markedly.[46] The fact that *after* 1780 the economy could finance both increasing industrialization and a large war expenditure, without serious inflation, confirms this view that the capital needs of early industrialization were modest.[47] Thus there seems to be little theoretical or historical justification for assuming that the industrial revolution in England was the result of a notable acceleration in capital accumulation.

One theory which should be mentioned, if only because it had the backing of J. M. Keynes, argues that the steady price rise between 1750 and 1790 inflated profits, increased savings and accelerated capital formation. Keynes wrote in *The Treatise on Money* that, "It is the teaching of this Treatise that the wealth of nations is enriched not during Income inflations, but during Profit inflations—at times, that is to say, when prices are running away from costs." E. J. Hamilton has provided historical backing for this thesis and has argued that the profit inflation after 1750 caused the industrial revolution. But disaggregating the price rise shows that money wages rose more than industrial prices and less than agricultural prices; if anything, there was pressure on industrial profits in the second half of the eighteenth century. More generally, two economists have argued, on theoretical and historical grounds, that nowhere in history is there evidence of a clear wage-lag that cannot be explained by real or monetary factors.[48]

TECHNICAL CHANGE—INVENTION

Many economists now believe that the rate of growth is a function of the rate of technical change and its application to industry.[49] Historically, however, it is difficult to separate technological progress and capital accumulation. Most new technology during the industrial revolution, for example, was embodied in new or improved capital goods; thus, there was a close relationship between investment, capital formation, technical progress and increases in output. However, if there was no great increase in *per capita* capital accumulation, the increase in *per capita* output must have come from the use of more productive or better organized equipment. But the use of better equipment presupposes invention and innovation, and the problems remain of determining why appropriate inventions were made when they were made, how knowledge of them spread,[50] and why and how entrepreneurs were able to embody those inventions in profitable enterprises when they did. The process of invention, however, has defied systematic analysis. T. S. Ashton has pointed out that although "invention appears at every stage of human history . . . it rarely thrives in a community of simple peasants or unskilled manual laborers."[51] Eighteenth century England had a relatively advanced society and economy and it is not surprising that invention could flourish there. However, what of its timing and direction? Certainly the *kind* of invention and the *frequency* of invention are conditioned by the environment, by the social context with its incentives and opportunities, by the state of growth of knowledge, by "the interaction of fundamental ideas and technical possibilities,"[52] and by the stimulus of practical problems. But such general acknowledgements, and a study of the inventions of the eighteenth century, do not reveal the sources of invention, nor, in many cases, reasons for the directions which invention took.[53] Nevertheless the connection between technical change and output in the eighteenth century can be discerned. A listing of the important technical advances of the century shows two things: (1) the advances are made on a broad front—in textiles, basic metallurgy, mining, transport, agriculture, and power production—suggesting that the revolution in technology was not the product of any single intellectual or industrial stimulus, but rather the result of a growing awareness of the potentialities generally of technical progress; (2) there were two important clusters of inventions, one early, one late in the century. The coke-smelting of iron, the Newcomen engine and Kay's flying shuttle all came before 1733. The great concentration, however, is after 1768: the Jenny (1768), the Water Frame (1769), the boring mill (1775), the improved steam engine (1776-1781), the mule (1779), the seed drill (1782), cotton printing machinery (1783), iron puddling (1784), the first useful threshing machine (1786) and the improved lathe (1794). Most of these inventions took time to spread, but in this period the time-lag between invention and innovation shortened, the "rate of improvement" in technology increased[54], the combined effect of so many inventions over such a wide field was cumulatively impressive, and the rapid application of three important inventions—iron puddling, cotton spinning and the steam engine—had immediate quantitative effects on the output of key sectors of the economy after 1780. The upturn in industrial production in the last quarter of the century followed these important technical changes.[55]

INNOVATION

If invention as a social process is difficult to analyze, innovation is narrowly economic in motivation. Innovation depends on favorable economic conditions; on the supply side, on the availability of appropriate factor supplies and their prices, and on the demand side, on the existence of appropriate markets.[56] Obviously the availability of factors depends both on the physical and human resources of an economy, and also on the flexibility of the factor market. In significant senses England had a freer society and a freer economy in the eighteenth century than other European economies; there was greater security for property and enterprise; there was greater social mobility; the prevalent social attitudes (religious, political and economic) were relatively more favorable towards change; there was an increasing breakdown of medieval and mercantilist restrictions on trade and industry; improved communications made transport of men and materials easier; Great Britain constituted the largest free trade area in Europe. A freer economy meant the more effective working of the price mechanism; prices became more flexible and price changes became more efficient in promoting capital and labor mobility. In such circumstances profit became a more certain measure of economic efficiency, and enterprise was rewarded, making relative price changes effective in quickly encouraging or discouraging production. Here again, insight came originally from Adam Smith, who argued that if capital formation caused progress, the rate of capital formation depended on a favorable institutional environment, especially on free trade and competition. Free trade widened the market, permitted international division of labor, and increased productivity. Monopoly, on the other hand, was "a great enemy to good management."[57] It would be difficult, however, to measure the rate of growth of "free enterprise" in the eighteenth century, although conceptually it could be measured, for example, by estimating the increasing proportion of total production which passed through the market. The untidy conclusion is that the English environment increasingly favored enterprise and was increasingly effective in rewarding and punishing it. Thus insofar as historians have interpreted the differing histories of national economies in terms of the supply and characteristics of their entrepreneurs,[58] as the history of the industrial revolution in England has been interpreted, it can be argued rather that growth was not created by, but allowed, enterprise to flourish.[59]

SOCIAL CHANGE

Crucial change in the eighteenth century was dependent, not only on more productive equipment, not only on more entrepreneurs, but also on changing values in society; in particular it was necessary to cross "a threshold level of acceptance of novel methods."[60] The changing values were reflected in changed social action that was economically significant: for example, at the top of the income structure more capital went into factories and less into country houses, while at the bottom more into new consumer goods and less in idleness, gin and a customary subsistance living standard. These switches in demand were the result partly of a rational economic reaction to price changes, but partly also of a radical revision of those traditional attitudes which discouraged the fuller use of human and material resources. Men's minds turned *generally* from traditionalism to risk-taking and profit-making, from the acceptance of a customary way of life to striving for extra income and extra consumption; and although these changes were not independent of the economic opportunities offering, the emergence of "pushing" entrepreneurs with "disruptive innovating energy"[61] was the result of social forces, of changes in English society which rationalized and secularized human attitudes to the point that the pursuit of wealth dominated the minds of a much larger segment of English society than before, and the acceptance (if not the welcoming) of change was general. Some of the characteristics of this society have been described in the previous section, but the analysis of eighteenth century social change and its relationship to eighteenth century economic growth depends not only on detailed research by the historians, not yet done, but also on the theoretical guidance of economists and sociologists. However, although economists recognize that the requirements for economic growth involve both economic and social (or cultural) change, they have been quite unable to incorporate social forces into their systematic theories of development.[62] Sociologists, similarly, although they have posited certain general conditions which encourage social change (for example, the alleged importance for change in a society of social conflict), and although they have devoted much effort to studying changes in social structure induced by industrialization, have raised more problems than they have solved; indeed, they look to history rather than to their own discipline for insight into the origins, the conditions, the rate and the consequences of social change. There is no help for the historian of the industrial revolution in sociology.[63] There is no doubt, however, as H. L. Beales has insisted, that "the analysis of the industrial revolution is still made too much in economic terms."[64] But until there is considerably more research into the social factors which influenced economic change in eighteenth-century England, the historian of the industrial revolution must be content to assume their importance and to disguise his ignorance with a series of now well-known generalizations about religion and secularism,[65] science and rationalism, law and social mobility, government and freedom, and the consequential economically beneficial changes in social structure and action.

GROWTH OF DEMAND

Adam Smith argued that the division of labor is limited by the extent of the market. "As it is the power of exchanging that gives occasion to the division of labor; so the extent of this division must always be limited by the extent of that power, or, in other words, by the extent of the market."[66] The importance of a high level and expansion of demand for growth was firmly postulated by Adam Smith, but over the long period of the classical dominance of economic theory, the importance of demand for growth was explained away by Say's law of markets, which postulated that production increased not only the supply of goods in the market but also the demand for them.[67] Only with J. M. Keynes in the 1930s was the thesis advanced and universally accepted by the economists that incomes and employment are largely dependent on investment, that consumer spending has direct effects on profits and the incentive to invest. Even before Keynes some historians, perhaps still students of Adam Smith, realized, in the words of the Hammonds, that "mass production demands popular consumption," and that "the command of a wide market is essential to the organization of large-scale industry."[68] But most historians of the industrial revolution, although implicitly recognizing the need to explain the disposal of an increasing output of consumer goods, have attributed greater importance to an increase in overseas trade than to an increase in home demand. The emphasis on international trade is understandable; there was a rapid expansion of exports in the third quarter of the eighteenth century,[69] and after a deceleration in the seventies a remarkable acceleration between 1780 and 1800; manufactures constituted a major part of exports, and a significant proportion of industrial output was exported; and the industries mainly dependent on the home economy expanded less rapidly than the major export industries.[70] However, much of the increased trade came from North America and the West Indies, colonies whose demand for English goods was largely derived from the English demand for colonial goods. Even so colonial trade was important because it increased the total size of the market available to English producers. It is not inappropriate, indeed, to speak of an Atlantic economy of the eighteenth century, with an aggregate market that permitted comparative advantage specialization in England which otherwise might not have been possible. The great foreign potential, nevertheless, was in Europe, with its 200 millions and "towards the end of the century, England's cotton and metal industries . . . were poised ready to invade not only the European but all other markets with their irresistible bundles of products of the Industrial Revolution."[71]

However, foreign trade could only have accounted for a small though significant proportion of total industrial production in the years leading up to the industrial revolution. The largest growth market must have been the home market, especially since in the eighteenth century market expansion usually preceded industrial expansion. As Mantoux wrote, "In those days progress in industry was almost impossible unless it was preceded by some commercial development."[72] It was the relentless growth of domestic demand which stimulated industrial growth over a wide field, demand which was local and obvious and which had immediate response from industrial producers. The steadily expanding level of aggregate domestic demand was more important for growth than the more erratic growth of foreign trade in the years before 1780. Evidence for rising real wages in the first half of the century has been reviewed by various writers,[73] and was noted by Adam Smith in 1776: "In

Great Britain the real recompense for labor, ... the real quantities of the
necessaries and conveniences of life which are given to the laborer, has increased considerably during the course of the present century."[74] This increase
in real wages owed much to agricultural improvements which date back well
into the seventeenth century, and to a series of good harvest after 1730, both
of which increased the disposable money income of the mass of Englishmen at
a critical stage of development.[75]

A more productive agriculture not only increased real incomes and released resources to industry, it allowed more people to survive and the population of England to grow. What role did increasing population play in the
industrial revolution? Historically population increase and economic growth go
together, but although economic growth has always been accompanied by
population growth, population growth has not always been accompanied by
economic growth. Not only did the histories of England and Ireland between
1750 and 1850 demonstrate this, but in the hundred years since 1850, also,
variations in the rate of growth of output in the countries of Europe have *not*
shown any close relationship with population movements.[76] Historians, economists and demographers are all interested in the relationship between industrialization and demographic change, for example during the industrial revolution, but this interest is frustrated by the absence of firm data on the population growth of the eighteenth century. It was almost certainly more food, the
result of widespread agricultural improvements, which was responsible for the
growth of population generally in Europe.[77] The combination in eighteenth
century England of improved agriculture *and* industrialization was unique; so
too was the rate of increase of English population. It would seem, therefore,
that population growth was the response to economic growth, and not an
independent variable. In so far as the figures allow a regional breakdown, they
confirm this view: the counties which were quickening industrially before the
industrial revolution and which later became the main centers of industrial
change, were already increasing their population faster than the rest of the
country in the first half of the century; with industrialization these differen-
tials increased.[78] Increasing population meant an increasing labor force, and
when this basic factor of production was better organized and equipped with
better tools, total output certainly rose, and if wage rates are any indication,
also *per capita* output.

"Natura non facit saltum"[79]

This summary of the economic historians' theories about the origins of the
industrial revolution, with a survey, with some help from the economists, of
the "forces making for growth" in the eighteenth century, has added little to
our understanding of the industrial revolution. It has demonstrated only that
the rise in eighteenth century output was the result in part of improved
organization and technology, and in part of expanding resources and the
growth of population, without having explained the process of invention and
its diffusion, or the reasons for the increase in population; it has stressed the

importance for industrialization of a changing society and new social values, without explaining how those changes came about; it has demonstrated the need there was for a growing demand, particularly in the home market, without analyzing how that demand grew and was sustained; it has argued that there was no great acceleration in capital formation as a prelude to, or as an accompaniment of the industrial revolution. The survey, moreover, has lead inevitably to the conclusion that the various "forces making for growth" in the eighteenth century were not autonomous variables, but rather manifestations of growth itself; this seems to have been particularly true of capital accumulation, innovation, and population growth. Does this mean that changing human attitudes, in particular the development of a rational ethic about wealth, and the emergence of business enterprises motivated by profit-making (and, thus, the willingness to take risks), were the promoters of the industrial revolution? We cannot say; but, again, it is reasonable to argue that because the profit motive depended on the possibility of making profits, this possibility was created by the economic changes of the eighteenth century. But do we need *an explanation* of the industrial revolution? Could it not be the culmination of a most unspectacular process, the consequence of a long period of slow economic growth?

In the policy writing about growth, two main conceptual models have been developed: the first, a sectoral model, in which a leading sector (or sectors) in a process of *unbalanced growth* activates the rest of the economy through backward linkages and technical diffusion;[80] the second, an aggregative model, in which, for example, the variation of a strategic variable, usually savings, has *general* impact throughout the economy, operating on a wide front on the aggregate capital-output ratio to produce *balanced growth*. The assumption today is that balanced growth, with simultaneous investment in all sectors of the economy, requires a plan and a strong government, but that unbalanced growth, 'the way that advanced countries of the Western world have in fact realized economic development',[81] is the natural outcome of a free-enterprise economy. But was England's development in the eighteenth century an example of unbalanced growth? Cannot the industrial revolution be explained more plausibly as the outcome of a process of balanced growth?[82] This growth was the product of long-term and wide-spread change in England: the rationalization of social attitudes; increasing knowledge and education; more and cheaper capital (the rate of interest had been falling from the early seventeenth century); greater factor flexibility and the more effective working of the price mechanism; wide-spread technical change (in both industry and agriculture); increasing factor supplies (population increase and more land—in America and at home, increasing raw material supplies) and fuller use of factors (fuller employment, less under-employment); better transport (which enabled, for example, trading in the winter months); the protection of infant industries (for example, silk and linen), which widened the industrial base of the economy.[83] There were also autonomous growth factors, for example the growth of foreign trade and the good harvests of the thirties and forties, whose impact was general. As the economy slowly expanded, so the market increased, giving incentive to the further division of labor and technical innovations, and to further growth. But what then becomes of the industrial revolution? What of the great discontinuity?

If one takes a long-term view of English economic development, say from 1700 to 1900 (or from 1750 to 1850, the traditional century of the industrial revolution), then it becomes obvious that there was in this period a radical shift in the structure of the economy, in the composition of total output, and in the distribution of employment, which gives concrete meaning to the idea of an industrial revolution. And in the rise of output central influence can be attributed to the great technical breakthroughs in industry of the period 1760 to 1800; it was these which allowed the acceleration of economic growth. Here perhaps the unbalanced growth concept helps. In the period *after* 1780 there were obvious growth sectors, sectors which were already important in the economy but which now grew faster, sectors with a large feedback which triggered off quantity responses in other industries, as well as disseminating technical change widely. The cumulative effect was to produce a different type of economy in a relatively short period of time; this transformation the historians have called *The Industrial Revolution*. Given the previous growth of the economy, however, "a turning-point" and "a take-off" were certain when the pressure of demand on agriculture and industry was cumulatively great enough to stimulate a sufficient number of important technical changes which would enable a large and sustained increase in *per capita* output.

FOOTNOTES

1. I am indebted to Professors E. F. Söderlund and L. E. Davis, and particularly to Dr A. R. Hall, for criticism and advice during the writing of this paper.

2. J. H. Clapham "The Transference of the Worsted Industry from Norfolk to the West Riding," *The Economic Journal*, XX (1910), p. 195.

3. Good examples of now questioned dogma are (a) the relationship between enclosure and labor supply, (b) the influence of medicine on the death rate, (c) the yeoman origins of entrepreneurs, (d) the unqualified assumption that there was a laissez faire policy during the industrial revolution. Untested dogma, still to be investigated thoroughly, include the following: (a) the assumed importance of international trade as providing the main or crucial increase in demand during the industrial revolution, (b) the assumption that there was a marked increase in *per capita* savings (investment) in the eighteenth century, (c) the assumption that there was a turning point, (d) the assumptions that in the eighteenth century social overheads were financed by market funds and industrial investment by profits. Further research may show that these latter assumptions are correct; at the moment to assert their truth is to be dogmatic.

4. See Carlo Cipolla, *The Economic History of World Population* (Pelican Books: London, 1962), pp. 24-31, who also argues (p. 29) that the industrial revolution created a "deep breach ... in the continuity of the historical process."

5. See Preface to *Money, Credit and Commerce* (London, 1923), p. vi, where Marshall stated his intention to complete his *Principles* with a further volume on "the possibilities of social advance."

6. See for example, the following books by economists on economic growth with historical sections: G. M. Meier and R. E. Baldwin, *Economic Development. Theory, History, Policy* (New York, 1957), part 2; B. Higgins, *Economic Development. Problems, Principles and Policies* (London: 1959), part 3; A. K. Cairncross, *Factors in Economic Development* (London, 1962), parts II and III.

7. I am generalizing here a remark of H. T. Davis about Marx in his *The Analysis of Economic Time Series* (Bloomington: Indiana, 1941), p. 571.

8. *Past and Present,* no. 17 (April 1960), pp. 71-81.

9. A. Toynbee, *Lectures on the Industrial Revolution of the Eighteenth Century in England* (London, 1884).

10. P. Mantoux, *The Industrial Revolution in the Eighteenth Century* (English translation of the French original of 1906, London, 1928).

11. T. S. Ashton, *The Industrial Revolution, 1760-1830* (Home University Library: Oxford, 1948).

12. W. Bowden, *Industrial Society in England towards the End of the Eighteenth Century* (New York, 1925).

13. C. R. Fay, *Great Britain from Adam Smith to the Present Day* (London, 1928).

14. H. L. Beales, *The Industrial Revolution, 1750-1850* (London, 1928).

15. H. Heaton, "Industrial Revolution," *Encyclopaedia of the Social Sciences* (New York, 1948), vol. 8, pp. 3-13.

16. C. Beard, *The Industrial Revolution,* (London, 1901).

17. W. Cunningham, *The Growth of English Industry and Commerce in Modern Times,* vol. III, *Laissez Faire* (Cambridge, 1882); W. J. Ashley, *The Economic Organization of England* (London, 1914), ch. VII; G. Unwin, *Samuel Oldknow and the Arkwrights. The Industrial Revolution at Stockport and Marples* (Manchester, 1924): J. L. and B. Hammond, *The Rise of Modern Industry* (London, 1925), part II; J. H. Clapham, 'The Industrial Revolution and the Colonies', *Cambridge History of the British Empire,* vol. II (Cambridge, 1940); G. N. Clark, *The Idea of the Industrial Revolution* (Glasgow, 1953); A. Redford, *The Economic History of England, 1760-1860* (London, 1931); E. Lipson, *The Growth of English Society* (London, 1949); W. H. B. Court, *Concise Economic History of Britain* (Cambridge, 1954); J. D. Chambers, *The Workshop of the World* (Home University of Library: Oxford, 1961); and A. H. John, *The Industrial Development of South Wales, 1750-1850* (Cardiff, 1950).

18. W. W. Rostow, *The Process of Economic Growth* (Oxford, 1960, enlarged edition of 1953 original); P. Deane and W. A. Cole, *British Economic Growth, 1688-1959. Trends and Structure* (Cambridge, 1962); and H. J. Habakkuk and P. Deane, 'The Take-off in Britain', *The Economics of Take-Off into Sustained Growth,* ed. W. W. Rostow (London, 1963).

19. Toynbee, *op. cit.,* pp. 64, 204-5.

20. Cunningham, *op. cit.,* p. 610.

21. Ashley, *op. cit.,* p. 136.

22. Mantoux, *op. cit.,* pp. 487, 137, 190.

23. Redford, *op. cit.,* p. 3.

24. Bowden, *op. cit.*, p. 65.

25. E. W. Gilboy, "Demand as a Factor in the Industrial Revolution," *Facts and Factors in Economic History* (Harvard University Press, 1932), p. 639. This is an important and neglected essay, partly, no doubt, because of the rarity of the volume in which it is published.

26. Lipson, *op. cit.*, p. 189 *et seq.*

27. Ashton, *op. cit.*, pp. 21, 22, 11.

28. Habakkuk and Deane, *op. cit.*, pp. 77-80.

29. Deane and Cole, *op. cit.*, pp. 82-97.

30. A. H. John, "Aspects of English Economic Growth in the First Half of the Eighteenth Century," *Essays in Economic History*, vol. II, ed. E. M. Carus-Wilson (London, 1962), p. 373.

31. J. D. Chambers, "Population Change in a Provincial Town: Nottingham 1700-1800," *Studies in the Industrial Revolution*, ed. L. S. Pressnell (London, 1960), p. 101.

32. Rostow, *op. cit.*, chapters 11 and 12.

33. G. S. L. Tucker, 'English Pre-Industrial Population Trends', *Economic History Review*, 2nd ser., XVI, 2 (December 1963).

34. Deane and Cole, *op. cit.*, ch. VIII.

35. But see S. Lilley, *Men, Machines and History* (London, 1948), pp. 207-26, for a rare attempt to measure "the relative invention rate."

36. J. U. Nef, *War and Human Progress* (London, 1950) discusses the turning point in ch. 15.

37. To this work, for example, S. Kuznets has devoted his academic life.

38. A. Smith, *The Wealth of Nations* (Cannan Edition, London, 1904), vol. I, p. 325.

39. W. Cunningham, for example, was "inclined to think that this [capital formation] may be advantageously treated as the dominating factor in Economic History."

40. A. Lewis, *The Theory of Economic Growth* (London, 1955), p. 208.

41. See, for example, the article of A. Fishlow, "Empty Economic Stages," *The Economic Journal*, LXXV (March 1965).

42. See, for example, A. Maddison, *Economic Growth in the West* (London, 1964), chapter III.

43. See H. Heaton, "Financing the Industrial Revolution," *Bulletin of the Business Historical Society*, XI (February 1937) and S. Pollard, "Fixed Capital in the Industrial Revolution," *The Journal of Economic History*, XXXIV (September 1964).

44. *Ibid.*, pp. 299, 314; also, "Investment, Consumption and the Industrial Revolution," *Economic History Review*, 2nd ser., XI, 2 (December 1958), pp. 215-16.

45. M. Postan, "Recent Trends in the Accumulation of Capital," *Economic History Review*, 1st ser., VI, (October 1935), p. 2.

46. Deane and Cole, *op. cit.*, p. 304.

47. I am indebted to Professor G. S. L. Tucker for this point.

48. J. M. Keynes, *A Treatise on Money* (London, 1930), vol. II, ch. 30 and E. J. Hamilton, 'Profit Inflation and the Industrial Revolution', *Quarterly Journal of Economics*, LVI (1941-2), p. 257 *et seq.*, for the profit-inflation

theory; R. A. Kessel and A. A. Alchian, "The Meaning and Validity of the Inflation-Induced Lag of Wages," *American Economic Review*, L, 1 (March 1960) for criticism.

49. For example, R. Solow, S. Fabricant and A. Abramovitz appear to do so.

50. Very little systematic historical work has been done on technical diffusion; for example, at the general level of eighteenth century technical sophistication, how much technical change was *independent technical evolution* rather than *diffusion* is not known.

51. Ashton, *op. cit.*, p. 15.

52. A. C. Crombie (ed.), *Scientific Change* (London, 1963), p. 4.

53. The classical theory of the direction of invention argues that inventive effort is distributed according to relative factor prices, i.e., is either capital, labor or raw-material saving in bias according to relative prices and price changes. And although Ashton (for the eighteenth century) and Habakkuk (for the nineteenth) have tried to demonstrate this thesis, the attempts are not convincing. A chronological chart of inventions over these two centuries shows no pattern at all, let alone a systematic relation to factor prices. Ashton, *op. cit.*, p. 91; H. J. Habakkuk, *American and British Technology in the 19th. Century* (Cambridge, 1962).

54. W. E. Salter, *Productivity and Technical Change* (Cambridge, 1960), p. 6, used the term "rate of improvement" to indicate "a given change in technical knowledge."

55. See T. S. Ashton, *An Economic History of England. The Eighteenth Century* (London, 1955), p. 125.

56. J. A. Schumpeter has argued that growth is determined by the rate of innovation, a function of entrepreneurial activity, and that innovations appear discontinuously in groups or swarms; such a swarm began the industrial revolution. *The Theory of Economic Development* (Harvard, 1951), p. 223.

57. Adam Smith, *op. cit.*, I, 148.

58. D. Landes, for example, attributes France's relative economic retardation in the nineteenth century to entrepreneurial shortcomings; "French Entrepreneurship and Industrial Growth in the Nineteenth Century," *Journal of Economic History*, IX, 1 (May 1949).

59. As does Charles Wilson, "The Entrepreneur in the Industrial Revolution in Britain," *History*, XLII (June 1957). It is remarkable *about Europe* that industrialization there was seldom hindered by lack of entrepreneurs or capital.

60. Fishlow, *op. cit.*, p. 123.

61. The words are those of A. H. Cole.

62. However, see E. E. Hagen, *On the Theory of Social Change; How Economic Growth begins* (Homewood: Illinois, 1962) for an attempt.

63. See T. Bottomore, *Sociology. A Guide to Problems and Literature* (London, 1962), ch. 17, for a discussion of the sociological literature on "factors in social change."

64. Beales, *op. cit.*, Introduction to 1958 edition, p. 20.

65. See, for example, the critical examination of the alleged influence of Protestantism on economic life in K. Samuelsson, *Religion and Economic Life* (English translation, Stockholm, 1961).

66. Adam Smith, *op. cit.*, I, p. 19.

67. J. A. Schumpeter, *History of Economic Analysis* (London, 1954), p. 615 *et seq.* for a discussion of 'Say's Law of Markets'.

68. J. L. and B. Hammond, *op. cit.*, p. 67.

69. R. Davis, "English Foreign Trade, 1700-1774," *Economic History Review*, 2nd ser., XV, 2 (December 1962), p. 295.

70. Deane and Cole, *op. cit.*, pp. 41-50; also E. B. Schumpeter, *English Overseas Trade Statistics 1697-1808* (Oxford, 1960), p. 12.

71. Davis, *op. cit.*, p. 298.

72. Mantoux, *op. cit.*, p. 93.

73. See, in particular, E. W. Gilboy, *Wages in Eighteenth Century England* (Harvard, 1934), and A. H. John, "Aspects of English Economic Growth in the First Half of the Eighteenth Century," *op. cit.*, p. 365.

74. Adam Smith, *op. cit.*, I, p. 200.

75. The questions of whether *an agricultural revolution* is a necessary prerequisite of *an industrial revolution,* and whether agriculture can be *a driving force* in *economic growth,* are still debated by the economists. Economic history shows that in Europe industrialization was preceded usually by a rise in agricultural productivity, but that the growth of the agricultural and non-agricultural sectors were intimately linked in a process of general economic growth (for example, through the industrial demand for agricultural raw materials). The economists' treatment of the problem is reviewed in C. Eicher and L. Witt (Editors), *Agriculture in Economic Development* (New York, 1964), especially Part I.

76. Maddison, *op. cit.*, p. 29 *et seq.*

77. However P. E. Razzeil has argued that it was the decline in the deaths from small-pox (for medical reasons—inoculation) which caused the population growth after c. 1740; see his forthcoming "Population Change in Eighteenth Century England: A Reinterpretation," *Econ. Hist. Rev.,* 2nd ser., XVIII,2.

78. Deane and Cole, *op. cit.*, ch. III.

79. The motto of Alfred Marshall's *Principles of Economics* (London, 1890), which he translated as "economic evolution is gradual and continuous in each of its numberless routes."

80. A. O. Hirschman, *The Strategy of Economic Development* (Yale, 1958), has argued persuasively, and has made popular, the theory that economic imbalance is a stimulus to growth.

81. S. Enke, *Economics for Development* (London, 1964), p. 332.

82. It was Dr A. R. Hall, (Australian National University) who, in a private communication ("Reflections on the Industrial Revolution") convinced me that the industrial revolution could have been "a consequence of a long period of slow economic growth"; he did not, however, base his argument explicitly on the "balanced growth" thesis.

83. Professor R. Davis has pointed out that tariffs became increasingly protective after 1690, so that by 1720 there was a fully protective system.

SUGGESTED READINGS

PART I. THE SOCIAL SCIENCE PERSPECTIVE

Logic and Function of the Social Sciences

Bronowski, J., *The Common Sense of Science.* New York: Vintage Books, 1953.

Kuhn, Thomas S., *The Structure of Scientific Revolutions.* Chicago: University of Chicago Press, 1962.

Raison, Timothy (Ed.), *The Founding Fathers of Social Science.* Baltimore: Penguin Books, 1963.

Redfield, Margaret Park, *Human Nature and the Study of Society.* Chicago: University of Chicago Press, 1962.

Thompson, Arthur W., *Gateway to the Social Sciences.* New York: Henry Holt & Co., 1959.

Methodology and the Social Sciences

Bart, Pauline and Linda Frankel, *The Student Sociologist's Handbook.* Cambridge, Mass.: Schenkman Publ. Co., Inc., 1971.

Braithwaite, R. B., *Scientific Explanation.* Cambridge: University Press, 1968.

Brown, Robert, *Explanation in Social Science.* Chicago: Aldine Publishing Co., 1963.

Hillway, Tyrus, *Introduction to Research.* Boston: Houghton-Mifflin Co., 1964.

Kaplan, Abraham, *The Conduct of Inquiry.* San Francisco: Chandler Publ. Co., 1964.

Madge, John, *The Tools of Social Science.* Garden City, New York: Anchor Books, Doubleday and Co., Inc., 1965.

The Social Sciences and Society

Braybrooke, David, *Philosophical Problems of the Social Sciences.* New York: The Macmillan Co., 1965.

Mills, C. Wright, *The Sociological Imagination.* Middlesex, England: Penguin Books, Ltd., 1970.

Redfield, Margaret Park (Ed.), *The Social Uses of Social Science.* Chicago: University of Chicago Press, 1963.

Sanders, Marion K., *The Professional Radical: Conversations with Saul Alinsky.* New York: Harper & Row, 1970.

Vidich, Arthur J. and Joseph Bensman, *Small Town in Mass Society* (Chapter 14). Princeton: Princeton University Press, 1968.

Weber, Max, *Essays in Sociology.* (Chapter: "Science as a Vocation.") Oxford University Press, 1946.

Waitzkin, Howard, "Truth's Search for Power: the Dilemmas of the Social Sciences" *Social Problems,* Vol. 15, No. 4, Spring, 1968.

PART II. THE URBANIZATION OF MAN

The Scope of the Problem

Fava, Sylvia, *Urbanism in World Perspective.* New York: Thomas Crowell, 1968.

Meadows, Paul and Ephraim H. Mizreechi, *Urbanism, Urbanization, and Change: Comparative Perspectives.* (Section 1). Reading, Mass.: Addison-Wesley Publ. Co., 1969.

The City and its Environment

Adams, Robert McC., *The Evolution of Urban Society.* Chicago: Aldine Publ. Co., 1966.

Braidwood, Robert J and Gordon R. Willey, *Courses Toward Urban Life: Archeological Considerations of Some Cultural Alternates.* Chicago: Aldine Publ. Co., 1962.

Braidwood, Robert J. and Charles A. Reed, "The Achievement and Early Consequences of Food Production: A Consideration of the Archeological and Natural-Historical Evidence." *Cold Spring Symposia on Quantitative Biology,* Vol. XXII, 1957.

Marquis, Stewart, "Ecosystems, Societies, and Cities" *American Behavioral Scientist* Vol. XI, No. 6, July-August 1968, p. 11.

Sanders, William T. and Barbara J. Price, *Mesoamerica: The Evolution of a Civilization.* New York: Random House, 1968.

The Classic Preindustrial City

deBurgh, W. G., *The Legacy of the Ancient World.* Middlesex, England: Penguin Books, 1923.

DeCoulanges, Fustel, *The Ancient City.* Garden City, New York: Anchor Books, Doubleday and Co., Inc., 1890.

Sjoberg, Gideon, *The Preindustrial City.* Glencoe, Illinois: Free Press, 1960.

Greece

Kitto, H. D. F., *The Greeks.* Baltimore: Penguin Books, 1951.

Plato, *Republic of Plato,* translated, with notes and an interpretive essay by Allan Brown. New York: Basic Books, 1968, pp. 45-50.

Wycherley, R. E., *How the Greeks Built Cities.* Garden City, New York: Anchor Books, Doubleday and Co., Inc. 1969.

Rome

Africa, T. W., *Rome of the Caesars.* New York: Wiley, 1965.

Balsdon, J. P. V. D., *Roman Civilization.* Baltimore: Penguin Books, 1965.

Barrow, R. H., *The Romans.* Baltimore: Penguin Books, 1949.

Dudley, Donald, *Urbs Roma.* New York: Phaedon, 1967.

Richmond, I. A., *Roman Britain.* Baltimore: Penguin Books, 1955.

Rostovtzeff, M., *Rome.* London: Oxford University Press, 1960.

The Medieval City

Brandt, William, *The Shape of Medieval History.* New Haven: Yale University Press, 1966.

Dannenfeldt, Karl H., *The Renaissance, Medieval or Modern.* Lexington, Mass.: D. C. Heath & Co., 1959.

Pirenne, Henri, *Medieval Cities.* Garden City, New York: Anchor Books, Doubleday and Co., Inc., 1956.

Havighurst, Alfred F. (Ed.), *The Pirenne Thesis: Analysis, Criticism, and Revision.* Lexington, Mass.: D. C. Heath and Co., 1969.

Rowling, Marjorie, *Everyday Life in Medieval Times.* London: Batsford, 1968.

von Martin, Alfred, *Sociology of the Renaissance.* New York: Harper & Row, 1963.

White, Lynn, *Medieval Technology and Social Change.* Oxford: Oxford University Press, 1962.

Zacour, Norman, *Introduction to Medieval Institutions.* New York: St. Martin's Press, 1969.

The Transformation to the Industrial City

Bendix, Reinhard, and Seymour Lipset, *Class, Status and Power.* (Chapters 1 and 2). New York: The Free Press, 1966.

Burns, Tom (Ed.), *Industrial Man.* Baltimore: Penguin Books, 1969.

Cox, Oliver, *Capitalism as a System.* New York: Monthly Review Press, 1964.

Cox, Oliver, *Foundations of Capitalism.* New York: Philosophical Library, 1959. Heath, 1959.

Green, Robert W., *Protestantism and Capitalism.* Lexington, Mass.: D. C. Heath, 1959.

Hobsbawm, E. J., *Industry and Empire.* Baltimore: Penguin Books, 1968.

Sombart, Werner, *Luxury and Capitalism.* Ann Arbor: University of Michigan Press, 1967.

Taylor, Philip A. M., *The Industrial Revolution in Britain.* Lexington, Mass.: D. C. Heath, 1958.